The Encyclopedia of
Franchises
and
Franchising

The Encyclopedia of Franchises and Franchising

by
Dennis L. Foster

Facts On File
New York • Oxford

The Encyclopedia of Franchises and Franchising

Facts On File, Inc.   Facts On File Limited
460 Park Avenue South   or   Collins Street
New York, NY 10016   Oxford OX4 1XJ
USA   United Kingdom

Library of Congress Cataloging-in-Publication Data

Foster, Dennis L.
  The encyclopedia of franchises and franchising.
  Bibliography: p.
  Includes index.
  1. Franchises (Retail trade)—Dictionaries. I. Title.
HF5429.23.F673 1989   381'.13'03   89-11774
ISBN 0-8160-2081-7

British CIP data available on request from Facts On File.

Facts On File books are available at special discounts when
purchased in bulk quantities for businesses, associations,
institutions or sales promotiion. Please contact the Special
Sales Department of our New York office at 212/683-2244
(dial 800/322-8755 except in NY, AK or HI).

Manufactured by Maple-Vail Manufacturing Group
Printed in the United States of America

10 9 8 7 6 5 4 3 2 1

This book is printed on acid-free paper.

Contents

Dedicated to the memory of
Victor T. Foster

Preface Franchising is a multi-billion dollar industry involving many millions of business owners, bankers, financial analysts, investors, accountants, attorneys, ad men, government workers, and, not the least of all, white-and blue-collar employees. Yet, franchising is also an integral and sometimes controversial component of American culture — both a purveyor and a reflection of public tastes in food, fashion, consumption, and lodging. Cleary, an exhaustive A-to-Z compendium of franchise facts and issues is long overdue.

Franchising defies precise categorization: at once a business method, a legal entity, a cultural influence, a financial tool, and an industry, franchising more than any other business phenomenon has managed somehow to pervade almost every aspect of life in almost every inhabitable spot of the planet.

An American Phenomenon

Franchising is first of all an American invention. By all acouunts, money and commerce were invented by the ancient Phoenicians, but not until Isaac Singer unleashed a horde of traveling salesman on America's farmers' daughters in the 1880s, had anyone thought to sell to another the "privilege" of marketing a product. Actually, Ben Franklin had sold enterprising Philadelphia youths territorial franchises to distribute his *Poor Richard's Almanac* for a franchise fee of ten cents. But their investments failed to meet at least one test of the modern definition of a franchise — a licensed trademark. In contrast, Singer's franchisees bought not just a sales territory, but also the right to use the Singer Sewing Machine name.

The word "franchise" means a right or privilege, and in its simplest form, franchising is nothing more than selling someone a right to use a particular trademark to market an exclusive product. But to a contemporary franchise corporation commanding an enormous financial empire, franchising has come to mean much more. Besides a trademark license and an exclusive product or service, a modern franchise entails an entire business methodology as well.

It is not uncommon for a franchisor to deliver to fee-paying franchisees complete "turn-key" operations fully stocked, equipped, promoted, and ready to run. When the franchise company hands over the keys to the front door, it also turns over its secrets for succeeding in business — secrets which apparently elude the two thirds of all small business owners who fail.

How important is the franchise method to the American free enterprise system? Consider this astonishing statistic: according to the Industry and Trade Administration of the U.S. Department of Commerce, 95 percent of the franchises that were open five years ago are still in business today.

Franchise operators owe their success to the fact that franchising uniquely weds a knowedgable big-time operator with an entrepreneurially motivated small-time operator. It is a scientifically validated fact that franchise owners work harder than middle managers and rank-and-file department heads. Thus, the franchise method performs equally well for franchisors and franchisees alike.

A Complex Legal Entity

Lawyers like to think of a franchise as a legal entity and nothing more. To be sure, franchising involves an intricate legal relationship between the franchisor and the franchisee — a relationship made more complex by prolific federal and state regulations. But franchise laws and rules have performed bravely on behalf of the small-time operator. When the sweeping franchise regulations adopted by the U.S. Federal Trade Commission went into effect in July of 1979, more than half of the so-called franchise opportunities advertised in the Wall Street Journal vanished from the classified pages overnight!

But the legal issues involved in franchising embrace more than regulations and laws. A franchise relationship must work for both parties, or it works for neither. Franchise law is more than a specialty practiced by a relative handful of American attorneys; it is a delicate art involving a myriad of details, precautions, variables, and options.

Yet, if a franchise were only a legal entity, without financial, marketing, management, and cultural elements, it would be little more than a lawyer's fancy words printed in small letters on a ream of paper.

Social Catalyst

It is often said that nature imitates art; i.e., that fashions and trends are invented by designers, rather than by the public at large. While it may be true that franchises follow trends, they also create and influence them. The most obvious example is fast food, the product most commonly associated with franchising — and for good reason. According to a survey by the National Restaurant Association, 90 percent of all meals taken in public are eaten at fast-food restaurants. For better or worse, it was franchising that invented, propogated, refined, and redefined fast food, a commodity that prior to the 1920s did not even exist.

Perhaps no franchised product has ever surpassed in impact the worldwide cultural influence of Coca-Cola. The soft drink's bottling franchises extend from Moscow to Bora Bora. Since the end of World War II, overseas the Coke trademark has been virtually synonymous with American life and American influence. Not only in food and beverages, but also in other important economic sectors such as lodging, convenience retailing, apparel merchandising, and automotive services, franchises have grown so influential as to be in a position to dictate public tastes, consumption habits, and industry prices.

A Financial Phenomenon

Besides influencing American life and business, major franchise corporations of the likes of McDonald's Corp., Pepsico, and Marriott Corp. are highly prized investments. The stock of most successful franchisors, as well as that of the most successful franchisees, is traded on a public exchange. Besides well known franchise names, others whose fortunes were once made in franchising or who currently own franchise subsidiaries are also carefully watched by investors: stocks like Standard Oil of Ohio, Hilton, and General Foods.

But after the October, 1987 stock-market crash, more investment capital began flowing into franchise outlets than into the stocks of their franchisors. In 1988, the average McDonald's outlet grossed over half a million dollars, the average Kentucky Fried Chicken outlet, more than $300,000, and the average Holiday Inn outlet, $2 to $5 million. "Absentee" investment in franchise businesses has become a virtual mainstay of venture capital groups and fund managers.

With the high success rate of franchise outlets, financial institutions favor franchise investments over other types of business financing. Small Business Investment Companies (SBICs), commercial finance companies, venture capitalists, profit sharing funds, and conventional lenders are more willing to lend money to finance franchise outlets today than at any previous time.

An Industry Apart

It is fashionable in franchise circles to say that franchising is not an industry, but rather a method of business expansion. Although it is true that franchising may ideally achieve the growth objectives of an individual company in search of expansion, it is impossible to ignore the collective impact of franchise businesses on the American economy.

Franchise businesses represent more than a third of all U.S. retail trade, accouting for an estimated $670 billion in 1988. In its annual report on franchise business, Franchising in the Economy, the Department of Commerce enumerates the various segments of the franchise industry by category. Fast food franchises continue to set the pace, with automotive franchises and various retail trades also exhibiting financial muscle. The report's author, department spokesman Andrew Kostecka, describes franchising as "the last avenue of the American dream." Time magazine predicts that by the end of the century, franchising will be "the primary method of doing business in America."

In a time when concerns over import/export imbalances are pronounced, the American franchise industry serves as a predictable pillar buttressing a sometimes unpredictable retail economy.

About This Book

Considering the immense economic, cultural, legal, historical, and social impact of franchising in the modern world, surprisingly little information exists on this subject, other than listings and reviews of franchise offerings. When Facts On File asked me to create a sequel to *The Rating Guide to Franchises*, the first "insider's" glance at the multi-billion dollar franchise industry, I immediately envisioned a single, comprehensive reference devoted not just to companies involved in franchising but also to the concepts, principles, practices, history, people, events, associations, laws, regulations, social issues, and terminology behind the franchise phenomenon.

If any book can be said to be truly "indispensable" to anyone currently involved, or thinking about getting involved in franchising, this is the book. Besides expanding on several basic ideas expressed in *The Rating Guide to Franchises*, this encyclopedia also builds on (but by no means supplants) my other books about franchising, *The Complete Franchise Book: What You Must Know But Are Rarely Told About Buying or Starting Your Own Franchise* and *Franchising For Free: Owning Your Business Without Investing Your Own Cash*.

The encyclopedic entries are organized in alphabetical order by keyword, with those consisting entirely of initials located at the front of their respective letter categories. In other words, you will find "A&W," "AAA," and "AAMCO" at the front of the As, and "TCBY" and "TGIF" at the front of the Ts. Investment data relating to all the franchises, a ranking of the top 100 chains, and separate category listings can be found in the appendix.

The investment data are summarized in tabular form for easy reference. The data fields include year founded, initial fee, royalty percentage, advertising fee, minimum investment, and total outlets. The investment data appear in alphabetical order by franchise tradename. The top 100 chains are ranked in descending order by number of outlets.

Franchises and investment data are continually subject to change. Although every effort has been made to assure that this work reflects the most current information at press time, some variance is unavoidable. Every day, new outlets open and others close their doors. Franchisors merge, change their names, are acquired, or go out of business. Existing fees are raised or lowered, and new ones are adopted. New laws, regulations, and court interpretations change the way franchising is practiced.

**A&W
to
Avis**

A&W Headquartered in Dearborn, Michigan, a franchisor of fast-food restaurants.

A&W has been franchising since 1925, one of the earliest businesses to adopt the franchise method of expansion. The "secret" recipe for A&W root beer was originated by an Arizona pharmacist, who reputedly blended 16 different barks, berries, herbs and spices to create the basic syrup. An entrepreneur named Roy Allen purchased the recipe in 1918 and began selling root beer from a walk-up concession on a busy street corner in Lodi, California. The outlet's only product was root beer, sold at a nickel a mug.

In the four years that followed, Allen opened three more stands in Sacramento, California — one with uniformed carhops serving customers in their cars. In 1922, Allen teamed up with an employee, Frank Wright to open three new restaurants in Houston, Texas under the name A&W Root Beer. Allen bought out Wright's interest in the company in 1924, the same year in which the A&W trademark appeared on the register of the U.S. Patent and Trademark Office. Allen began franchising the following year. The first master franchises sold for $2,000, but A&W's primary revenues were derived from the sale of root beer concentrate to franchisees.

A&W founders Roy Allen (left) and Frank Wright (right)

Few companies have played a more historic role in the evolution of the modern food and beverage industry. The Lodi root beer stand was probably the first fast-food restaurant in America, and the Sacramento carhop outlet was undoubtedly the first drive-in. J. Willard Marriott, who was destined to become one the world's most successful hoteliers, started out in 1927 as an A&W franchisee in the Washington, D.C. area.

The first A&W outlets, like this 1925 Salt Lake City stand, sold only root beer, at five cents a mug. Note the early uniformed carhops holding trays on the far left.

In 1950, having franchised 450 restaurants, Roy Allen retired, selling the company to a Nebraska businessman, Gene Hurtz. In 1963, A&W was acquired by J. Hungerford Smith Company, the firm which since 1921 had manufactured the concentrate for A&W root beer. A&W changed hands again three years later when United Fruit Company, now called United Brands, took over JHS.

In January, 1982, a California shopping mall developer, A. Alfred Taubman, purchased A&W Restaurants, Inc. and undertook an extensive program to revitalize the chain's facilities and image.

In May, 1986, A&W Brands, a separate company which franchises the bottling and distribution rights to A&W root beer, was acquired for $74 million by two Texas financiers, Thomas O. Hicks and Robert B. Haas. By the end of the year, Hicks and Haas had also taken over Seven-Up for $240 million and Dr. Pepper for $416 million.

A typical A&W Restaurant franchisee operates a family-oriented fast-food restaurant bearing the recognizable trademark of the franchisor's popular root beer. It is estimated that of the franchisor's 525 outlets currently operating, all except ten are franchise units.

A&W Restaurants, Inc., One Park Lane Blvd., 500 East, Dearborn, MI 48126. Telephone: (313) 271-9300

The distinctive barrel-shaped root beer stands of the 1930s (above) have metamorphosed into the sleek, contemporary familystyle A&W restaurants of today (below).

AAA Employment Headquartered in St. Petersburg, Florida, a franchisor of employment placement agencies.

Founded in 1957, AAA has been franchising since 1957. A typical AAA franchisee operates a personnel recruitment and employment agency for all types of job categories, ranging from domestic to executive positions. In the franchisor's business system, job applicants are responsible for paying their own placement fees, based on two week's starting salary. Approximately a third of the franchisor's 130 active outlets are franchise units.

AAA Employment, 5533 Central Ave., St. Petersburg, FL 33710. Telephone: (813) 343-3044

AAMCO Headquartered in Bala Cynwyd, Pennsylvania, a franchisor of automobile transmission repair shops.

Founded in 1963, AAMCO has been franchising since its inception. A typical AAMCO franchisee operates a transmission repair and service outlet, marketing only products authorized by the franchisor. The company's tradename is derived from the initials of its founder, Anthony A. Martino, who left the firm in 1972 to found MAACO Auto Painting and Bodyworks, whose franchise outlets also bear Martino's initials. The AAMCO chain encompasses 920 outlets, none of which are company owned.

AAMCO Transmissions, Inc., One Presidential Blvd., Bala Cynwyd, PA 19004. Telephone: (215) 668-2900

ABC Seamless Headquartered in Fargo, North Dakota, a franchisor of building siding products.

Founded in 1973, ABC Seamless has been franchising since 1978. A typical ABC Seamless franchisee operates a marketing business devoted to the franchisor's proprietary line of seamless siding equipment. Of the franchisor's 280 outlets currently operating, all except six are franchise units.

ABC Seamless, Inc., 2004 1st Ave. South, Fargo, ND 58103. Telephone: (800) 732-6577

ACA Joe Headquartered in San Francisco, California, a franchisor of retail apparel stores.

Founded in 1983, ACA Joe has been franchising since the following year. A typical ACA Joe franchisee operates a clothing boutique specializing in adult casual wear manufactured entirely of natural fabrics. The initials ACA are derived from the airline code for Acapulco, reminiscent of the company's Mexico-influenced designs and fabrics. Of the franchisor's 160 outlets currently operating, about a hundred are franchise units.

ACA Joe, 915 Front St., San Francisco, CA 91411. Telephone: (415) 986-5850

ASI Sign Systems Headquartered in New York City, a franchisor of sign making outlets.

Founded in 1978, ASI has been franchising since the following year. A typical ASI franchisee operates a commercial sign business specializing in architectural signs, building directories, and planning services. None of the franchisor's 34 outlets are company-owned.

ASI Sign Systems, 548 W. 28th St., New York, NY 10001

Acc-u-Tune Headquartered in Mountain View, California, a franchisor of automobile tune-up centers.

Founded in 1975, Acc-u-Tune has been franchising since 1980. A typical Acc-u-Tune franchisee operates an auto service boutique specializing in quick tune-ups, oil changes, lubrication, and brake service. Of the franchisor's 18 outlets currently operating, seven are franchise units.

Acc-u-Tune, 2510 Old Middlefield Way, Mountain View, CA 94043. Telephone: (415) 968-8863

Adams, Annie Book dealer and franchisor of retail "pre-read" book outlets. The founder of Annie's Book Stop, Adams reputedly had no business background or know-how when she started her first book-swapping store, with no thoughts of franchising whatsoever.

The self-avowed "bookaholic," housewife, and mother of six got the idea in a book store in which a corner had been devoted to trading used paperbacks. With the idea of starting a store devoted entirely to book swapping, Adams rented a small retail space in Westborough, Massachusetts. With a two-page in the Worcester Telegram, Annie's "Book Swap" opened to a crowd of local paperback junkies.
In 1979, Adams opened two more Book Swaps in nearby Acton and Natick. Two years later, by popular demand, the successful dealer of "pre-read" books began selling franchises to other "bookaholics." In 1984, she changed the name of her shops briefly to Swap to Stop, finally settling on Annie's Book Stop. With more than a hundred outlets, Adams sold the chain in 1988 to a small east coast publishing house. *See Annie's Book Stop.*

Adia Personnel Services Headquartered in Menlo Park, California, a franchisor of personnel employment agencies.

Founded in 1957, Adia has been franchising since 1976. A typical Adia franchisee operates a personnel recruitment and placement business with dual emphasis on both temporary and permanent employment. The chain consists of 460, a hundred of which are franchise units.

Adia Personnel Services, 64 Willow Pl., Menlo Park, CA 94025. Telephone: (800) 343-2342

Advantage Payroll Service Headquartered in Auburn, Maine, a franchisor of business payroll services.

Founded in 1967, Advantage has been franchising since 1983. A typical Advantage franchisee operates a commercial payroll preparation service utilizing the franchisor's computer processing system. All 17 of the Advantage Payroll outlets currently open and operating are franchise units.
Advantage Payroll Service, P.O. Box 1330, Auburn, ME 04210. Telephone: (800) 852-0030

Adventureland International Headquartered in Salt Lake City, Utah, a franchisor of videocassette rental outlets.

Founded in 1981 by two former soup salesman, Adventureland has been franchising since the following year. Founders Brent Smith and Martin Ehman opened the first outlet as a "hobby" for their wives. Within five years, they had franchised more than 300 storees. In 1986, Adventureland International Corp. acquired Video Biz, the second largest video rental chain, nearly doubling the franchise organization.

A typical Adventureland franchisee operates a videocassette rental business utilizing the franchisor's purchasing and inventory systems. The company is distinguished by its refusal to handle X-rated adult movies. Of the 800 Adventureland outlets currently operating, all except one are operated under franchise licenses.

Adventureland International Corp., 4516 S. 700 East, Ste. 260, Salt Lake City, UT 84107. Telephone: (801) 266-9679

Affordable Used Car Rental Headquartered in Key Port, New Jersey, a franchisor of used-car rental outlets.

Founded in 1981, Affordable has been franchising since its inception. A typical Affordable franchisee operates a discount car rental business based on a fleet of used cars and trucks. Of the franchisor's 140 outlets currently operating, all are franchise units.

Affordable Used Car Rental System, Inc., 88A W. Front St., Key Port, NJ 07735. Telephone: (800) 631-2290

Aid Auto Stores Headquartered in Inwood, New York, a franchisor of retail automotive parts outlets.

Founded in 1951, Aid Auto has been franchising since 1966. A typical Aid Auto franchisee operates a self-service store devoted to auto parts, tools, batteries, chemicals, and accessory items. Of the franchisor's 86 outlets currently operating, all except one are franchise units.

Aid Auto Stores, P.O. Box 1100, Inwood, NY 11696. Telephone: (516) 371-4330

Air Brook Limousine Headquartered in Rochelle Park, New Jersey, a franchisor of personal services outlets.

Founded in 1969, Air Brook has been franchising since 1971. A typical Air Brook franchisee operates a private limousine service. At the end of 1988, the chain boasted 120 outlets, all operated under franchise licenses.

Air Brook Limousine, P.O. Box 123, Rochelle Park, NJ 07662. Telephone: (201) 368-3974

Ajax Rent A Car Headquartered in Los Angeles, California, a franchisor of car rental agencies.

Founded in 1969, Ajax has been franchising since 1971. A typical Ajax franchisee operates a rental lot specializing in passenger cars ranging from economy size vehicles to luxury sedans. The parent company is no longer accepting applications for new franchises. It is estimated that of the franchisor's 1,600 outlets currently operating, all except eight are franchise units.

Alabama, Franchise Regulations To date, the Alabama legislature has not passed any generally applicable franchise investment law.

Franchises offered for sale in Alabama are subject to the Deceptive Trade Practices Act, which forbids any misrepresentation in the sale of "seller-assisted marketing plans." This definition embraces more than simply franchises, but includes any type of business opportunity or venture in which the seller provides "significant assistance" to the buyer. If the seller or franchisor helps to secure customers for the buyer's outlet, or assists in advertising, product selection, or promotion, the offering is subject to the Deceptive Trade Practices law. The law applies if either the franchisor or the franchisee is located in Alabama.

Alabama law does not require franchisors to register or file disclosures with any state regulatory agency. In the absence of such a requirement, the federal Franchise Rule applies, requiring franchisors to furnish prospective franchisees with a disclosure document prescribed by the Federal Trade Commission ten business days before any franchise sale is made. *See Franchise Rule.*

Alaska, Franchise Regulations The Alaska legislature has not adopted any generally applicable franchise investment law. However, gasoline dealers are governed by the Gasoline Products Leasing Act, which requires certain disclosures to be furnished to service station owners before a gasoline leasing agreement may be executed. The same law regulates the conduct of the lessor during the term of the franchise and also governs terminations and nonrenewals.

In other industries, Alaska law does not require franchisors to register or file disclosures with any state regulatory body. In the absence of such a requirement, the federal Franchise Rule applies, requiring franchisors to furnish a disclosure document prescribed by the Federal Trade Commission to prospective franchisees ten business days before a franchise sale is made. *See Franchise Rule.*

All American Hero Headquartered in Ft. Lauderdale, California, a franchisor of fast-food outlets.

Founded in 1980, All American Hero has been franchising since its inception. A typical All American Hero franchisee operates a fast-food operation devoted to hot and cold specialty sandwiches, including the franchisor's own submarine-style "Hero" sandwich and Philadelphia steak sandwiches. Of the franchisor's 50 outlets currently operating, none are company owned.

All American Hero, 2200 W. Commercial Blvd. Ste. 100, Ft. Lauderdale, FL 33309. Telephone: (305) 486-7000

Allison's Place Headquartered in Los Angeles, California, a franchisor of retail apparel stores.
Founded in 1980, Allison's has been franchising since 1985. A typical Allison's franchisee operates a mall or stip-center outlet devoted to women's clothing and accessories offered at discount prices. About a third of the franchisor's 230 active outlets are franchise units.
Allison's Place, 3161 E. Washington St., Los Angeles, CA 90023. Telephone: (213) 267-0663

Almost Heaven Hot Tubs Headquartered in Renick, West Virginia, a franchisor of specialty retail outlets.

Founded in 1971, Almost Heaven has been franchising since 1978. A typical franchisee operates a retail sales outlet for hot tubs, portable spas, saunas, and related products. The franchise is distinguised by a low initial investment with no ongoing fees or royalties. All of the franchisor's 975 outlets currently operating are franchise units.

Almost Heaven Hot Tubs, Rte. 5 FY, Renick, WV 24966. Telephone: (304) 497-3163

Aloette Cosmetics Headquartered in Malvern, Pennsylvania, a franchisor of cosmetic sales territories.

Founded in 1978, Aloette has been franchising since its inception. A typical Aloette franchisee operates a direct-sales business devoted to the franchisor's proprietary line of cosmetics, skin products, and health and beauty aids. All except one of the franchisor's 108 outlets are franchise units.

Aloette Cosmetics, 345 Lancaster Ave., Malvern, PA 19355. Telephone: (215) 644-8200

Alphagraphics Printshops of the Future Headquartered in Tucson, Arizona, a franchisor of document duplication outlets.

Founded in 1970, Alphagraphics has been franchising since 1980. A typical Alphagraphics franchisee operates a retail printing center specializing in duplicating services, offset printing, and desktop publishing services. In addition to conventional duplication and printing equipment, franchise shops also offer self-service design and typesetting with Apple Macintosh computers. The Alphagraphics chain is comprised of 230 outlets, all except eight of which are franchise units.

Alphagraphics Printshops of the Future, 3760 N. Commerce Dr., Tucson, AZ 85719. Telephone: (800) 528-4885

American Advertising Distributors Headquartered in Mesa, Arizona, a franchisor of direct-mail advertising services.

Founded in 1976, AAA has been franchising since the following year. A typical AAA franchisee operates an advertising sales operation utilizing direct-mail coupons. Of the 115 AAA outlets currently operating, all except one are franchise units.

American Advertising Distributors, Inc., P.O. Box AAD 16964, Mesa, AZ 85211. Telephone: (800) 528-8249

American Arbitration Association (AAA) A national association of arbitration boards established to resolve business disputes.

The AAA membership consists of local and state arbitration boards available to intervene in legal and contractual disputes and negotiate objective settlements between the parties. Arbitrators are usually attorneys who volunteer to help resolve legal disputes under the Association's guidelines.

Arbitration offers both parties in a dispute the benefit of resolving a conflict through a disinterested third party. In addition, arbitration usually results in speedy and relatively low-cost resolutions to problems that otherwise would entail lengthy and expensive court trials.

Both parties in a dispute or litigation must agree in advance to be bound by the arbitrator's decision. An arbitration clause may be included in a franchise agreement, stipulating that any disputes between franchisor and franchisee will be resolved by arbitration through the American Arbitration Association and/or or one of its member arbitrators. *See arbitration.*

American International Headquartered in Dallas, Texas, a franchisor of car rental agencies.

Founded in 1969, AI has been franchising since its inception. A typical AI franchisee operates an automobile rental outlet with a fleet of 75 to 200 vehicles. Featuring discount prices and off-airport locations, the chain steadily established a foothold in the competitive car rental market, with franchises in 38 states and 25 foreign countries. All of the franchisor's 1,500 outlets are franchise units.

American International Rent A Car Corp., 4801 Spring Valley Rd., Ste. 120B, Dallas, TX 75244. Telephone: (214) 233-6530

American Leak Detection Headquartered in Palm Springs, California, a franchisor of building maintenance services.

Founded in 1975, ALD has been franchising since 1984. A typical ALD franchisee operates a maintenance service specializing in detection and repair of concealed water and gas leaks, utilizing the franchisor's proprietary process and equipment. Of the 95 ALD outlets currently operating, none are company owned.

American Leak Detection, Inc., 1750 E. Arenas Rd., Ste. 1, Palm Springs, CA 92262. Telephone: (619) 320-9991

American Speedy Printing Centers Headquartered in Bloomfield Hills, Michigan, a franchisor of document duplication outlets.

Founded in 1976, American Speedy has been franchising since 1877. A typical American Speedy franchisee operates a retail printing center combining quick-print and high-speed duplication services with personal computer services such as word processing and mail list management. The chain has 508 franchised outlets.

American Speedy Printing Centers, 2555 Telegraph Rd., Bloomfield Hills, MI 48013. Telephone: (800) 521-4002

Americlean Mobile Power Wash Headquartered in Orlando, Florida, a franchisor of exterior maintenance services.

Founded in 1985, Americlean has been franchising since its inception. A typical Americlean franchisee operates a commercial exterior cleaning and restoration service utilizing the franchisor's patented "power-wash" equipment and techniques. Of the franchisor's 90 outlets currently operating, all are franchise units.

Americlean Mobile Power Wash & Restoration, 943 Taft Vineland Rd., Orlando, FL 32924. Telephone: (800) 262-WASH

am/pm Mini-Markets Headquartered in Los Angeles, California, a franchisor of retail convenience markets.

Founded in 1980, am/pm has been franchising since its inception. A typical am/pm franchisee operates a convenience store, usually on the same premises as a gasoline service station, retailing a limited selection of groceries, microwave foods, beverages, and sundries. The chain's outlets are widely associated with Atlantic Richfield stations. Approximately three fourths of the franchisor's 750 active outlets are franchise units.

Atlantic Richfield Company, 515 S. Flower St., Los Angeles, CA 90071. Telephone: (213) 486-3939

Annie's Book Stop Headquartered in Westborough, Massachusetts, a franchisor of retail book stores.

Founded in 1974 as the Book Swap, Annie's has been franchising since 1981. A typical Annie's franchisee operates a retail book exchange specializing in mass-market paperbacks and "pre-read" books. The start-up stock includes approximately 25,000 titles, delivered to the franchisee's outlet in the company's distinctive, red "Magic Wagon" van. In 1988, the franchisor was acquired by an east coast publishing house. All except one of the franchisor's 100 active outlets are franchise units.

Annie's Book Stop, 15 Lackey St., Westborough, MA 01581. Telephone: (617) 366-9547 See Adams, Annie.

Antitrust Any type of legislation or court ruling opposing trusts, monopolies, or large combinations of business and capital that restrain or threaten free trade. Since the turn of the century, all three branches of the federal government have consistently taken measures to preserve competition in the free enterprise system, through antitrust laws, agencies, and court decisions. The Federal Trade Commission was established by the U.S. Congress in 1914 to police monopolies and assure competition in commerce. The FTC Act declared unlawful "unfair methods of competition," but the Sherman Antitrust Act, more than any other federal legislation, set the ground rules for the modern system of competition. The Sherman Act is repeatedly cited by the courts in settling antitrust issues, such as price fixing, territoriality, and tie-in arrangements.

Price Fixing

Price fixing is one of the earliest trade practices ruled illegal under the Sherman Act. Under the Act, any attempt by a distributor or wholesaler to restrict the prices at which products are sold by dealers or other resellers is per se illegal. A franchisor cannot set any minimum, maximum, or fixed prices whatsoever for the goods and services offered to customers by franchisees. Franchisors can suggest prices, but may not encourage, discourage, punish, or reward franchisees for complying or failing to comply with the suggested price list.

Territorial Restrictions

Another common practice in franchising that is subject to scrutiny under antitrust laws is the designation of a restricted territory in connection with a franchise.

Franchisors can generally limit the use of trademarks and signs to specific geographic areas, but they cannot restrict franchisees from carrying on business outside a particular area. Most of the allowable restrictions that apply to a franchise territory restrain the franchisor, rather than the franchisee. A franchisor can promise not to compete with the franchisee within a designated territory, by agreeing not to open other franchise outlets or company-owned stores in the area. However, the franchisee cannot be restricted from selling to customers outside the territory, even in another franchisee's territory.

Tie-in Arrangements

An illegal "tie-in arrangement" is a contract that requires a franchisee, without justification, to purchase products from the franchisor or the franchisor's designated supplier. For example, a franchisor in the restaurant business cannot force its franchisees to purchase napkins and other supplies from the franchisor's wholesale supply subsidiary. However, franchisors can require franchisees to purchase a franchised product that is unique and cannot be acquired from other sources.

In numerous franchise disputes, franchisees have complained of being forced or coerced into buying fixtures, equipment, and supplies from a designated source at prices higher than those paid for the same items elsewhere. Although tie-in arrangements are usually struck down by today's courts, franchisors can set quality standards and specifications for the products purchased by franchisees for their own use or resale. *See Federal Trade Commission, Price Fixing, Tie-In Arrangments.*

Applause Video Corp. Headquartered in Omaha, Nebraska, a franchisor of videocassette rental outlets.

Founded in 1983, Applause Video has been franchising since 1985. A typical Applause Video franchisee operates a specialty retail store devoted to videocassette and VCR rentals and sales. More than half of the 48 Applause Video outlets currently operating are operated under franchise licenses.

Applause Video Corp., 2622 S. 156th Circle, Omaha, NE 68130. Telephone: (402) 330-1000

Application for Franchise In an era of increasing "business-format" franchising and decreasing "tradename-only" franchising, franchisors normally grant franchises to individuals, based on aptitudes, attitudes, skills, and experience. To be sure, a small percentage of franchisors may be willing to sell a franchise to anyone desiring to buy one. But, for the most part, franchisors can and must be highly selective. Outlet failures and dissention among the ranks of franchisees constitute severe burdens to any franchise organization. To qualify prospective franchisees, almost every franchisor actively recruiting today requires some form of *application for franchise* to be completed. Commonly, a prospective franchisee must submit an application before the franchisor will furnish the Uniform Franchise Offering Circular, or UFOC (a disclosure document prescribed by federal regulations, providing information about the franchisor, the franchise business, and the franchise agreement).

A typical application for franchise consists of three parts: (1) personal data, (2) financial data, (3) references. In addition, some application forms include essay-type questionnaires or space for supplemental information about prospective partners or investors.

Personal Data

In many respects, an application for franchise is similar to an employment application, requesting the full name, personal and business address and telephone, birth date, and other personal data about the prospective franchisee. Almost all applications require the applicant to provide details regarding his or her education and prior business background, including, names, places, dates, and degrees or titles.

Financial Data

To assess the applicant's financial capability or creditworthiness, every application for franchise includes a financial questionnaire or statement of net worth. In this section, the prospective franchisee must document his or her assets, such as any equity in real estate holdings, personal property, and monies in savings and checking accounts; and liabilties, such as any outstanding loans or other debts, credit card balances, and taxes payable.

Typically, franchisors multiply an applicant's stated assets and net worth by 80 percent, the proportion that a conventional lending institution might use to determine the maximum amount of a loan. Usually, franchisors will have the financial information verified by an independent credit or background checking service.

References

The applicant's personal and professional references help the franchisor assess the prospective franchisee's work stability and esteem by others. Three references are commonly required, but, in some instances, as many as five to ten may be requested.

The three parts of the application for franchise are illustrated in the sample.

See Franchise Rule, Recruitment, Uniform Franchise Offering Circular.

FRANCHISE APPLICATION

NAME _____
            Last   First   Middle Initial

ADDRESS _____
            Street   City   State   Zip

How long have you resided at the above address? _____

BUSINESS ADDRESS _____

BUSINESS TELEPHONE (   ) _____ RESIDENCE TELEPHONE (   ) _____

MARITAL STATUS _____ NO. OF DEPENDENTS _____ DATE OF BIRTH _____

U.S. Citizen: ☐ Yes ☐ No   Have you ever been convicted of a crime or pleaded nolo contendere? ☐ Yes ☐ No

Nearest Relative _____ Address _____

EDUCATION

High School _____ City/State _____

College _____ City/State _____

Graduate _____ Degree _____

EMPLOYMENT HISTORY

Most recent: _____
           Employer Name   Location   Position

2. _____

3. _____

4. _____

5. _____

EXPERIENCE *(Indicate any special experience you may have in):*

Sales (years) _____

Bookeeping/Accounting _____ Retail _____ Management _____

PERSONAL REFERENCES

1. _____

2. _____

PERSONAL FINANCIAL STATEMENT

This is a statement of: _____ my individual financial status

_____ the financial status of my spouse and me

ASSETS

Cash on hand $ _____

Accounts receivable _____

Stocks and bonds _____

Notes receivable _____

Cashable insurance _____

Real estate _____

Other (specify) _____

_____

_____

TOTAL _____

LIABILITIES

Notes payable $ _____

Accounts payable _____

Credit card _____

Mortgage _____

Taxes due _____

Contracts payable _____

Other _____

_____

_____

TOTAL _____

NET WORTH $ _____

Other income (e.g. spouse) _____

_____

Real estate payments or rent _____

_____

Have you ever reorganized due to insolvency or inability to pay debts?   ☐ Yes   ☐ No

If yes, explain _____

_____

Arbitration Resolution of a legal or contract dispute by a disinterested third party. Arbitration is an alternative to court action, in which both parties in a dispute agree to be bound by the decision of an independent arbitrator.

In disputes between a franchisor and a franchisee, a third- party arbitrator, such as the *American Arbitration Association*, can usually render a decision much faster and at far less cost than the courts. In addition, most arbitration hearings are conducted in private, out of public view, minimizing the potential for negative publicity for either party.

Approximately one fourth of the franchise agreements currently in use include arbitration clauses stipulating that any applicable dispute between franchisor and franchisee will be decided by independent arbitration. Under such clauses, both parties agree to submit any grievances or disputes to the designated arbitrator and to be bound by whatever decision is finally rendered.

From the franchisee's standpoint, arbitration helps to assure fair practices by the franchisor, which invariably constructs its franchise agreement to favor its own rights, as opposed to the franchisee's. From the franchisor's perspective, an agreement to submit to arbitration helps control litigation costs and enhances the ethical image of the franchise industry in general.

The International Franchise Association encourages its members to use negotiation and arbitration wherever possible to resolve franchisor-franchisee disputes. *See American Arbitration Association.*

Arby's Headquartered in Atlanta, Georgia, a franchisor of fast-food restaurants.

Founded in 1964, Arby's has been franchising since 1965. A typical Arby's franchisee operates a retail fast-food outlet serving packaged meals with both on-premises dining and take-out facilities. Once devoted exclusively to roast beef sandwiches, the current Arby's menu is designed to compete against hamburger, chicken, and sandwich outlets. The franchisor's system-wide sales currently exceed $1 billion. It is estimated that of the franchisor's 2,000 outlets currently operating, all except 200 are franchise units.

Arby's, Inc., 3495 Piedmont Rd., Ten Piedmont Ctr., Ste. 700, Atlanta, GA 30305. Telephone: (404) 262-2729

Arizona, Franchise Regulations The Arizona legislature has not passed any generally applicable franchise investment law. However, three statutes regulate franchise relationships in three industries.

The Petroleum Products Franchises Act regulates the franchise relationship between petroleum distributors and gasoline dealers. The law controls business practices and contract terms, limiting the ability of distributors to exercise undue control or terminate the franchise without reasonable grounds.

The Motor Vehicle Act regulates franchisors who supply automobile and motorcycle dealers. The rights of liquor wholesalers and suppliers to terminate franchise agreements are restricted by the Termination of Beer and Liquor Franchises Act. Arizona law does not require franchisors to register or file disclosures with any state regulatory body. In the absence of such a requirement, the federal Franchise Rule applies, requiring franchisors to furnish a disclosure document prescribed by the Federal Trade Commission to prospective franchisees ten business days before a franchise sale is made. *See Franchise Rule.*

Arkansas, Franchise Regulations The rights of franchise holders in Arkansas are protected by the Franchise Practices Act, which prevents franchisors from terminating a franchise without good cause. The law also forbids franchisors from refusing to renew franchise agreements upon their expiration, except for good cause. The same law prohibits "fraud and deceit" in the offer or sale of franchises.

In addition, the rights of service station owners are protected by the Gasoline Distributors and Dealers Act. Wholesalers of farm equipment are regulated by the Farm Equipment Retailer Act.

Arkansas law does not require franchisors to register or file disclosures with any state regulatory body. In the absence of such a requirement, the federal Franchise Rule applies, requiring franchisors to furnish a disclosure document prescribed by the Federal Trade Commission to prospective franchisees ten business days before a franchise sale is made. *See Franchise Rule.*

Armstrong World Industries Headquartered in Lancaster, Pennsylvania, a franchisor of retail floor covering outlets.

Founded in 1867, Armstrong has been franchising since 1985. A typical Armstrong franchisee operates a flooring products business devoted to the franchisor's proprietary line of floor and ceiling tiles and accessories. Of the franchisor's 275 outlets currently operating, none are company-owned.

Armstrong World Industries, P.O. Box 3001, Lancaster, PA 17604. Telephone: (717) 397-0611

Arthur Murray Schools of Dancing Headquartered in Coral Gables, Florida, a franchisor of recreational dancing schools.

Founded in 1912, Arthur Murray has been franchising since 1938. Over the century, franchisees have managed to remain competitive by adapting to changing dance and social trends, teaching everything from the Charleston to the Twist. The primary focus has consistently remained on ballroom dancing. A typical Arthur Murray franchisee operates a dance instruction studio specializing in ballroom steps. The chain currently consists of 225 outlets, all of which are franchise units.

Arthur Murray Franchised Schools, 1077 Ponce de Leon Blvd., Coral Gables, FL 33134. Telephone: (305) 445-9645

Athlete's Foot, The Headquartered in Atlanta, Georgia, a franchisor of retail shoe stores.

Founded in 1972, TAF has been franchising since the following year. A typical TAF franchisee operates a specialty boutqiue with a wide selection of sports footwear, ranging from baseball and golf cleats to tennis and jogging shoes. Eighty percent of the franchisor's 500 outlets are franchise units.

The Athlete's Foot, 3735 Atlanta Industrial Parkway, Atlanta, Georgia 30331. Telephone: (404) 696-3400

Athletic Attic Headquartered in Gainesville, Florida, a franchisor of retail sports apparel stores.

Founded in 1973, AA has been franchising since the following year. A typical AA franchisee operates a specialty boutique with a athletic orientation and motif. Stores specialize in sneakers, cleats, jogging suits, and athletic shirts and jackets. Founded by a college track coach and a former sprinter, the company sets aside a portion of its profits to sponsor amateur track and field competitions. Of the franchisor's 175 outlets currently operating, all but 15 are franchise units.

Athletic Attic, P. O. Box 14503, Gainseville, FL 32604. Telephone: (904) 377-5289

Athletic Training Equipment Headquartered in Santa Cruz, California, a franchisor of baseball recreation and training outlets.

Founded in 1971, ATE has been franchising since 1983. A typical ATE franchisee operates a baseball batting practice facility, with both indoor and outdoor facilities, and automated pitching machines which serve batting practice at varying speed and skill levels. All except one of the franchisor's 55 active outlets are franchise units.

Athletic Training Equipment, 115 Post St., Santa Cruz, CA 95060. Telephone: (800) 547-6273

Atlantic Personnel Services Headquartered in Wilmington, North Carolina, a franchisor of personnel employment agencies.

Founded in 1982, Atlantic has been franchising since 1985. A typical Atlantic franchisee operates a personnel recruitment and placement business focusing on permanent employment opportunities. Of the franchisor's 36 outlets currently operating, all except one are franchise units.

Atlantic Personnel Services, 4806 Shelly Dr., Wilmington, NC 8405. Telephone: (800) 558-5883

Automotive Industry Franchises Automotive sales, service, and reconditioning outlets are among the oldest businesses established through the franchise method of expansion. After assembling his first motorcar in 1896, Henry Ford began selling the mass-produced Model T through franchised dealerships as early as 1909. Since, franchising has been used to open outlets that sell, fuel, service, restore, customize, clean, and rent motor vehicles of all sizes and shapes.

Regulation of automotive franchises is divided into three segments. The rights of automobile and farm equipment dealers are governed by state motor vehicle, automobile dealership, and farm equipment retailer laws. The petroleum industry, including service station franchises, is regulated by separate state laws which prohibit termination or refusal to renew a gasoline service station franchise without reasonable notice and good cause. Other franchises not affected by these specialized statutes fall under state and federal franchise regulations, including the FTC's Franchise Rule.

Excluding automobile dealers and gasoline service stations, franchises in the automotive industries fall into five general categories: (1) motor vehicle parts and equipment; (2) motor vehicle service, repair, and maintenance; (3) motor vehicle cleaning and restoration; (4) motor vehicle painting and body work; (5) car and truck rental and leasing. The following table lists the largest franchise chains in each category, ranked by estimated number of outlets.

A. Largest Motor Vehicle Parts & Equipment Franchise Chains

Franchisor	Outlets
1. Western Auto	2,500
2. Uniroyal Goodrich	2,200
3. Goodyear Tire	1,700
4. Big O Tires	280
5. Mighty Distributing	220
6. Champion Auto	125
8. Penn Jersey	85
9. Aid Auto	70
10. Fantasy Coachworks	25

B. Largest Motor Vehicle Service, Repair, & Maintenance Franchise Chains

Franchisor	Outlets
1. Midas International	2,010
2. AAMCO Transmission	920
3. Meineke Discount Muffler	820
4. NOVUS Windshield Repair	500
5. Jiffy Lube	450
6. Precision Tune	375
7. Lee Myles Transmission	150
8. Cottman Transmission	145
9. Sparks Tune-Up	140
10. Mr. Transmission	135

C. Largest Motor Vehicle Cleaning & Restoration Franchise Chains

Franchisor	*Outlets*
1. Sparky Coin-Op	160
2. Classic Car Wash	90
3. Perma-Shine Car Care	40
4. Hanna Auto Wash	30
5. American Mobile Wash	20

D. Largest Motor Vehicle Painting & Body Work Franchise Chains

Franchisor	*Outlets*
1. MAACO Auto Painting	450
2. Ziebert	375
3. Sunshine Polishing Systems	250
4. Tuff-Kote Dinol	170
5. Tidy Car	160

E. Largest Car & Truck Rental Franchise Chains

Franchisor	*Outlets*
1. Budget	3,100
2. Hertz	1,660
3. American International	1,500
4. Avis	1,200
5. Thrifty	590

AutoSpa Headquartered in Great Neck, New York, a franchisor of automotive service outlets.

Founded in 1980, AutoSpa has been franchising since 1983. A typical AutoSpa franchisee operates a retail service business specializing in quick oil change and lubcrication. About two thirds of the franchisor's 50 outlets currently operating are franchise units; the remainder are company-owned.

AutoSpa, 343 Great Neck Rd., Great Neck, NY 11021. Telephone: (718) 899-2126

Avis Rent A Car Headquartered in Garden City, New York, a franchisor of retail car rental agencies.

Founded in 1946, Avis has been franchising since its inception. A typical Avis franchisee operates a car rental lot featuring a broad range of passenger and utility vehicles, from economy cars to luxury sedans and vans. The franchise program includes used car sales and truck rental and leasing. Founded by franchise and car rental pioneer Warren Avis, the chain was sold to a Hertz franchisee in 1954 and acquired, in 1986, by Wesray Capital. The franchisor is reportedly no longer recruiting new franchisees. It is estimated that of the franchisor's 1,200 outlets currently operating, less than a third are franchise units.

Avis Rent A Car System, 900 Old Country Rd., Garden City, NY 11530

B

**Barnes
to
Business Format**

Barnes, Joan Operator and franchisor of preschool centers. The founder of Gymboree Corporation, Barnes virtually created and dominated an entirely new child-services industry consisting of developmental learning centers for preschoolers.

Barnes was a 29-year-old mother of two in 1976, when she opened the first Gymboree exercise center for children. She had a keen interest in the psychomotor and emotional development of infants, toddlers, and preschoolers. In the 1960s and early 1970s, a rash of parenting books had appeared, examining the formative stages of childhood development and enouraging mothers to become involved in early childhood play. Barnes created the Gymboree concept at the San Rafael, California Community Center, where she was in charge of children's programs. With a $3,000 investment from a colleague, she began opening her own preschool centers, providing an environment to promote self-confidence and self-esteem for parents and toddlers alike.

At Gymboree, using specially designed equipment, children from three months to four years of age participate with their parents in planned exercise programs and inventive play. Barnes' standardized repertoire includes special limbering exercises for infants, called "boogies." Encouraged to play freely in a

Joan Barnes, founder and chairwoman of Gymboree Corporation.

spacious environment equipped with plentiful play equipment, children acquire social and leadership skills which ostensibly help cultivate future academic achievement.

Barnes had opened eight Gymboree schools of her own, when an experienced franchise executive, Robert Jacob, persuaded her to begin franchising in 1980. Working capital for the expansion program was supplied by an investment firm in the San Francisco Bay Area, which continues to hold a 35 percent interest in Gymboree. In eight years, Barnes sold more than 300 franchises, generating over $1 million in annual fees and royalties.

Gymboree Corporation also operates 34 retail stores which market active wear, toys, books, audio and video tapes, and at-home play equipment.

Barnes, 50 percent owner of the franchising corporation, has an estimated personal net worth of more than $2 million. A company spokesman estimates that at least 35,000 children participate in the Gymboree program today.

Her book, *Gymboree: Giving Your Child Physical, Mental, and Social Confidence Through Play*, was published by Doubleday, under the Dolphin imprint, in 1981.

See Gymboree.

Barter Exchange Headquartered in Austin, Texas, a franchisor of commercial bartering service.

Founded in 1983, Barter Exchange has been franchising since the following year. A typical Barter Exchange franchisee operates a bartering service in which member companies exchange goods or services with other members. Of the franchisor's 18 outlets currently operating, all except one are franchise units.

Barter Exchange, 1106 Clayton Lane, Ste. 480W, Austin, TX 78723. Telephone: (800) 448-7233

Baskin-Robbins Headquartered in Glendale, California, a franchisor of retail ice cream shops.

Baskin-Robbins was founded by two brothers-in-law, Burton Baskin and Irvine Robbins. On December 6, 1945, Robbins opened a retail store in Glendale, California, called Snowbird, specializing in 21 exotic flavors of ice cream. The following year, he and Baskin formed a partnership to distribute Robbins' product line through a multi-outlet chain. Baskin called his stores Burton's Ice Cream.

In 1948, the expansion-minded relatives sold their first franchise under the name Baskin-Robbins. The partners purchased their own dairy in 1951, in Burbank, California, to assure control over manufacturing and new-product development. In 1953, the "31 Flavors" motif and trademark were instituted, giving the organization its unique market niche and flair. Conceived by two west coast advertising designers, Ralph Carson and Jack Roberts, the Baskin-Robbins logo featured chocolate and cherry polka dots and a bold number 31, representing a different ice cream flavor for every day of the month.

The 1,000th Baskin-Robbins outlet opened in 1970. Irvine Baskin died in 1967 at the age of 54, and the company was purchased by J. Lyons & Co. Ltd. of London, England in 1973. Burton Robbins retired in 1978, when J. Lyons was acquired by Allied Brewery. The company was reorganized in 1986 as Baskin-Robbins, Inc.

The Baskin-Robbins chain and its constantly changing line of exotic dairy products have become a virtual American tradition. Since its inception, the company has developed more than 600 flavors of ice cream and received the highest rating in seven of the last eight "Taste of America" surveys conducted by *Restaurants and Institutions magazine*.

A typical Baskin-Robbins franchisee operates a retail ice cream parlor featuring the franchisor's private brand products. In 1982, the parent company was sued by a group of franchisees who argued their franchise contracts illegally forced them to buy only the franchisor's products for resale. The court ruled in favor of Baskin-Robbins, affirming the rights of franchisors to license outlets strictly for the purpose of distributing their own products. Of the franchisor's 3,450 outlets currently operating in the U.S., 2,300 are franchise units. Baskin-Robbins International operates another 900 outlets in 37 countries.

Baskin-Robbins, 31 Baskin-Robbins Pl., Glendale, CA 91201. Telephone: (818) 956-0031

Burton Baskin first began marketing ice cream from his own Burton's frozen food store (left), while his brother-in-law, Irvine Robbins, was setting up a small chain of Snowbird Ice Cream shops (below).

Baskin-Robbins Ice Cream/Silicorp Headquartered in Rexdale, Ontario, a franchisor of Canadian ice cream parlors.

Founded in 1971, Silicorp has been franchising since its inception. A typical Silicorp franchisee operates a retail ice cream parlor featuring the franchisor's proprietary line of 31 flavors of ice cream. Of the franchisor's 200 outlets currently operating, all except 11 are franchise units.

Baskin Robbins/Silicorp, 91 Skyway Ave., Ste. 200, Rexdale, Ont., Canada M9W 6C7. Telephone: (416) 675-3131

Bathcrest, Inc. Headquartered in Salt Lake City, Utah, a franchisor of specialty interior remodeling services.

Founded in 1979, Bathcrest has been franchising since 1985. A typical Bathcrest franchisee operates a remodeling business specializing in repair and resurfacing of porcelain bathtubs, sinks, and fixtures. The chain consists of 135 outlets, with only one company-owned unit.

Bathcrest, Inc., 2425 S. Progress Dr., Salt Lake City, UT 84119. Telephone: (801) 972-1110

Bath Genie Headquartered in Marlboro, Massachusetts, a franchisor of specialty interior remodeling services.

Founded in 1976, Bath Genie has been franchising since 1983. A typical Bath Genie franchisee operates a remodeling business specializing in the resurfacing of bathtubs, sinks, and tile fixtures. Of the franchisor's 32 outlets currently operating, all except one are franchise units.

Bath Genie, 109 E. Main St., Marlboro, MA 01752. Telephone: (617) 481-8338

Bathtique Headquartered in Rochester, New York, a franchisor of specialty retail outlets.

Founded in 1969, Bathtique has been franchising since its inception. A typical Bathtique franchisee operates a retail store devoted to bath accessories and gift items. Of the franchisor's 80 outlets currently operating, all except 21 are franchise units.

Bathtique, 247 Goodman St., Rochester, NY 14607. Telephone: (716) 442-9190

Becker Milk Company, Ltd. Headquartered in Scarboro, Ontario, a franchisor of Canadian retail convenience outlets.

Founded in 1957, Becker has been franchising since 1972. A typical Becker franchisee operates a convenience food store stocking dairy products, selected grocery items, and household supplies. Eighty four of the franchisor's 784 outlets currently operating are franchise units.

Becker Milk Co., 671 Warden Ave., Scarboro, Ont., Canada M1L 3Z7. Telephone: (416) 698-2591

Beefsteak Charlie's Restaurants Headquartered in New York City, a franchisor of food service outlets.

Founded in 1972, Beefsteak Charlie's has been franchising since 1975. A typical Beefsteak Charlie's franchisee operates a family-style steakhouse. Of the franchisor's 48 outlets currently operating, 33 are franchise units.

Beefsteak Charlie's Restaurants, 11 E. 26th St., 8th Fl., New York, NY 10010. Telephone: (212) 696-7700

Bellini Juvenile Designer Furniture Boutiques Headquartered in Englewood, New Jersey, a franchisor of retail furniture outlets.

Founded in 1982, Bellini has been franchising since 1984. A typical Bellini franchisee operates a retail hard-goods store specializing in imported "designer" furniture for enfants and children. Of the franchisor's 40 outlets currently operating, 34 are franchise units.

Bellini Juvenile Designer Furniture Boutiques, 15 Engle, Ste. 304, Englewood, NJ 07631. Telephone: (800) 332-3339

Ben & Jerry's Ice Cream Headquartered in Waterbury, Vermont, a franchisor of specialty fast-food outlets.

Founded in 1978, Ben & Jerry's has been franchising since 1981. A typical Ben & Jerry's franchisee operates an ice cream parlor featuring the franchisor's proprietary line of 34 flavors of "gourmet" ice cream. The outlet is distinguished by its nostalgic motif designed to attract an upscale clientele. Of the franchisor's 70 outlets currently operating, all except five are franchise units.

Ben & Jerry's Ice Cream, P.O. Box 240, Rte. 100, Waterbury, VT 05676. Telephone: (802) 244-5641

Benihana of Tokyo Headquartered in Miami, Florida, a franchisor of Japanese restaurants.

Founded in 1964 by a Japanese Olympic wrestler Rocky Aaoki, Benihana has been franchising since 1970. A typical Benihana franchisee operates a family-style restaurant with an Oriental ambience. Twenty percent of the franchisor's 50 outlets are franchise units.

Benihana of Tokyo, P. O. Box 020210, Miami, FL 33102. Telephone: (305) 593-0770

Best Inns of America Headquartered in Marion, Illinois, a franchisor of lodging outlets.

Founded in 1970, Best Inns has been franchising since 1982. A typical Best Inns franchisee operates an economy-priced motor inn utilizing standardized site-selection, architectural, and construction specifications. To reduce the initial investment and overhead, the motel is normally constructed on low-priced real estate and operated without food and beverage service. Of the franchisor's 25 outlets currently operating, nine are franchise units.

Best Inns of America, P.O. Box 1719, Marion, IL 62959. Telephone: (618) 997-5454

Better Homes Realty Headquartered in Walnut Creek, California, a franchisor of independent real estate sales offices.

Founded in 1964, Better Homes has been franchising since 1975. A typical Better Homes franchisee operates a licensed real estate brokerage specializing in residential listings. The franchisor does not own any of the 100 outlets in the Better Homes system.

Better Homes Realties, 710 S. Broadway, Ste. 200A, Walnut Creek, CA 94596. Telephone: (415) 937-9001

Big O Tires Headquartered in Englewood, Colorado, a franchisor of retail tire outlets.

Founded in 1962, Big O has been franchising since 1964. A typical Big O franchisee operates an automotive tire store merchandising the franchisor's proprietary product line and augmented by services such as wheel alignments, tire rotation, and balancing. Of the franchisor's 300 outlets currently operating, all but 15 are franchise units.

Big O Tires, P.O. Box 3206, Englewood, CO 80155. Telephone: (303) 779-9991

Binex Headquartered in Sacramento, California, a franchisor of commercial accounting services.

Founded in 1965, Binex has been franchising since 1967. A typical Binex franchisee operates an accounting and tax preparation service based on the franchisor's standardized computer processing system. All 60 of the Binex outlets currently open and operating are franchise units.

Binex Corp., 4441-E Auburn Blvd., Sacramento, CA 95841. Telephone: (916) 483-8080

Blue Chip Cookies Headquartered in San Francisco, California, a franchisor of specialty bakery goods outlets.

Founded in 1982, Blue Chip has been franchising since 1985. A typical Blue Chip franchisee operates a retail bakery goods shop specializing in "gourmet" cookies freshly prepared on the premises from the franchisor's proprietary ingredients. Of the franchisor's 47 outlets currently operating, 26 are franchise units.

Blue Chip Cookies Franchise Corp., 124 Beale St., Ste. 401, San Francisco, CA 94109. Telephone: (415) 928-2583

Boardwalk Fries Headquartered in Ellicott City, Maryland, a franchisor of fast-food outlets.

Founded in 1981, Boardwalk has been franchising since 1983. A typical Boardwalk franchisee operates a fast-food stand specializing in french fried potatoes, barbequed beef, and beverage service. Of the franchisor's 65 outlets currently operating, all except five are franchise units.

Boardwalk Fries, 8307 Main St., Ellicott City, MD 21043.

Big Boy Restaurants Headquartered in Washington, DC, a franchisor of family-style restaurants.

Founded in 1936 as Bob's Big Boy, the chain has been franchising since 1946. Bob Wian opened the first Bob's restaurant in 1934, specializing in his double-decker Big Boy sandwich. He began franchising in the late 1930s and a decade later, transformed his hamburger stands into car-hop drive-ins. The restaurants were so integral to American life in post-war America, that Time magazine featured the chain's cartoon advertising symbol, Big Boy, on its cover.

A typical Big Boy franchisee operates a full-service coffee shop featuring a diversified menu. The franchisor is a subsidiary of Marriott Corporation, which is presently converting its franchised Howard Johnson's restaurants into modern Big Boy outlets. All except one of the franchisor's 780 outlets currently operating are franchise units.

Big Boy Restaurants, One Marriott Dr., Washington, DC 20058. Telephone: (301) 897-7863 *See Howard Johnson.*

Bojangles of America Headquartered in Charlotte, North Carolina, a franchisor of fast-food outlets.

Founded in 1976, Bojangles has been franchising since the following year. Expansion began in earnest in 1982, when the chain was acquired by Horn and Hardart Company. A typical Bojangles franchisee operates a fast-food restaurant featuring Cajun-style chicken and an upscale dining environment with both sit-down and drive-up facilities. Besides chicken, the menu features rice and biscuits, hamburgers, specialty sandwiches, "home-style" fried potatoes, and breakfast orders. More than half of the 380 Bojangles restaurants currently operating are franchise units.

Bojangles of America, P.O. Box 240239, Charlotte, NC 28224. Telephone: (704) 527-2675

Bonanza Restaurants Headquartered in Dallas, Texas, a franchisor of food service outlets.

Founded in 1963, Bonanza has been franchising since its inception. A typical Bonanza franchisee operates a family-style restaurant with a limited menu devoted to steaks, seafood, chicken, and salads. All except two of the 610 Bonanza outlets currently in business are franchise units.

Bonanza Restaurants, 8080 N. Central Expwy., Ste. 500, Dallas, TX 75206. Telephone: (800) 527-6832

Boston Pizza International, Inc. Headquartered in Richmond, British Columbia, a franchisor of food service outlets.

Founded in 1963, Boston Pizza has been franchising since its inception. A typical Boston Pizza franchisee operates a specialty restaurant devoted to pizza and beverage sales, with full table service in additon to take-out and delivery service. Of the franchisor's 76 outlets currently operating in Canada, all except two are franchise units.

Boston Pizza International, Inc., 212-6011 Westminster Hwy., Richmond, B.C., Canada V7C 4V4. Telephone: (604) 270-1108

Bredeaux Pisa Headquartered in Corning, Iowa, a franchisor of fast-food outlets.

Founded in 1985, Bredeaux has been franchising since its inception. A typical Bredeaux franchisee operates a fast-food pizza restaurant. Seventy three of the franchisor's 85 outlets that are currently operating are franchise units.

Bredeaux Pisa, P.O. Box 333, Corning, IA 50841.

Bresler's 33 Flavors Ice Cream Shops Headquartered in Des Plaines, Illinois, a franchisor of specialty fast-food outlets.

Founded in 1930, Bresler's has been franchising since 1963. A typical Bresler's franchisee operates an ice-cream parlor devoted to the franchisor's multiflavored ice cream and yoghurt products. Of the franchisor's 300 outlets currently operating, all except one are franchise units.

Bresler's, 999 E. Touhy Ave., Ste. 333, Des Plaines, IL 60018. Telephone: (800) 535-3333

Budget Rent a Car Headquartered in Chicago, Illinois, a franchisor of automobile rental offices.

The first Budget Rent a Car location was establishedi n 1958, by the late Morris Mirkin, in a Los Angeles storefront. It was Mirkin's belief that the major car rental companies of the day charged more than a typical family could afford. His outlet opened with 15 used cars, offered for rent at four dollars per day and four cents per mile — less than half the fees charged by Hertz and Avis. He chose the name Budget to appeal to the cost-conscious car renter, but also to reflect his own financial situation.

It did not take Mirkin long to realize that car rental customers demanded new cars and were willing pay a higher price to rent them. In 1959, he appealed to a cousin, Jules Lederer, for assistance. Lederer formed a leasing company to fund the purchase of a hundred new Chevrolets, and Mirkin opened three more locations in Los Angeles and San Diego. In 1960, Lederer organized Budget Rent A Car Corporation to franchise rental outlets.

The first Budget franchisee was Irwin "Bick" Bickson, a Chicago man, who opened with 37 cars. Other outlets opened in quick succession in Phoenix and Houston and within a year, 15 Budget franchises had been established. That same year, Bickson sold his Chicago franchise and opened one in Hawaii.

The chain expanded into Europe in 1964, with the opening of a Budget rental outlet in Zurich. A sublicensing program was initiated for master distributors, spurring rapid expansion. By the end of the year, Budget was represented in 42 states and all Canadian provinces. In 1968, the first Budget franchises opened in the Caribbean, South Africa, and on Cyprus.

In 1968, Budget was acquired by Transamerica Corporation for an undisclosed price. Morris Belzberg, a native of Calgary, Alberta who had entered the scene as the first Canadian franchisee, was named president of the franchising corporation in 1969. By then, the chain had proliferated to 636 outlets.

In 1986, the company was sold by Transmerica in a leveraged buyout by a group of independent investors headed by Belzberg and the Fulcrum II Limited Partnership, formed by Gibbons, Green, van Amerongen. Budget's stock appeared on the public stock exchange on May 22, 1987, with an initial offering of 3.2 million shares at a price of $14 per share. In the fall of 1988, the company announced plans to return to private ownership.

A typical Budget franchisee operates a car rental agency with a fleet of 30 to 100 vehicles. It is estimated that of the franchisor's 3,200 outlets currently operating, all except five percent are franchise units.

Budget Rent A Car Corp., 200 N. Michigan Ave., Chicago, IL 60601. Telephone: (312) 580-5000 *See Lederer, James.*

In 1959, Budget began renting new Chevrolets in Los Angeles at $5 per day and 5 cents per mile. Budget Rent-a-Car was incorporated in 1960.

*What every stylish Budget counter represen-
tative was wearing in 1966.*

Budgetel Franchises International, Inc. Headquartered in Milwaukee, Wisconsin, a franchisor of lodging outlets.

Founded in 1936, Budgetel has been franchising since 1986. A typical Budgetel franchisee operates an economy-priced motor inn. Of the 63 Budgetel outlets currently operating, ten are franchise units.

Budgetel Franchises International, Inc., 212 W. Wisconsin Ave., Milwaukee, WI 53203. Telephone: (414) 272-6020

Building Inspector of America Headquartered in Wakefield, Massachusetts, a franchisor of real estate inspection services.

Founded in 1985, Building Inspector has been franchising since its inception. A typical Building Inspector franchisee operates a property inspection business for residential and commercial real estate listed for resale. Of the franchisor's 41 outlets currently operating, none are company owned.

Building Inspector of America, 684 Main St. Wakefield, MA 01880. Telephone: (800) 321-4677

Burger King Headquartered in Miami, Florida, a franchisor of fast-food outlets.

Founded in 1951, Burger King has been franchising since 1957. Burger King originated as InstaBurger King, founded by two Jacksonville restaurant equipment salesmen, Keith Kramer and Mathew Burns. Their fast-food system was based on a unique broiler which automated hamburger cooking and streamlined the preparation process. The first franchise was purchased by two Cornell graduates, David Edgerton and James McLamore. The enterprising restaurant operators completely redesigned the InstaBurger system, including the automatic broiler, and introduced a hamburger with quarter-pound beef patties, dubbed "the Whopper."

In 1957, Edgerton and McLamore began franchising their own system, which they called Burger King, on a regional basis. In 1962, they succeeded in buying out InstaBurger King and expanded their franchising efforts nationwide. J. Jeffrey Campbell is the current chairman of Burger King Corp., which boasts the second largest hamburger chain and tenth most recognizable brand name in the United States.

A typical Burger King franchisee operates a fast-food restaurant specializing in "charcoal broiled" hamburgers and specialty sandwiches. Since 1982, the company's emphasis has shifted from franchising to company-owned outlets, acquisitions, and limited partnerships. Of the franchisor's estimated 4,500 outlets currently operating, about two thirds are franchise units.

Burger King, P.O. Box 520783, Miami, FL 33152. Telephone: (305) 596-7011

Business Format Franchising The practice of granting franchises in conjunction with standardized operating, marketing, and/or management methods.

In contrast to *trademark* or *tradename-only* franchising, in which a franchisor grants only the right to sell a trademarked product or service, a business-format franchise involves a combination of a trademark, a training program, an operations manual, systematic management procedures, and other "significant control or assistance" by the franchisor.

In 1986, the International Franchise Association (IFA) commissioned John Naisbitt, a consultant and author of a best-selling nonfiction book, *Megatrends*, to conduct a study on franchising trends. The author concluded that tradename-only and product franchising has declined steadily since 1972, while business-format franchising has increased. His list of the ten most popular formats included restaurants, non-food retail outlets, lodging establishments, convenience markets, business services, automotive products and services, retail food outlets, car rental agencies, construction and home improvement outlets, and recreational and travel services.

A typical business format franchise has the following elements:

1. Licensed Trademark

The franchisee receives the right to use the franchisor's trademark, name, logo, or other commercial symbol, thus taking advantage of the parent company's reputation and image. For example, a franchisee licensed to use the McDonald's trademark benefits from major national television advertising and the image of an industry giant.

2. Training Program

The franchisee receives training in operating the franchise business, usually at the franchisor's headquarters or at a designed site. Industry-wide, franchise training programs range from two days to six months. A typical curriculum consists of the following subjects: industry background; outlet development; accounting, purchasing and inventory methods; product preparation, manufacturing, or merchandising; sales and marketing; advertising and promotion; staff hiring and training. Additional technical or industry-specific training may also be offered, depending on the business and the franchise.

Refresher courses, periodic seminars, and annual conferences are also common elements of a franchise training system.

3. Operations Manual

The franchisor's know-how and experience are usually documented in a confidential operations manual loaned to franchisees for the term of the franchise. A good manual includes detailed policies, procedures, and techniques for starting and developing the outlet, ordering initial supplies and inventory, pricing and merchandising, preparing or selling products, outlet management, hiring and training staff, personnel policies, bookkeeping techniques, and technical aspects of the business.

Many franchise operations manuals are divided into series, with separate volumes devoted to daily operating procedures, management policies, marketing and advertising, technical operations, and so forth.

4. Specifications, Blueprints, and Designs

Franchisors often provide specifications and designs for building and operating the outlet. Examples include architectural plans, construction blueprints, and designs for fixtures and signs. Franchisors may also provide approved supplier lists, suggested or mandatory opening inventory lists, and detailed specifications for equipment and ingredients, where applicable.

Food service franchisors commonly provide franchisees with "secret" recipes or ingredients, such as premade dough for bakery goods or patented syrups for bottled soft drinks.

5. Advertising Systems

More than half of franchisors administer or provide for a cooperative advertising fund, to which franchisees contribute a small percentage of their outlets' gross revenues. This pool is generally used to finance major national or regional campaigns to the benefit of all franchisees.

Franchisors may also assist individual outlet owners through the preparation of standard advertising materials, such as fliers, commercials, or camera-ready artwork for newspaper or magazine advertisements. Most franchise agreements force franchisees to abide by their franchisors' advertising standards and to use only artwork and language approved by the franchisor's advertising department.

6. Ongoing Assistance

A typical business format franchise includes provisions for ongoing assistance, such as on-site troubleshooting and guidance by a field manager or consultant. Franchisees may also have access to company advisers via a toll-free "hotline."

As franchisors improve their business systems and operating methods, they invariably share innovations with their franchisees or upgrade the image of their outlets.

In consideration of the benefits of a business format franchise, the franchisee pays a fee. The franchise fee usually has two components: (1) an initial fee, due upon signing of the franchise agreement, and (2) an ongoing fee, most often a royalty based on the outlet's gross sales. *See Franchise, Franchisee, Franchising, Operating Manual, Franchise Fee.*

Business Organization One of the first decisions faced by any business owner is how to organize the business. There are legal as well as tax considerations which must enter into this decision. Franchisees are well advised to seek and rely on competent counsel, such as a small business attorney, CPA, or other licensed advisor, before deciding on a particular form of organization.

Normally, a business is conducted as one of three entities: (1) sole proprietorship, (2) partnership, or (3) corporation.

Tax Considerations

In general, a business operated as a sole proprietorship does not pay income taxes. Instead, the sole proprietor reports profits or losses from the business on his own income tax return.

Profits from a corporation are usually taxed both to the corporation and again to the individual shareholders when profits are distributed as dividends. A competent attorney should be consulted to determine the legal, organizational, and tax implications of incorporation. Most franchise agreements stipulate certain conditions and actions required when a franchise business is organized as a corporation.

Following is a general discussion of the distinguishing traits, advantages, and drawbacks to each form of business organization.

Franchises Operated as Sole Proprietorships

The sole proprietorship is the simplest form of business organization. The business has no separate identity from its owner's. Its liabilities are the owner's personal liabilities. Income from a sole proprietorship is part of the owner's total gross reportable income.

The proprietor must report all income from the business on federal and state tax returns. In addition, the owner is subject to self-employment tax.

The Internal Revenue Service allows sole proprietors to deduct such expenses as advertising, bank charges, equipment depreciation, insurance, office supplies, rent, utilities, and other costs of doing business.

Franchises Operated as Partnerships

In a general partnership, each partner shares both the liabilities and the assets of the business. Each is taxed according to his or her share of the profits. As with a sole proprietor, the partner must report all income form the business on state and federal tax returns, and may have to pay self-employment tax in addition to income tax.

The partnership must also submit a separate tax return disclosing the profits, draws, and advances paid out to the partners. Similarly, partners are jointly and severably liable for all liabilities of the business.

In a limited liability partnership, only the general partners have direct responsibility for the debts and liabilities of the business. The limited partners receive a share of the profits, which are then taxed as ordinary income.

Franchises Operated as Corporations

When a business is operated as a corporation, profits are taxed to the corporation. When profits are distributed in the form of dividends, these are taxed to the individual shareholders. However, the corporation is a separate entity, a legal "person" by and of itself. In general, the corporation, not its shareholders, is responsible for the liabilities of the business. In some instances, the officers and directors of a small corporation may be held liable for debts of the business and the actions of employees.

In a sub-Chapter S corporation, the corporation is not taxed, but shareholders must report their share of profits and losses on their gross income statements when reporting tax liabilities.

To form a corporation, all shareholders must transfer money or property, or both, to the corporation in exchange for stock entitling each shareholder to a portion of the profit. Stock may generally not be given in exchange for services. But stock may be issued in return for cancellation of indebtedness for past services performed.

A competent attorney experienced in small businesses and closely held corporations should be consulted in all matters pertaining to the formation of a corporation, issuance of stock, and reporting of tax liabilities.

Usually, a franchisee's election to incorporate is governed by certain provisions in the franchise agreement. A franchise is normally granted to an individual, in reliance on his or her character, aptitude, business skill, management ability, and other qualities. The franchisee must assign the franchise to the newly formed corporation. The assignment usually requires the franchisor's prior approval, but approval will not be reasonably withheld.

The following stipulations are typical:

1. Control of ownership

The franchisee you must own and control the majority of the ownership (equity) and voting power of the corporation. This provision protects both the franchisor and the franchisee against the involuntary wrenching of control from by other shareholders.

2. Management control

The franchisee must actively manage and direct the corporation. In other words, the franchisee must be the corporation's chief executive officer.

3. Exclusive business

The corporation must not be engaged in any other business besides the franchise business.

4. Stock legend

The stock certificates of the corporation may not bear any trademark or symbol of the franchisor, unless they are accompanied by a statement that the stock is stock in a franchise (not stock in the franchising corporation).

All stock certificates must bear a legend stating that the transfer of the stock is limited, or such other legend as is required by the appropriate state or federal corporate regulatory agency for stock in a corporate franchisee.

5. Personal guarantee

The franchisee must usually sign a personal guarantee stating that he or she will be empowered to act on behalf of the new corporation and will personally guarantee all the liabilities, debts, and obligations under the franchise agreement.

6. Corporate documents

Upon organizing the corporation, the franchisee must usually submit the following items to the franchisor:

A. A Resolution of the Board of Directors stating full acknowledgement and approval of the franchise agreement;

B. A list of all shareholders, stating their names, addresses, and the number of shares owned by each;

C. A list of all officers and directors;

D. A copy of the Articles of Incorporation, Corporate Bylaws, and other corporate resolutions.

**California
to
Cutlery World**

California, Franchise Regulations California was the first state to enact a franchise investment law calling for full disclosure of pertinent information about franchisors, franchise businesses, and franchise agreements. In 1971, the legislature adopted the Franchise Investment Act, requiring registration and disclosure by all franchisors operating in California. Other state laws protect the rights of franchisees to renew their franchise agreements on expiration and to join trade associations and cooperatives.

The Franchise InvestmentLaw

Before offering or selling a franchise in the state, a franchisor must first prepare a disclosure document prescribed by the statute, then file the information, along with the franchise agreement, financial statements, and related documents, with the California Department of Corporations. The Corporations Commissioner must approve the registration and all proposed advertisements to be used in the state, before the franchisor may proceed to advertise the franchise.

In addition to a disclosure document, franchisors are also required to submit the following items to the Department of Corporations:

1. Application for registration of the franchise offering;
2. Salesman disclosure form;
3. Consent to service of process;
4. Auditor's consent to use of audited financial statements;
5. Cross-reference sheet showing the location in the franchise agreement of the key items in the disclosure document.

The disclosure document prescribed by the 1971 law was later adopted by a consortium of midwestern securities commissioners attempting to devise a uniform method of complying with various state franchise investment laws. The resulting format, the *Uniform Franchise Offering Circular*, or UFOC, today fulfills the requirements of most states which regulate the offer and sale of franchises, including California. There are minor variations and differences in language required by the California statute, including a different cover page.

The disclosure document or UFOC must be furnished to a prospective franchisee at least ten business days before a franchise sale is made.

Other State Franchise Laws

The Franchise Relations Act was passed to protect the rights of franchisees regarding termination and renewal of the franchise agreement. The law prohibits franchisors from terminating a franchise without good cause and provides franchisees with the opportunity to correct any default before a termination is attempted. Franchisors must provide notice of any intention not to renew a franchise agreement at least 180 days prior to the expiration date. The same law provides a franchisee whose outlet is converted from a franchise to a company-owned store with the right to receive monetary compensation for his investment.

An amendment to the Franchise Investment Law, titled Franchisee's Right to Join Trade Association, permits franchisees to join trade associations or cooperatives, regardless of any restrictions in their franchise agreements.

For information about state franchise laws, regulations, and filing requirements, or to report possible violations, contact: Department of Corporations, 600 S. Commonwealth Ave., Los Angeles, CA 90005. Telephone: (213) 736-2741.

California Closet Company Headquartered in Woodland Hills, California, a franchisor of space organizing systems.

Founded in 1978, California Closet has been franchising since 1982. A typical California Closet franchisee operates a retail store devoted to a unique line of products designed for organizing confined spaces, primarily closets, storage rooms, and garages. Of the franchisor's 87 outlets currently operating, all except three are franchise units.

California Closet Company, 6409 Independence Ave., Woodland Hills, CA 91367. Telephone: (818) 888-5888

California Smoothie Headquartered in Wayne, New Jersey, a franchisor of fast-food outlets.

Founded in 1973, CS has been franchising since 1981. A typical CS franchisee operates a fast-food service with a health-diet flair devoted to frozen yoghurt products, fruit shakes, and specialty salads. Of the franchisor's 38 outlets currently operating, 28 are franchise units.

California Smoothie, 1700 Rte. 23, Ste. 120, Wayne, NJ 07470.

CameraAmerica Headquartered in Overland Park, Kansas, a franchisor of specialty retail outlets.

Founded in 1974, CameraAmerica has been franchising since 1984. A typical CameraAmerica franchisee operates a retail store devoted to photographic equipment and supplies, and featuring one-hour photofinishing service. Of the franchisor's 95 outlets currently operating, all except five are franchise units.

CameraAmerica Franchising, Inc., 10895 Lowell, Ste. 150, Overland Park, KS 66210. Telephone: (913) 451-6177

Canterbury of New Zealand Headquartered in Foster City, California, a franchisor of specialty apparel outlets.

Founded in 1904, CNZ has been franchising since 1985. A typical CNZ franchisee operates a clothing store devoted to sports, athletic, and exercise fashions for men, women, and children. Of the franchisor's 70 U.S. and overseas outlets currently operating, all except four are franchise units.

Canterbury of New Zealand, 101 Lincoln Center Dr., Ste. 125, Foster City, CA 94404. Telephone: (415) 349-7792

Caps Nursing Service Headquartered in Oakville, Ontario, a franchisor of nursing employment agencies.

Founded in 1978, Caps has been franchising since 1983, exclusively in Canada. A typical Caps franchisee operates a recruitment and placement agency specializing in nursing personnel for both domestic and institutional employment. Of the 11 Caps outlets currently operating, 10 are franchise units.

Caps Nursing Service, 250 Wyecroft Rd., No. 8, Oakville, Ont., Canada L6K 3T7. Telephone: (416) 844-5588

Captain D's Seafood Headquartered in Nashville, Tennessee, a franchisor of fast-food outlets.

Founded in 1969, Captain D's has been franchising since its inception. A typical Captain D's franchisee operates a fast-food restaurant specializing in seafood, with both sit-down and drive- up facilities. Of the franchisor's 590 outlets currently operating, 248 are franchise units.

Captain D's Seafood, 1727 Elm Hill Park, Nashville, TN 37210. Telephone: (615) 361-5201

Car-X Muffler Headquartered in Chicago, Illinois, a franchisor of automotive muffler and brake outlets.

Founded in 1971, Car-X has been franchising since 1973. A typical Car-X franchisee operates an auto service facility specializing in exhaust and brake system service, sales, and installation. Of the franchisor's 120 outlets currently operating, 71 are franchise units.

Car-X Muffler and Brake, 8430 W. Bryn Mawr, Ste. 400, Chicago, IL 60631. Telephone: (312) 836-1500

Carbone's Pizzeria Headquartered in St. Paul, Minnesota, a franchisor of fast-food outlets.
Founded in 1953, Carbone's has been franchising since 1957. A typical Carbone's franchisee operates an Italian-style fast-food operation with a limited menu featuring freshly prepared sandwiches and hot pizza. Of the franchisor's 32 outlets currently operating, all except six are franchise units.

Carbone's Pizzeria, 55 E. Wentworth Ave., West St. Paul, MN 55102. Telephone: (800) 233-5396

Career Blazers Headquartered in New York City, a franchisor of personnel employment agencies.

Founded in 1949, Career Blazers has been franchising since 1987. A typical Career Blazers franchisee operates a personnel recruitment and placement business handling both permanent and temporary employment. The chain presently consists of four company-owned outlets and one franchise unit.

Career Blazers, 500 Fifth Ave., New York, NY 10110. Telephone: (212) 719-3232

Carl's Jr. Restaurants Headquartered in Anaheim, California, a franchisor of fast-food outlets.

Founded in 1941 by Carl Karcher, Carl's Jr. has been franchising since 1984. A typical Carl's Jr. franchisee operates a limited-menu restaurant specializing in hamburgers, specialty sandwiches, and salads and featuring both drive-up and dine-in facilities. Entrees range from traditional-style "Famous Star" and "Super Star" hamburgers to barbequed chicken with smoked hickory sauce. The menu also features such contemporary offerings as batter-fried zuccini and a self-service salad bar for sit-down patrons. Of the franchisor's 460 outlets currently operating, 70 are franchise units.

Carl Karcher Enterprises, 1200 N. Harbor Blvd., Anaheim, CA 92801. Telephone: (714) 774-5796

Carline Muffler Headquartered in Cambridge, Ontario, a franchisor of muffler service and repair outlets.

Founded in 1981, Carline has been franchising since its inception. A typical Carline franchisee operates an automotive exhaust system sales and service facility. The franchise chain consists of 90 outlets, all of which are franchise units.

Carline Muffler, 500 Conestoga Blvd., Cambridge, Ont., Canada N1R 5T7. Telephone: (519) 621-3360

Carpet Town Headquartered in Hollywood, California, a franchisor of retail flooring outlets.

Founded in 1954, Carpet Town has been franchising since 1962. A typical Carpet Town franchisee operates a carpeting sales and installation business. Of the franchisor's 26 outlets currently operating, only seven are franchise units.

Carpet Town, 937 Citrus Ave., Hollywood, CA 90038. Telephone: (213) 466-7175

Carpeteria Headquartered in Valencia, California, a franchisor of retail floor covering outlets.

Founded in 1960, Carpeteria has been franchising since 1972. A typical Carpeteria franchisee operates a carpet sales and installation business based on the franchisor's inventory selection and purchasing system. Of the franchisor's 70 outlets currently operating, 44 are franchise units.

Carpeteria, 28159 Stanford, Valencia, CA 91355.

Case Law Law which derives its authority from court decisions; in contrast to statutory law, which refers to laws enacted by legislative bodies.

The term "case law" applies to decisions rendered by federal and state appellate judges. Appellate courts, also called "courts of appeals," are courts that hear cases appealed from lower trial courts. The decisions and opinions of the appellate judges are published in "reporters."

When a case has been decided by a lower trial court, the decision may be appealed to an appellate court. For example, a case decided in a federal district court may be appealed to a federal court of appeals. The appellate court has the authority to re-decide the case, based on arguments presented by the opposing parties.

After both parties to the lawsuit, or *litigation*, have submitted briefs and presented arguments, the judge, or in some cases, a panel of judges, renders its decision to reverse or affirm the decision of the lower court. When a panel of judges votes to render a decision, the view of the judges who voted in favor of the winning decision is called the "majority opinion." Likewise, the views held by the judges who voted against the winning decision are called the "minority opinion."

The courts have helped to shape franchising practices in numerous ways. Several landmark decisions established the groundrules for price fixing, tie-in arrangements, vicarious liability, and quality standards.

Price Fixing

In *Coors Brewery v. U.S. Federal Trade Commission* and again in *U.S. v. Parke Davis & Co.*, the courts ruled that franchisors and other contractors may not fix the prices at which franchisees sell products to the public. Any minimum, maximum, or fixed price constitutes illegal price fixing.

Tie-In Arrangements

In *Siegel v. Chicken Delight*, the Supreme Court declared that franchisors may not, without reasonable justification, force franchisees to purchase equipment and supplies from designated suppliers. But, in *Krehl v. Baskin-Robbins*, the court upheld the right Baskin-Robbins to obligate franchisees to purchase and sell only its private brand of ice cream. The distinguishing factor, said the court, is whether a product is trademarked, unique, and not generally available from other sources.

Vicarious Liability

In 1986, a Docktor Pet franchisee was sued by a customer who had bought what he thought was a purebred Doberman Pincher. The store had misrepresented the dog's authenticity, and the franchisor was held to be *vicariously liable* for the conduct of its franchisee. In another landmark case involving Avis Rent A Car, an appellate court declared that the franchisor was equally liable for an accidental death caused by one of its franchisees. But a district court in Kansas found that a gasoline franchisor was not vicariously liable for a franchisee's racial discrimination against a customer.

Quality Standards

In *Ramada Inns v. Gadsden Motel Co.*, a federal appellate judge ruled that franchisors have the right to require their franchisees to upgrade their outlets to meet new quality standards. Ramada Inns had terminated a franchisee for deficiencies under the franchise agreement and instructed the owner to cease using the franchisor's trademark. When the franchisee failed to comply, Ramada was awarded more than $250,000 in damages for injuries to its reputation.
See *Price Fixing, Tie-in Arrangements, Statutory Law.*

Celluland Headquartered in San Diego, California, a franchisor of cellular telephone outlets.
Founded in 1985, Celluland has been franchising since the following year. A typical Celluland franchisee operates a retail telephone store specializing in cellular mobile phones and carrier services. Of the 21 Celluland outlets currently operating, all except one are franchise units.
Celluland, 5812 Miramar Rd., San Diego, CA 92121. Telephone: (619) 455-1600

Century 21 Real Estate Headquartered in Irvine, California, a franchisor of independent real estate sales offices.
Founded in 1971, Century 21 has been franchising since its inception. By selling area franchises for large geographical territories to master franchisees, the chain proliferated rapidly, opening an average of 400 outlets per year. The company is presently a subsidiary of Metropolitan Life Insurance Co., which funnels mortgage services to real estate buyers through the chain's outlets.
A typical Century 21 franchisee operates a real estate brokerage utilizing the franchisor's trademark, signage, national relocation service, and computer-based referral system. All of the estimated 7,000 Century 21 outlets currently operating owned by independent franchisees.
Century 21, P.O. Box 19564, Irvine, CA 92713. Telephone: (714) 553-2100

Chad's Rainbow Headquartered in Richardson, Texas, a franchisor of retail children's book and toy outlets.

Founded in 1981, Chad's Rainbow has been franchising since 1983. A typical Chad's Rainbow franchisee operates a retail store specializing in educational toys, children's books, and related learning tools. The outlet is distinguished by its emphasis on products for development and learning for children of preschool-to-elementary-school age. All of the franchisor's 30 outlets currently operating are franchise units.

Chad's Rainbow, 1778 N. Plano Rd., Ste. 120, Richardson, TX 75081. Telephone: (214) 680-9787

Champion Auto Stores Headquartered in New Hope, Minnesota, a franchisor of retail automotive parts outlets.

Founded in 1956, Champion has been franchising since 1961. A typical Champion franchisee operates a retail business marketing auto parts, tires, batteries, performance products, and tools. Of the franchisor's 130 outlets currently operating, all except 14 are franchise units.

Champion Auto Stores, 5520 County Rd. 18 N, New Hope, MN 55428. Telephone: (612) 535-5984

Check-X-Change Headquartered in Portland, Oregon, a franchisor of check-cashing outlets.

Founded in 1979, Check-X-Change has been franchising since 1985. A typical Check-X-Change franchisee operates a fee-based check-cashing and personal business service center. The chain consists of 58 outlets, all operated under franchise licenses.

Check-X-Change, 111 SW Columbia, Ste. 1080, Portland, OR 97201. Telephone: (800) 423-3371

Chem-Clean Headquartered in Freeport, Maine, a franchisor of furniture restoration outlets.

Founded in 1967, Chem-Clean has been franchising since 1969. A typical Chem-Clean franchisee operates a furniture restoration business utilizing the franchisor's patented paint-removal process. Of the franchisor's 62 outlets currently operating, all except one are franchise units.

Chem-Clean Furniture Restoration Centers, Rte. 11, Box 285, Freeport, ME 04032. Telephone: (207) 865-9007

Chem-Dry Carpet, Drapery, and Upholstery Cleaning Headquartered in Cameron Park, California, a franchisor of interior maintenance services.

Founded in 1975 by Robert D. Harris, Chem-Dry has been franchising since 1977. Harris is also the chief executive of Harris Research, Inc., which manufactures the chemical solutions used by franchisees. A typical Chem-Dry franchisee operates a mobile fabric-cleaning and stain-removal business specializing in carpeting, window coverings, and upholstery materials, utilizing the franchisor's patented cleaning process. All of the estimated 1,840 Chem-Dry outlets currently in business are franchise units.

Chem-Dry, 3330 Cameron Park Dr., Ste. 700, Cameron Park, CA 95682. Telephone: (800) 841-6583; California: (800) 821-3240

Chez Chocolat Headquartered in Winston-Salem, North Carolina, a franchisor of retail confection outlets.

Founded in 1986, Chez Chocolat has been franchising since its inception. A typical Chez Chocolat franchisee operates a retail food shop devoted to packaged chocolate candy and nuts. Of the franchisor's 52 outlets currently operating, all except six are franchise units.

Chez Chocolat, 4198 N. Cherry St., Drawer 11025, Winston-Salem, NC 27116. Telephone: (919) 761-1961

Chicken Delight Headquartered in Winnepeg, Manitoba, a franchisor of fast food outlets.

Until 1954, franchising in the food service industry was largely confined to ice cream and root beer. A scrap iron dealer named A. L. Tunick converted an abandoned oil cooker into a high-pressure deep fat frier, capable of cooking fried chicken in one third the time required by conventional equipment. Inspired by the success of early food-service franchisors such as Bob's Big Boy and Dairy Queen, Tunick built a fried chicken restaurant franchise around his innovative cooker, calling his new outlets Chicken Delight. Ten years later, the chain of several hundred restaurants was acquired by Consolidated Food.

A typical Chicken Delight franchisee operates a convenience restaurant specializing in fried chicken and take-out service. Of the franchisor's 90 outlets currently operating, all except 10 are franchise units.

Chicken Delight, 395 Berry St., Winnipeg, Man., Canada R3M 0K6. Telephone: (204) 885-7570

Children's Orchard Headquartered in Newbury Port, Massachusetts, a franchisor of retail apparel outlets.

Founded in 1980, Children's Orchard has been franchising since 1984. A typical franchisee operates a clothing boutique specializing in apparel for infants and children. All of the 16 Children's Orchards outlets currently operating are franchise units.

Children's Orchard, 253 Low St., Newbury Port, MA 01950

Church's Fried Chicken Headquartered in San Antonia, Texas, a franchisor of fast food outlets.

Founded in 1952, Church's has been franchising since 1976. A typical Church's franchisee operates a convenience restaurant specializing in fried chicken. It is estimated that of the franchisor's 1,500 outlets currently operating, about a fourth are franchise units.

Church's Fried Chicken, Inc., P.O. Box BH001, San Antonio, TX 78230. Telephone: (512) 737-5760

Chrysler, Walter (1875-1940) Industrialist and automobile franchisor.

Born at Wamego, Kansas on April 2, 1875, Chrysler was fascinated with railroads from an early age and, while still a teenager, went to work as an apprentice in a machine shop for the Pacific Union Railroad. He spent the better part of fifteen years working for various railroads as a machinist, until 1901, when he signed on as roundhouse foreman for the Denver, Rio Grande and Western Railroad.

After the turn of the century, Chrylser adopted a keen interest in automtobiles and, in 1912, he took a cut in pay to work as a manager for the Buick Motor Company division of General Motors in Detroit. He left Buick four years later, in a dispute with General Motors president William Duran and, in a reorganization, re-emerged as president of Maxwell Motor Company.

Chrylser used his new company as the springboard to introduce an innovative new line of automobiles, culminating, in 1924, with the car that bore his name. The Chrylser automobile featured four-wheel hydaulic brakes, a high-compression engine, and a number of other engineering improvements. The following year, the company officially became Chrysler Corporation.

As a result of the founder's aggressive engineering and marketing programs, the Chrylser trademark became one of the most recognizable in America, as franchised dealers channeled millions of passenger cars to market. In 1928, Chrysler bought out the Dodge Brothers and began manufacturing two new models, the De Soto and the Plymouth. No long afterward, the automaker built the Chrylser building in New York, at the time the world's tailest manmade structure.

His autobiography, *Life of an American Workman*, was published in 1937.

Cindy's Cinnamon Rolls Headquartered in Fallbrook, California, a franchisor of specialty bakery goods outlets.

Founded in 1985, Cindy's has been franchising since the following year. A typical franchisee operates a retail bakery goods store specializing in freshly baked cinnamon rolls. All 41 of the Cindy's outlets currently operating are franchise units.

Cindy's Cinnamon Rolls, 1667 S. Mission Rd., Ste. G, Fallbrook, CA 92028

Clarion Resorts Headquartered in Silver Spring, Maryland, a franchisor of lodging outlets.

Founded in 1941, Clarion has been franchising since its inception. A typical franchisee operates an executive-style hotel or mid-luxury vacation resort distinguished by deluxe accommodations offered at competitive rates. Amenities may include a swimming pool, meeting and banquet rooms, exercise facilities, and on-premises food and beverage service. Of the franchisor's 950 Clarion, Quality, and Comfort outlets currently operating, all except 11 are franchise units.

Clarion Resorts, 10750 Columbia Pk., Silver Springs, MD 20901. Telephone: (301) 236-5080

Classy Maids Headquartered in Madison, Wisconsin, a franchisor of interior maintenance services.

Founded in 1980, Classy Maids has been franchising since 1985. A typical Classy Maids franchisee operates a full-service housecleaning business. All of the franchisor's 30 outlets currently operating are franchise units.

Classy Maids, 722 Acewood Blvd., Madison, WI 53714. Telephone: (608) 249-2496

Clemens, Samuel (1835-1910) American humorist and author, known familiarly by the pen name "Mark Twain." His fictional account of Tom Sawyer selling a franchise to Huck Finn to whitewash a fence predated the first McDonald's franchise by almost a hundred years.

Born in Florida, Missouri on November 30, 1835, Clemens grew up in the tiny village of Hannibal, on the shores of the Mississippi River. The river and its culture heavily influenced his later literary work. Publishing was Clemens' lifeblood. At the tender age of 12, he went to work as a printer's apprentice and, from 1851 to 1853, he labored in various capacities for his brother's newspaper.

In 1861, Clemens moved west to Virginia City, Nevada, where he hired on as a reporter for the *Territorial Enterprise*. Writing as Mark Twain, his most productive literary years fell in the period between 1869 and 1994. One of his most memorable passages is a scene in *The Adventures of Tom Sawyer*, in which the enterprising Tom sells his playmates the "privilege" of whitewashing a fence, for an apple core and other considerations — a bona fide act of franchising.

Ben Rogers, munching contently on an apple on his way to the old swimming hole, comes across Tom Sawyer busily whitewashing his aunt's fence.

> "Hello, old chap," says Ben. "You got to work, hey?"
> Tom wheels suddenly and says:
> "What do you call work?"
> "Why ain't that work?"
> "Well, maybe it is, and maybe it ain't."

Ben decides he'd like to try his hand at the whitewashing, But Tom denies him the privilege. Exasperated, Ben offers Tom the core of his apple, then finally, the whole fruit.

Like a modern-day franchisor, Tom was quick to capitalize on a good thing:

"And when the middle of the afternoon came, from being a poor poverty-stricken boy in the morning, Tom was literally rolling in wealth. He had (beside a kite, in good repair, a dead rat, and a string to swing it with) twelve marbles, part of a jews' harp, a piece of blue bottleglass to look through, a spool cannon, a key that wouldn't unlock anything, a fragment of chalk, a glass stopper of a decanter, a tin soldier, a couple of tadpoles, six firecrackers, a kitten with only one eye, a brass door-knob, a dog collar — but no dog — the handle of a knife, four pieces of orange peel, and dilapidated old window sash."

What made Tom Sawyer such a successful franchisor was his application of a franchise sales strategy well known in marketing circles today: reverse selling.

"Tom told himself that it was not such a hollow world, after all. He had discovered a great law of human action, without knowing it — namely, that in order to make a man or a boy covet a thing, it is only necessary to make the thing difficult to attain."

Samuel Clemens, a.k.a. Mark Twain, envisioned the franchise method of marketing in his Adventures of Tom Sawyer.

Club Nautico Headquartered in Ft. Lauderdale, Florida, a franchisor of marine recreation facilities.
Founded in 1981, Club Nautico has been franchising since 1985. A typical Club Nautico franchisee operates a powerboat rental outlet catering to recreational customers. Of the franchisor's 55 outlets currently operating, 37 are franchise units.
Club Nautico, 5450 NW 33rd Ave., Ft. Lauderdale, FL 33309. Telephone: (305) 739-9800

Color-Glo Headquartered in Minneapolis, Minnesota, a franchisor of interior maintenance services.
Founded in 1970, Color-Glo has been franchising since 1984. A typical Color-Glo franchisee operates a mobile fabric restoration business specializing in cleaning, dyeing, and restoring carpet and upholstery. Of the franchisor's 240 outlets currently operating, all except three are franchise units.
Color-Glo, 7111 Ohms Lane, Minneapolis, MN 55435. Telephone: (800) 328-6347

Coast to Coast Stores Headquartered in Denver, Colorado, a franchisor of retail hardware outlets.

Founded in 1928, Coast to Coast has been franchising since its inception. A typical Coast to Coast franchisee operates a retail hardware store utilizing the franchisor's trademark, merchandising system, and advertising. All but ten of the 965 Coast to Coast outlets currently operating nationwide are franchise units.

Coast to Coast, 501 S. Cherry St., Denver, CO 80222. Telephone: (303) 377-8400

Coca Cola A well known soft drink trademark and, arguably, the most successful franchised product worldwide.

With a 29-percent share of the United States soft drink market, Coca Cola is truly "Number One" among soft drink bottling franchises. A staggering 60 percent of the company's sales originate from overseas franchises. Coca Cola has maintained its lead through two world wars, a depression, sugar shortages, FDA litigation, bottling changes, changes in popular tastes and trends, and competition from Pepsi-Cola's twelve ounce bottles.

Undoubtedly the most successful product ever exported from America, Coca Cola is not only a universally recognized franchise trademark, but also a profound cultural phenomenon. Coke is locally produced and bottled by franchisees from Moscow to Bora Bora. The franchisor, known by franchisees as "Big Coke," has received applications for franchises on the moon.

Coca Cola originated in 1886, as a cure-all elixer concocted by a Georgia pharmacist, John S. Pemberton. A blend of cola nut, oils from the coca leaf, a pinch of caffeine, and miscellaneous herbs, the tonic was first promoted as a hangover remedy. At the Turn of the Century, cocaine use was widespread among the American public, particularly in the post-Civil War South, and Pemberton's elixer was one of many cocaine-based tonics. In fact, the first popular nickname for Coca Cola was not "Coke," but rather "Dope," and the horse-drawn wagons from which the soft drink was sold were known as "Dope Wagons." Eventually, the cocaine was replaced by caffeine, which is still used today to provide the soft drink's "kick."

According to popular legend, carbonation was added as an afterthought, when a soda fountain clerk mistakenly mixed soda water, instead of tap water, with the Coca Cola syrup. Pemberton's bookkeeper, Frank Robinson, used his talents at caligraphy to scrawl the familiar "Coca Cola" logo which adorns the distinctive, curved soft-drink bottle to this day.

Pemberton's destiny was to include neither fame nor fortune. Shortly before his death, he sold the rights to his "Intellectual Beverage and Temperance Drink" to an Atlanta drug store owner, Asa Candler, for $1200. An astute businessman with a bold vision, Candler made Coca Cola a household word. Before his relatives and fellow stockholders sold the company against his will in 1919, he succeeded in spreading the soft drink across the United States and Great Britain. But Candler's efforts were limited to selling Coke to soda fountain operators, and in a legendary transaction, he sold nationwide bottling rights for the sum of one dollar. The buyers, two young Chattanooga lawyers, Benjamin Franklin Thomas and Joseph Brown Whitehead, eventually resold their franchise to a syndicate of three banks for $25 million.

Robert Woodruff, who became president of Coca Cola in 1923, controlled the soft drink's fate for the next thirty years. Where Candler "put Coca Cola on its feet", Woodroff "gave it wings." During World War II, he built Coca Cola bottling factories around the globe to supply American troops with "the pause that refreshes," and at war's end, the Coke factories remained wherever the troops had been stationed. Woodroff encouraged international divisions based on local ownership with foreign adaptations.

Throughout the soft drink's history, the recipe for the Coca Cola syrup has remained a carefully guarded "secret," supposedly passed by whisper between family members. Despite early advertisements that admonished the public to "Ask for Coca Cola by its full name only," the company eventually accepted the slang word "Coke," for which a second trademark was obtained in the early 1940s.

In the late 1950s, Coca Cola introduced three additional brands to keep abreast of competition: Sprite, Tab, and Fanta. Coca Cola and its sister soft drinks are produced by independent bottling com-

The distinctive curved shape of the Coca-Cola bottle has become a mainstay of American life.

panies operated under franchise agreements with the franchisor, "Big Coke." A hallmark of the Coca Cola franchise is an exclusive territory granted to the franchisee "in perpetuity." Today, the Coca Cola franchise empire remains one of the most powerful and influential economic, political, and social forces at work in the U.S. and world economies.

Colorado, Franchise Regulations To date, the Colorado legislature has not adopted any generally applicable franchise investment law. However, the relationship between automobile wholesalers and dealers is regulated by the Automobile Dealers law.

Colorado law does not require franchisors to register or file disclosures with any state regulatory body. In the absence of such a requirement, the federal Franchise Rule applies, requiring franchisors to furnish a disclosure document prescribed by the Federal Trade Commission to prospective franchisees ten business days before a franchise sale is made.
See Franchise Rule.

Coit Drapery and Carpet Cleaners Headquartered in Burlingame, California, a franchisor of interior maintenance services.

Founded in 1950, Coit has been franchising since 1962. A typical Coit franchisee operates a mobile fabric-cleaning business devoted to floor and window coverings, utilizing the franchisor's standardized equipment and operating procedures. Of the franchisor's 63 outlets currently operating, all except nine are franchise units.

Coit Drapery and Carpet Cleaners, 897 Hinckley Rd., Burlingame, CA 94010. Telephone: (800) 243-8797; California: (415) 342-6023

Comfort Inns Headquartered in Silver Spring, Maryland, a franchisor of lodging outlets.

Founded in 1941, Comfort has been franchising since its inception. The franchisor also licenses outlets under the trade names Quality Inns and Clarion Resorts. A typical Comfort Inn franchisee operates an economy-priced motor inn on a low-to-moderately priced property, accessible from a major thoroughfare and offering sanitary, attractively furnished accommodations at competitive rates. Of the franchisor's 950 Comfort Inn, Quality Inn, and Clarion Resort outlets currently operating, all except 11 are franchise units.

Comfort Inns, 10750 Columbia Pk., Silver Spring, MD 20901. Telephone: (301) 236-5080

Command Performance Headquartered in Wilmington, Massachusetts, a franchisor of hair care salons.

Founded in 1976, Command Performance has been franchising since its inception. At one point in its history, the franchisor boasted more than a thousand licenses. A typical Command Performance franchisee operates a retail hairstyling salon for men and women, in an environment characterized by a contemporary, upscale decor and high-tech furnishings. Of the franchisor's 267 outlets currently operating, all except two are franchise units.

Command Performance, 335 Middlesex Ave., Wilmington, MA 01887. Telephone: (617) 658-6586

Commerce, U.S. Department of The U.S. Department of Commerce, or simply, the **Commerce Department**, established by federal law as the ninth office of the President's Cabinet.

History and Scope

A bill creating the Department of Commerce and Labor was signed into law by President Theodore Roosevelt on February 14, 1903. The secretary of the department was charged with overseeing interstate commerce and labor practices on behalf of the President. Early notoriety visited the cabinet post in 1906, when Roosevelt appointed Oscar S. Straus of New York City as the department's secretary. Straus was the first Jew to be appointed to the Cabinet.

In 1913, Congress divided the department into two separate entities, the Department of Commerce and the Department of Labor, each receiving full Cabinet status.

The Commerce Department and Franchising

As the purveyor of U.S. commerce and trade, the Commerce Department is also a federal clearinghouse for franchise information. Among other activities, the Department maintains statistics relating to the strength and number of franchise organizations in every segment of U.S. industry. The department's vested interest in the economy is reflected in its hearty endorsement of franchising as a business practice and as a cornerstone of the retail trade. One publication issued by the department called franchising "the last avenue of the American dream," citing an annual growth rate among franchise units of 6 percent.

Department analyst Andrew Kostecka is widely regarded as the federal government's leading authority on franchising. Mr. Kostecka is a frequent speaker at trade association conventions and seminars both in North America and in Europe, and the author of the deparment's annual survey of franchising, *Franchising in the Economy*.

The Commerce Department also publishes the *Franchise Opportunities Handbook*, a comprehensive directory listing the names, addresses, telephone numbers, and descriptions of virtually every franchisor operating in the United States.

Both publications are available for a nominal charge from: Superintendent of Documents, U. S. Government Printing Office, Washington, DC 20402. See Antitrust.

Theodore Roosevelt was a dedicated trust-breaker, as well as the target of innumerable, usually unflattering, caricatures.

Communications World Headquartered in Golden, Colorado, a franchisor of retail business communications outlets.

Founded in 1979, CW has been franchising since 1982. A typical CW franchisee operates a retail store specializing in facsimile transmission devices, telephone systems, and other telecommunications products. The chain consists of 65 outlets, 52 of which are franchise units.

Communications World, 14828 W. 6th Ave., Ste. 13B, Golden, CO 80401. Telephone: (303) 279-8200

Comprehensive Accounting Headquartered in Aurora, Illinois, a franchisor of bookkeeping/accounting services.

Founded in 1949 by Leo G. Lauzen, Comprehensive has been franchising since 1965. A typical franchisee operates an accounting, tax preparation, and business consulting service catering to "medium size"companies. Customers of the outlet include corporations, small businesses, attorneys, medical practices, and self-employed individuals. All of the 340 Comprehensive Accounting outlets currently open and operating are franchise units.

Comprehensive Accounting Corp., 2111 Comprehensive Dr., Aurora, IL 60605. Telephone: (800) 323-9000

CompuFund National Mortgage Network Headquartered in Santa Ana, California, a franchisor of loan information services.

Founded in 1984, CompuFund has been franchising since its inception. A typical CompuFund franchisee operates a mortgage loan office utilizing the franchisor's computer-based information network. Franchisees have access to current, timely data regarding loan packages and lenders to match with the varying needs of prospective borrowers. None of the chain's 120 outlets are company owned.

CompuFund National Mortgage Network, 3700 S. Susan St., Ste. 250, Santa Ana, CA 92683. Telephone: (714) 545-9101

Computerland Headquartered in Oakland, California, a franchisor of specialty retail outlets.

Founded in 1976, Computerland has been franchising since its inception. Despite a history of ownership disputes, management turnover, and litigation, Computerland remains the largest and most recognizable chain of specialty computer stores. A typical Computerland franchisee operates a retail store devoted to personal computers, peripheral devices, and a limited selection of software and books. Each outlet must individually qualify to market major product lines such as IBM, Apple, Compaq, and Hewlett-Packard hardware. The store's customer base includes small businesses, corporate accounts, schools, and consumers. Of the franchisor's estimated 800 outlets currently operating, all except one are franchise units.

Computerland Corp., 2901 Peralta Oaks Court, Oakland, CA 94605. Telephone: (415) 465-2000

Connecticut, Franchise Regulations Franchisors operating in the state of Connecticut are governed by the Business Opportunity Investment Act, which requires registration and disclosure of pertinent information about the franchisor, franchise business, and franchise agreement. Other state laws protect the rights of franchisees to renew their franchise agreements on expiration, and the rights of service station owners and liquor dealers.

The Business Opportunity Investment Law

Before offering or selling a franchise in the state, a franchisor must first prepare a disclosure document prescribed by the statute, then file the information, along with the franchise agreement, financial statements, and related documents, with the Connecticut Securities Division. The Securities Commissioner must approve the registration before the franchisor may proceed to offer or sell franchises.

In addition to a disclosure document, franchisors are also required to submit the following items to the Securities Division:
1. Application for registration of the franchise offering;
2. Salesman disclosure form;
3. Consent to service of process;
4. Auditor's consent to use of audited financial statements;
5. Cross-reference sheet showing the location in the franchise agreement of the key items in the disclosure document.

The disclosure document devised by a consortium of midwestern securities commissioners as a uniform method of complying with state franchise investment laws, the *Uniform Franchise Offering Circular*, or UFOC, fulfills the disclosure requirements of the Connecticut law. There are minor variations and differences in language required by the Connecticut statute, including a different cover page. *(See Uniform Franchise Offering Circular.)*

The disclosure document or UFOC must be furnished to a prospective franchisee at least ten business days before a franchise sale is made.

Other State Franchise Laws

The Franchising Fairness Law provides franchisees with additional rights regarding termination and renewal of the franchise agreement. The law prohibits franchisors from terminating or refusing to renew a franchise except for good cause and only after the franchisee has a reasonable opportunity to correct a default.

The rights of service station owners under franchise agreements are regulated by the Petroleum Product Franchisors law. The Liquor Dealers law governs the relationship between liquor wholesalers and retailers.

For information about state franchise laws, regulations, and filing requirements, or to report possible violations, contact: Securities Division, State Office Building, Hartford, CT 06115. Telephone: (203) 566-4257.

Conroy's Headquartered in Long Beach, California, a franchisor of retail florists.

Founded in 1964 by Chris Conroy, Conroy's has been franchising since 1974. A typical Conroy's franchisee operates a retail floral ship based on a standardized merchandising program. The outlet is distinguished by its streetside display of brightly colored floral merchandise designed to attract the attention of motorists. Of the 75 Conroy's outlets currently operating, all except one are franchise units.

Conroy's, 6621 E. Pacific Coast Hwy., Long Beach, CA 90803.

Cookie Factory Bakeries Headquartered in Lombard, Illinois, a franchisor of specialty bakery goods outlets.

Founded in 1974, Cookie Factory has been franchising since its inception. A typical Cookie Factory franchisee operates a retail bakery goods shop featuring freshly prepared cookies, muffins, croissants, and pastries. Of the franchisor's 46 outlets currently operating, all except four are franchise units.

Cookie Factory Bakeries, 651 E. Butterfield Rd., Ste. 503, Lombard, IL 60148.

Copeland, Alvin American restaurateur and franchisor of fast-food chicken outlets. Founder of Popeyes Famous Fried Chicken and Biscuits, Copeland owns and operates 80 restaurants and oversees a franchise chain of 600 independently owned outlets.

Copeland was a 16-year-old grocery clerk in New Orleans, when his brother Gilbert offered him a job in a doughnut shop. Alvin set out to learn the franchise business and, in 1966, decided to start his own fried chicken restaurant. He tried and failed with two different restaurants, before finally hitting on the right combination of preparation and location. He named the fast-food stand Popeye's Mighty Good Fried Chicken, after Popeye Doyle, the main character in the movie *The French Connection.*

Later, Copeland obtained a license from King Features to use the name and image of the brawling, spinach-guzzling Popeye the Sailor cartoon character.

Within ten months after the first Popeye's outlet opened, Copeland was earning $5,000 a week, prompting the enterprising youth to open a second outlet across town. In the two years that followed, he

Alvin Copeland, founder and chairman of Popeye's Famous Fried Chicken and Biscuits, and owner of Copelands of New Orleans.;

opened 24 restaurants altogether, all financed with his own capital. Today, Copeland's holding company, A. Copeland's Enterprises, Inc. operates 80 fried chicken outlets. His subsidiary, Popeyes Famous Fried Chicken and Biscuits, franchises outlets to independent owner/operators, with approximately 600 restaurants currently open. The third largest fired chicken chain, Popeyes operates in 35 states and five foreign countries, grossing $250 million annually. The outlet's product is distinguished from competition by its Cajun-style preparation.

Copeland also owns an upscale New Orleans eatery, Copeland's, which features a menu of 100 different food and beverage selections.

Copy Mat Headquartered in Emeryville, California, a franchisor of document duplication outlets.

Founded in 1973, Copy Mat has been franchising since 1984. A typical Copy Mat franchisee operates a retail duplication center devoted to self-service document copying with high-speed duplicating equipment. All of the 50 Copy Mat outlets currently in business are franchise units.

Copy Mat, 2000 Powell St., Ste. 1300, Emeryville, CA 94608.

Cost Cutters Headquartered in Minneapolis, Minnesota, a franchisor of hair care salons.

Founded in 1982, Cost Cutters has been franchising since its inception. A typical Cost Cutters franchisee operates a retail haircutting salon, with ten full-time and five part-time employees. The outlet has a distinctive family orientation, catering to men, women, and children alike. Of the franchisor's 290 outlets currently operating, all except 25 are franchise units.

Cost Cutters Family Hair Care Shops, 300 Industrial Blvd. NE, Minneapolis, MN 55413. Telephone: (612) 331-8500

Coustic-Glo Headquartered in Minneapolis, Minnesota, a franchisor of interior maintenance services.

Founded in 1970, Coustic-Glo has been franchising since 1980. A typical Coustic-Glo franchisee operates a residential/commercial maintenance business specializing in surface cleaning, care, and restoration of walls and ceilings. All of the 240 Coustic-Glo outlets currently in business are franchise units.

Coustic-Glo, 7111 Ohms Lane, Minneapolis, MN 55435. Telephone: (800) 328-6347

Coverall Headquartered in San Diego, California, a franchisor of interior maintenance services.

Founded in 1982, Coverall has been franchising since its inception. A typical Coverall franchisee operates a commercial janitorial cleaning service. Of the franchisor's 900 outlets currently operating, all except nine are franchise units.

Coverall, 3111 Camino Del Rio North, Ste. 305, San Diego, CA 92108. Telephone: (800) 537-3371

Crossland Furniture Restoration Headquartered in Sylvania, Ohio, a franchisor of furniture restoration outlets.

Founded in 1944, Crossland has been franchising since 1977. A typical Crossland franchisee operates a furniture restoration business devoted to stripping, repairing, refinishing, and upholstering used furniture. Of the franchisor's 110 outlets currently operating, all except one are franchise units.

Crossland Furniture Restoration Studios, 5679 Monroe St., Ste. 208, Sylvania, OH 43560. Telephone: (419) 882-6950

Crusty's Pizza Headquartered in Oak Park, Michigan, a franchisor of fast-food outlets.

Founded in 1957, Crusty's has been franchising since 1971. A typical Crusty's franchisee operates a fast-food pizza restaurant devoted to take-out service. Of the franchisor's 200 outlets currently operating, all except six are franchise units.

Crusty's Pizza, 20700 Greenfield Rd., Oak Park, MI 48237. Telephone: (313) 968-1900

Culligan Water Conditioning Headquartered in Northbrook, Illinois, a franchisor of water treatment services.

Founded in 1936, Culligan has been franchising since 1938. A typical Culligan franchisee operates a retail outlet and route service devoted to water treatment systems utilizing the franchisor's proprietary line of equipment and supplies. Of the franchisor's 806 outlets currently operating, all except 24 are franchise units.

Culligan Water Conditioning, 1 Culligan Pkwy., Northbrook, IL 60062. Telephone: (312) 498-2000

Cultures Fresh Food Restaurants Headquartered in Toronto, Ontario, a franchisor of fast-food outlets.

Founded in 1977, Cultures has been franchising since 1980. A typical Cultures franchisee operates a fast-food restaurant with a health-food flair and a limited menu featuring frozen yoghurt, fresh bakery goods, specialty sandwiches, soups, and salads. Of the franchisor's 60 outlets currently operating, all except 11 are franchise units.

Clutures Fresh Food Restaurants, 162 Cumberland St., Ste. 232, Toronto, Ont., Canada M5R 1A8. Telephone: (416) 968-1440

Cutlery World Headquartered in Chatannoga, Tennessee, a franchisor of specialty retail outlets.

Founded in 1966, Cutlery World has been franchising since 1976. A typical Cutlery World franchisee operates a retail store devoted to brand-name cutlery and accessories, ranging from kitchen and hunting knives to wet stones, scissors, and gift items. Of the 185 Cutlery World outlets currently operating, 27 are operated under franchise licenses.

Cutlery World, 2841 Hickory Valley Rd., Chatannoga, TN 37422

**Dairy Queen
to
Durant**

Dairy Queen Headquartered in Minneapolis, Minnesota, a franchisor of fast-food outlets.

Founded in 1940, DQ has been franchising since 1944. The soft-ice-cream chain whose name became a virtual household word originated in 1938, when two Moline, Illinois men, J. F. McCullough and his son Alex, developed the dairy product today known as "Dairy Queen" soft serve. The McCulloughs made arrangements with Sherb Noble, the owner of a retail ice cream shop in nearby Kakkakee, to market-test the new product. When Noble ran an "All You Can Eat For Ten Cents" sale on a hot afternoon in August, more than 1,600 customers lined up to sample the goods.

J. F. McCullough coined the term "Dairy Queen" in 1940, when the first outlet of the same name, owned by Noble, opened in Joliet, Illinois. The heart of the Dairy Queen system was a unique freezer which poured soft ice cream into a cone, invented by a man named Harold Oltz. Oltz sold the manufacturing rights to McCullough, who installed the first unit in a retail outlet in Davenport, Iowa.

Due to sugar shortages during World War II, expansion was forestalled until 1944, when a farm equipment salesman named Harry Axene stepped into the picture. Axene and McCullough formed a partnership to franchise Dairy Queen outlets nationwide. With the aid of a cone manufacturer in Chicago, they recruited a group of 26 investors, each of whom paid $25,000 to $50,000 for the first master franchises. Within four years, the Dairy Queen chain had burgeoned to 2,500 outlets.

From 1947 until 1955, the Dairy Queen organization proliferated from 100 stores to more than 2,600 franchise outlets. In 1962, several master area franchisees pooled their assets to form International Dairy Queen, Inc. and its wholly owned subsidiary, American Dairy Queen Corporation. The company adopted the Brazier food line in 1968, teaming the soft dairy product with traditional fast-food fare such as hot dogs and hamburgers.

International Dairy Queen acquired Karmelkorn Shoppes, Inc. in 1986 and the Orange Julius chain in 1987. A typical DQ franchisee operates a fast-food restaurant distinguished by the franchisor's soft ice cream in cones, shakes, sundaes, parfaits, and frozen drinks. The outlet's popular dessert fare is supplemented by a limited menu of hamburgers, hot dogs, sandwiches, and complete meals. Dairy Queen outlets vary in size and seating capacity, but most are free-standing establishments with both sit-down and take-out service.

In 1988, outlets began marketing the company's own brand of frozen yogurt. Specially designed "Treat Centers" house Dairy Queen, Karmelkorn, and Orange Julius concessions in a single facility.

Of the franchisor's 5,000 worldwide outlets currently operating, all except five are franchise units. Dairy Queen, P.O. Box 35286, Minneapolis, MN 55435. Telephone: (612) 830-0312

Early Dairy Queen outlets were characterized by tile roofs, Greek pillars, and frozen-icycle awnings.

Dan Hanna Headquartered in Portland, Oregon, a franchisor of automatic carwash outlets.

Founded in 1954, Hanna has been franchising since 1985. A typical Hanna franchisee operates a full-service car wash facility, using the franchisor's automated equipment and supplies. Of the franchisor's 50 outlets currently operating, only a handful are franchise units.

Dan Hanna Auto Wash, 2001 Hanna, Portland, OR 97222. Telephone: (503) 659-0361

David's Cookies Headquartered in New York City, a franchisor of specialty baked goods outlets.

Founded in 1979 by David Liederman, David's Cookies has been franchising since 1983. Liederman, a law-school graduate and French-trained chef, had tried and failed with two other businesses, a private sauce company and a restaurant, before he opened his first cookie shop to the acclaim of New York food critics.

A typical David's Cookies franchisee operates a retail bakery goods shop specializing in chocolate chip cookies prepared from the franchisor's "secret" dough, using genuine Swiss chocolate. Each outlet also offers a private line of David's ice cream, yoghurt, brownies, and beverages. Of the franchisor's estimated 200 outlets currently operating, all except one are franchise units.

David's Specialty Food Products, 12 E. 42nd St., New York, NY 10017. Telephone: (212) 682-0210

Days Inn of America Headquartered in Atlanta, Georgia, a franchisor of lodging outlets.

Founded in 1970, Days Inn has been franchising since the following year. The chain was the brainchild of an Atlanta real estate developer, Cecil B. Day, who started out with a group of six no-frills motels. A Days Inn executive, Richard Kessler, happened to be in Florida when he noticed a flurry of construction activity in the Orlando vicinity. Kessler moved quickly to open new outlets in the area, sowing the seeds for the fifth largest lodging organization in the United States. With 18 units in Orlando and 50 others throughout Florida, Days Inn is the major host to visitors to America's most popular tourist attraction, Disney World.

In 1984, the company-owned units were acquired by Reliance Capital, an investment group headed by a New York financier, Saul Steinberg. Steinberg's group resold the chain to a second outfit, Integrated Resources, which solicited individual investors to repurchase the outlets. At present, fewer than ten percent of the chain's outlets are company owned.

A typical Days Inn franchisee operates an economy lodging establishment designed to attract the mid- to higher-priced hotel patron by providing comparable quality accommodations and amenities at lower rates. The premises may include a swimming pool, meeting facilities, and food and beverage service. Of the estimated 700 Days Inn outlets currently open and operating, all except 60 are franchise units.

Days Inn of America, 2751 Buford Highway NE, Atlanta, GA 30324. Telephone: (404) 728-4145

Debit One Mobile Bookkeeping Headquartered in Springfield, Missouri, a franchisor of on-site bookkeeping services.

Founded in 1983, Debit One has been franchising since the following year. A typical Debit One franchisee operates a mobile accounting and tax preparation service. Of the 77 Debit One outlets currently operating, all except four are franchise units.

Debit One, 10317 NW Prairie View Rd., Kansas City, MO 64153. Telephone: (800) 331-2491

Deck the Walls Headquartered in Houston, Texas, a franchisor of specialty retail outlets.

Founded in 1979, DTW has been franchising since its inception. A typical DTW franchisee operates a retail store merchandizing posters, prints, and art works in conjunction with a custom picture framing service. Ninety percent of the chain's 254 outlets currently operating are franchise units.

Deck the Walls, P.O. Box 4586, Houston, TX 77210. Telephone: (800) 231-6337; Texas: (713) 890-5900

Decorating Den Headquartered in Bethesda, Maryland, a franchisor of mobile interior-decorating outlets.

Founded in 1969, Decorating Den has been franchising since 1974. A typical Decorating Den franchisee operates a home interior-decorating business based from a specially equipped van. Utilizing a diverse selection of drapery, carpet, wall and windowcovering samples, the outlet offers in-home decorating and counseling services without a retail site or inventory. The Decorating Den chain consists of 720 outlets, none of which are company-owned.

Decorating Den Systems, Inc., 4630 Montgomery Ave., Bethesda, MD 20814. Telephone: (301) 652-6393

Delaware, Franchise Regulations The Delaware legislature has not enacted any generally applicable franchise investment law. However, the Franchise Security Act provides franchisees with certain rights relating to the termination and renewal of the franchise agreement.

The law prohibits franchisors from terminating or refusing to renew a franchise without just cause or in bad faith. Delaware law does not require franchisors to register or file disclosures with any state regulatory body. In the absence of such a requirement, the federal Franchise Rule applies, requiring franchisors to furnish a disclosure document prescribed by the Federal Trade Commission to prospective franchisees ten business days before a franchise sale is made.
See Franchise Rule.

DeLuca, Fred Entrepreneur and sandwich shop franchisor. Cofounder of Subway Sandwiches and Salads, DeLuca successfully transformed a small, corner sandwich shop into a 2,000-outlet business empire.

DeLuca was 17 in 1965, when he was looking for ways to finance his college education. A family friend, a nuclear physicist named Peter Buck, suggested opening a sandwich shop. DeLuca agreed to run the shop, and Buck wrote out a check for $1,000 to get the business off the ground. Their venture, Pete's, opened in Bridgeport, Connecticut in August, 1965. When customers failed to throng into the shop, the partners decided to open a second store in nearby Fairfield to enhance their visibility.

Cutting corners, they continued opening sandwich shops over the next eight years, adopting the name Subway Sandwiches. DeLuca posed as a starving student to buy refrigerators at $15 each and stood on street corners passing out advertising fliers to motorists. Once he began selling franchise locations in 1974, expansion began in earnest. The 100th Subway outlet opened in 1978. Today, DeLuca and Buck, who remains a passive investor in the business, oversee a massive chain of 2,000 sandwich shops in 41 states and the Persian Gulf region. System-wide sales are reported at approximately $140 million annually.

DeLuca attributes the company's phenomenal success to keeping things simple. The sandwich shops do no cooking or frying, and menu is limited to ten varieties of submarine sandwiches. Salads are made from essentially the same ingredients, simplifying operations and containing costs.

Fred DeLuca, cofounder of Subway Sandwiches and Salads, one of the fastest growing fast-food chains of the 1980s.

Denny's, Inc. Headquartered in La Mirada, California, a franchisor of food service outlets.

Founded in 1953, Denny's has been franchising since 1984. When the company sold its first franchise in 1985, the chain had already grown to become one of the largest roadside restaurant organizations in the United States. A typical Denny's franchisee operates a family-style restaurant and coffee shop with a diversified breakfast, lunch, and dinner menu.

Of the franchisor's 1,390 outlets currently operating, 190 are franchise units.

Denny's, Inc., 16700 Valley View Ave., La Mirada, CA 90637. Telephone: (714) 739-8100

Descamps Headquartered in New York City, a franchisor of specialty retail outlets.

Founded in 1980, Descamps has been franchising since the following year. A typical Descamps franchisee operates a retail store specializing in household linen products. The outlet is distinguished by its French-style motif and product line. Of the franchisor's 195 outlets currently operating, 170 are franchise units.

Descamps, 454 Columbus Ave., New York, NY 10024. Telephone: (212) 302-3620

Dial-A-Gift, Inc. Headquartered in Salt Lake City, Utah, a franchisor of direct-mail merchandising outlets.

Founded in 1980, Dial-A-Gift has been franchising since 1984. A typical Dial-A-Gift franchisee operates a gift-wire service marketing gifts and novelties to catalog consumers. Orders are filled by local outlets which stock candies, cakes, gourmet foods, ceramic dishes, beverages, and other specialty gift items. Of the franchisor's 130 outlets currently operating, almost all are franchise units.

Dial-A-Gift, Inc., 2265 E. 4800 South, Salt Lake City, UT 84117. Telephone: (801) 278-0413

Dictograph Security Systems Headquartered in Florham Park, New Jersey, a franchisor of building security services.

Founded in 1965, Dictograph has been franchising since the following year. A typical Dictograph franchisee operates a sales and installation service devoted to electronic security and surveillance systems for commercial and residential buildings. Of the chain's 72 outlets currently in business, all except four are franchise units.

Dictograph, 26 Columbia Turnpike, Florham Park, NJ 07932. Telephone: (201) 822-1400

Diet Center, Inc. Headquartered in Rexburg, Idaho, a franchisor of weight-control counseling centers.

Since its inception in 1972, Diet Center has grown into the largest franchised weight control program in the world, with over 2,300 centers in the United States and Canada. According to the company, more than 5 million men, women, and children have undergone the Diet Center program. Every month, an estimated 60,000 new dieters begin the program to collectively shed a million pounds.

Diet Center was spawned by one individual's personal bout with her own weight problem. Sybil Ferguson was nearly 60 pounds overweight in 1970, when she was forced to postpone a necessary surgerical procedure because, in spite of her weight condition, she was also suffering from malnutrition. Through intensive personal research and with the help of her doctor, Sybil developed a nutrition-based weight loss program that successfully restored her health allowed her to permanently lose her excess weight.

Diet Center's corporate headquarters originated in the Ferguson's suburban home but has since relocated to more spacious, rustic quarters in Rexburg.

Roger and Sybil Ferguson

When Ferguson began helping friends do what she had done, physicians in her locality began referring overweight patients to her. Her husband Roger devised the Diet Center franchise program in 1971 and served as president of the Rexburg, Idaho company. By 1976, Diet Center had grown to 120 centers, when the company was nearly wiped out by a flood.

In 1977, the Diet Center Counselor Training School relocated from Idaho to Carefree, Arizona and was renamed the Diet Center International Training Headquarters. The school graduates over 600 counselors per year.

The company formed its own advertising agency, Ferguson & Associates, in 1978. Two year later, Ferguson Laboratories opened in Rexburg, Idaho's only FDA-licensed pharmaceutical manufacturing plant. The lab was destroyed by fire in 1988 and never rebuilt.

In 1983, *The Diet Center Program*, written by Sybil Ferguson, was published by Little, Brown, and Company, eventually reaching number seven on the New York Times best-seller list. Her sequel, *The Diet Center Cookbook*, was published in 1986.

In 1985, with more than 2,000 outlets, Diet Center, Inc. became a subsidiary of American Health Companies, Inc., and the Fergusons' son, Michael, assumed the presidency. The company has awarded approximately $200,000 in grants to fund research into the basic causes of obesity. An International Scholarship Program was instituted in 1986 for undergraduates majoring in nutrition or dietetics.

In 1988, American Health Companies and Diet Center, Inc. were acquired by CDI Holdings, Inc. and DC Acquisition Corporation, organized by the Thomas H. Lee Company of Boston. Shortly afterward, Sybil Ferguson was named Diet Center president.

A typical DCI franchisee operates a personal weight-loss center offering daily counseling and weekly support groups as part of a "five-phase" plan. The program stresses motivational support, behavior modification practices, and nutrition education. Franchisees also market name-brand vitamins, diet supplements, and low-calorie salad dressings and snack foods. All of the 2,330 Diet Center outlets currently open and operating are franchise units.

Diet Center, Inc., 220 S. 2nd West, Rexburg, ID 83440. Telephone: (208) 356-9381

The Diet Center program is based on a controlled regimen of health assessment and nutritional counseling

Dip 'N Strip Headquartered in Denver, Colorado, a franchisor of furniture restoration outlets.

Founded in 1970, Dip 'N Strip has been franchising since the following year. A typical Dip 'N Strip franchisee operates a furniture restoration business utilizing the franchisor's process for stripping and refinishing wood and metal surfaces. Of the franchisor's 280 outlets currently operating, all except one are franchise units.

Dip 'N Strip, 2141 S. Platte River Dr., Denver, CO 80223. Telephone: (303) 781-8300

Dipper Dan Ice Cream Shoppes Headquartered in St. Petersburg, Florida, a franchisor of specialty fast-food outlets.

Founded in 1963, Dipper Dan has been franchising since 1965. A typical franchisee operates a fast-food business specializing in cookies, candy, doughnuts, and 32 flavors of hand-dipped ice cream. None of the 250 Dipper Dan outlets currently operating are company-owned.

Dipper Dan Ice Cream Shoppes, P.O. Box 47068, St. Petersburg, FL 33743. Telephone: (813) 323-7927

District of Columbia, Franchise Regulations To date, the District of Columbia has not adopted any generally applicable franchise investment law. However, the rights of service station owners operating under franchise agreements are protected by the Retail Service Stations statute.

The District of Columbia does not require franchisors to register or file disclosures with any regulatory body. In the absence of such a requirement, the federal Franchise Rule applies, requiring franchisors to furnish a disclosure document prescribed by the Federal Trade Commission to prospective franchisees ten business days before a franchise sale is made.

See Franchise Rule.

Docktor Pet Headquartered in Wilmington, Massachusetts, a franchisor of retail pet stores.

Founded in 1966, Docktor Pet has been franchising since 1967. A typical Docktor Pet franchisee operates a pet boutique featuring dogs, cats, birds, tropical fish, other domesticated animals, pet supplies, equipment, cages, and pet training services. Of the franchisor's 270 outlets currently operating, all except three are franchise units.

Docktor Pet, 355 Middlesex Av., Wilmington, MA 01887. Telephone: (617) 658-7840

Dollar Rent A Car Headquartered in Los Angeles, California, a franchisor of automobile rental outlets.

Founded in 1966, Dollar has been franchising since 1968. A typical Dollar franchisee operates a car rental facility at or near a major airport or downtown area. Of the franchisor's estimated 1,600 outlets, all but nine are franchise units.

Dollar Systems, 6141 W. Century Blvd., Los Angeles, CA 91356. Telephone: (213) 766-8100

Domestic Aide Headquartered in Overland Park, Kansas, a franchisor of interior maintenance services.

Founded in 1976, Domestic Aide has been franchising since 1984. A typical Domestic Aide franchisee operates a full-service housecleaning business. Of the franchisor's 30 outlets currently operating, all except one are franchise units.

Domestic Aide, 8717 W. 110th St., Ste. 750, Overland Park,KS 66210. Telephone: (800) 433-4519

Domino's Pizza Headquartered in Ann Arbor, Michigan, a franchisor of fast-food outlets.

Founded in 1960 by Thomas Monaghan, Domino's has been franchising since 1967, growing into one of the largest franchise fast-food chains in the United States. Monaghan was an architecture student when he bought a modest pizza restaurant named Dominick's, for $900. To reduce overhead costs, he converted the operation into a delivery-only service. When he changed the restaurant's name to Domino's Pizza, Monaghan was sued by the Domino Sugar Co. for trademark infringement. He faced bankrupcty on three separate occasions, before a federal court finally ruled in the pizza operator's favor.

Twenty years after licensing the first Domino's Pizza franchise to a former delivery driver, Monaghan had become America's undisputed pizza king. A typical Domino's franchisee operates a fast-food business devoted to pizza delivered free to customers' homes. Domino's eschews sit-down facilities to concentrate exclusively on delivery service. Franchisees guarantee their customers 30-minute delivery. The product is kept warm en route inside specially installed ovens. About two thirds of the franchisor's estimated 4,600 outlets are franchise units.

Domino's Pizza, 30 Frank Lloyd Wright Dr., P.O. Box 997, Ann Arbor, MI 48104-0997. Telephone: (313) 668-6055

Dr. Nick's Transmissions Headquartered in Melville, New York, a franchisor of automotive transmission outlets.

Founded in 1971, Dr. Nick's has been franchising since 1978. A typical Dr. Nick's franchisee operates a retail transmission repair service. All 30 of the Dr. Nick's outlets currently operating are franchise units.

Dr. Nick's Transmissions, 150 Broadhollow Rd., Melville, NY 11747. Telephone: (516) 385-0330

Dr. Pepper Popular soft drink and franchise trademark.

Dr. Pepper originated in Waco, Texas in 1885, at a corner drug store operated by Wade Morrison. But the concoction was named after another drug store owner in Virginia, where Morrison had worked as a pharmacist. Allegedly, Morrison had been fired from his job and driven from Virginia for having fallen in love with Dr. Pepper's daughter.

R. S. Lazenby, a Texas ginger-ale producer, perfected the cherry-tasting syrup used to mix the soda. The numerals "10, 2, 4" which appeared on the Dr. Pepper label for decades, were vestiges of a 1920's advertising slogan, "Drink a bite to eat at 10 - 2 & 4 o'clock."

In 1986, industry frontrunner Coca-Cola offered $480 million for Dr. Pepper, the fourth-largest soft drink franchisor. The takeover attempt occurred almost simultaneously with a bid by second-ranked Pepsico to acquire Seven-Up. The mergers were blocked by the FTC, which unanimously ruled that the twin acquisitions would severely restrict competition in the soft drink industry.

In the wake of the landmark FTC decision, Dr. Pepper was acquired in a leveraged buyout by two Texas financiers, Thomas Hicks and Robert Haas, who bought out Seven-Up in a similar deal two months later.

Drake Personnel Headquartered in San Francisco, California, a franchisor of personnel employment agencies.

Founded in 1951, Drake has been franchising since 1987. Atypical Drake franchisee operates a full-service employment agency with dual emphasis on both temporary and permanent placement, utilizing a computer-based job search system developed by the franchisor. Prospective job candidates are tested for "projected performance" prior to acceptance. Temporary-help services are handled by the franchisor's Office Overload division. Of the 235 Drake Personnel outlets currently operating, ten are franchise units.

Drake Personnel, 595 Market St., Ste. 2150, San Francisco,CA 94105. Telephone: (800) 458-5621. In Canada: (416) 967-7700

Drug Emporium, Inc. Headquartered in Columbus, Ohio, a franchisor of specialty retail outlets.

Founded in 1977, Drug Emporium has been franchising since the following year. A typical Drug Emporium franchisee operates a retail drug store devoted to health and beauty aids and cosmetics, and stressing high volume and low margins to enable discount pricing. Of the franchisor's 150 outlets currently operating, slightly more than half are franchise units.

Drug Emporium, Inc., 7760 Olentangy River Rd., Columbus, OH 43085. Telephone: (614) 888-6876

Dryclean-USA, Inc. Headquartered in Miami, Florida, a franchisor of dry cleaning outlets.

Founded in 1976, Dryclean-USA has been franchising since the following year. A typical Dryclean-USA franchisee operates a retail dry cleaning business based on a standardized site design and equipment package, and uniform operating standards. Of the franchisor's 245 outlets currently operating, approximately 170 are franchise units.

Dryclean-USA, 9100 S. Dadeland Blvd., Ste. 1110, Miami, FL 33156. Telephone: (305) 667-3488

Duds 'N' Suds Headquartered in Ames, Iowa, a franchisor of laundromats.

Founded in 1982, DNS has been franchising since 1984. A typical DNS franchisee operates a self-service laundromat featuring a lounge with entertainment facilities for patrons. Of the 80 outlets currently operating, all except one are franchise units.

Duds 'N' Suds, P.O. Box B, Welch Station, Ames, IA 50010. Telephone: (800) 222-3837

Dunhill Personnel System Headquartered in Carle Place, New York, a franchisor of personnel employment agencies.

Founded in 1952, Dunhill has been franchising since 1961. A typical Dunhill franchisee operates a personnel recruitment and placement business utilizing the franchisor's national computer system to match applicants to suitable job opportunities. The outlet caters to 55 different occupational categories, ranging from data processing to chemical engineering. Of the 340 Dunhill offices currently operating, all except nine are franchise units.

Dunhill Personnel System, One Old Country Rd., Carle Place, NY 11514. Telephone: (800) 247-4881

Dunkin' Donuts Headquartered in North Brunswick, New Jersey, a franchisor of fast-food outlets.

Founded in 1950, Dunkin' Donuts has been franchising since 1956. A typical Dunkin' Donuts franchisee operates a fast-food service specializing in doughnuts and coffee, based on the franchisor's standarized site design and product specifications. Each shop prepares its own baked goods from ingredients selected by the franchisor. Of the franchisor's 1735 outlets currently operating, all except eight are franchise units.

Dunkin' Donuts, 825 George Rd., North Brunswick, NJ 08902.

Duraclean International Headquartered in Deerfield, Illinois, a franchisor of interior maintenance services.

Founded in 1930, Duraclean has been franchising since 1945. A typical Duraclean franchisee operates a home cleaning business specializing in carpet and drapery cleaning and restoration, utilizing the franchisor's standardized equipment, chemical products, and cleaning techniques. Of the 615 Duraclean outlets currently in business, all except one are franchise units.

Duraclean International, 2151 Waukegan Rd., Deerfield, IL 60015. Telephone: (312) 945-2000

Durant, William Crapo Industrialist, automaker, and franchisor of General Motors automobiles.

Born in Boston on December 8, 1861, Durant grew up in Flint, Michigan. In 1886, with his associate, J. Dallas Dort, he organized the Durant-Dort Carriage Company. The new enterprise rapidly became the world's largest manufacturer of buggies, shipping 150,000 carriages per year.

In 1904, Durant bought the Flint Wagon Works, a company which had previously acquired the rights to an automobile designed by David D. Buick. The following year, Durant formed a new organization, Buick Motor Company, to begin manufacturing of the new horseless carriage. He formed General Motors in 1910 and also took over Cadillac, Oldsmobile, and Oakland.

Forcibly removed from the helm of General Motors, he joined forces with Louis Chevrolet in 1911, to create a new automobile. Four years later, Chevrolet lost interest in the project and sold his interests to Durant. The Chevrolet automobile would become one of the most recognizable franchised products of the twentieth century.

After organizing the Chevrolet Motor Company in 1915, Durant successfully regained control of General Motors in 1916. In the stock market crash of 1929, he lost most of his personal wealth, once estimated at $120 million.

By the 1960s, automobile dealers under contract to General Motors represented the single largest franchise organization in America.

One of Durant's earliest successes was the popular Buick passenger automobile.

**ELS
to
European Tanspa**

ELS International Headquartered in Culver City, California, a franchisor of educational service outlets.

Founded in 1961, ELS has been franchising since 1981. A typical ELS franchisee operates a tutoring service specializing in remedial English. Of the franchisor's 34 outlets currently operating, 13 are franchise units.

ELS International, Inc., 5761 Buckingham Pky., Culver City, CA 90230. Telephone: (213) 642-0982

ERA Electronic Realty Associates Headquartered in Overland Park, Kansas, a franchisor of independent real estate sales offices.

Founded in 1972, ERA has been franchising since 1975. A typical ERA franchisee operates a licensed real estate listing and sales business utilizing the franchisor's trademark, signs, and advertising. Franchisees offer nationwide property listings, residential and commercial sales and leasing, service contracts, and financing programs. The ERA network consists of 2,840 outlets, none of which are company owned.

ERA, 4900 College Blvd., Overland Park, KS 66211. Telephone: (800) 255-6000

Earl Keim Realty Headquartered in Troy, Michigan, a franchisor of real estate sales offices.

Founded in 1958, Earl Keim has been franchising since 1970. A typical Earl Keim franchisee operates a real estate brokerage under the umbrella of the franchisor's trademark and advertising. None of the franchisor's 90 outlets currently operating are company owned.

Earl Keim Realty, 1740 W. Big Beaver, Ste. 200, Troy, MI 48084. Telephone: (313) 649-0200

Econo Lodges of America Headquartered in Charlotte, North Carolina, a franchisor of lodging outlets.

The company's management attributes the chain's rapid expansion to its memorable slogan "Spend the night, not a fortune." Founded in 1969, Econo Lodge has been franchising since its inception. A typical Econo Lodge franchisee operates a new or previously owned economy-priced hotel based on the franchisor's specifications, designs, and trademark. The average outlet has 100 rooms and offers attractive accommodations at reduced rates, by controlling costs through the elimination of amenities such as uniformed bell service, banquet facilities, and food and beverage service. Of the franchisor's 440 outlets currently operating, all except six are franchise units.

Econo Lodges of America, 6135 Park Rd., Ste. 200, Charlotte, NC 28210. Telephone: (704) 554-0088

Econo Lube N' Tune Headquartered in Newport Beach, California, a franchisor of automobile service outlets.

Founded in 1973, Econo Lube has been franchising since its inception. A typical Econo Lube franchisee operates an auto maintenance business specializing in quick oil changes, lubrication, and tune-ups. Of the franchisor's 115 outlets currently operating, 104 are franchise units.

Econo Lube N' Tune, 4911 Birch St., Newport Beach, CA 92658. Telephone: (714) 851-2259

Ehman, Martin D. Entrepreneur, salesman, and franchisor of video rental outlets. Cofounder and chairman of the board of Adventureland, Inc., Ehman and his partner, Brent Smith, transformed their wives' hobby into a multimillion-dollar business empire.

Ehman was a sales manager for the Campbell Soup Company in 1981 when his wife, Deanna Ehman, teamed up with Connie Smith to open the first Adventureland store in Pleasant Grove, Utah. Connie's husband, Brent, was also a former soup salesman who had jumped ship to a videocassette rental outfit. The owners were able to recoup their $10,000 initial investment in the first three months. Soon afterward, Martin and Brent began selling franchises, charging a $5,000 initial fee with no ongoing royalty obligations.

By 1983, the partners had franchised a hundred outlets in 17 states. Catering to families, Adventureland prohibits franchise owners from handling pornographic tapes or X-rated movies. In 1986, the franchisor acquired its closest competitor, Video Biz, to become the largest home video rental organization in America, with annual sales of $40 million.

El Chico Restaurants Headquartered in Dallas, Texas, a franchisor of food service outlets.

Founded in 1940, El Chico has been franchising since 1965. A typical El Chico franchisee operates a specialty restaurant and beverage service with a Mexican decor and menu. About one third of the 96 El Chico outlets currently operating are franchise units.

El Chico Restaurants, 12200 Stemmons Fwy., Ste. 100, Dallas, TX 75234. Telephone: (214) 241-5500

El Pollo Asado Headquartered in Phoenix, Arizona, a franchisor of fast-food outlets.

Founded in 1983, EPA has been franchising since 1984. A typical EPA franchisee operates a fast-food restaurant specializing in charbroiled chicken. Of the franchisor's 47 outlets currently operating, 25 are franchise units.

El Pollo Asado, 3420 E. Shea Blvd., Ste. 150, Phoenix, AZ 85028. Telephone: (602) 998-0941

Employers Overload Headquartered in Minneapolis, Minnesota, a franchisor of temporary employment agencies.

Founded in 1947, Employers Overload has been franchising since 1984. A typical Employers

Overload franchisee operates a personnel recruitment and placement agency specializing in temporary employment. Of the franchisor's 72 outlets currently operating, 62 are franchise units.

Employers Overload, Inc., 8040 Cedar S., Minneapolis, MN55420. Telephone: (800) 854-2345

Empress Travel Headquartered in New York City, a franchisor of retail travel agencies.

Founded in 1957, Empress Travel has been franchising since 1974. A typical Empress Travel franchisee operates a retail travel agency which books air reservations, tour packages, cruises, hotel space, and other travel arrangements. The agency derives income from commissions on airline, hotel, cruise, and car rental reservations. Of the franchisor's 60 outlets currently operating, all but five are franchise units.

Empress Travel, 5 Penn Plaza, New York, NY 10001. Telephone: (212) 563-0560

Endrust Industries Headquartered in Pittsburgh, Pennsylvania, a franchisor of automobile rustproofing outlets.

Founded in 1969, Endrust has been franchising since 1978. A typical Endrust franchisee operates a retail automobile detailing and reconditioning business based on a standardized product line and service system. Of the franchisor's 85 outlets currently operating, none are company-owned.

Endrust Industries, 1725 Washington Rd., Pittsburgh, PA 15241. Telephone: (412) 831-1255

Entre Computer Centers Headquartered in McLean, Virginia, a franchisor of specialty computer stores.

Founded in 1981, Entre has been franchising since the following year. A typical Entre franchisee operates a retail store specializing in computer hardware and software. The outlet is distinguished by its "business-consulting" approach to marketing and sales. Of the franchisor's 195 outlets currently operating, all except 11 are franchise units.

Entre Computer Centers, 1430 Spring Hill Rd., McLean, VA 22102. Telephone: (703) 749-3275

Ernies's Wine & Liquors Headquartered in South San Francisco, California, a franchisor of retail liquor, wine, and beer outlets.

Founded in 1938, Ernie's has been franchising since 1960. A typical Ernie's franchisee operates a retail liquor store based on the franchisor's wholesale purchasing and inventory-control system. Of the franchisor's 40 outlets currently operating, all except one are franchise units.

Ernie's Wine & Liquors, 305 Littlefield Ave., South San Francisco, CA 94080. Telephone: (415) 583-7663

European Tanspa Headquartered in Downers Grove, Illinois, a franchisor of tanning salons.

Founded in 1982, ET has been franchising since 1983. The organization was acquired in 1986 by a group of nine salon owners headed by Sandy Lindholm, the company's current chief executive. A typical ET franchisee operates a retail tanning salon based on a standardized equipment package and site design furnished by the franchisor. The average salon has three tanning rooms with six tanning beds. Of the franchisor's 125 outlets currently operating, none are company-owned.

European Tanspa, 1911 Ogden Ave., Downer's Grove, IL 60515. Telephone: (312) 963-2626

Everything Yogurt/Bananas Headquartered in Staten Island, New York, a franchisor of fast-food outlets.

Founded in 1976, EY has been franchising since 1982. A typical EY franchisee operates a fast-food restaurant devoted to yoghurt products. Each outlet features a menu of frozen yoghurt, desserts, and drinks, in addition to full-scale dinner entrees,such as salads, vegetable dishes, quiches, and pasta, all prepared with yoghurt. Of the franchisor's 185 outlets currently operating, all except five are franchise units.

Everything Yogurt, 304 Port Richmond Ave., Staten Island, NY10302. Telephone: (718) 816-7800

Express Services, Inc. Headquartered in Oklahoma City, a franchisor of personnel employment agencies.

Founded in 1970, ESI has been franchising since 1985. A typical ESI franchisee operates an employment agency offering both temporary-help and permanent-placement services. Of the franchisor's 105 outlets currently operating, none are company-owned.

Express Services, Inc., 6300 NW Expressway, Oklahoma City, OK 73132. Telephone: (800) 652-6400

Famous Amos
to
Fuddrucker's

Famous Amos Chocolate Chip Cookies Headquartered in Van Nuys, California, a franchisor of specialty bakery goods outlets.

Founded in 1975, Famous Amos has been franchising since 1982. A typical Famous Amos franchisee operates a retail bakery goods shop featuring the franchisor's proprietary chocolate chip cookies. Of the franchisor's 70 U.S., Canadian, and foreign outlets currently operating, all except three are franchise units.

Famous Amos Chocolate Chip Cookie Corp., 14553 Delano St., Ste. 202, Van Nuys, CA 91411. Telephone: (800) 354-2667

Fantastic Sam's Headquarted in Memphis, Tennessee, a franchisor of hair care salons.

Founder Samuel Ross opened his first haircutting parlor in 1974 and began franchising two years later. Over the next 15 years, he would license more than a thousand franchisees. A typical Fantastic Sam's franchisee operates a haircutting and styling salon catering to families. Salon employees adopt cartoon-character nicknames and greet arriving customers with coffee, bubblegum, and balloons. The business format is based on a patented haircutting process and a standardized package of equipment and procedures. Of the 1,275 Fantastic Sam's outlets currently operating, all but one are franchise units.

Fantastic Sam's, P.O. Box 18845, Memphis, TN 38181. Telephone: (901) 363-8624

Fashion Crossroads Headquartered in Burbank, California, a franchisor of women's apparel stores.

Founded in 1933, Fashion Crossroads has been franchising since 1940, under the name Mode O' Day. A typical franchisee operates a women's apparel and accessories outlet, featuring inventories selected by the franchisor's fashion consultants and furnished to franchisees on consignment. Of the franchisor's 480 outlets, all but 30 are franchise units.

Fashion Crossroads, 2130 North Hollywood Way, Burbank, CA 91505. Telephone: (818) 843-4340

Courtesy Jack in the Box Restaurants

Fast Food Food prepared in quantity, usually by means of a standardized system, and dispensed quickly at low-cost service outlets. In contrast to a full-service restaurant, a typical fast-food outlet eschews table service and dispenses meals from a service counter or window.

Fast food restaurants are an outgrowth of the "car hop" drive-in restaurants which rose to popularity in the 1940s and 50s. The drive-ins offered the unique scenario of uniformed waitresses, often on roller skates, serving customers in their automobiles.

The invention of the drive-in restaurant is widely attributed to Roy Allen and Frank Wright, whose first venture into food service was a roadside stand which sold only root beer. They opened their first A&W outlet in Lodi, California in 1918 and, amazed at the little stand's success, added hot dogs and sandwiches to the menu and instituted car-hop service. In 1925, Allen and Wright licensed the world's first fast-food franchise to a Texas man, for $2,000.

The success of the new drive-in concept did not escape the notice of other restaurant operators. In the 1930s, two brothers, Maurice and Richard McDonald, opened a similar outlet in the Los Angeles area, specializing in hot dogs and pork sandwiches. The idea of selling hamburgers did not occur to them until the 1950s, when they devised their unique "Speedy Service System" for turning out burgers with

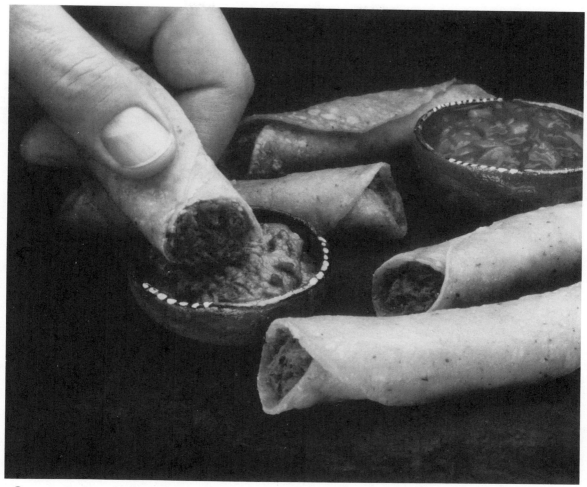

Courtesy Jack in the Box Restaurants

assembly-line efficiency. The McDonald sold their first franchise to a Phoenix man in 1952. Neither brother was serious about expanding the business and, in 1961, they sold all their rights to the McDonald's concept to a milkshake machine salesman named Ray Kroc. Under Kroc's reins, McDonald's and fast food became household words.

The 1950s were boom years for the fast-food industry. The first Jack in the Box drive-through restaurants sprang up in southern California in 1950, followed in the southeastern U.S. by InstaBurger King, which later shortened its name to Burger King. In 1952, Kentucky colonel Harlan Sanders shared his recipe for southern-style poultry with a friend, Pete Harmon, who urged Sanders to consider selling franchises. Not coincidentally, Harmon became the first Kentucky Fried Chicken franchisee.

In 1958, America's fast-food love affair was heated up by Pizza Hut, the first in a long line of pseudo-Italian eateries. In 1962, Taco Bell made a splash with pseudo-Mexican food. Five Five years later, a college student named Thomas Monaghan scraped together $900 to buy a run-down pizza parlor named Dominick's. Over the next two decades, he would specialize exclusively in home delivery, change the name to Domino's, and create the world's largest chain of pizza franchises.

Monaghan owed his success to increasing public concern over health and nutrition in the 1970s and

80s, which prompted a shift toward food prepared with fresher and more nutritious ingredients. During this period, Subway Sandiches and Salads, founded by a medical student and a nuclear physicist, became one of the fastest growing fast-food chains in history.

In both number of outlets and total sales volume, the largest fast-food chain today remains McDonald's, discounting Pepsico, which owns the Kentucky Fried Chicken, Taco Bell, and Pizza Hut organizations. Viewed as a separate entity, the KFC chain boasts the second largest number of outlets, followed by Pizza Hut, Dairy Queen International, Baskin-Robbins, Hardee's, and Taco Bell.

The 20 largest fast-food chains are ranked in the following table.

Largest Fast-Food Franchisors by Number of Outlets

1. McDonald's (13,900)
2. Kentucky Fried Chicken 10,200)
3. Pizza Hut (6,000)
4. Dairy Queen International (5,000)
5. Domino's Pizza (4,600)
6. Burger King (4,500)
7. Wendy's International (3,650)
8. Baskin-Robbins (3,300)
9. Hardee's Food System (3,000)
10. Taco Bell (2,760)
11. SUBWAY Sandwiches & Salads (2,400)
12. Little Caesar's Pizza (2,000)
13. Dunkin' Donuts (1,735)
14. Long John Silver's (1,500)
15. Arby's (1,500)
16. Church's Fried Chicken (1,500)
17. Sonic Drive-Ins (1,100)
18. Jack in the Box Restaurants (940)
19. Orange Julius (745)
20. Pizza Inn (690)

Fat Boy's Bar-B-Q Headquartered in Cocoa, Florida, a franchisor of food service outlets.

Founded in 1959, Fat Boy's has been franchising since 1968. A typical Fat Boy's franchisee operates a specialty restaurant featuring a diversity of barbecue-style cuisine. Of the 34 Fat Boy's outlets currently operating, all except two are franchise units.

Fat Boy's Bar-B-Q Restaurants, 1550 W. King St., Cocoa, FL 32926. Telephone: (305) 636-1000

Federal Trade Commission (FTC) A federal regulatory body established by Congress and granted sweeping authority to regulate business practices in the United States. Today, the FTC also serves as the federal watchdog over the offer and sale of franchises.

History and Scope

The FTC was created when the Federal Trade Commission Act became law on September 26, 1914. The new commission absorbed and superceded the federal Bureau of Corporations. Its mission was to prevent monopolies and preserve competition in commerce. President Woodrow Wilson hailed the new law as an important safeguard of the free enterprise system, a means "to make men in a small way of business as free to succeed as men in a big way" and to "kill monopoly in the seed."

Section Five of the Act begins:

> *Unfair methods of competition in commerce, and unfair or deceptive acts or practices in commerce, are declared unlawful.*

The law provides the FTC with the power to make regulations and issue rules which have the full impact and enforcement of federal law. The FTC is further empowered to bring legal proceedings against any person or company that transgresses a FTC regulation or rule.

On December 21, 1978, the Commission drafted an amendment to Title 16 of the Code of Federal Regulations, which deals with Commerce and Trade. The amendment was aimed at promulgating a trade regulation rule relating to the sale of franchises and business opportunity ventures. The new Franchise Rule went into effect on October 21, 1979, requiring franchisors to disclose certain pertinent information to prospective franchisees before any sale is made.

The FTC and Franchising

FTC Rule 436.1 declares:

> *...it is an unfair or deceptive act or practice within the meaning of Section 5 of the Federal Trade Commission Act for any franchisor or franchise broker: (a) to fail to furnish any prospective franchisee with the following information accurately, clearly, and concisely stated, in a legible, written document at the earlier of the "time for marking of disclosures" or the first "personal meeting"...*

By "the following information," the Rule refers to a document disclosing 20 points of information about the franchisor, the franchise business, and the franchise agreement. (See *Disclosure Document, Franchise Rule*). The Rule defines the "time for the making of disclosures" as ten business days before a franchise sale is made.

The FTC's Franchise Rule also affects the manner in which franchisors may make any claims regarding actual or potential sales or earnings of a prospective franchisee.

Information regarding FTC rules and regulations affecting franchise offerings can be obtained from: Federal Trade Commission, 6th and Pennsylvania Avenue N.W., Washington, DC 20580. Telephone inquiries may be directed to: (202) 376-2805.

The Federal Trade Commission also publishes an informative pamphlet, *Franchise Business Risks* (Consumer Bulletin No. 4), advising prospective franchisees about potential pitfalls. The publication is available for a nominal charge from: Superintendant of Documents, U. S. Government Printing Office, Washington, DC 20402.

Financing Many, if not most, franchises are started with financial assistance from a third party, such as a bank, savings and loan, investment firm, leasing company, financial partner, or venture capitalist. In addition, approximately 20 percent of all franchisors offer some form of direct or indirect financial assistance to franchisees.

Franchisors and franchisees use financing for any of four general purposes: (1) seed capital, (2) start-up capital, (3) working capital, (4) expansion capital.

Seed capital is an investment in an idea, as opposed to an established business. This type of financing is used to fund the development of the idea itself. *Start-up capital* is an investment in a new business for which there is a business plan and management team already in place. This type of financing is used for such purposes as real estate purchases, building construction, equipment, fixtures, and opening inventory. *Working capital* is money applied to keeping an ongoing business afloat. This type of financing is used to pay wages and salaries, make lease payments, and replenish inventory and supplies. *Expansion capital* is an investment in a merger, acquisition, diversification, or market expansion program. This type of financing is used to expand a business beyond its present markets and territories.

A prospective franchisee seeking financing to open a franchise outlet is usually looking for start-up capital, money available for the initial investment. Five sources of start-up financing are commonly used by franchisees: (1) conventional lenders, (2) the Small Business Administration, or SBA, (3) Small Business Investment Companies, or SBICs, (4) finance companies, and (5) franchisors which offer direct or indirect financial assistance.

Conventional Lenders

The most common source of start-up capital for small businesses, including franchise outlets, is a conventional lending institution, such as a bank, savings and loan, or credit union. Commercial loans are generally available at prevailing interest rates, subject to the creditworthiness of the borrower and current economic conditions. To guarantee the loan, the borrower must usually commit personal property, such as equity in a home, or the assets of the business, as collateral.

The major advantage of obtaining financing from a conventional lender is widespread availability of funds at prevailing interest rates. Some potential drawbacks include difficulty in qualifying in the absence of substantial property to pledge as collateral and, usually, a payback period of 15 to 30 years, saddling the business with lengthy debt service.

The Small Business Administration

The SBA has provided numerous franchisees with start-up capital over the last three decades. This federal agency provides both direct and indirect financial assistance to small business owners. To qualify for a SBA loan, a borrower must first be turned down by conventional lenders.

The SBA also licenses banks and finance companies to lend money to small businesses, guaranteeing repayment with federal funds. More than 1,000 conventional lending institutions currently participate in the SBA-guaranteed loan program.

An advantage to SBA or SBA-guaranteed assistance is the fact that the agency favors franchise outlets over other types of small business. Franchise businesses are four times more likely to succeed than other, independently owned enterprises. A drawback is the lengthy application process, from six to as much as twelve months.

Small Business Investment Companies

SBICs are independent investment firms which are licensed by the SBA to invest in small businesses. Some of these firms specialize in or favor franchise outlets. Many limit their investments to a particular industry or trade, such as lodging, fast food, or electronics.

A variation of the SBIC is the Minority Enterprise Small Business Investment Company, or MESBIC, which invests exclusively in minority-owned businesses.

Whereas a lender loans money to creditworthy franchisees at prevailing interest rates, a SBIC or MESBIC may make an outright equity investment, purchasing from 5 to 50 percent of the ownership. Such firms may also lend start-up, working, or expansion capital to business owners who might not otherwise qualify for commercial loans, but usually at higher-than-prevailing rates.

Finance Companies

An alternative source of financing consists of finance companies, leasing firms, and propery management businesses which arrange for partial funding of the franchisee's investment. For example, a credit

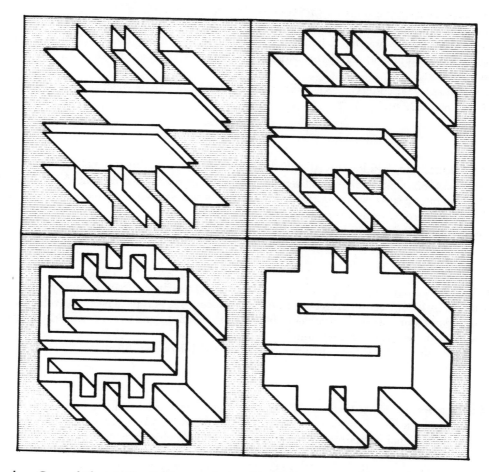

company, such as General Electric Credit Corporation or Westinghouse Credit Corporation, may provide financing for inventory, equipment, or fixtures. Leasing companies may purchase equipment or real estate to lease back to the franchisee. Property management firms may invest in real property required by the franchisee, either through conventional financing or through a leaseback program.

Financial Assistance from a Franchisor

Each year, hundreds of franchise outlets are opened with the benefit of direct or indirect financing from a franchisor. A small percentage of franchisors offer 100-percent franchising of the franchisee's entire initial investment, including working capital. Others may finance a portion of the investment, or merely the initial fee. Still others provide assistance by leasing equipment or real estate, or offering credit terms for purchases of supplies and opening inventory.

Many franchisors have arrangements with third parties, such as finance companies, leasing firms, or product distributors, to finance all or part of the initial investment. A franchisor who offers any form of financial assistance to franchisees, either through itself or through a third party, must disclose the details in section 10 of the Uniform Franchise Offering Circular (UFOC). The prescribed disclosures must include the terms, interest rates, and conditions of the financing, as well as information regarding the source. Under federal regulations, franchisors must tell whether they receive any "kickbacks" from third-party lenders who offer financing to franchisees.

See *Small Business Administration, Small Business Investment Company, Minority Enterprise Small Business Investment Company, Franchise Rule,* Uniform Franchise Offering Circular.

First Choice Haircutters Headquartered in Mississauga, Ontario, a franchisor of hair care salons.

Founded in 1980, First Choice has been franchising since 1982. A typical First Choice franchisee operates a retail, family-oriented haircutting and styling salon utilizing the franchisor's standardized process, techniques, equipment, and decor. More than half of the 200 First Choice outlets currently operating are franchise units.

First Choice Haircutters, 6535 Millcreek Dr., Ste. 64, Mississauga, Ont., Canada L5N 2M2. Telephone: (800) 387-8335

Flakey Jake's, Inc. Headquartered in Bellevue, Washington, a franchisor of food service outlets.

Founded 1982, Flakey Jake's has been franchising since the following year. A typical Flakey Jake's franchisee operates a specialty restaurant featuring hamburger sandwiches, chicken, and barbecued spare ribs. The chain currently has 25 franchise units.

Flakey Jake's, Inc., 15015 Main St., Ste. 202, Bellevue, WA 98007

Fleet Feet Headquartered in Sacramento, California, a franchisor of sports and foot wear stores.

Founded in 1976, Fleet Feet has been franchising since 1978. A typical Fleet Feet franchisee operates a specialty apparel store devoted to athletic shoes, sports apparel, and accessories. All except two of the franchisor's 24 outlets are franchise units.

Fleet Feet, Inc., 2408 J. St., Sacramento, CA 95814. Telephone: (916) 442-7223

Florida, Franchise Regulations The Florida legislature has not adopted any generally applicable franchise investment law. However, the Franchises and Distributorship Law prohibits franchisors from making any intentional misrepresentation in the offer or sale of a franchise.

For information about the law, or to report possible violations, contact: Division of Consumer Services, 110 Mayo Bldg., Tallahassee, FL 32301. Telephone: (904) 488-2221.

Florida law does not require franchisors to register or file disclosures with any state regulatory body. In the absence of such a requirement, the federal Franchise Rule applies, requiring franchisors to furnish a disclosure document prescribed by the Federal Trade Commission to prospective franchisees ten business days before a franchise sale is made.
See Franchise Rule.

Flowerama of America Headquartered in Waterloo, Iowa, a franchisor of retail florists.

Founded in 1967, Flowerama has been franchising since 1972. The chain originated as a floral supply business started by two horticulturists, Maurice and Herbert Frink, of Cedar Falls, Iowa. A typical Flowerama franchisee operates a retail flower, plant, and gift store merchandising cut flowers, floral arrangements, potted plants, and related gift items. Each franchisee leases a"turn-key" flower store, completely developed by the franchisor prior to opening. Of the 88 Flowerama outlets currently operating, all except 11 are franchise units.

Flowerama of America, 3165 W. Airline Hwy., Waterloo, IA50703. Telephone: (319) 291-6004

Foliage Design Systems Headquartered in Ocala, Florida, a franchisor of specialty interior decoration outlets.

Founded in 1971, FDS has been franchising since 1980. A typical FDS franchisee operates a sales and leasing business devoted to interior foliage plants used as interior design elements in offices and homes. Of the franchisor's 38 outlets currently operating, all except three are franchise units.

Foliage Design Systems, 1553 SE Fort King, Ocala, FL 32671. Telephone: (904) 732-8212

Food Service Franchising The category of franchising made up of retail food service businesses.

The idea of offering food and beverage service for pay is almost as old as humankind, but the premise of sanitary, affordable food service is a relatively modern concept. The early inns of Biblical times were usually no more than private residences which offered travelers a hot meal, a jug of wine, and a bench or cot to sleep on. Sanitation was of little concern, and the prices were prohibitive to all except the wealthy or desparate.

The first public establishment devoted exclusively to food service opened in Paris in 1765. On an oak plaque over the entrance was carved the following inscription:

Venite ad me omnes qui stomacho laboratis et ergo restaurabo vos.

("Come to me all whose stomachs growl and I shall replenish you.") The term "restaurant" is derived from this plaque, specifically from the Latin word restaurabo ("I shall replenish"). Throughout the colonial period, American eateries were created in the European image as country inns or taverns catering to travelers, but not to the general public. For the average citizen, food service came of age during the Industrial Revolution of the 1880s.

The first cafeteria opened in New York in 1885. When sandwiches became popular in the 1920s, and soda fountains in the 1930s, eating out became a national pastime. The first franchised food service establishment originated from an A&W root beer stand opened in southern California in 1918. An early A&W franchisee, J. Willard Marriott, would become one of the most successful hotel and restaurant operators in America.

Meanwhile, across the continent in Quincy, Massachusetts, a patent medicine dealer named Howard Johnson was tinkering with a hand-cranked freezer in the basement of his corner drugstore, creating the nation's first line of multi-flavored ice cream. In 1925, with his soda fountain the talk of the town, Johnson converted the entire store into a restaurant. Four years later, he opened his second fast-food parlor, which would serve as the prototype for the Howard Johnson restaurant chain.

Bob Wien opened his first Big Boy restaurant in 1934, sewing the seeds for a new era of affordable, sanitary, family- style dining establishments.

Food Service Categories

Food service outlets, franchised or otherwise, may be classified into four categories: classical, specialty, family-style, and fast-food.

Classical restaurants, often called "gourment" restaurants, emphasize classical cuisine in the European tradition, prepared by a highly skilled chef with a lifetime of apprenticeship. The hallmarks of a classical restaurant are elegant surroundings, a well trained, highly disciplined staff, sophisticated cuisine, and equally sophisticated prices. There are no known examples of franchised classical restaurants.

Specialty restaurants are the most prevalent type of full- service dining establishment, with the largest share devoted to ethnic foods such as Italian, Chinese, Japanese, Mexican, German, or Swedish cuisine. A typical specialty restaurant has a limited menu which, like the decor, is centered around a theme. Prices are usually reasonable, ranging from moderate to high. Benihana's of Tokyo and Tony Roma's A Place for Ribs are examples of successful specialty restaurant chains.

Family-style restaurants include coffee shops and cafeterias. Modest in personality, atmosphere, and price, this type of eatery features dependable, predictable food and service. The menu may be limited or diversified, but the hallmark of the family-style restaurant is moderate pricing. A typical decor incorporates padded booths, a counter with stools, and natural lighting from ample window space. Bob's Big Boy, Denny's, and Rax are examples of successful family-style restaurant chains.

Fast-food restaurants account for roughly 90 percent of all meals taken in public. Franchise chains represent two thirds of the eateries in this category. Most are self-service outlets which feature convenience, a limited menu, and low prices. The most successful fast-food chains are McDonalds, Kentucky Fried Chicken, and Wendy's International.

See *Fast Food*.

Food-N-Fuel Headquartered in Arden Hills, Minnesota, a franchisor of retail convenience outlets.

Founded in 1978, Food-N-Fuel has been franchising since the following year. A typical franchisee operates a convenience food store combined with gasoline service. Of the 100 Food-N-Fuel outlets currently operating, all except 21 are franchise units.

Food-N-Fuel, 4366 Round Lake Rd. West, Arden Hills, MN 55112

Ford, Henry (1863-1947) Industrialist, automaker, philanthropist, and automobile franchisor.

Born on July 30, 1863 in Dearborn, Michigan, Ford went to work while still a teenager, as a machinist for the Edison Illuminating Company. By 1899, he had risen to chief engineer. Fascinated by the idea of horseless carriages, he created his own "gasoline buggy" in 1892 and, four years later, assembled a more elaborate vehicle, called the Quadricycle, in a shed in the back of his farmhouse. When completed, the vehicle was reportedly too large for the shed door and had to be taken apart and reassembled outside.

With $100,000 in borrowed capital, Ford organized the Ford Motor Company in 1903. When the first Ford automobile appeared shortly thereafter, the young company was sued for patent infringement by the Association of Licensed Automobile Manufacturers, representing inventor George B. Selden. Ford finally setted in 1911, but by then, company sales had topped $10 million per year.

In 1908, Ford unveiled his masterpiece, the Model T, which succesfully captured a previously unimagined market for sporting and luxury cars. By 1927, more than 15 million "Tin Lizzies" had been distributed across America through independent Ford franchise dealers.

For an industrialist, Henry Ford was an innovator and humanitarian. He instituted the first voluntary minimum wage ($5 per day) for Ford workers. But, his was also the last automobile manufacturer to yield to unionization by the United Auto Workers.

When Ford Motor Company finally introduced the Model A in 1927, the company was already six years behind competition in engineering accomplishment. In 1932, the automaker recaptured its former glory by marketing the V-8 engine.

In 1918, Ford ran unsuccessfully for the U.S. Senate and, a year later, turned over the presidency of FMC to his son, Edsel Bryant. He established the humanitarian Ford Foundation in 1936 and briefly returned to corporate life upon his son's death in 1943. He handed over the reigns to his grandson, Henry Ford II, in 1945.

Ford's biography, *My Life and Work*, appeared in 1922.

Ford Model T The first "modern" automobile, devised by Henry Ford and manufactured by Ford Motor Company, and one of the most influential franchised products in history.

The Model T Ford made its first appearance on October 1, 1909. When the last Tin Lizzie rolled off the assembly line on May 31, 1927, a total of 15,007,033 units had been manufactured. Perhaps more significantly, the debate over the practicality of the new-fangled "horseless carriage" had come to an end, and American life in general had been altered forever by a simple mode of transportation. Henry Ford's Model T was the single most instrumental development in bringing about the automotive revolution.

According to popular legend, Henry Ford was inspired as a youth with both the invention of the automobile and the concept of mass production. On the contrary, he invented neither the automobile nor mass production, but rather a packaging concept capable of capturing the public imagination. In fact, Ford came a breath away from selling his foundering company to Jim Durant, the owner of General Motors, in 1908. Only after extensive trial and error did Ford finally stumble across the formula of selling a single, "basic black", no-frills product in large quantity at a low price. Undoubtedly, luck also played a prominent role in Ford's destiny as the "father of the modern automobile."

The first motorcars were slow to catch on. The main obstacle to both manufacturing and performance was the cumbersome weight of the vehicles after assembly. A breakthrough occured in Florida in 1908, when Ford happened by accident across a piece of metal salvaged from a demolished French racecar. The metal turned out to be a new type of lightweight steel, which Ford adopted as the basic fabric of the Model T.

The first Model T sold for $950. By 1916, Ford was able to sell 534,000 cars for $360 a piece, raise his workers' wages, and still earn a $59 million profit. Ford's phenomenon was not only the first, truly affordable car but also the first "sporty" car designed primarily for touring. The Model T came in one color: black. As Ford told the nation, "any customer can have a car painted any color he wants so long as it is black."

Because it was the chosen car of the ordinary working man, the Model T became a symbol of economic democracy. When the sleek, comfortable, slightly European-looking automobile was finally replaced, never again would its quality, distinction, and price competitiveness be matched by any Ford product. And Never again would Henry Ford be the undisputed king of the motor industry.

Foremost Liquors Headquartered in Chicago, Illinois, a franchisor of retail liquor, wine, and beer outlets.

Founded in 1949, Foremost has been franchising since its inception. A typical Foremost franchisee operates a retail liquor store or a discount liquor supermarket, utilizing a standardized inventory and purchasing system. None of the 76 Foremost outlets currently operating are owned by the franchisor.

Foremost Sales Promotions, 5252 N. Broadway, Chicago, IL 60640. Telephone: (312) 334-0077

Fortunate Life Headquartered in Charlottesville, Virginia, a franchisor of weight-loss centers.

Founded in 1983, Fortunate Life has been franchising since its inception. A typical Fortunate Life franchisee operates a personal weight-loss business based on a standardized program of diet and nutrition counseling. The center markets a line of diet and health products to enrollees in the program. All but one of the franchisor's 45 outlets are franchise units.

Fortunate Life Weight Loss Centers, P.O. Box 5604, Charlottesville, VA 22905. Telephone: (800) 446-6003

F-O-R-T-U-N-E Franchise Corporation Headquartered in New York City, a franchisor of personnel recruitment agencies.

Founded in 1959, Fortune has been franchising since 1969. A typical Fortune franchisee operates a management recruitment agency specializing in middle-management and upper-echelon positions.

All of the franchisor's 50 outlets are franchise units. Fortune Franchise Corp., 655 Third Ave., Ste. 1805, New York, NY 10017. Telephone: (800) 221-4864

Foster's Donuts Headquartered in Ventura, California, a franchisor of fast-food outlets.

Founded in 1970, Foster's has been franchising since 1980. A typical Foster's franchisee operates a specialty bakery goods shop specializing in freshly prepared doughnuts and beverage service. The chain presently consists of 55 outlets, none of which are company-owned.

Foster's Donuts, 3583 Maples St., Ste. 120, Ventura, CA 93003. Telephone: (805) 642-5844

Foster's Freeze International Headquartered in Arroyo Grande, California, a franchisor of fast-food outlets.

Founded in 1946, Foster's Freeze has been franchising since the following year. A typical Foster's Freeze franchisee operates a fast-food restaurant specializing in soft ice cream, hamburgers, hot dogs, sandwiches, and beverage service. Of the franchisor's 200 outlets currently operating, all except four are franchise units.

Foster's Freeze International, P.O. Box 266, Arroyo Grande, CA 93420. Telephone: (805) 481-9577

Four Star Pizza Headquartered in Washington, Pennsylvania, a franchisor of fast-food outlets.

Founded in 1981, Four Star has been franchising since 1985. A typical Four Star franchisee operates a fast-food pizza/sandwich shop specializing in home-delivery service. The chain is composed of 85 outlets, 65 of which are franchise units.

Four Star Pizza, P.O Box 1370, Washington, PA 15301.

Four Seasons Greenhouses Headquartered in Holbrook, New York, a franchisor of home-improvement products.

Founded in 1978 by two brothers, Chris and Joe Esposito, Four Seasons has been franchising since 1985. The company currently maintains manufacturing and distribution facilities in 14 countries. A typical Four Seasons franchisee operates a commercial/retail "Design and Remodeling Center" devoted primarily to modular greenhouse systems. The outlet focuses on solarium additions to homes and commercial buildings such as restaurants and lodging establishments, but franchisees also market windows, doors, and home remodeling products. The Four Seasons chain currently boasts 250 outlets, of which all except five are franchise units.

Four Seasons Greenhouses, 5005 Veterans Memorial Hwy., Holbrook, NY 11741. Telephone: (800) 521-0179

Fox's Pizza Den Headquartered in New Kensington, Pennsylvania, a franchisor of specialty fast-food outlets.

Founded in 1971, Fox's has been franchising since 1974. Atypical Fox's franchisee operates a fast-food restaurant devoted to pizza, specialty sandwiches, and beverage service. Of the franchisor's 115 outlets currently operating, none are company-owned.

Fox's Pizza Den, 122 Carrie Ann Dr., New Kensington, PA 15068. Telephone: (412) 733-7888

Franchise A right, license, or privilege granted by one entity to another. The term "franchise" is derived from *franc*, an Old French word for "free." Originally, the Middle English term referred to the privileges granted by a government to its citizens. Even today, politicians can be heard fervently defending the public franchise to vote. But in modern usage, the word "franchise" is most often encountered in reference to a license granted by a company to an independent reseller to merchandise or distribute the company's products or services.

To most people, a franchise is a place where double-decker hamburgers or southern fried drumsticks are served from behind a brightly lit counter. Technically, a fast-food restaurant is not a franchise at all, but rather a franchise outlet. In this case, the term "franchise" refers to the right or privilege to open the restaurant. The owner receives this privilege by purchasing a franchise from the "franchisor," a company that sells to qualified individuals franchises to open fast-food restaurants.

As an example, consider someone who purchases a franchise to open a McDonald's restaurant. The franchisor, McDonald's Corporation, owns the McDonald's trademarks along with all the plans, blueprints, designs, recipes, and operating methods associated with a McDonald's restaurant. To open a McDonald's restaurant of his own, a businessman must first obtain a franchise from the franchisor. The businessman, the "franchisee," pays a fee to McDonald's Corporation and puts up the money to build the restaurant. In return, the franchisor permits the businessman to use the company's trademarks and puts the businessman through a training program.

Franchises are not limited to fast food or the restaurant industry. Retail stores, hotels, amusement parks, auto repair shops, car rental agencies, real estate companies, banks, travel agencies, and trade schools, all can be opened and operated under franchises granted by successful corporations.

General Definition

A business franchise, often referred to as a *business format franchise*, has three characteristics: (1) an identity, usually derived from a registered trademark, (2) a business format, consisting of specifications, quality standards, and prescribed methods of operation, and (3) a financial relationship between two parties. The person or entity which grants the franchise is referred to as the "franchisor," and the person or entity who receives the franchise is the "franchisee." The identity and business format are normally owned by the franchisor. The franchisee pays the franchisor a consideration for the franchise.

The International Franchise Association defines a franchise in the following terms:

> A *franchise is a continuing relationship between franchisor and franchisee in which the sum total of the franchisor's knowledge, image, success, manufacturing, and marketing techniques are supplied to the franchisee for a consideration.*

The franchisee pays a financial consideration to the franchisor and invests the money required to start the business. The franchisor supplies know-how, a recognizable identity, and marketing experience. The franchisee must usually abide by the franchisor's quality standards and product specifications. Yet, despite this relationship, franchisor and franchisee are not partners in business; the franchisee is the exclusive owner of the outlet and the franchise under which it is operated.

Legal Definition

Both federal and state laws refer to an entity as a "franchise." Exactly what constitutes such an entity is defined differently in each of the applicable statutes. The federal definition is found in Federal Trade Commission Rule 436.2, under Paragraph 6160, *Definitions*, as follows:

> *(a) The term "franchise" means any continuing commercial relationship created by any arrangement or arrangements whereby . . . a person offers, sells, or distributes to any*

person goods, commodities, or services which are (1) identified by a trademark, service mark, trade name, advertising or other commercial symbol . . . or (2) directly or indirectly required or advised to meet the quality standards prescribed by another person where the franchisee operates under a name using the trademark, service mark, trade name, advertising or other commercial symbol . . .

Thus, first of all, a franchise consists of a trademark, logo, or trade name granted by the franchisor to the franchisee. For example, the franchisee who acquires a franchise from McDonald's Corporation receives the right to erect the McDonald's sign on the restaurant. Likewise, other franchisees receive the right to operate under such trade names as Hertz, Holiday Inn, and Baskin-Robbins.

The federal definition also includes the following qualification:

(B)(1) The franchisor exerts or has the authority to exert a significant degree of control over the franchisee's method of operation, including but not limited to, the franchisee's business organization, promotional activities, management, marketing plan or business affairs; or (2) the franchisor gives significant assistance to the franchisee in the latter's method of operation . . .

Thus, a franchise also involves "a significant degree of control" and "significant assistance" by the franchisor. The element of control takes the form of mandatory operating procedures, quality standards, and specifications relating to the type and make of products offered by the franchisee. The franchisor provides assistance in the form of a training program, an operating manual, and ongoing consultation in periodic visits to the franchisee's outlet.

The third component of a franchise, as defined by the Federal Trade Commission, is a financial relationship, explained in the next part of the definition:

(2) The franchisee is required as a condition of obtaining or commencing the franchise operation to make a payment or a commitment to pay to the franchisor, or to a person affiliated with the franchisor . . .

Simply stated, the FTC rule defines a franchise as a business relationship between a franchisor and a franchisee involving the following factors: (1) a trademark license, (2) quality standards, (3) management controls, (4) operating assistance, (5) payment of a franchise fee. The simplest type of franchise is an arrangement by which a manufacturer or distributor sells to a dealer the right to sell or resell trademarked products. A "business format" franchise is one which includes instruction in business methods, participation in joint promotion or advertising, or other elements prescribed by the franchisor.

Trademark License

A license to use a trademark or trade name does not, *per se*, constitute a franchise, but a trademark license is an integral element of any franchise relationship. The franchisee receives the right to distribute products or services bearing the franchisor's trademark, or to conduct a business under a trademark owned by the franchisor.

In general, a franchise permits the franchisee to use the franchisor's name, logo, trademark, or commercial symbol to identify either the franchisee's business or the products and services marketed under the franchise.

Managements Controls and Operating Assistance

Types of control or assistance offered or prescribed by franchisors typically include training in the operation of the business, selection or approval of the site, production or selling techniques, bookkeeping practices, personnel policies, promotional assistance, sales territories, and specifications pertaining to quality and workmanship. Such controls or assistance are often referred to as "a community of interest" between franchisor and franchisee "in marketing goods and services."

The contract between the franchisor and the franchisee, commonly referred to as the "franchise agreement," normally spells out the restrictions imposed on the franchisee by the franchisor. The franchisor's advice and specifications pertaining to the operation of the business and the marketing of products and services are usually contained in a manual, or series of manuals, called the "Franchise Operating Manual."

For example, the franchise agreement may restrict the franchisee from owning another business in direct competition with the franchise outlet. The operating manual may cover, among other subjects, accounting practices, maintenance procedures, sales and marketing, advertising, personnel hiring and training, and inventory control.

Franchisee Fees

The FTC Rule does not consider a relationship or contract to be a franchise unless a financial consideration is paid by the franchisee. Specifically, the total payment or obligation during the first six months of the franchisee's operation must exceed $500. If this condition is not met, the arrangement is not a true franchise under FTC requirements and is therefore exempt from the federal rules governing franchises.

Business Opportunities

Certain types of "business opportunities" offered for sale to the general public may fall under the FTC rules, as well. In general, any business relationship which meets the following three conditions is considered a franchise under the federal definition: (1) the franchisee sells goods or services supplied by the franchisor, or by suppliers designated by the franchisor; (2) the franchisor secures the franchisee's outlet, customers, or, in the case of vending machines or display racks, locations; (3) the franchisee pays a consideration to the franchisor (more than $500 within six months after the franchise business has commenced).

This requirement covers product distributors, vending machine routes, and rack jobbers, even though a trademark is not associated with the arrangement. If a business relationship involves any form of "significant control or assistance," such as a marketing plan, operating manual, or training program, the federal franchise rules may be invoked.

Exemptions

Both federal and state rules and laws exempt certain types of enterprises and business relationships from the definition of a franchise. At the federal level, these exceptions include employer-employee relationships, general partnerships, cooperative associations, single-unit licenses, and departments within a department store. In addition, "fractional franchises" (franchises accounting for no more than 20 percent of the gross receipts of the franchisee) are also exempted from the FTC rules.

Different exemptions are granted by the various state laws. For example, California law exempts franchises involved in the petroleum industry, mainly, gasoline service stations, as well as franchises for bank credit card services.

State Definitions

The legal definition of a franchise differs in the states which individually regulate franchising practices. The respective statutory definition is found in the following state laws and rules:

Arkansas

        Arkansas Franchise Practices Act, Section 2(a)

California

        California Corporations Code, Section 31005(a)
        California Civil Code, Section 1812.201
        California Business and Professions Code, Section 20001

Connecticut

        Connecticut General Statutes, Section 42-133(e)
        Connecticut General Statutes, Section 36-504

Delaware

        Delaware Code Annotated, Title 6, Section 2551

Florida

        Florida Statutes, Section 817.416

Georgia

        Georgia Code, Section 10-1-410

Hawaii

        Hawaii Revised Statutes, Section 482E-2

Illinois

        Illinois Revised Statutes, Chapter 121 1/2

Indiana

        Indiana Code 23-2-2.5-1

Iowa

        Iowa Code, Section 523B.1

Kentucky

        Kentucky Revised Statutes, Section 367.801

Louisiana

        Louisiana Revised Statutes, Section 51:1821

Maine

        Maine Revised Statutes, Section 32-4391

Maryland

        Maryland Annotated Code, Section 56-345
        "   "   "   Section 56-401

Michigan

        Michigan Compiled Laws, Section 445.1502
        "   "   "   Section 445.902

Minnesota
>Minnesota Statutes, Section 80C.01

Mississippi
>Mississippi Code, Section 75-24-51

Missouri
>Missouri Revised Statutes, Section 407.400

Nebraska
>Nebraska Revised Statutes, Section 59-1703
>"   "   "   Section 87-402

New Jersey
>New Jersey Revised Statutes, Section 56:10-3

New Hampshire
>New Hampshire Revised Statutes, Section 358-E:1

New York
>New York General Business Law, Article 33, Section 681.1

North Dakota
>North Dakota Century Code, Section 51-19-02

Ohio
>Ohio Revised Code, Section 1334.01

Oklahoma
>Oklahoma Statutes, Title 71, Chapter 4, Section 802

Oregon
>Oregon Revised Statutes, Section 650.005

Rhode Island
>Rhode Island General Laws, Section 19-28-3

South Carolina
>South Carolina Code, Section 39-57-20

South Dakota
>South Dakota Laws, 1985, HB 1076, Section 1

Texas
>Texas Revised Civil Statutes, Title 79, Article 16.05

Utah
>Utah Code, Section 13-15-2

Virginia
>Virginia Code, Section 13.1-559

Washington
     Washington Revised Code, Section 19.100.010

Wisconsin
     Wisconsin Statutes, Section 553.03
     "   "   "   Section 135.02

See *Franchise Agreement, Franchise Fee, Franchise Rule, Franchisee, Franchisor, Uniform Franchise Offering Circular.*

Franchise Agreement A contract between franchisor and franchisee granting a franchise and setting forth the mutual obligations of the parties. The franchise agreement, more than any other element of a franchise, defines the relationship between franchisor and franchisee and sets the stage for their joint success.

Objectives of the Franchise Agreement

From the franchisor's perspective, the franchise agreement is an instrument for creating uniformity in quality standards from one franchise outlet to another. The franchisee is more likely to view the agreement as a means of enforcing the franchisor's obligations to train and assist the franchisee. In reality, both parties have rights and obligations under the franchise agreement aimed at maintaining uniformity and protecting their respective interests.

The franchisor uses the franchise agreement to obligate the franchisee to adhere to the franchisor's standards, specifications, policies, and procedures. The agreement also protects the franchisor's trademarks and trade secrets licensed to the franchisee. Most agreements seek to restrict the franchisee from engaging in any business or activity that is detrimental to, or in direct competition with, the franchise outlet.

From the franchisee's point of view, the agreement should obligate the franchisor to provide the assistance promised by the franchise sales representative. Typically, these services include a training program, assistance with selecting a site for the business, help with hiring and training of personnel, the provision of a franchise operating manual, and ongoing consultation in the form of periodic visits to the outlet by the franchisors qualified representative.

Very often, the franchise agreement bestows territorial rights on the franchisee. In some cases, the franchisee may have expansion rights within the territory or, based on the achievement of a certain sales level or quota, the right to acquire additional territories. In the case of *subfranchising* or *area franchising,* the agreement must spell out the financial, as well as business, relationship between the franchisor and the subfranchisor or area franchisee.

Although there are numerous different franchise agreements in use by franchisors, most contracts are designed to deal with several common aspects of the franchise relationship.

Territorial Rights

People who purchase franchises to start businesses often expect or demand exclusive rights to a designated territory. Aside from granting rights to the franchisee, the agreement also imposes certain restrictions upon the franchisor.

An "exclusive" territory is one in which the franchisor agrees not to open another outlet in competition with the franchisee's outlet. In addition, the franchisor is prohibited from granting a franchise to another party besides the franchisee inside the territory.

The territory may be *static*; that is, it may remain the same throughout the duration of the franchise agreement. Or, it may be subject to revision based on the franchisee's sales performance. For example, if the franchisee reaches a certain quota, he may have the right to expand the territory. Conversely, if the outlet falls below a certain sales level, the franchisor may have the right to reduce the franchisee's exclusive territory.

There are no rules or regulations governing the boundaries or size of a franchise territory, which may encompass an entire continent or may be confined to a street corner. But, generally, the courts have held that franchisees may not be prohibited from selling to customers outside their exclusive territories.

Franchise Fees

The franchise agreement is the instrument by which the franchisor obligates the franchisee to pay an initial fee and any ongoing fees while the contract is in effect.

The *initial fee* is payable by the franchisee when the franchise agreement is signed. This amount is usually paid as a lump sum directly to the franchisor. Other fees may also be payable upon signing, such as a separate tuition fee for the franchise training program and/or a fee for selecting or approving the site for the franchisee's outlet.

Ongoing fees are also typical of a franchise relationship, and the franchisee's obligation to pay them is an integral part of the franchise agreement. These fees may include a franchise royalty, to be calculated as a set percentage of the franchisee's gross sales receipts, and a contribution to a national or regional advertising fund administered by the franchisor.

The agreement may also obligate the franchisee to pay other types of fees and payments, such as charges for special services or assistance, payments to franchisee associations, costs of auditing the franchisee's business, mandatory minimum advertising expenditures, and contract renewal fees. The franchisee may also be obligated to pay transfer fees, in the event the franchise should be sold or assigned.

Uniformity of Standards

Much of the verbage in the franchise agreement is devoted to the enforcement of uniformity among franchisees. Recognizing that consumers place a high priority on sameness, franchisors seek with extraordinary rigor to achieve and maintain uniform standards of sanitation, appearance, decor, and service throughout their franchise systems.

The franchisee may be restricted as to the goods and services that may be offered for sale by the franchise business. For example, a franchisee who operates a family hotel may be prohibited by the franchise agreement from also operating an amusement park on the same premises.

Most franchise agreements require the franchisee to comply with the franchisor's standards relating to all aspects of the outlet's premises. The franchisor, for example, may have the right to select or approve the site where the business will be established. Further, the franchisor may insist upon approving or directly overseeing the construction or remodeling of the premises. Some agreements go so far as to place all planning, architecture, and construction in the hands of the franchisor, with little or no participation or input by the franchise. Indeed, many franchisees view the franchisor's willingness to undertake site construction as a benefit of the franchise relationship.

The agreement may also stipulate such standards as the business hours of the outlet; the grooming and appearance of employees; the use and specification of signs, logos, and advertising displays; and minimum insurance requirements.

The franchisor typically requires each of its franchisees to attend a franchise training school. New McDonald's franchisees, for example, attend Hamburger U., where they master the nuances of the burger business; Swensen's Ice Cream franchisees, not surprisingly, attend Sundae School.

Besides the franchisee himself, the manager of the outlet and designated employees may also be obligated to complete the pre-opening training program. In most cases, the cost of attending the training program must be borne by the franchisee.

The franchisor's trade secrets are documented in a franchise operating manual provided to the franchisee for the term of the agreement. In most cases, the agreement requires the franchisee to return the manual, along with all bulletins, updates, and revisions, when the agreement is terminated or expires. The franchisor may reserve the right to make changes to the business system and to the operating manual after the franchise agreement has been signed. A typical agreement obligates the franchisee to accept and implement such changes at the franchisee's own expense. For example, if the franchisor decides to change the appearance, decor, and furnishings of its outlets, the franchisee may be required to conform to the new specifications, regardless of the cost.

Quality Control

Many franchise agreements contain provisions aimed at quality control in the procurement and sale of products or in the performance of services by franchisees. It is common for a franchisee to be obligated to purchase products, equipment, and supplies only from suppliers who meet the franchisor's standards. Typically, the franchisor will reserve the right to approve any suppliers with whom the franchisee may wish to do business. Although the franchisor may supply products to franchisees, the franchisor is prohibited by law from designating itself as the franchisee's *sole* supplier.

For example, Baskin-Robbins at one time required its franchisees to purchase ice cream products solely from the franchisor and from no other supplier. The courts, however, ruled that franchisees were free to purchase from any supplier who could meet the franchisor's standards and specifications, not just from Baskin-Robbins.

Invariably, franchisors use the franchise agreement as a mechanism for prescribing specifications and procedures governing the methods by which the franchisee operates the business. For example, the franchisee may be obligated to use the franchisor's purchasing, bookkeeping, or inventory system, or to use only advertising materials prepared or approved by the franchisor's ad department.

A common provision in franchise agreements bestows upon the franchisor the right to inspect the franchisee's business and records, either with or without prior notice. If the franchisor suspects that the franchisee has been concealing income to avoid royalty payments, the franchisor may have the right to audit the franchisee's books. If any deficiencies are uncovered, the franchisee is usually obligated to pay for the expense of the audit.

Many franchise agreements require the franchisee to submit financial statements, reports of gross sales, and other records to the franchisor periodically. In addition, the franchisee may be obligated to use a standard accounting system or a designated computer software program to keep the outlet's books.

Protection of Trade Secrets

Besides a familiar trademark, pre-opening assistance, and the right to sell a product or service, every franchisee also obtains certain trade secrets along with a business format franchise. For example, a Coca-Cola® Bottling Company franchisee receives the "secret formula" for concocting New Coke® or Classic Coke® ; and a Domino's Pizza franchisee delivers hot pizza stored in specially manufactured ovens inside each delivery van.

The recipes, formulas, inventory systems, merchandising techniques, accounting programs, customer accounts, and, often, computer software programs developed by the franchisor and acquired by the franchisee, all are trade secrets. Obviously, the value of the franchise is derived in large part from the protection of these secrets. Hence, a sound franchise agreement obligates the franchisee to help guard the secrecy of the systems and techniques on which the franchise system was built.

The franchisee and his employees are typically prohibited from disclosing the franchisor's trade secrets to any unauthorized party. The employees of the outlet may be required to sign an oath of confidentiality, vowing to keep all information about the business in strict confidence.

A hallmark of the franchise agreement is the *covenant not to compete*. During the term of the franchise and for a specified period thereafter, the franchisee may be restricted from engaging in any business in direct competition with the franchise outlet. Generally, a period of one or two years after the expiration or termination of the agreement is considered "reasonable."

Assistance and Supervision

The franchise agreement spells out exactly what assistance and supervision is to be provided by the franchisor both before and after the outlet has commenced business. Typically, these items items include: provision of a training program to the franchisee and designated employees of the outlet; assistance or approval in selecting a site for the outlet; ongoing consultation in the form of written communications, telephone assistance, and personal visits by a field manager; annual workshops, conventions, or seminars for franchisees; refresher training courses.

Franchise Term

The "term" of the franchise refers to the length of time for which the agreement will remain in effect. When the term has passed, the franchise agreement automatically expires, unless it has been renewed. Normally, a contract may not be terminated prior to its expiration, except under extraordinary circumstances.

Most franchises have a fixed term, with ten years being the average. Approximately fifteen percent of the franchise agreements currently in effect have indefinite terms; that is, they never expire. Fewer than five percent have a term of less than five years.

Renewal

The franchise agreement may provide the franchisee with the right to renew the franchise upon expiration. This right may be subject to any number of conditions, including upgrading of the outlet's premises, completion by the franchisee of a refresher training course, or payment in full for any outstanding debts. For example, when Holiday Inns decided to upgrade the image of its hotels, as each agreement came up for renewal, the company required franchisees to refurbish their establishments from the inside out. The costs of the improvements, as well as a separate renewal fee, may be imposed on the franchisee.

Transfer and Assignment

To preserve its control over the franchise system, the franchisor usually restricts the franchisee from transfering or assigning the franchise to an unauthorized party. Conversely, the franchisor rarely gives up his rights to transfer his own obligations to others. A "transfer" takes place when the franchise is sold or given away. The agreement is subsequently "assigned" to the purchaser or recipient. Transfer and assignment also occur if someone seizes possession of the business through legal action, e.g., as payment for an outstanding debt, or if the business is inherited by a relative of the franchisee upon the franchisee's death.

The franchisor normally reserves the right to approve any assignment of the franchise. Simply stated, if the franchisee desires to sell the business, the buyer must meet with the franchisor's approval. Further, if the franchisee should happen to die, his heirs must also be approved as franchisees by the franchisor. The buyer or heir must meet the same qualifications as anyone else whom the franchisor accepts into the organization. Any such "assignee" must usually execute a new franchise agreement, complete the franchisor's training course, and, often, pay a transfer fee. The new owner normally assumes any debts or other obligations of the previous franchisee.

The agreement may provide the franchisor with the right of *first refusal* regarding any proposed transfer. In other words, the franchisor may have the option to purchase the franchise on the same terms and at the same price as those offered by another buyer. For example, assume a franchisee receives an offer from an independent party to purchase the business for $375,000. Exercising its right of first refusal, the franchisor can buy the franchisee's business at the same price, preventing the sale to the outside buyer.

If the franchisor declines to match the offer, the franchisee can proceed with the sale. The buyer, of course, may have to meet with the franchisor's approval as an assignee.

Termination of the Franchise

Although, technically, the franchise agreement should remain in effect until its term has lapsed, every franchise agreement contains certain provisions for termination by either the franchisor or the franchisee. These provisions are based on "defaults" by one of the parties. The defaulting party normally has a reasonable period in which to "cure" the default.

The franchisee should have the right to terminate the agreement if the franchisor has breached the contract and, after a reasonable time, has not corrected the problem or made amends. Most agreements will specify numerous grounds permitting termination by the franchisor. For example, the agreement might be subject to termination by the franchisor if the franchise abandons the business; attempts to make an unauthorized transfer of the franchise; discloses the franchisor's trade secrets to an unauthorized party; violates the covenant not to compete; or, after a reasonable period, fails to correct a default relating to the franchisor's mandatory standards, specifications, and procedures.

A severe default, such as abandoning the franchise or making an unauthorized assignment, is often tied to immediate termination without notice. In the case of a default relating to operating standards — e.g., grooming and appearance of employees — the franchisee should be given reasonable notice and ample opportunity to cure the default, before termination becomes an issue.

Obligations on Termination

It is common for franchise agreements to place additional obligations on franchisees even after termination or expiration. For example, the former franchisee may be forced to give up the telephone number or even the location of the business. Whenever a franchise is temrinated, the franchisee is obligated to cease using the franchisor's operating system, manuals, advertising materials, trademarks, and other items associated with the franchise.

See *Franchise, Franchisee, Franchisor, Uniform Franchise Offering Circular.*

Example Franchise Agreement

FRANCHISE AGREEMENT

1. Grant of Franchise

A. [Franchisor name] (the "Franchisor") hereby grants to _____
whose business address is _____
(the "Franchisee") a license to use the trade name "[Trade name]" and the trade marks associated therewith, and a franchise to operate a [Trade name] outlet (the "Outlet") in the geographical market identified in Exhibit A of this agreement.

B. Franchisee shall use the trade name and marks in the conduct of a [outlet description], and franchisee's place of business shall incorporate the name [Trade name].

C. The name of any corporation operating this franchise may include the name "[Trade name]" or any other trade mark owned or licensed by franchisor, but only with the written consent of franchisor.

2. Exclusive Territory

Franchisor shall not, while this agreement is in force, conduct a similar operation, or grant a similar franchise to any other franchisee, within the territory defined in Exhibit A.

3. Term

This agreement shall continue for a period of [length of term] years from the date hereof, and shall be automatically renewed for an additional term, unless at least six (6) months before the expiration of this agreement, franchisee gives to franchisor notice in writing of termination at the end of the term.

4. Development and Opening

Within ninety (90) days of the execution of this agreement, franchisee shall do or cause the following to be done:

A. Secure all financing required to develop the outlet;

B. Complete all arrangements for a site for the outlet. Franchisor shall have the right and option to approve the selected site prior to the development and opening of the outlet.

C. Execute a lease for the premises in which the outlet shall be operated, and deliver to the franchisor a true and correct copy;

D. Obtain all licenses and permits required to conduct the business;

E. Obtain all improvements, fixtures, supplies, and inventory.

5. Payments

A. Franchise Fee Franchisee shall make payment to franchisor the sum of $_____

Dollars ($_____) upon execution of this agreement, receipt of which is hereby acknowledged. In return for this payment, franchisee shall receive the right to do business as a licensed _____ franchise under the terms of this agreement, and to receive the services and assistance hereinafter set forth. The initial fee shall be fully earned by the franchisor and is nonrefundable.

6. Advertising

A. Franchisee agrees to use all advertising designs, materials, media, and methods preparation described by or which conform to franchisor's standards and specifications.

B. Franchisee shall refrain from using any advertising designs, materials, media, and methods of preparation which do not meet franchisor's standards and specifications.

C. Franchisor shall make available to franchisee any assistance that may be required, based on the experience and judgment of franchisor, in the design, preparation, and placement of advertising and promotional materials for use in local advertising.

D. Franchisor shall administer the Franchisee Cooperative Advertising Fund, and direct the development of all advertising and promotional programs. The content of the advertising, as well as the media in which the advertising is to be placed and defined advertising area, shall be at the discretion of the franchisor.

7. Trade Marks

A. Franchisor shall make available to franchisee franchisor's trade names and marks. For the purpose of this agreement, "the marks" shall be defined as all symbols, logos, trade marks, and trade names owned and/or under application by franchisor.

B. Franchisee agrees that its rights to use the marks are derived solely from this agreement, and franchisee shall not derive any right, title, or interest in the marks, other than a license to use them in connection with the franchise outlet while this agreement is in force,

C. Franchisee shall use the name and service marks only in such manner as prescribed by franchisor and in no other way.

D. Franchisee shall immediately notify franchisor of any apparent infringement of the use of the marks.

E. If it becomes advisable at any time in franchisor's sole discretion to discontinue or modify the use of any mark, franchisee agrees to comply within a reasonable time after notice thereof by franchisor.

8. Products, Supplies, and Equipment

Franchisee understands and acknowledges that every detail of the franchise system is important to franchisor, to franchisee, and to other franchises to develop and maintain high and uniform standards of quality, cleanliness, appearance, services, courses, and techniques, and to protect and enhance the reputation and goodwill of the franchise system. Franchisee accordingly agrees:

(1) To use all course materials, supplies, goods, signs, equipment, methods of exterior and interior design and construction, and methods of recruitment and instruction prescribed by or which conform to franchisor's standards and specifications.

(2) To refrain from using or offering any courses, materials, supplies, goods, signs, equipment, and methods of recruitment and instruction which do meet with franchisor's standards and specifications.

(3) To offer any such classes of products or services as shall be expressly approved for sale in writing by franchisor, and to offer all classes of products or services that have been designated as approved by franchisor.

(4) To purchase all products, supplies, equipment, and materials required for conduct of the franchise operation from suppliers who demonstrate, to the reasonable satisfaction of franchisor, the ability to meet all of franchisor's standards and specifications for such items; who possess adequate capacity and facilities to supply franchisee's needs in the quantities, at the times, and with the reliability requisite to an effective operation, and who have been approved, in writing, by the franchisor. Franchisee may submit to franchisor a written request for approval of a supplier not previously approved by franchisor.

9. Standards and Procedures

A. Management Standards

Franchisee agrees to comply with franchisor's standards with respect to products or services, customer solicitations, equipment, and facility maintenance, as documented in franchisor's Franchise Operating Manual for franchise outlets.

B. Personel Standards

Franchisee shall hire only efficient, competent, sober, and courteous employees for the conduct of the business, and shall pay their wages, commissions, and other compensation with no liability thereof on the part of the franchisor. Franchisee shall require all employees to comply with franchisor's standards for grooming and appearance.

C. Best Efforts

Franchisee agress to devote his/her best efforts to the operation of the outlet and to the supervision of its employees. Franchisee agrees that it will not engage in any other business activity which may conflict with the obligations of this agreement or impair the operation of the outlet.

D. Insurance

Franchisee shall, at his own expense, procure and maintain in full force and effect during the entire term of this agreement, comprehensive public, fire damage, product and motor vehicle liability insurance in the amount of One Million Dollars ($1,000,000) for each person and Three Million Dollars ($3,000,000) for each occurrence of bodily and personal injury, death and property damage. Fire damage insurance shall be sufficient to cover repair or replacement of all equipment, inventory, tools, and supplies normally required to operate the outlet, as specified in franchisor's operating manual. Franchisor shall be named as an additional insured under all such insurance policies, as its interests may appear, and contain a waiver by the carrier of all subrogation rights against franchisor. Maintenance of insurance under this paragraph shall not relieve franchisee of liability under the default provisions set forth in this agreement.

10. Training and Assistance

A. Franchisor agrees to provide personal training to franchisee, to furnish an operating manual, to make promotional and other recommendations, and to furnish franchisee, at franchisee's place of business, a qualified supervisor for not less than three (3) days during the initial six-day period of franchisee's operation.

B. Franchisor shall loan to franchisee for the term of this agreement an operating manual containing the standards, specifications, procedures, and techniques of the franchise system, and may, at its sole discretion, revise, from time to time, the contents of the manuals, incorporating new standards, specifications, procedures, and techniques.

C. Franchisor agrees to furnish franchisee with the following:

(1) guidelines and approval for the location of a suitable site for the outlet. By providing such guidelines and approval, franchisor in no way promises, warrants, or otherwise represents that the site location is the optimal location for the outlet;

(2) assistance in negotiating a lease for the outlet, when appropriate;

(3) assistance is planning the layout of the outlet;

(4) assistance in the conduct of a Grand Opening promotion for the outlet.

11. Business Conduct

A. All representations made by franchisee to others shall be completely factual. Franchisee agrees to abide by all laws, regulations, and codes.

B. Franchisee agrees to protect, defend, and indemnify franchisor and to hold franchisor harmless from and against any and all costs, expenses, including attorney's fees, court costs, losses, liabilities, damages, claims and demands of every kind or nature, arising in any way out of the occupation, use or operation, of any fixtures, equipment, goods, merchandise, or products used or sold at the outlet.

C. Franchisee will not divulge any business information, whether written or oral, received from franchisor or from any meetings of other of franchisor's franchisees, until such time as disclosure to the public may be required by the nature of the information. Such information may include, but is not limited to, promotional material or plans, expansion plans, new products, marketing information, costs or other financial data.

12. Inspections

A. Franchisor shall have the right to inspect franchisee's outlet and records, provided, however, that franchisee shall have been given reasonable advance notice. Franchisee agrees to cooperate fully with representatives of the franchisor making any such inspection.

13. Relationship of the Parties

A. Franchisee shall be an independent contractor, and nothing in this agreement shall be construed as to create or imply a fiduciary relationship between the parties, nor to make either party a general or specific agent, legal representative, subsidiary, joint venturer, or servant of the other.

B. Franchisee is in no way authorized to make a contract, agreement, warranty, or representation on behalf of franchisor to create any obligation, express or implied, on behalf of franchisor.

C. Franchisee shall be responsible for his/her own taxes, including without limitation any taxes levied upon the outlet.

14. Assignment of Franchise

Franchisee's rights in the franchise may be assigned only as follows:

A. Upon franchisee's death, the rights of franchisee in the franchise shall pass to franchisee's next of kin or other beneficiaries, provided that such next of kin or other beneficiaries shall agree in written form satisfactory to franchisor to assume all of franchisee's obligations under this agreement.

B. Franchisee may sell his interests in the franchise to another party, provided that the following conditions are met:

(1) The assignee is of good moral character, meets franchisor's normal qualifications for franchisees of franchisor, will comply with franchisor's training requirements, and enters into any and all direct agreements with franchisor that franchisor is then requiring of newly franchised persons.

(2) all monetary obligations of franchisee hereunder are fully paid, and franchisee executes a general release of all claims against franchisor, its officers, and directors;

(3) The assignee pays franchisor for its legal, training, and other expenses in connection with the assignment;

(4) franchisee has first offered to sell his franchise to franchisor upon the same terms as the purchaser has offered franchisee in writing, and franchisor has refused the offer or failed to accept it for a period of thirty (30) days;

(5) franchisee shall reaffirm a covenant not to compete in favor of franchisor;

C. Franchisee may assign and transfer his rights hereunder to a corporation without, however, being relieved of any personal liability, provided that the following conditions are met:

(1) the corporation is newly formed and shall conduct no other business but the franchise business, which shall continue to be managed by franchisee;

(2) franchisee owns the controlling stock interest in the corporation and is the principal executive officer thereof;

(3) the articles of incorporation, by-laws and other organizational documents of the corporation shall recite that the issuance and assignment of any interest therein is restricted by the terms of this agreement, and all issued and outstanding stock certificates of such corporation shall bear a legend reflecting or referring to the restrictions of this agreement;

(4) all stockholders of the corporation guarantee, in written form satisfactory to franchisor, to be bound jointly and severally by all provisions of this franchise agreement;

(5) franchisee shall not use any mark in a public offering of his securities, except to reflect his franchise relationship with franchisor.

15. Termination

If franchisee defaults under the terms of this agreement and such default shall not be cured within thirty (30) days after receipt of written notice to cure from franchisor, then, in addition to all other remedies at law or in equity, franchisor may immediately terminate this agreement. Termination under such conditions shall become effective immediately upon receipt by franchisee of a written notice of termination. Franchisee shall be considered to be in default under this agreement if:

(1) franchisee fails to open the business within the time specified in Section 4 of this agreement;

(2) franchisee abandons the franchise;

(3) franchisee attempts to assign this agreement without prior written approval of franchisor;

(4) franchisee misuses or makes an unauthorized use of the mark in a manner which materially impairs the goodwill of the franchisor;

(5) franchisee has made a material misrepresentation to franchisor before and after being granted the franchise;

(6) franchisee discloses or reproduces any portion of the franchisor's operating manual to any unauthorized party;

(7) franchisee fails to abide by his covenant not to compete as provided in this agreement;

(8) franchisee fails to comply substantially with any of the requirements imposed upon franchisee by this agreement.

16. Rights and Obligations of the Parties Upon Termination or Expiration

A. On termination or expiration of this agreement, franchisee shall do or cause to be done the following:

(1) promptly pay all amounts owed to franchisor which are then unpaid;

(2) immediately cease to use any and all marks and names, and any other trade secrets, confidential information, operating manuals, slogans, signs, symbols, or devices forming part of the franchise system or otherwise used in connection with conduct of the franchise outlet.

(3) immediately return to franchisor all advertising materials, operating manuals, plans, specifications, and other materials prepared by franchisor and relative to the franchise system.

B. Covenent not to compete

Franchisee, its officers, directors, and shareholders agree during the term of this agreement, or upon expiration or termination, or nonrenewal for any reason, they shall not have any interest as an owner, partner, director, officer, employee, manager, consultant, shareholder, representative, agent, or in any other capacity for any reason for a period of two (2) years after the occurrence of said events in any business or activity involving the conduct of a proprietary post-secondary educational institution or training school or program, or proposing to engage in the conduct of a proprietary post-secondary educational institution or training school or program, except with the written permission of franchisor.

Franchisee acknowledges that this covenant is reasonable and necessary and agrees that its failure to adhere strictly to the restrictions of this paragraph will cause substantial and irreparable damage to franchisor. Franchisee hereby acknowledges, therefore, that any violation of the terms and conditions of this covenant shall give rise to an entitlement to injunctive relief.

17. Enforcement and Construction

A. Severability

The paragraphs of this agreement are severable, and in the event any paragraph or portion of the agreement is declared illegal or unenforceable, the remainder of the agreement shall be effective and binding on the parties.

B. Notice

Whenever, under the terms of this agreement, notice is required, the same shall be deemed delivered if delivered by hand to whom intended, or to any adult person employed by franchisee at franchisee's place of business, or upon deposit in any U.S. depository for mail delivery, addressed to franchisee or franchisor at their respective business addresses.

C. Specific performance.

Nothing contained herein shall bar the franchisor's or franchisee's right to obtain specific performance of the provisions of this agreement and injunctive relief against threatened conduct that will cause it loss or damages, under customary equity rules, including applicable rules for obaining retraining orders and preliminary injunctions.

D. Governing law

This agreement is entered into and shall be construed in accordance with the laws of the state of Arizona, as of the date of execution of this agreement.

E. Successors

This agreement shall inure to the benefit of and be binding upon the executors, administrators, heirs, assigns and successors in interest of the parties.

Agreed to and executed on this _____ day of _____, 198__, by and between the parties whose signatures appear below.

_____
Franchisee

Its:_____

_____
Franchisor

Its: _____

Franchise Fee The financial consideration paid to a franchisor by a franchisee.

Almost any form of payment by the franchisee to the franchisor is considered a franchise fee, including any fee for training, advertising, deposits, signs, or royalties. Commonly, the franchise fee has three forms: (1) an initial fee, (2) an ongoing royalty, and (3) an ongoing advertising fee.

Initial Fees

The initial fee is normally paid by the franchisee upon signing the franchise agreement, as a stipulation for starting the business associated with the franchise. Typically, the initial fee is applied by the franchisor toward the costs of training the franchisee and assisting with business planning and start-up. Some state laws require franchisors to itemize the cost components of the initial fee, in an attempt to minimize the amount of "blue sky," or unjustifiable costs, included in the total. In addition, the Securities Exchange Commission prohibits corporations which sell franchises from including initial fees as income until the fees "are fully earned" by the franchisor; that is, until the franchisor has fulfilled all its obligations to the respective franchisees, and the franchisees have commenced operation.

Initial fees charged by franchisors range from a few hundred dollars for a newspaper route to more than a hundred thousand for a well known hotel or resort franchise. The average initial fee is $16,200.

Ongoing Fees

Besides an initial fee, virtually every franchise also includes an ongoing payment, typically, a royalty based on the gross revenues of the franchisee's outlet or business. Ongoing royalties range from one half of one percent of a travel agency's gross receipts to fifteen percent of a retail store's gross income. The average royalty is five percent.

In lieu of a royalty, a fixed fee may be payable by the franchisee at weekly or monthly intervals. In some cases, the ongoing fee is hidden in the franchisor's markup of goods or supplies which the franchisor sells to franchisees.

Advertising Fees

An advertising fee is a separate payment by the franchisee for promotional assistance. Typically, advertising fees may be accrued in a joint national or regional fund, to finance major promotional campaigns on behalf of all the contributing franchisees. The most common type of advertising fee is a royalty on gross revenues of the franchisee's outlet, but a set fee for promotional assistance is permissible.

See Franchise, Franchise Rule, Franchisee, Uniform Franchise Offering Circular.

Franchise Rule Also, **Federal Trade Commission Rule.** FTC Rule 436 (Code of Federal Regulations, Title 16, Chapter I, Subchapter D, Part 436), formally titled the "Disclosure Requirements and Prohibitions Concerning Franchising and Business Opportunity Ventures," created by the Bureau of Consumer Protection and adopted by the Federal Trade Commission, effective October 21, 1979.

The most sweeping franchise reform ever implemented at the federal level, the Franchise Rule was introduced in response to widespread abuses in connection with the sale of franchises. Prior to the time the Rule was adopted, the very word "franchise" was almost synonymous with consumer fraud. Nearly any kind of spurious business venture could be perpetrated on an unsuspecting, and largely unprotected, public.

The Franchise Rule dealt with these abuses by requiring franchisors and franchise brokers to furnish prospective franchisees with pertinent information about the franchisor, the franchise business, and the terms of the franchise agreement. Additional information is required to substantiate any claims of actual or potential earnings made to any prospective franchise buyer or in any advertisement. These disclosures must be made before any sale is consummated, in a format prescribed by the Rule. Although the Rule requires the material facts of the franchise offering to be disclosed in writing, it does not require franchisors to register or file the offering with the FTC or any other federal agency.

Businesses Affected by the Rule

The Franchise Rule covers two types of "continuing commercial relationships" defined as "franchises" by the FTC.

The first type is any business relationship which has all three of the following traits: (1) the franchisee operates under a trademark, name, or commecial symbol licensed by the franchisor and markets products or services in compliance with the franchisor's standards of quality or performance; (2) the franchisor has "significant control" over the franchisee's method of operation, or provides "significant assistance" to the franchisee; and (3) the franchisee pays a fee to the franchisor. If the franchise fees (or any related fees or payments) total less than $500 during the first six months after the franchisee's outlet opens, the offering is exempt from the Rule.

The second type of commercial relationship governed by the Franchise Rule is one which meets the following three tests: (1) the franchisor or an affiliate of the franchisor supplies the franchisee with products or services; (2) the franchisor helps to secure customers for the franchisee's business, or to secure locations for vending machines or rack displays; (3) the franchisee pays a fee to the franchisor. The same $500 limit applies to franchise offerings in this category.

Under these definitions, a contractual relationship may still be governed by the Rule, even though it may be called a "business opportunity" or "joint venture," rather than a franchise.

Disclosure Requirements

The Franchise Rule requires all franchisors who meet the foregoing tests to furnish a *disclosure document* to prospective franchisees before any sale is made. In this context, "prospective franchisee" means any person or company to whom a franchisor offers to sell a franchise.

The disclosure document is modeled after the **Uniform Franchise Offering Circular**, or UFOC, created in 1977 by a consortium of midwestern securities commissioners attempting to devise a uniform method of complying with individual state franchise investment laws. Today, the terms UFOC, offering circular, and disclosure document are used interchangeably to refer to the written disclosures required by the Franchise Rule and the laws of individually regulated states.

The disclosure document is required to contain information on the following 20 subjects:

1. Identifying information about the franchisor;
2. Business experience of the franchisor's directors and key executives;
3. The franchisor's business experience;
4. Litigation history of the franchisor and its directors and key executives;
5. Bankruptcy history of the franchisor and its directors and key executives;
6. Description of the franchise;
7. Money required to be paid by the franchisee to obtain or commence the franchise operation;
8. Continuing expenses to the franchisee in operating the franchise business that are payable in whole or in part to the franchisor;
9. A list of persons who are either the franchisor or any of its affiliates, with whom the franchisee is required or advised to do business;
10. Real estate, property, or services which the franchisee is required to purchase, lease, or rent, and a list of any persons from whom such transactions must be made;
11. Description of consideration paid (such as royalties, commissions, etc.) by third parties to the franchisor or any of its affiliates as a result of a franchisee's purchase from such third parties;
12. Description of any franchisor assistance in financing the purchase of a franchise;
13. Restrictions placed on a franchisee's conduct of its business;

14. Required personal participation by the franchisee;
15. Termination, cancellation, and renewal of the franchise;
16. Statistical information about the number of franchises and their rate of termination;
17. Franchisor's right to select or approve a site for the franchise;
18. Training programs for the franchisee;
19. Celebrity involvement with the franchise;
20. Financial information about the franchisor.

The Franchise Rule prohibits franchisors from claiming, without reasonable proof, that franchisees can attain any actual or potential sales or earnings levels. If such earnings claims are made, they must be presented in a prescribed format and accompanied by a legend cautioning prospective franchisees.

All of the required disclosures must be made in a single document, which may not include any other information not prescribed by the Rule. Whenever a material change occurs in the information required to be disclosed, a quarterly revision must be prepared.

Time Frames

The Franchise Rule defines the 'time for making of disclosures' as follows:

> *. . . ten (10) business days prior to the earlier of (1) the execution by a prospective franchisee of any franchise agreement or any other agreement imposing a binding legal obligation on such prospective franchisee . . . or (2) the payment by a prospective franchisee . . . of any consideration in connection with the sale or proposed sale of a franchise.*

Simply stated, the disclosure document must be provided to the franchisee at least ten business days before the sale is made. No franchise agreement or related contract may be executed, or any payment accepted by the franchisor, until the ten-day waiting period has lapsed.

Penalties for Violation

The Federal Trade Commission Act declares unlawful any "unfair methods of competition in commerce, and unfair or deceptive acts or practices in commerce." The Franchise Rule cites this law and further declares that "it is an unfair or deceptice act or practice" for a franchisor to fail to abide by the prescribed disclosure requirements. Specifically, it is a federal crime to:

1. to fail to furnish the prescribed disclosure document to any prospective franchisee, within the time frames established by the Rule;
2. to make any representations about actual or potential sales, income, or profits of existing or prospective franchises except in the manner prescribed by the Rule;
3. to make any oral or advertised claim or representation which is inconsistent with the information in the offering circular;
4. to fail to furnish a copy of the franchise agreement to any prospective franchisee, within the time frames established by the Rule;
5. to fail to return any refundable deposits or down payments to prospective franchisees.

Those who violate the Franchise Rule are subject to civil penalties of up to $10,000 per violation. Moreover, any person injured by a violation of the Rule may be entitled to recover monetary damages.

The UFOC and the Franchise Rule

Although the terms UFOC and disclosure document are generally used interchangeably, there are slight differences in the form of disclosure required by the federal Franchise Rule and the Uniform Franchise Offering Circular adopted by individually regulated states.

The UFOC generally fulfills the requirements of the 15 states which have laws requiring franchise registration and disclosure. The UFOC format is not identical to the disclosure format prescribed by the federal Rule. Besides minor differences in language, the state-mandated UFOC requires more disclosure on some subjects than the federal Franchise Rule. However, the two formats are quite similar and designed to achieve the same result, regardless of the minor variations. Thus, the FTC considers that the UFOC fulfills the disclosure requirements of the Franchise Rule, provided that the franchisor complies with the prescribed time frames.

However, complying with the federal Rule does not obviate the franchisor from also having to comply with any applicable state franchise investment laws. In instances where the state law is more severe than the Franchise Rule, the state law takes precedence.

Exemptions from the Rule

Franchises and other continuing commercial relationships which do not fall into the two categories defined by the Franchise Rule are exempt from the disclosure requirements. They are not, however, exempt from other aspects of the Federal Trade Commission Act which forbids "unfair and deceptive business practices."

For example, a franchise which does not cost the franchisee anything, or results in less than $500 during the first six months of operation, is not covered by the Franchise Rule.

A second type of exemption is granted to *fractional franchises*, ones which account for less than 20 percent of the franchisee's total dollar volume. To qualify as a fractional franchise, the the franchisee's directors or executive officers must have at least two years experience in the type of business in which the franchise is engaged.

Exemption from the federal Rule has no affect on a franchisor's obligations under any applicable state franchise investment laws.

Franchisee (Also **franchise holder** or **franchise owner**) An individual, partnership, group, or company to which a franchisor grants a franchise. In franchise agreements and other documents, the term "franchisee" generally refers to both males and females and is used interchangeably in reference to individuals or companies.

Under the federal definition of a franchise, a franchisee typically receives two elements from the franchisor:

1. A license to use the franchisor's trademark, name, or commercial symbol;
2. Some form of "significant control or assistance" in the operation of the franchise business.

In return for these elements, the franchisee pays a fee to the franchisor — typically, an initial fee for the right to commence the business plus an ongoing fee or royalty based on the outlet's sales.

Rights of a Franchisee

Various state and federal laws provide franchisees with certain rights not enjoyed by other contractors. Federal regulations require franchisors to disclose important information about the franchisor, the franchise business, and the franchise agreement before a franchise may be sold. (See *Franchise Rule*.) Various state laws also furnish franchisees with the right to renew their franchise agreements upon expiration and protect franchisees from involuntary termination.

The franchise agreement establishes most of the franchisee's rights with regard to the franchise business. Typically, a franchisee receives the following rights in consideration of the initial fee and any ongoing franchise royalties or fees:

1. Trademark license

The franchisee receives the right to use the franchisor's trademarks, name, logo, or other commercial symbols. In some instances, the franchise covers the right to sell a product bearing a trademark; e.g., Coca-Cola ® or Baskin-Robbins Ice Cream ® . In a typical business-format franchise, the franchisee receives the right to use a particular trade name in the operation of the business; e.g., Hertz Rent A Car or Holiday Inn.

2. Standardized business system

Most franchisees receive "significant control or assistance" in the form of a training program, a franchise operating manual, and ongoing consultation from the franchisor's field experts. Franchise training programs range from a few days to several weeks in length. The franchisor's experience and know-how are usually documented in a confidential operating manual covering the management and operation of the franchise outlet. Other types of assistance may include annual or quarterly seminars and conferences, assistance with advertising and promotion, and inventory or accounting systems.

Obligations of a Franchisee

Uniform of standards are generally regarded as critical elements of a franchise organization. Consumers patronize a franchise outlet because of an assurance that the level of performance, quality, and service will be largely the same from one outlet to another.

To maintain uniformity among outlets, franchisors frequently obligate their franchisees to adhere to strict standards and sppecifications. Typically, a franchisee is obligated to abide by the following rules:

1. Maintain high standards of integrity and ethical business conduct.

2. Promote a favorable image in all conduct with the public, customers, and persons with whom they come into contact.

3. Provide a high level of customer service.

4. Maintain in full force all licenses, permits, certificates, and other applicable documentation required by community and state laws and regulations to conduct their businesses.

5. Promptly and accurately pay all fees and royalties due to their franchisors.

6. Pay all monies owed to suppliers for products and supplies promptly and accurately.

7. Maintain their places of business in a clean, orderly, and functional condition at all times; and keep all equipment, inventory, and supplies in proper working condition.

8. Maintain a clean, attractive, efficient customer area, with proper safeguards and security.

9. Maintain fair but rigorously enforced personnel policies to promote a favorable image to the public.

10. Maintain all records, tax, information, employee data, and books required to fulfill local,state, and federal requirements.

11. Complete their franchisor's training programs.

12. Determine a site for the business, obtain applicable lease(s) or financing, and commence improvements within the stipulated time after signing the franchise agreement.

13. Open the franchise outlet for business within the stipulated time after signing the franchise agreement.

14. Maintain business liability, comprehensive public and motor vehicle liability insurance as specified in the franchise agreement or operating manual.

15. Adhere to all franchise standards and specifications for advertising, inventory,quality, service, performance, working hours, and procedures.

Franchise Reports

Besides adhering to quality standards, franchisees are also usually required to furnish their franchisors with various reports. The following types of reports are typical:

1. Weekly Summary

A summary of the outlet's sales may be required weekly.

2. Monthly Recap

A recap of weekly sales may be required monthly.

3. Operating Statement (Profit and Loss Sheet)

A statement of the outlet's income and expenses, showing the businesses profits or losses, may be required monthly, quarterly, or annually.

4. Proforma Operating Statement (Projected Profit and Loss Sheet)

A projection of the outlet's future income and expenses, showing anticipated profits or losses, may also be required monthly, quarterly, or annually.

5. Federal Tax Return(s)

Franchisees may be required to submit a true and accurate copy of their federal tax return(s), or those portions relating to the franchise business, within a reasonable time after the date of filing.

6. Miscellaneous Reports

In addition, franchisees may be required to submit any of the following occurrences in writing, within a reasonable time after the event:

A. Changes in ownership

If the franchise outlet is operated by a corporation, the franchisee may be required to report the names and addresses of any new shareholders, or address changes of any existing shareholders.

B. Changes in management

Franchisees may be required to promptly report any changes among the principal management of the franchise outlet.

C. Equipment failures

Franchisees may be required to promptly report breakdowns or damage to any equipment that is vital to the operation of the business.

D. Trademark infringements

The franchise agreement may obligate franchisees to assist in protecting the franchise name and trademarks, by promptly reporting any apparent infringement or unauthorized use by others.

Outlet Maintenance

Franchisees are typically required to maintain the condition and appearance of their franchise outlets in a manner that is consistent with the quality standards of the franchise network. Franchisees may also be required to provide for all routine and normal maintenance and repair; replacement of worn-out or obsolete accessories, fixtures, equipment, signs, equipment, obsolete or unsellable inventory; and periodic refurbishing.

Franchisors often prohibit their franchisees from making any material alterations to the outlet or business system without prior approval in writing from the franchisor. This prohibition may include any alteration to the layout, accessories, fixtures, signs, or equipment.

Appearance and Grooming of Employees

The franchise agreement may stipulate that employees of the outlet must maintain their appearance and grooming on the job in amanner consistent with the quality standards of the franchisor, and that they exhibit neatness, cleanliness, and a friendly, professional demeanor in the presence of customers.

Books and Records

Franchisees are invariably required to maintain accurate records to document, determine, and demonstrate income and expenses; calculate tax liability; determine profitability; and compute the franchise royalty and co-op ad fund contribution. Federal law does not require any particular form of record keeping. However, franchisees may be required to maintain such books and records as may be necessary for efficient operation and sound financial control, or to comply with local, municipal, county, state, or other laws or regulations. This list may include sales tax accounts, employee payroll records, motor vehicle records, and employee business expense records.

Inspections and Audits

To assure uniform standards of image, conduct, and performance, franchisors usually reserve the right to periodically evaluate their franchisees' outlets. In personal inspections by a field manager or other representative, franchisees may be monitored for adherence to the franchisor's standards, specifications, policies, and procedures. In addition, the outlet may be subject to an unnanounced audit of its books and records.

If the franchisor should discover a discrepancy in the reporting of franchise royalties or other fees, the franchisee may be held responsible for paying all costs associated with the audit.

See *Franchise, Franchise Agreement, Operating Manual.*

Franchising The practice of granting trademark or business format franchises, including the exercise of ongoing rights and obligations under a franchise agreement. The term "franchising" is often used interchangeably to denote the act of either buying or selling a franchise. In a broader sense, the "franchising industry" refers to a large segment of the U.S. economy, accounting for approximately forty percent of all domestic retail trade.

Franchising as a Growth Strategy

Technically, franchising is not an industry, but rather a method of product distribution and/or business expansion. A business contemplating expansion faces four classical alternatives: (1) vertical market expansion, (2) diversification, (3) acquisition or merger, (4) franchising. A company expands *vertically* when it devises new applications for its existing product line. For example, a manufacturer of business computer systems attacks vertical markets when it attempts to sell the same products to medical laboratories or farms. Another expansion strategy is to *diversify* the company's sources of income, by devising new products or entering new industries. For example, a petroleum refinery diversifies when it expands into the insurance, finance, and real estate fields. Both expansion objectives can often be achieved by *acquiring* or *merging* the business with another company.

Franchising, as a growth strategy, provides a business with the ability to rapidly enter and, frequently, dominate new markets, by increasing the distribution channels, or "outlets." Franchising also permits the company to diversify its sources of income, by deriving franchise fees and royalties to supplement the sale of existing products. By utilizing working capital supplied by independent, entrepreneurially motivated franchisees, franchisors minimize their own capital risk in expanding.

To franchise, a company must have a unique or competitive product associated with a trademark, a successful *business format* that can be easily replicated and transferred to others, or both. Typically, a franchise program includes a well known or memorable trade name and logo, a training program for franchisees, architectural plans and product specifications, operating procedures, management controls, and assistance with purchasing, inventory, marketing, and advertising. For the right to implement the franchisor's refined "business operating system," the franchisee pays a fee, usually an initial fee upon signing the franchise agreement, with an obligation to pay ongoing royalties based on gross sales of the outlet.

It is a common practice for the franchisee to supply the working capital to secure a site, construct the premises, and develop the outlet. To handle the initial investment, franchisees often borrow the funds or obtain investment money from a venture capitalist or other source. The franchisee is literally the owner of the outlet, although its operation may be governed to a large extent by the franchise agreement.

Franchising in the Economy

Since the economic boom years of the 1950s, the success rate of franchised businesses has been nothing short of phenomenal. More than 90 percent of all franchise outlets survive at least five years, whereas two thirds of all other independently owned businesses fail, most in a year or less. The practice of franchising ideally taps the entrepreneurial motives of individuals who desire to be their own bosses, while generating an ongoing source of income to the franchisor. The franchisee derives self-esteem, an opportunity for self-management, and an asset of lasting value. The franchisor achieves the ability to dramatically expand its avenues of distribution and, in many instances, to diversify its existing product lines.

The Singer Company is widely credited with the first application of this expansion method, employing it as early as the 1850s. General Motors, Coca-Cola, Holiday Inn, Hertz, and McDonald's all rose to international prominence through the franchise method of marketing and expansion.

Franchising was largely unregulated prior to 1971, when California enacted the first state franchise investment law to shield investors against potential fraud. Today, 15 states have similar statutes on their books, requiring registration and disclosure by franchisors. In 1979, the Federal Trade Commission adopted sweeping regulations governing franchising practices throughout the United States. When the federal rules went into effect, more than half of the so-called "franchisors" with business-opportunity advertisements in the Wall Street Journal seemingly vanished overnight.

As a growth mechanism for business, franchising knows few equals. The Department of Commerce reports that franchise outlets have a 20-percent higher productivity rate than comparable company-owned stores. As a franchise chain proliferates, contributions to a cooperative advertising fund are used to underwrite lavish national advertising programs which bestow the small-time operator with a competitive footing equal to that of industry giants.

Today, franchising represents more than a third of the entire U.S. retail economy. The U.S. Department of Commerce predicts that more than half of all retail trade will be conducted by franchise businesses by the end of the century. Over the last two decades, overall franchise revenues have increased by an average of ten percent per year. By 1990, total sales should exceed $870 billion.

Once considered a uniquely American practice, franchising made significant inroads abroad during the 1980s. Although more than 80 percent of the world's franchises are confined to the United States, the remainder is dispersed among 80 countries on all five continents. The popularity of franchise establishments overseas is evidenced by a 300-seat Kentucky Fried Chicken restaurant in Beijing, China, located within view of the Palace of Heavenly Gates. A McDonald's outlet situated in a historical building in Belgrad has become a posh nighttime gathering place for Yugoslavian youths. Adventurers in the South Pacific can rent jeeps from a Hertz office on the remote island of Bora Bora.

Franchising as a Consumer Trend

The franchising phenomenon is rooted in the concern of a mobile, consumer-oriented society for the security of sameness. Americans frequent franchise establishments because of a subconscious assurance of uniform standards. For example, patrons of a franchised hotel chain are assured of a comparable level of service, accommodations, and rates at virtually any location. Similarly, fast-food patrons seek a uniform level of comfort, sanitation, and meal preparation among all the outlets of a particular chain. Before the widespread franchising of hotels and restaurants, roadside lodging and dining establishments were feared and eschewed by the average traveler. Today, it is estimated that 90 percent of American travelers have spent at least one night in a Holiday Inn; enough hamburgers have been sold by McDonald's restaurants to serve every man, woman, and child in the world.

To capitalize on the public's search for uniformity, franchisors typically require franchisees to adhere to rigid quality standards and mandatory specifications. Key to the public acceptance of franchised products is the ability to cater to the median in public tastes and preferences. In repeated market tests, consumers consistently chose a bland, flavorless hamburger over more savory entries.

Because franchising both cultivates and caters to sameness, the practice is subject to social criticism for encouraging mediocrity. Certainly, no franchise restaurant is likely to be awarded four stars by any serious food critic, nor will any franchise motel likely attain the former glory of the Waldorf-Astoria or Palace Hotel. Nevertheless, in a society which tolerates, but does not necessarily encourage, individuality, franchising will indisputably remain a powerful economic and social influence into the next century.

Franchisor (Also, **franchiser**) In general, any person, company, government, or other entity which grants a right or privilege to another. The legal definition of a "franchisor" is derived from Federal Trade Commission Rule 436.2, which states:

> The term "franchisor" means any person who participates in a franchise relationship as a franchisor . . .

The Rule further defines "franchise relationship" as any business relationship involving a trademark license, "significant control or assistance," and payment of a fee exceeding $500 within six months (See *Franchise, Franchise Rule*). Thus, in the business sense, a franchisor is a person, partnership, company, or association which, for a financial consideration, licenses a trademark or trade name to another party and provides quality standards, training, an operating manual, or other assistance.

Benjamin Franklin was probably the first franchisor, marketing his popular *Poor Richard's Almanack* through newspaper couriers. A newspaper route is a classical distribution franchise, charging fees from independent couriers for the marketing rights to designated territories.

Isaac Merrit Singer, the inventor of the modern sewing machine, is commonly regarded as the forerunner of trademark franchising. As early as 1851, Singer and his partner, Edward Clark, sold territories to independent traveling salesmen to hawk the company's trademarked sewing machines. In timeworn fables about traveling salesmen and midwestern farmer's daughters, the traveling salesmen were most likely Singer Company franchisees.

Automobile manufacturers and petroleum distributors were among the earliest franchisors of the 20th century. Ford Motor Company, General Motors, and Chrysler began franchising car dealerships almost as soon as the first "horseless carriages" began rolling off the assembly lines. The advent of the automobile gave rise to the modern service station and made Standard Oil of Ohio, founded by John D. Rockefeller in 1870, an international giant in franchising. Hertz Rent A Car, founded in 1918, began franchising in 1921.

Pioneering franchisors also included soft drink distributors, such as Coca-Cola, Pepsi-Cola, Dr. Pepper, and A&W. The first A&W root beer stand opened in 1919, effectually "inventing" the fast-food franchise. Franchisors in the restaurant, retail, and automobile service industries flourished in the Depression years of the lates 1920s and early 1930s, among them, Ben Franklin Stores, Tru-Valu Hardware, and Western Auto Supply stores. Motel franchisors and fast-food operators enjoyed a boom in the 1950s, as postwar America took to the nation's highways in an era of widespread mobility. Dunkin' Donuts began establishing roadside coffee shops in 1950, and the first Holiday Inn opened in Tennessee in 1952. Three years later, a malted milk machine salesman named Ray Kroc acquired the rights to franchise a drive-through hamburger stand owned by two brothers, Mac and Dick MacDonald, launching what would become the world's largest and most famous fast-food chain. "Kentucky colonel" Harlan Sanders, who had operated a successful southern fried chicken chain since 1930, began franchising in earnest in 1956.

The world's largest hotel chains, Hilton and Sheraton, became franchisors in the 1960s. Convenience food stores also proliferated in that decade, led by The Southland Corporation's 7-Eleven chain.

In the 1970s and 1980s, changing public attitudes and tastes spawned a new breed of franchisors in a wide cross section of industries, from computer systems to aerobic dancing. Fast food continues to dominate the franchise economy, but with a new character reflecting modern culinary preferences. Public preoccupation with fitness and grooming also influenced franchising in the 1980s. The fastest growing franchisors over the last decade include Subway Sandwiches, Domino's Pizza, and Pepsico-owned Pizza Hut, but also Jazzercise exercise studios, Diet Center weight reduction clinics, and Fantastic Sam's haircutting parlors.

Pepsico, which owns the Kentucky Fried Chicken, Pizza Hut, and Taco Bell chains, is the largest franchisor, with approximately 18,500 fast-food outlets. McDonald's Corporation, with nearly 14,000 outlets, is the largest single chain, with approximately 3,500 restaurants in more than 50 foreign countries.

Largest U.S. Franchisors by Number of Outlets

1. Pepsico (18,960 total)
   Kentucky Fried Chicken (10,200)
   Pizza Hut (6,000)
   Taco Bell (2,760)
2. McDonald's (13,900)
3. 7-Eleven Stores (12,000)
4. H&R Block (8,800)
5. Century 21 Real Estate (7,000)
6. Dairy Queen International (5,000)
7. Domino's Pizza (4,600)
8. Burger King (4,500)
9. ServiceMaster (3,875)
10. Jazzercise (3,380)
11. Wendy's International (3,650)
12. Budget Rent A Car (3,600)
13. Baskin-Robbins (3,450)
14. Hardee's Food System (3,000)
15. ERA Electronic Realty Associates (2,840)
16. SUBWAY Sandwiches & Salads (2,400)
17. Diet Center, Inc. (2,330)
18. Midas Discount Muffler (2,200)
19. Little Caesar's Pizza (2,000)
20. Arby's (2,000)
21. Chem-Dry (1,840)
22. Western Auto (1,800)
23. Realty World (1,760)
24. Dunkin' Donuts (1,735)
25. Dollar Rent A Car (1,600)
    Hertz Rent A Car (1,600)
    Holiday Inns (1,600)
28. Goodyear Tire (1,570)
29. Long John Silver's (1,500)
    Arby's (1,500)
    Church's Fried Chicken (1,500)
32. National Video (1,400)
    RE/MAX (1,400)
    American Internationl Rent A Car (1,400)
35. Denny's (1,390)
36. JaniKing (1,300)
    Red Carpet Realty (1,300)
38. PIP Postal Instant Press (1,120)
    Packy the Shipper (1,120)
40. Sonic Drive-Ins (1,100)
    Ben Franklin Stores (1,100)
42. TCBY "The Country's Best Yogurt" (1,075)
43. Nutri System, Inc. (1,000)
    One Hour Martinizing (1,000)
    Kwik Copy (1,000)
46. Almost Heaven Hot Tubs (975)
47. Coast to Coast Stores (965)
48. Quality Inn/Comfort Inn (950)
49. Jack in the Box (940)
50. AAMCO Transmission (920)

Franklin, Benjamin Printer, author, inventor, scientist, diplomat, public official, and franchisor.

Born in Boston on January 17, 1706, Ben Franklin was probably the first American entrepreneur to use the franchise method of distribution. The tenth and youngest offspring of a chandler, he went to work as an apprentice for his brother, a printer, at the age of 15. A year later, his brother began publishing a newspaper, the *New England Courant*, for which the younger Franklin frequently wrote small essays, eventually getting arrested for publically criticizing a Massachusetts official.

In 1723, he pulled up stakes and migrated to Philadelphia, where he arrived penniless and unemployed. Finding a position in the printing shop of Samuel Keimer, Franklin established his own printing business five years later. His business prospered for many years afterward.

In 1732, Franklin began publishing *Poor Richard's Almanack*, becoming America's first best selling author, distributing 10,000 copies per year through franchised delivery agents. Reportedly, Franklin commanded a franchise fee of ten cents for the rights to distribute his phenomenally successful almanac. Thus, besides inventing the Franklin stove, coauthoring the Declaration of Independence and the U.S. Constitution, and discovering electricity, Ben Franklin probably also "invented" the franchise marketing method.

Poor Richard's Almanack derived its success from Franklin's translation of pithy, literary maxims into homespun colonial American vernacular. For instance, he is credited with the morals: "God helps those who help themselves" and "Never leave until tomorrow that which you can do to-day." His fictional spokesman, "Richard Saunders," also proclaimed: "A man has three faithful friends: an old wife, an old dog, and ready money."

Ben Franklin, the father of franchising, was elected to the Hall of Fame in 1900.

Poor Richard's Almanack was distributed by independent couriers who purchased franchise "routes"

Franklin's Printing and Office Supplies Headquartered in Atlanta, Georgia, a franchisor of retail printing and office supply outlets.

Founded in 1971, Franklin's has been franchising since 1977. A typical Franklin's franchisee operates a retail store combining quick-printing services with the merchandising of office supplies. The outlet's printing services include high-speed duplication, offset printing, and desktop publishing services. None of the 92 Franklin's Printing outlets are company owned.

Franklin's Printing and Office Supplies, 135 International Blvd., Atlanta, GA 30303. Telephone: (800) 554-5699

Freedom Rent-A-Car Headquartered in Bartlesville, Oklahoma, a franchisor of automobile rental outlets.

Founded in 1981, Freedom has been franchising since 1983. A typical Freedom franchisee operates a discount car rental business. All except one of the franchisor's 160 outlets are franchise units.

Freedom Rent-A-Car, P.O. Box 2345, Bartlesville, OK 74005. Telephone: (800) 331-0777

Freshens Premium Yogurt Headquartered in Atlanta, Georgia, a franchisor of fast food outlets.

Founded in 1985, Freshens has been franchising since the following year. A typical Freshens franchisee operates a fast-food operation specializing in frozen yogurt products. Of the franchisor's 85 outlets currently operating, all but five are franchise units.

Freshens Premium Yogurt, 4000 Cumberland Pkwy., Bldg. 300, Ste. C, Atlanta, GA 30339

Friendship Inns International Headquartered in North Bergen, New Jersey, a franchisor of lodging outlets.

Founded in 1960, Friendship has been franchising since 1985. The chain originated as a referral organization comprised of 380 independent hotel operators who paid annual dues to participate in cooperative promotional programs. Hotel operator Al Olshan acquired the rights to the Friendship Inn trade name in 1985 and began converting member hotel to franchisees. A typical Friendship franchisee operates a full-service lodging establishment catering to the mid-priced hotel patron. Franchisees participate in a national reservation system and adhere to the franchisor's standards for sanitation, appearance, and maintenance. The Friendship chain consists of 135 outlets, all of which are franchise units.

Friendship Inns International, 2627 Paterson Plank Rd., North Bergen, NJ 07047. Telephone: (201) 863-3443

Frontier Fruit and Nut Company Headquartered in Norton, Ohio, a franchisor of retail confection outlets.

Founded in 1976, Frontier has been franchising since 1978. A typical Frontier franchisee operates a retail food shop specializing in candy, nuts, and dried fruit confections. Of the franchisor's 260 outlets currently operating, more than two thirds are franchise units.

Frontier Fruit and Nut Co., 3823 Wadsworth Rd., Norton, OH 44203. Telephone: (216) 825-7835

Frusen Gladje Headquartered in Lindenhurst, New York, a franchisor of specialty fast-food outlets.

Founded in 1980, Frusen Gladje has been franchising since the following year. A typical Frusen Gladje franchisee operates an ice cream parlor devoted to the franchisor's proprietary line of premium ice cream. Of the franchisor's 35 outlets currently operating, none are company-owned.

Frusen Gladje, 424 E. John St., Lindenhurst, NY 11757. Telephone: (516) 884-0024

Fuddruckers Headquartered in San Antonio, Texas, a franchisor of food service outlets.

Founded in 1980, Fuddruckers has been franchising since 1983. A typical Fuddruckers franchisee operates a specialty restaurant with a resort-style decor and a menu devoted to "gourmet" hamburger sandwiches. Of the franchisor's 106 outlets currently operating, 65 are franchise units.

Fuddruckers Franchising, Inc., 3636 Medical Dr., San Antonio, TX 78229. Telephone: (512) 692-0040

G. Fried Carpetland
to
Gymboree

G. Fried Carpetland Headquartered in Westbury, New York, a franchisor of retail flooring outlets.

Founded in 1889, GFC has been franchising since 1971. A typical GFC franchisee operates a carpeting sales and installation business. Of the franchisor's 26 outlets currently operating, all except one are franchise units.

G. Fried Carpetland, 800 Old Country Rd., Westbury, NY 11590. Telephone: (516) 333-3900

Gallery of Homes Headquartered in Orlando, Florida, a franchisor of independent real estate sales offices.

Founded in 1935, Gallery of Homes has been franchising since its inception. A typical Gallery of Homes franchisee operates residential listing and sales business under the franchisor's trademark. Franchisees offer a broad range of real estate services, from listings to financial guidance. Of the franchisor's 260 outlets currently operating, none are company owned.

Gallery of Homes, P.O. Box 2900, Orlando, FL 32802. Telephone: (800) 241-8320

General Business Services Headquartered in Germantown, Maryland, a franchisor of accounting support services.

Founded in 1962 by an entrepreneur named Bernard Browning, GBS has been franchising since its inception. A typical GBS franchisee operates a counseling and financial management service catering to small business owners and self-employed individuals. The outlet offers accounting/bookkeeping support, as well as qualified advice on organizational, tax, and financial matters. All of the 600 GBS outlets currently operating are franchise units.

General Business Services, 20271 Goldenrod Lane, Germantown, MD 20874. Telephone: (800) 638-7940

Gelato Classico Headquartered in San Francisco, California, a franchisor of ice cream parlors.

Founded in 1976, Gelato Classico has been franchising since 1982. A typical Gelato Classico franchisee operates a retail ice cream parlor marketing the franchisor's private brand of "Italian-style" premium ice cream. Twenty different flavors may be offered at any time, including such purported delicacies as Coppa Mista (a rich blend of vanilla, chocolate, and pistachio), Joseph Saint-Almond, and

Crema de Limone. Besides ice cream, most outlets also serve expresso coffee, tea, and soft drinks. Of the franchisor's 30 outlets currently operating, all but four are franchise units.

Gelato Classico Italian Ice Cream, 369 Pine St., Ste. 90,San Francisco, CA 94104. Telephone: (415) 433-3111

Georgia, Franchise Regulations To date, the Georgia legislature has not adopted any generally applicable franchise investment law. However, an amendment to the Securities Law requires area franchisees and subfranchisors operating in the state to register as securities salesmen. Dealers in the petroleum, farm machinery, and construction equipment industries are protected by separate laws.

Georgia law does not require franchisors to register or file disclosures with any state regulatory body. In the absence of such a requirement, the federal Franchise Rule applies, requiring franchisors to furnish a disclosure document prescribed by the Federal Trade Commission to prospective franchisees ten business days before a franchise sale is made. Business opportunity ventures are regulated by the secretary of state. To report possible fraudulent or deceptive practices, contact: Secretary of State, Corporation Department, Peachtree Center South, 225 Peachtree St. N.E., Atlanta, GA 30303. Telephone: (404) 656-2185. *See Franchise Rule.*

Gibraltar Transmissions Headquartered in Lake Success, New York, a franchisor of automotive service outlets.

Founded in 1977, Gibraltar has been franchising since the following year. A typical Gibraltar franchisee operates an auto service business specializing in transmission service, repair, and maintenance. Of the franchisor's 80 outlets currently operating, all except three are franchise units.

Gibraltar Transmissions, 1 Hollow Ln., Lake Success, NY 11042. Telephone: (516) 365-5090

Gingiss Formalwear Headquartered in Chicago, Illinois, a franchisor of tuxedo sales and rental outlets.

Founded in 1936, Gingess has been franchising since 1968. A typical Gingess franchisee operates a retail store specializing in men's formal apparel. The company's list of past celebrity customers includes Liberace, Bob Hope, and Conrad Hilton. Of the franchisor's 235 outlets currently operating, all but 25 are franchise units.

Gingess Formalwear, 180 N. LaSalle St., Chicago, IL 60601. Telephone: (800) 621-7125

Giorgio Headquartered in Montreal, Quebec, a franchisor of specialty restaurants.

Founded in 1977, Giorgio has been franchising since 1985. A typical Giorgio franchisee operates a full-service restaurant specializing in fine Italian cuisine. Of the franchisor's 30 outlets currently operating, two thirds are franchise units.

Giorgio, 222 St. Laurent Blvd., Montreal, Que., Canada H2Y2Y3. Telephone: (514) 845-4221

Gloria Jean's Coffee Bean Headquartered in Arlington Heights, Illinois, a franchisor of specialty food outlets.

Founded in 1979, Gloria Jean's has been franchising since 1985. A typical Gloria Jean's franchisee operates a retail shop devoted to "gourmet" coffees, teas, and related products and accessories. Of the franchisor's 37 outlets currently operating, 27 are franchise units.

Gloria Jean's Coffee Bean Franchising Corp., 12C W. College Dr., Arlington Heights, IL 60004. Telephone: (312) 253-0580

Godfather's Pizza Headquartered in Omaha, Nebraska, a franchisor of fast-food outlets.

Founded in 1973, Godfather's has been franchising since the following year. A typical Godfather's franchisee operates a fast-food pizza restaurant featuring both thin-crust and deep-dish pizza prepared with a variety of meat and vegetable toppings. Of the franchisor's 810 outlets currently operating, 615 are franchise units.

Godfather's Pizza, 9140 W. Dodge Rd., Omaha NE 68114. Telephone: (402) 391-1452

Goodyear Tire Headquartered in Akron, Ohio, the world's largest tire manufacturer and franchisor of automotive tire and merchandise dealerships.

The Goodyear Tire and Rubber Company was founded with high expectations on August 28, 1898 by an engineer named Frank Sieberling, to produce rubber bicycle and carriage tires. The company was named after Charles Goodyear, the American inventor who perfected the process of vulcanizing rubber. Goodyear discovered the process by accident, after dropping some India rubber and sulphur on the hot surface of his kitchen stove. He died in poverty in 1860, but he will long be remembered for one of the most significant developments of the 19th century.

By 1920, Akron, Ohio had become the "Rubber Capital" of the world, largely due to Frank Sieberling and the company he named in honor of Charles Goodyear. With the advent of the "horseless carriage," Sieberling had expanded from bicycle tires into car tires. Although he had run the company from its inception, he did not become its president until 1906.

The first Goodyear tire was designed in 1900 by Paul Weeks Litchfield, a graduate of Massachusetts Institute of Technology, who had never owned an automobile himself. His design for a cross-hatched, diamond-shaped tread pattern became the model for all subsequent tire treads. In 1908, a Goodyear consultant devised an automatic tire-building machine, enabling the manufacturer to double its output and sales. The following year, the company developed the first airplane tire, which was selected for the inaugural U.S. airmail flight in 1911.

In 1921, the curtain abruptly fell on the Sieberling era. When the "Little Napoleon," as some affectionately called him, met his Waterloo, the company he founded nearly collapsed. A massive reorganization was completed on May 12, resulting in the resignation of the entire board, with the exception of Litchfield and one other director.

Litchfield assumed the presidency on March 29, 1926, beginning what developed into a 30-year term as Goodyear's chief executive. His association with the company would span nearly 60 years.

The company first began sponsoring racing cars as a promotional gimmick in the early 1900s. But no Indianapolis 500 winner ever rolled to victory on Goodyear tires until A. J. Foyt accomplished the feat in 1967. A year later, Boby Unser repeated the accomplishment and by 1975, virtually every car in the race rode on Goodyear tires.

The company's "aerial ambassadors," the Goodyear blimps, have become virtual American traditions. When the United States was brought into World War II, the company's blimp fleet was called into action to help patrol and protect the coastal waters. On the morning of August 16, 1942, the Goodyear airship Ranger took off from Treasure Island in the San Francisco Bay on a routine antisubmarine patrol

At the Goodyear tire plant in Akron, Ohio, tires were originally manufactured by hand

mission. Several hours later, residents of nearby Daly City were astonished to see the blimp light softly on a suburban street. The airship and its armaments were perfectly intact, but the two-man crew were nowhere to be found. The mystery of the "ghost" blimp has never been solved.

The Goodyear fleet presently includes the airships Columbia, America, Mayflower, and Europa, all common sights in the skies over North America and Europe, particularly at World's Fairs and sporting events.

Following World War II, the company's sales doubled from 1945 until 1955, when annual revenues reached nearly $1.4 billion. That same year, Frank Sierbling died at the age of 95. A year later, 80-year-old Paul Litchfield stepped down as chief executive, staying on as chairman of the board until 1959.

Throughout the "go go" 60s and turbulent 70s, Goodyear expanded globally on numerous fronts. New production facilities in Europe and Asia allowed the company to keep pace with accelerating demand for improved transportation. Automobile registrations doubled in the U.S. in the 1960s, and replacement tire sales increased more than 40 percent. Goodyear tires landed on the moon in 1971, with the NASA Apollo mission. The experimental cart towed around the lunar surface by the astronauts was equipped with specially made, 16-inch Goodyear "moon tires" — developed by the joint efforts of hundreds of Goodyear engineers.

A typical Goodyear dealer operates a retail automotive tire and service business merchandising only Goodyear products and other brands approved by the franchisor. Besides tires, Goodyear stores also perform light auto maintenance, including tune-up services, brake repair, and lubrication. Of the franchisor's 1,570 outlets currently operating, 660 are owned by independent dealers.

Goodyear Tire and Rubber Co., 144 E. Market St., Akron, OH 44315. Telephone: (216) 796-3467

Note that in this early photo depicting a shipment of new tires behing hauled to market, neither truck nor trailer have tires themselves.

Gourmet Cup, The Headquartered in Abbotsford, British Columbia, a franchisor of specialty retail outlets.

Founded in 1985, TGC has been franchising since the following year. A typical TGC franchisee operates a retail store specializing in fine coffees and coffee-brewing accessories. Of the franchisor's 20 outlets currently operating, all but two are franchise units.

The Gourmet Cup, P.O. Box 490, Abbotsford, BC, Canada V2S5Z5. Telephone: (604) 852-8771

Grand Slam USA Headquartered in Santa Cruz, California, a franchisor of baseball batting practice facilities.

Founded in 1976, Grand Slam has been franchising since 1984. A typical Grand Slam franchisee operates a recreational outlet for baseball players and enthusiasts, featuring automatic pitching machines of varying speeds and difficulty. All of the franchisor's 57 outlets are franchise units.

Grand Slam USA, P.O. Box 1573, Santa Cruz, CA 95060. Telephone: (800) 331-4337

Grandy's Headquartered in Lewisville, Texas, a franchisor of fast-food outlets.

Founded in 1973, Grandy's has been franchising since 1977. A typical Grandy's franchisee operates a fast-food restaurant specializing in chicken and barbecued ribs. The outlet also offers a breakfast menu.

Of the franchisor's 205 outlets currently operating, 95 are franchise units.

Grandy's, 997 Grandy's, Lewisville, TX 75067. Telephone: (214) 221-3780

Ground Round, The Headquartered in Weymouth, Massachusetts, a franchisor of family-style restaurants.

Founded in 1969, TGR has been franchising since the following year. A typical TGR franchisee operates a family restaurant specializing in "gourmet" hamburger ensembles. Of the franchisor's 200 outlets currently operating, about a fifth are franchise units.

The Ground Round, 541 Main St., Weymouth, MA 02190.

Grease Monkey Headquartered in Denver, Colorado, a franchisor of automotive service outlets.

Founded in 1978, Grease Monkey has been franchising since its inception. A typical Grease Monkey franchisee operates a quick oil-change and lubrication business, based on a standardized site design and equipment package. Of the franchisor's 131 outlets currently operating, all except five are franchise units.

Grease Monkey, 1660 Wynkoop, Ste. 1160, Denver, CO 80202. Telephone: (303) 543-1660

Great Clips Headquartered in Minneapolis, Minnesota, a franchisor of hair care salons.

Founded in 1984, Great Clips has been franchising since its inception. A typical Great Clips franchisee operates a retail haircutting establishment catering to both men and women. Of the franchisor's 160 outlets currently operating, all except one are franchise units.

Great Clips, Inc., 3601 W. 77th St., Minneapolis, MN 55435. Telephone: (612) 893-9088

Great Expectations Headquartered in Jericho, New York, a franchisor of hair care salons.

Founded in 1955, Great Expectations has been franchising since 1974. The franchisor is currently owned and operated by CutCo Industries, the parent company of the HairCrafters and Cut & Curl chains. A typical Great Expectations franchisee operates a retail hair care salon with a cosmopolitan, high-tech image, catering to a youthful clientele. None of the franchisor's estimated 300 outlets are company-owned.

Great Expectations Precision Haircutters, P.O. Box 265, Jericho, NY 11753. Telephone: (516) 334-8400

Great Frame Up Systems Headquartered in Franklin Park, Illinois, a franchisor of specialty retail outlets.

Founded in 1971, Great Frame Up has been franchising since 1975. A typical Great Frame Up franchisee operates a retail store merchandising custom picture framing supplies, art goods, and posters. Of the franchisor's 95 outlets currently operating, all except three are franchise units.

The Great Frame Up Systems, Inc., 9335 Belmont Ave., Franklin Park, IL 60131. Telephone: (800) 55-FRAME

Guarantee Carpet Cleaning and Dye Company Headquartered in Jacksonville, Florida, a franchisor of interior maintenance services.

Founded in 1969, Guarantee has been franchising since the following year. A typical Guarantee franchisee operates a mobile home-maintenance business specializing in carpet cleaning and restoration, utilizing the franchisor's techniques, chemicals, and equipment. The Guarantee chain consists of 564 outlets, with only one company-owned unit.

Guarantee Carpet Cleaning and Dye Co., 2953 Powers Ave., Jacksonville, CA 32207. Telephone: (904) 733-8211

Gymboree Headquartered in Burlingame, California, a franchisor of recreational centers for children.

Founded in 1977 by Joan Barnes, Gymboree has been franchising since 1980. The Gymboree concept originated in 1976, when Barnes instituted a development program for toddlers at a community center in San Rafael, California, a suburb of San Francisco on the north side of the Golden Gate Bridge. A coworker invested $3,000 and encouraged her to open a private center of her own. The first Gymboree centers opened in the San Francisco Bay area and, later, branched into the Los Angeles vicinity.

Venture Partners, a venture-capital firm headquartered in nearby Menlo Park, initially staked $300,000 to fuel the expansion of Gymboree centers nationwide. The group's total investment to date reprotedly exceeds $1 million.

From 1980 to 1985, Gymboree Corporation more than doubled its annual revenues every year, expanding to more than 220 centers and emerging as a dominant force in the child-services industry.

A typical Gymboree franchisee operates an exercise and play center designed for child development with parent participation. The outlet houses colorful play equipment such as balance beams, slides, mats, trampolines, and parachutes, for structured exercise, games, and singing by groups of ten to twenty parent-child pairs led by trained Gymboree staff members. Parents pay an average of $50 to $60 for a dozen sessions.

The Gymboree program is divided into three levels: Babygym, for tots from three months to one year; Gymboree, for toddlers from one year to 30 months; and Gymgrad, for kids from 30 months to four years. The therapeutic learning program is modeled after a parenting system developed by pyschologist Burton L. White in the 1960s. White's method is based on so-called "benign neglect" which provides children with ample play space, toys, and personal freedom under a parent's watchful, but not overprotective, eyes. White had observed that children reared in this way surpass other children in self-esteem, social skills, and academic achievement.

Of the 350 Gymboree centers currently operating in the U.S., Canada, France, Australia, and Israel, all except five are franchise units. In addition, 34 Gymboree retail stores merchandise the company's private-label apparel, books, play equipment, and videocassettes.

Gymboree Corp., 577 Airport Blvd., Ste. 400, Burlingame, CA 94010. Telephone: (415) 692-8080
See Barnes, Joan.

Parent-child interaction at Gymboree

**H&R Block
to
Huntington**

H&R Block Headquartered in Kansas City, Missouri, a franchisor of tax preparation outlets.
Founded in 1946, H&R Block has been franchising since 1958, growing to become one of the largest and most recognizable franchise organizations in the world. A typical H&R Block franchisee operates a tax preparation service specializing in personal income tax, usually in conjunction with a related business such as an accounting, bookkeeping, or real estate office. Of the estimated 8,800 H&R Block outlets currently operating, more than half are franchise units.
H&R Block, 4410 Main St., Kansas City, MO 64111. Telephone:(816) 753-6900

HairCrafters Headquartered in Jericho, New York, a franchisor of hair care salons.
Founded in 1955 under the name Cut & Curl, HairCrafters has been franchising since 1968. The parent company, CutCo Industries, acquired the Great Expectations chain in 1984. A typical HairCrafters franchisee operates a retail haircutting and styling business based on a standardized format and decor package. Of the franchisor's estimated 400 outlets currently operating, all except 40 are franchise units.
HairCrafters, P.O. Box 265, Jericho, NY 11753. Telephone: (516) 334-8400

Hampton Inns Headquartered in Memphis, Tennessee, a franchisor of lodging outlets.
Founded in 1983, Hampton Inns has been franchising since the following year. A typical Hampton Inns franchisee operates a mid-price hotel designed to attract clientele of higher priced lodging establishments. Each outlet features such traditional amenities as on-premises food and beverage service, meeting rooms, and recreational facilities. Of the franchisor's 180 outlets currently operating, all except 23 are franchise units.
Hampton Inns, 6699 Great Oak Rd., Ste. 100, Memphis, TN 38138. Telephone: (901) 756-2811

Handle With Care Packaging Stores Headquartered in Englewood, Colorado, a franchisor of packaging and shipping outlets.
Founded in 1980, HWC has been franchising since 1984. A typical HWC franchisee operates a service business devoted to custom packaging and shipping. Outlets also derive income from sales of packaging supplies, boxes, and filler. Of the franchisor's 190 outlets currently operating, all are franchise units.

Handle With Care Packaging Stores, 8480 E. Orchard Rd., Ste. 4900, Englewood, CO 80111. Telephone: (800) 525-6309

Hardee's Food Systems, Inc. Headquartered in Rocky Mount, North Carolina, a franchisor of fast-food outlets.

Founded in 1960, Hardee's has been franchising since the following year. The chain originated from a system of charcoal-broiling hamburgers conceived by Wilber Hardee, a restaurant owner in Greenville, North Carolina. The system was based in part on a specially designed charcoal broiler and a high-speed milkshake machine capable of turning out 360 shakes an hour. The outlet design was geared for high-volume walk-up service. Hardee called his concept the "Jet Service Drive-In System." With two investors, James Gardner and Leonard Rawls, Jr., Wilber formed Hardee's Drive-Ins, Inc. in 1960.

The first restaurant based on the Jet Service system opened in Rocky Mount in 1961 on the corner of Church Street and Falls Road. "It went great," Wilber was quoted in the Greensboro Daily News. "It went so damn great...my profit was 9500 bucks and that was big, big money for that time." The first Hardee's franchise was sold to two South Carolina men, Charles Bradshaw and Jerry Richardson. The menu featured "charco-broiled" hamburgers for 15 cents, french fries for a dime, and milk shakes for 20 cents.

Gardner formed a partnership with two brothers, Nick and Bayo Boddie, to build a second franchise outlet in Rocky Mount in 1962. That same year, Hardee's made headlines in Augusta, Georgia when the company altered its standard building design in order to save a 150-year old Magnolia tree growing on the property.

Hardee's stock appeared on the public stock exchange at noon on August 13, 1963, at an initial offering of $4 per share. The first overseas outlet, Hardee's Schnellrast, opened in Heidelburg, Germany in 1965. The following year, James Gardner made a successful run for the United States Congress. The company made fortes into the chicken business in 1968, with the opening of Yogi Bear Honey Fried Chicken. Hardee's Food System, Inc. was now opening new outlets at the rate of one every ten days.

In 1970, the Kellog Company entered into a joint venture to expand the chain into Australia. Flexing its financial muscles, the Hardee's organization acquired the 200-unit Sandy's hamburger chain in 1972, bringing the systemwide total to 640.

JET SERVICE
DRIVE-IN SYSTEM

A Canadian conglomerate, Imasco, Ltd., completed a successful takeover bid in 1981, beating out Pepsico and Pet, Inc. The following year, the revitalized chain bought out the 650-unit Burger Chef organization from General Foods Corp. Systemwide sales topped $2 billion for the first time in 1985.

A typical Hardee's franchisee operates a fast-food restaurant with a blue-collar orientation and a limited menu featuring specialty sandwiches, hamburgers, and soft drinks. The menu features hot ham and cheese sandwiches, mushroom-cheese hamburgers, and Hardee's traditional Big Roast Beef Sandwiches. About two thirds of the estimated 3,000 Hardee's outlets in the United States are franchise units.

Hardee's Food Systems, Inc., 1233 N. Church St., Rocky Mount, NC 27801. Telephone: (919) 977-8706

Hasty Markets Headquartered in Toronto, Ontario, a franchisor of Canadian retail convenience outlets.

Founded in 1981, Hasty has been franchising since 1982. A typical Hasty franchisee operates a convenience food store open 24 hours a day. Of the franchisor's 135 outlets currently operating, all except 20 are franchise units.

Hasty Markets, 33 Bloor St. East, Ste. 201, Toronto, Ont., Canada M4W 3H1. Telephone: (416) 922-7849

Hawaii, Franchise Regulations Franchisors operating in the state of Hawaii are governed by the Franchise Investment Law, which requires registration and disclosure of pertinent information about the franchisor, franchise business, and franchise agreement. The same law protects the rights of franchisees to renew their franchise agreements on expiration, and forbids franchisors from termiminating or refusing to renew a franchise without good cause.

Before offering or selling a franchise in the state, a franchisor must first prepare a disclosure document prescribed by the statute, then file the information, along with the franchise agreement, financial statements, and related documents, with the Director of Regulatory Agencies. In addition to a disclosure document, franchisors are also required to submit the following items:

1. Application for registration of the franchise offering;
2. Salesman disclosure form;
3. Consent to service of process;
4. Auditor's consent to use of audited financial statements;
5. Cross-reference sheet showing the location in the franchise agreement of the key items in the disclosure document.

The disclosure document devised by a consortium of midwestern securities commissioners as a uniform method of complying with state franchise investment laws, the *Uniform Franchise Offering Circular*, or UFOC, fulfills the disclosure requirements of the Hawaii law. There are minor variations and differences in language required by the Hawaii statute, including a different cover page.

The disclosure document or UFOC must be furnished to a prospective franchisee at least ten business days before a franchise sale is made. For information about state franchise laws, regulations, and filing requirements, or to report possible violations, contact: Directory of Regulatory Agencies, 1010 Richards St., Honolulu, HI 96813. Telephone: (808) 548-6521.

See Uniform Franchise Offering Circular.

Headquarters Companies Headquartered in San Francisco, California, a franchisor of shared-tenant business offices and services.

Founded in 1967, HQ has been franchising since 1978. A typical HQ franchisee operates a rental office facility offering business supports services to tenants. Of the franchisor's 72 outlets currently operating, all are franchise units.

Headquarters Companies, 120 Montgomery St., Ste. 1040, San Francisco, CA 94804. Telephone: (415) 781-5000

Healthcare Recruiters International Headquartered in Dallas, Texas, a franchisor of personnel recruitment agencies.

Founded in 1977, HRI has been franchising since 1985. A typical HRI franchisee operates a management recruitment agency specializing in executives of health-care institutions. All of the franchisor's 36 outlets currently operating are franchise units.

Healthcare Recrutiers International, 5420 LBJ Fwy., Dallas, TX 75240.

Health Force Headquartered in Westbury, New York, a franchisor of nursing-care employment agencies.

Founded in 1975, Health Force has been franchising since 1982. A typical Health Force franchisee operates a temporary employment business devoted to nursing-care personnel for both in-home services and health care institutions. Of the 50 Health Force outlets currently operating, 42 are franchise units.

Health Force, 1600 Stewart Ave., Westbury, NY 11590. Telephone: (516) 683-6000

Health Mart, Inc. Headquartered in Carrollton, Texas, a franchisor of retail drug stores.

Founded in 1981, Health Mart has been franchising since 1983. A typical Health Mart franchisee operates a full-service drug store with a broad inventory of health and beauty products and sundries, including the franchisor's own private-labeled merchandise lines. The chain consists of 466 outlets, none of which are company owned.

Health Mart, Inc., 1220 Senlac Dr., Carrollton, TX 75006. Telephone: (214) 446-0909

Heavenly Ham Headquartered in Atlanta, Georgia, a franchisor of specialty food outlets.

Founded in 1984, Heavenly Ham has been franchising since the following year. A typical Heavenly Ham franchisee operates retail outlet specializing in the franchisor's private brand of packaged honey)glazed hams. Of the franchisor's 27 outlets currently operating, all except one are franchise units.

Heavenly Ham, 365 Northridge Rd., Ste. 230, Atlanta, GA 30338. Telephone: (404) 399-0511

Heidi's Frozen Yogurt Shops Headquartered in Laguna Hills, California, a franchisor of specialty food outlets.

Founded in 1982, Heidi's has been franchising since 1983. A typical Heidi's franchisee operates a retail shop specializing in the franchisor's proprietary line of frozen yoghurt products. Of the franchisor's 90 outlets currently operating, all except seven are franchise units.

Heidi's Frozen Yogurt Shops, 24422 Avenida de la Carlota, Laguna Hills, CA 92653. Telephone: (714) 770-1664

Help-U-Sell, Inc. Headquartered in Salt Lake City, Utah, a franchisor of real estate counseling services.

Founded in 1976, Help-U-Sell has been franchising since its inception. The franchise company is a subsidiary of Mutual Benefit Life Insurance Co. A typical Help-U-Sell franchisee operates a real estate marketing and counseling business offering support services and advice to homeowners seeking prospective buyers for their property. For a set fee, the outlet provides guidance in pricing and advertising the property, conducting open houses, and closing sales. Of the 353 Help-U-Sell outlets currently operating, all except one are franchise units.

Help-U-Sell, Inc., 57 W. 200 South, Salt Lake City, UT 84101. Telephone: (800) 345-1990

Hertz Rent-A-Car Headquartered in Parsippany, New Jersey, a franchisor of automobile rental outlets.

The Hertz system originated in 1918, when founder Walter Jacobs purchased a modest rental fleet of a dozen Ford Model T passenger cars. A self-taught mechanic, Jacobs serviced and repaired the fleet himself. By 1923, Hertz had become a million-dollar operation and, two years later, the company began selling franchises. A typical Hertz franchisee operates a retail car rental facility at an airport, downtown, or resort location. Of the franchisor's estimated 1,600, approximately 1,000 are franchise units.

Hertz Rent-A-Car, 7 Estin Rd., Parsippany, NJ 07054. Telephone: (212) 980-2600

Hickory Farms of Ohio Headquartered in Maumee, Ohio, a franchisor of specialty food and gift outlets.

Founded in 1926, Hickory Farms began franchise operations in 1960. The chain is presently a subsidiary of General Host Corp. A typical Hickory Farms franchisee operates a retail outlet devoted to specialty, traditional, and gift food products. Each store markets a selection of popular and exotic cheeses, meats, crackers, candy, nuts, fruit preserves, and beef sausages. Hickory Farms outlets range from inventory-stocking stores with fast-food service to small kiosks operated in regional shopping malls on a seasonal basis. Slightly less than half of the 340 Hickory Farm outlets in North America are franchise units.

Hickory Farms of Ohio, P.O. Box 219, Maumee, OH 43537. Telephone: (419) 893-7611

Hillary's Headquartered in Broomall, Pennsylvania, a franchisor of retail ice cream outlets.

Founded in 1976, Hillary's has been franchising since 1979. A typical Hillary's franchisee operates a retail ice cream parlor featuring the franchisor's special product line. Of the franchisor's 26 outlets currently operating, all except five are franchise units.

Hillary's, 838 Sussex Blvd., Broomall, PA 19008.

Hilton, Conrad Hotelier, oilman, and founder of the franchise organization of lodging establishments bearing his name.

Born on December 25, 1887 in San Antonio, New Mexico, Hilton attended St. Michael's College and New Mexico School of Mines, graduating in 1909. As a youth, he met late night trains stopping in San Antonio and escorted passengers to his father's sprawling ranch adobe house, where five rooms were set aside for guests. The room rate was a dollar per night, including meals.

Following a short stint in business with his father, the 25-year-old Conrad made a successful run for the New Mexico legislature as a Republican. Leaving public service a year later, he went to work as a cashier in the New Mexico State Bank of San Antonio, eventually rising to the presidency. He saw service as a second lieutenant in the first World War.

In 1919, Hilton went to Cisco, Texas intending to buy a bank. Instead, he ended up buying a hotel, the Mobley, which became the cornerstone of the Hilton hotel empire. In 1925, he set out to build a new hotel in Dallas, but ran out of money before construction was completed. When the project was finished, Hilton operated the establishment under a lease contract.

When the depression struck, he had already acquired a modest chain of eight hotels in the southwest. In a period when more than 80 percent of the nation's hotels went into bankruptcy, Hilton managed to hold onto five of his, by using profits from his oil lease investments to keep the lodging establishments afloat.

Conrad Hilton

In 1939, Hilton began building new hotels, while setting out to acquire the most famous of America's "Golden Age of Hotels." In 1942, he acquired the Town House in Los Angeles and, a year later, the Roosevelt and Plaza hotels in New York City. He consummated his plan by taking over the Palmer House in Chicago and in 1949 achieved his lifelong ambition of owning the Waldorf-Astoria in New York City.

In 1946, he organized his chain of lodging establishments as the Hilton Hotel Corporation and, in the succeeding years, bought or built luxury hotels around the world under the Hilton name. In 1954, he acquired controlling interest of his primary competitor, the Statler hotel chain, for $111 million. He turned over the management reins to his son, Barron Hilton, in 1966, staying on as chairman of the board.

Since the 1960s, franchising has provided the primary expansion of Hilton Inns in the United States. The overseas operation, Hilton International, was sold to a separate group of investors in 1967.

Hilton's autobiography, *Be My Guest*, appeared in 1957. He died in 1979 at the age of 91.

Hilton Inns Headquartered in Beverly Hills, California, a franchisor of lodging outlets.

Founded in 1925 by hotel pioneer Conrad Hilton, Hilton Inns began franchising in 1965. The chain's first lodging establishment was the Mobley hotel in Cisco, Texas, which Hilton bought in 1919 on the way to buy a bank. He constructed the first hotel bearing his own name in Dallas in 1925. In 1938, Hilton purchased the lease of the historic Sir Francis Drake hotel in San Francisco, his first property outside the state of Texas. In the 1940s, he added the Town House in Los Angeles, the Roosevelt and Plaza in New York City, and the Palmer House and the Stevens in Chicago to his chain.

Hilton Hotels Corporation was formed in 1946 and listed on the public stock exchange with Conrad Hilton as president. Three years later, the company acquired the world's most famous hotel, the Waldorf-Astoria in New York City. Shortly afterward, the Caribe Hilton, the chain's first overseas property, opened in San Juan, Puerto Rico, signaling the inception of the Hilton International subsidiary. Construction of the first Hilton hotel in Europe, the Castellana, was completed in 1953. The company bought out the Statler Hotel Company, its closest competitor, in 1954, in what was then the largest acquisition in the history of the hotel industry. The franchising subsidiary, today known as Hilton Inns, was organized in 1965 as Statler Hilton Inns.

Conrad Hilton's son, Barron Hilton, assumed the company's presidency in 1966. That same year, the chain's big red "H" logo was adopted to adorn the chain's properties. Shortly after taking the reins, Barron Hilton managed to convince his father to sell off the chain's international properties. In 1967, the sale of Hilton International was completed to TWA. Ironically, the overseas chain was later acquired by TWA's most formidable competitor, United Airlines.

In 1970, the company purchased the Las Vegas Hilton (the largest in the world, with 3,174 guest rooms) and the Flamingo Hilton, to utilize the hotels' gambling income to supply working capital. Prudential Life Insurance Company invested heavily in the company in 1975, purchasing a 50-percent interest in six hotels for over $83 million. Two years later, Hilton sold off the Waldorf-Astoria for $35 million.

To compete with firm's prior international division, the company formed a new subsidiary, Conrad International, in 1982. The first Conrad hotel opened on the Gold Coast of Australia the following year. In 1984, Hilton completed construction of the 1600-room Anaheim Hilton and Towers, adjacent to the Anaheim Convention Center, the largest lodging establishment in Southern California. The Hilton Hawaiian Village and the San Francisco Hilton opened in 1988.

Hilton Hotels Corporation is today a publicly held international lodging company with approximately 300 properties. Since 1969, most of the new units which have opened under the Hilton banner have been franchise outlets. Presently, franchises account for approximately 55 percent of the chain's total hotel rooms.

A typical Hilton Inns franchisee operates an executive-class lodging establishment catering to business travelers and upscale vacationers. The average outlet has 170 rooms, with banquet facilities, meeting rooms, food and beverage service, and uniformed bell service.

Besides franchising, Hilton also administers a management leaseback program under which the company sells part of its equity in an existing hotel, but continues to manage the property for a percentage of room revenues and profits.

Hilton Inns, P.O. Box 5567, Beverly Hills, California 90210. Telephone: (213) 205-4407

Hindman, W. James Entrepreneur, collegiate football coach, and franchisor of quick-change automotive oil service outlets.

In 1979, Hindman was head football coach at Western Maryland College, when he took his Cadillac to a service station to have the oil changed. When he returned eight hours later, he found that, due to a switch in service orders, the car's oil not been changed, but its interior had been almost completely disassembled. The disgruntled coach promptly bought a tiny chain of quick-change automotive oil service shops.

The parent company, Jiffy Lube, had been franchising with limited success since 1970. After learning the business, Hindman sold off a nursing care business in which he had previously invested, to finance a $3 million expansion program. With another $6 million from independent investors, he began buying up real estate for future Jiffy Lube sites. In 1983, Lindman speeded the program along by selling "area development" franchises, granting large geographical territories to investors willing to open multiple outlets.

By 1985, Jiffy Lube had burgeoned to 300 outlets, with gross annual revenues of $14.5 million. The chain is currently the largest organization of its type, in a period in which auto service "boutiques" specializing in limited services such as fast oil change or "instant" tune-up service are outpacing traditional full-service repair shops. Hindman continues to control 75 percent of the franchising company.

Holiday Inns Headquartered in Memphis, Tennessee, a franchisor of lodging outlets.

Founded in 1952, Holiday Inns has been franchising since 1954. Since 1984, the company has pursued an aggressive, system-wide campaign to upgrade both its image and operating standards, by terminating inefficient franchises and closing substandard company-owned outlets. The Holiday Inn organization began in 1952, when Memphis entrepreneur Kemmons Wilson began building a chain of standardized hotels across the United States. At the time, Wilson perceived the roadside motel business as "the greatest untouched industry." The first Holiday Inn was located on the outskirts of Memphis, which is still home to the corporation's headquarters. The property had 120 guest rooms, each with a private bath, air conditioning, and telephone. Additional features included a swimming pool, free ice, free parking, and dog kennels. Children under 12 could stay free in the room with their parents. These amenities, considered standard in lodging establishments today, were revolutionary for the hotel industry at the time.

From its modest beginnings, the Holiday Inn system grew into the world's largest lodging chain, with more than 315,000 rooms in some 1,600 hotels in 50 states and 52 countries. The 100th Holiday Inn opened in Tallahasee, Florida in September, 1959. The corporation's stock was traded over the counter in August, 1957 and appeared on the New York Stock Exchange in September, 1963. The 1,000th property opened in San Antonio, Texas in 1968.

By the end of the 1960s, a new Holiday Inn hotel was being completed somewhere in the world at the rate of one every two and one half days. The company's first European hotel opened in 1968 in Leiden, Holland, and not coincidentally, the corporation changed its name from Holiday Inns of America to Holiday Inns, Inc.

When Kemmons Wilson retired in 1979, Roy E. Winegardner, who had joined the corporation five years earlier as first vice chairman, succeeded Wilson as chairman of the board. Winegardner brought with him division vice president Michael D. Rose, who was named executive vice president in 1979 and chairman of the board in 1983.

In 1979, Holiday Inns moved to acquire River Boat Casinos, Inc., which operates the Holiday Casino adjacent to the Holiday Inn-Center Strip in Los Vegas, and purchased the 300-unit Perkins Family Restaurant chain. In February, 1980, the company acquired Harrah's, making Holiday the largest casino operator in the nation. In 1982, the company began construction on the first Embassy Suite and Crowne Plaza hotels. The following year, Holiday began developing limited-service Hampton Inns.

The company changed its name again in 1985, to Holiday Corporation.

A typical Holiday Inns franchisee operates a full-service lodging establishment catering to vacationing family units and business travelers. The average outlet has 184 rooms in a four-to six-story structure on a 3.5-acre site, with 45 full-time and 12 part-time employees. Depending on the size of the property and the initial investment, the facilities may include a restaurant, cocktail lounge, swimming pool, banquet facilities, and meeting rooms. The prototypes for new outlets include both mid-rise and high-rise structures. The Holiday Inn chain is comprised of 1,600 outlets currently operating, of which 90 percent are franchise units.

Holiday Inns, 1023 Cherry Rd., Memphis, TN 38117. Telephone: (901) 762-8600.

*The original Holiday Inn sign was designed
in the 1950s to attract passers-by on the
nation's then-new interstate highway system*

The first Holiday Inn, constructed by Kemmons Wilson outside Memphis

Homes & Land Magazine Headquartered in Tallahassee, Florida, a franchisor of specialty publishing outlets.

Founded in 1973, Homes & Land has been franchising since 1984. A typical Homes & Land franchisee operates an advertising sales and publishing business devoted to community real estate listings. The chain presently consists of 264 franchised outlets.

Homes & Land Magazine, 2365 Centerville Rd., Tallahassee, FL32308. Telephone: (904) 385-3310

Hometrend, Inc. Headquartered in Denver, Colorado, a franchisor of independent real estate sales offices.

Founded in 1979, Hometrend has been franchising since its inception. A typical Hometrend franchisee operates a licensed real estate brokerage utilizing the franchisor's trademark and advertising.

Hometrend, Inc., 3600 S. Beeler St., Ste. 300, Denver, CO 80237. Telephone: (800) 241-0689

Hotels, Motels, and Resorts Lodging establishments, including hotels, motels, resorts, convention centers, and bed-and-breakfast inns, constitute the world's seventh largest industry, generating approximately $36 billion in annual sales. Franchises are an integral component of the worldwide lodging trade, dominating the budget motel industry and carrying the banners of the world's most famous hoteliers.

The earliest lodging establishments were the inns of Biblical times, which offered little more than a cot or bench in the corner of a stable to merchants and itinerants. European taverns combined food and beverage service with lodging, with little concern for sanitation. Beds as well as rooms had to be shared with other travelers, and the rates were steep.

The first hotels constructed in Europe were reserved for aristocrats, with prices that were prohibitive to the common citizen. In colonial America, most taverns were modeled after the European concept, providing simple food and beverage service without regard to sanitation or means.

The first dedicated lodging establishment in North America, the Tremont House, opened in New York in 1919, heralding the Golden Age of Hotels. The Tremont was followed by the Waldorf-Astoria in New York, the Plaza Hotel in Chicago, and the elegant Grand Hotel in San Francisco. The Great Depression all but wiped out the lodging industry, but one hotel operator, Conrad Hilton, managed to stay afloat as a result of his oil and gas investments.

Howard Johnson, a Massachusetts restaurateur, began opening family roadside motor lodges in 1936. With the end of World War II, the lodging trade exploded, as Americans took to the nation's highways. The first Holiday Inn opened in Tennessee in 1951. The three largest hotel chains, Hilton, Sheraton, and Statler took each other on in fierce competition. When the dust settled, Sheraton had acquired the entire Statler chain, forming the world's largest lodging organization.

The Hilton, Sheraton, Howard Johnson, and Holiday Inn names live on today in the franchises bearing their respective trademarks. But in the 1960s, a new type of lodging outlet entered the picture. Whereas traditional hotels were located on premium properties and offered food and beverage service in addition to room sales, the new breed of hotel eschewed expensive real estate and sold nothing but room space. Minimizing overhead, the budget motel chains rose rapidly to prominence; of the ten largest lodging organizations in the world today, half fall in the budget category.

Leading Lodging Franchisors by Number of Outlets

1. Holiday Inns (1,600)
2. Quality Inns International (950)
3. Days Inns of American (700)
4. Ramada Inn System (590)
5. Sheraton Inns (500)
6. Travelodge (470)
7. Howard Johnson Company (450)
8. Econo Lodges of America (440)
9. Super 8 Motels (430)
10. Hilton Inns (275)

HouseMaster of America Headquartered in Bound Brook, New Jersey, a franchisor of real estate inspection services.

Founded in 1971, HouseMaster has been franchising since 1979. A typical HouseMaster franchisee operates a building inspection service for residential real estate offered for sale. The chain currently boasts 100 outlets, all of which are franchise units.

HouseMaster of America, 421 W. Union Ave., Bound Brook, NJ 08805. Telephone: (800) 526-3939

House of Almonds Headquartered in Bakersfield, California, a franchisor of retail confection outlets.

Founded in 1968, House of Almonds has been franchising since 1986. A typical House of Almonds franchisee operates a retail food shop devoted to nuts, candy, and specialty gift items. Of the franchisor's 68 outlets currently operating, only one are franchise units.

House of Almonds, P.O. Box 9380, Bakersfield, CA 93389. Telephone: (805) 835-6537

Howard Johnson Company Headquartered in Fairfield, New Jersey, a franchisor of lodging establishments.

Founded in 1925, Howard Johnson has been franchising since 1935. The chain traces its roots to a small patent medicine store purchased by Howard D. Johnson in the Wollaston section of Quincy, Massachusetts in 1925. The store housed a soda fountain, to which Johnson added full meal service, and in 1928, he converted the store into a restaurant. The first Howard Johnson franchise was licensed to a restaurateur in Cape Cod during the Great Depression. The one hundredth "HoJo" outlet opened in 1940.

The company entered the lodging trade in 1954, franchising its first roadside inn in Savannah, Georgia. The founder's son, Howard Brennan Johnson, assumed the chain's presidency in 1959, guiding the company to public ownership. Howard Johnson Co. stock first appeared on the New York stock exchange in 1961. In June, 1980, the company was acquired by a British congolomerate, Imperial Group plc., which sold the chain to Marriott Corporation five years later. Shortly afterward, the lodging business and franchise restaurant system were acquired by Prime Motor Inns. Marriott retained the manufacturing operations and company-owned restaurants, which were converted to the Big Boy name.

Under Prime's ownership, Howard Johnson began a course of upgrading its existing lodging establishments and expanding into upscale, all-suite hotels. Besides franchising Howard Johnson hotels, Prime also owns and operates 129 hotels of its own, including outlets of other hotel chains such as Ramada Inns, Holiday Inns, and Sheraton. Curtis B. Bean, Howard Johnson Company's chief executive, is the former president of Holiday Corporation.

A typical Howard Johnson franchisee operates a "guest lodging facility" designed to appeal to all segments of the traveling public, providing accommodations of uniform standards at a reasonable rate. Besides sleeping rooms, each outlet also has a swimming pool, meeting rooms, recreational facilities, and a full-service food and beverage operation. Of the franchisor's 450 outlets currently operating, 412 are franchise units.

Howard Johnson Company, Inc., 700 Rte. 46 East, P.O. Box 2700, Fairfield, NJ 07007-2700. Telephone: (201) 882-1010

Huntington Learning Centers Headquartered in Oradell, New Jersey, a franchisor of educational service outlets.

Founded in 1977, Huntington has been franchising since 1985. A typical Huntington franchisee operates a personal tutoring service for learners of elementary-and secondary-school age, as well as adults who require remedial instruction. Of the franchisor's 90 outlets currently operating, all except 14 are franchise units.

Huntington Learning Centers, Inc., 660 Kinderkamack Rd., Oradell, NJ 07649. Telephone: (201) 261-8400

I

I Can't Believe It's Yogurt
to
Island Water Sports

I Can't Believe It's Yogurt Headquartered in Dallas, Texas, a franchisor of fast-food outlets.

Founded in 1977, ICBIY has been franchising since 1983. A typical franchisee operates a fast-food stand devoted to frozen yoghurt products developed by the franchisor. The ICBIY chain currently consists of 175 outlets, all of which are franchise units.

I Can't Believe It's Yogurt, 5005 LBJ Fwy., Ste. 1650, Dallas, TX 75244. Telephone: (214) 392-3012

Ice Cream Churn Headquartered in Atlanta, Georgia, a franchisor of specialty fast-food outlets.

Founded in 1974, ICC has been franchising since 1978. A typical ICC franchisee operates an ice cream parlor featuring the franchisor's 'dip' ice cream process and products. The chain currently is currently comprised of 530 outlets, all of which are franchise units.

Ice Cream Churn, 700 Miami Circle, Atlanta, GA 31008. Telephone: (912) 956-5880

Idaho, Franchise Regulations The Idaho legislature has not adopted any generally applicable franchise investment law. However, the rights of farm equipment, automobile, and and beer and wine dealers are protected under separate laws.

The Attorney General's Office oversees the sales of business opportunities and possible pyramid sales schemes. To report possible violations, contact: Attorney General, State House, Boise, ID 83720. Telephone: (208) 344-2400.

Idaho law does not require franchisors to register or file disclosures with any state regulatory body. In the absence of such a requirement, the federal Franchise Rule applies, requiring franchisors to furnish a disclosure document prescribed by the Federal Trade Commission to prospective franchisees ten business days before a franchise sale is made.

See Franchise Rule.

Illinois, Franchise Regulations Franchisors operating in the state of Illinois are governed by the Franchise Disclosure law, which requires registration and disclosure of pertinent information about the franchisor, franchise business, and franchise agreement. Other state laws protect the rights of automobile dealers and liquor store owners.

Before offering or selling a franchise in the state, a franchisor must first prepare a disclosure document prescribed by the statute, then file the information, along with the franchise agreement, financial statements, and related documents, with the Illinois Attorney General's Office. The Attorney General must approve the registration before the franchisor may proceed to offer or sell franchises.

In addition to a disclosure document, franchisors are also required to submit the following items:

1. Application for registration of the franchise offering;
2. Salesman disclosure form;
3. Consent to service of process;
4. Auditor's consent to use of audited financial statements;
5. Cross-reference sheet showing the location in the franchise agreement of the key items in the disclosure document.

The disclosure document devised by a consortium of midwestern securities commissioners as a uniform method of complying with state franchise investment laws, the *Uniform Franchise Offering Circular*, or UFOC, fulfills the disclosure requirements of the Illinois law. There are minor variations and differences in language required by the Illinois statute, including a different cover page.

The disclosure document or UFOC must be furnished to a prospective franchisee at least ten business days before a franchise sale is made.

For information about state franchise laws, regulations, and filing requirements, or to report possible violations, contact: Franchise Division, Attorney General's Office, 500 S. Second St., Springfield, IL 62706. Telephone: (217) 782-4465.

See Uniform Franchise Offering Circular.

In 'N Out Food Stores Headquartered in Detroit, Michigan, a franchisor of retail convenience stores.

Founded in 1976, In 'N Out has been franchising since 1981. A typical In 'N Out franchisee operates a convenience food store with a limited inventory of grocery items, household goods, automotive supplies, confections, and fast-food items. Of the franchisor's 50 outlets currently operating, 35 are franchise units.

In 'N Out Food Stores, 19215 W. 8-Mile Rd., Detroit, MI 48219. Telephone: (313) 255-0100

Inacomp Computer Centers Headquartered in Troy, Michigan, a franchisor of specialty retail outlets.

Founded in 1976, Inacomp has been franchising since 1981. A typical Inacomp franchisee operates a retail store marketing small business computer systems and software. Of the franchisor's 80 outlets currently operating, 33 are franchise units.

Inacomp, 1800 W. Maple Rd., Troy, MI 48084. Telephone: (313) 649-5580

Indiana, Franchise Regulations Franchisors operating in the state of Indiana are governed by the Franchise Registration Disclosure law, which requires registration and disclosure of pertinent information about the franchisor, franchise business, and franchise agreement. Other state laws protect the rights of automobile dealers and liquor store owners.

Before offering or selling a franchise in the state, a franchisor must first prepare a disclosure document prescribed by the statute, then file the information, along with the franchise agreement, financial statements, and related documents, with the Securities Commissioner. The registration must be approved before the franchisor may proceed to offer or sell franchises.

In addition to a disclosure document, franchisors are also required to submit the following items to the Securities Commissioner:

1. Application for registration of the franchise offering;
2. Salesman disclosure form;
3. Consent to service of process;
4. Auditor's consent to use of audited financial statements;
5. Cross-reference sheet showing the location in the franchise agreement of the key items in the disclosure document.

The disclosure document devised by a consortium of midwestern securities commissioners as a uniform method of complying with state franchise investment laws, the *Uniform Franchise Offering Circular*, or UFOC, fulfills the disclosure requirements of the Indiana law. There are minor variations and differences in language required by the Indiana statute, including a different cover page.

The disclosure document or UFOC must be furnished to a prospective franchisee at least ten business days before a franchise sale is made.

Other State Franchise Laws

The rights of automobile dealers under franchise agreements are regulated by the Motor Vehicle Code. The Alcoholic Beverages Code governs the relationship between beer distributors and liquor retailers.

For information about state franchise laws, regulations, and filing requirements, or to report possible violations, contact: Securities Commissioner, 102 State House, Indianapolis, IN 46204. Telephone: (317) 232-6684.

See Uniform Franchise Offering Circular.

Ink Well of America, The Headquartered in Columbus, Ohio, a franchisor of document duplication outlets.

Founded in 1972, The Ink Well has been franchising since 1981. A typical Ink Well franchisee operates a retail printing center devoted to quick printing, high-speed document copying, and supportive services. Of the 50 Ink Well outlets currently operating, all except three are franchise units.

The Ink Well of America, 2323 Lake Club Dr., Columbus, OH 43232. Telephone: (800) 235-2221

Insty Prints Headquartered in Minneapolis, Minnesota, a franchisor of instant printing shops.

Founded in 1965, Insty Prints has been franchising since its inception. A typical Insty Prints franchisee operates a retail quick printing shop catering to individuals as well as businesses, with emphasis on duplication services and printing of stationery, business cards, wedding invitations, and fliers. All of the franchisor's 350 outlets currently open and operating are franchise units.

Insty Prints Printing Centers, 1215 Marshall St. NE, Minneapolis, MN 55413. Telephone: (612) 379-0039

International Blimpie Company Headquartered in New York City, a franchisor of fast-food outlets.

Founded in 1964, International Blimpie has been franchising since 1971. A typical International Blimpie franchisee operates a fast-food operation devoted to specialty sandwiches prepared with ample portions of fresh ingredients. All of the chain's 320 outlets are franchise units.

International Blimpie Co., 740 Broadway, New York, NY 10003. Telephone: (212) 673-5900

International Franchise Association (IFA)   Founded in 1960, a trade association with a membership of more than 500 franchise organizations. The IFA lobbies for favorable legislation on behalf of franchisors and compiles and publishes information on a diversity of subjects relating to franchise marketing, organization, finance, and law.

The IFA *Directory of Membership* is available at a nominal charge from the International Franchise Association, 1350 New York Avenue N.W., Suite 900, Washington, DC 20005.

The IFA requires all members to abide by a Code of Ethics. Following are the six provisions of the code:

1. In the advertisement and grant of franchises or dealerships a member shall comply with all applicable laws and regulations and the member's offering circular shall be complete, accurate and not misleading with respect to the franchisee's or dealer's investment, the obligations of the member and the franchise or dealer under the franchise or dealership and all material facts relating to the franchise or dealership.

2. All matters material to the member's franchise or dealership shall be contained in one or more written agreements, which shall clearly set forth the terms of the relationship and the respective rights and obligations of the parties.

3. A member shall select and accept only those franchisees or dealers who, upon reasonable investigation, appear to possess the basic skills, education, experience, personal characteristics and financial resources requisite to conduct the franchised business or dealership and meet the obligations of the franchise or dealer under the franchise and other agreements. There shall be no discrimination in the granting of franchises based solely on race, color, religion, national origin or sex. However, this in no way prohibits a franchisor from granting franchises to prospective franchisees as part of a program to make franchises available to persons lacking the capital, training, business experience, or other qualifications ordinarily required of franchisees or any other affirmative action program adopted by the franchisor.

4. A member shall provide reasonable guidance to its franchisees or dealers in a manner consistent with its franchise agreement.

5. Fairness shall characterize all dealings between a member and its franchisees or dealers. A member shall make every good faith effort to resolve complaints by and disputes with its franchisees or dealers through direct communication and negotiation. To the extent reasonably appropriate in the circumstances, a member shall give its franchisee or dealer notice of, and a reasonable opportunity to cure, a breach of their contractual relationship.

6. No member shall engage in the pyramid system of distribution. A pyramid is a system wherein a buyer's future compensation is expected to be based primarily upon recruitment of new participants, rather than upon the sale of products or services.

International House of Pancakes Headquartered in North Hollywood, California, a franchisor of food service outlets.

Founded in 1958, IHP has been franchising since 1960. A typical IHP franchisee operates a family-style restaurant and coffee shop with a European ambience and specializing in pancakes and other breakfast items. The menu also features a variety of hot and cold lunches, dinners, and desserts. Wine and beer are served in some locations. Of the franchisor's 458 outlets currently operating, all except 57 are franchise units.

International House of Pancakes, Inc., 6837 Lankershim Blvd., North Hollywood, CA 91605. Telephone: (818) 982-2620

International Mergers and Acquisitions Headquartered in Scottsdale, Arizona, a franchisor of business brokerage services.

Founded in 1970, IMA has been franchising since 1979. A typical franchisee operates a brokerage operation catering to acquisition-minded businesses. All of the estimated 40 IMA outlets currently operating are owned by independent franchisees.

International Mergers and Acquisitions, 8100 E. Indian School Rd., Scottsdale, AZ 85251. Telephone: (602) 990-3899

Iowa, Franchise Regulations The Iowa legislature has not enacted any generally applicable franchise investment law. However, the rights of automobile dealers are protected by the Motor Vehicle Franchisors law.

Iowa law does not require franchisors to register or file disclosures with any state regulatory body. In the absence of such a requirement, the federal Franchise Rule applies, requiring franchisors to furnish a disclosure document prescribed by the Federal Trade Commission to prospective franchisees ten business days before a franchise sale is made.

See Franchise Rule.

Island Water Sports Headquartered in Deerfield Beach, Florida, a franchisor of specialty boutiques.

Founded in 1978, IWS has been franchising since 1984. A typical IWS franchisee operates a retail outlet devoted to beach accessories, equipment, and apparel. Of the franchisor's 25 outlets currently operating, all except three are franchise units.

Island Water Sports, 1985-A NE Second St., Deerfield Beach, FL 33441. Telephone: (305) 427-5665

J. Higby's
to
Just Pants

J. Higby's Yogurt and Treat Shoppes Headquarted in Rancho Cordova, California, a franchisor of fast-food outlets.

Founded in 1983, J. Higby's has been franchising since 1984. A typical J. Higby's franchisee operates a fast-food service with a specialty menu devoted to frozen yogurt, ice cream, cookies, and hot dogs. Of the franchisor's 94 outlets currently operating, all except four are franchise units.

J. Higby's, 1110 White Rock Rd., Rancho Cordova, CA 95670.

Jack In the Box Headquartered in San Diego, California, the fifth largest hamburger restaurant chain in the U.S., presently operated and franchised by Foodmaker, Inc.

The first Jack in the Box outlet opened in San Diego in 1950 as a drive-through hamburger stand. The chain had grown to 280 outlets by 1968 when it was acquired by Ralston Purina Company. Foodmaker, Inc. completed a leveraged buyout in 1985, and the following year, the company's stock appeared on the public exchange with an initial offering of 4.6 million shares.

Through the 1970s, the Jack in the Box marketing thrust was aimed primarily at families, serving small portions of traditional fast food items such as hamburgers, french fries, and milkshakes, with the added gimmick of placing orders to "Jack," the outlet's drive-through clown. In 1980, the chain shifted its focus to upscale adult consumers. The change was symbolized in a memorable television commercial in which an elderly spinster ferociously calls for the destruction of the "Jack" clown, followed by the explosion of a drive-through unit.

In the 1980s, the chain experimented with various fast-food innovations ranging from chicken sandwiches and croissants to trendy Mexican cuisine appealing to nutrition-conscious adult consumers. At any given time, Foodmaker has 15 to 20 new products in research and development.

A typical Jack in the Box franchisee operates a fast-food restaurant characterized by a flexible menu and drive-through facilities. Foodmaker, the chain's parent company, is known for its emphasis on market research and experimentation in menu development. The outlet caters to young working adults, the largest segment of the population which patronizes fast-food establishments. The menu centers around hamburgers but is periodically modified to reflect changing public tastes and consumption trends. At various times, Jack in the Box restaurants have featured shrimp, chicken, Mexican cuisine, and specialty sandwiches.

Although the chain has been in existence since the early 1950s, for more than 30 years only company-owned outlets were developed. Foodmaker began franchising in the 1980s in an effort to remain competitive with rival chains. Not all owners of franchise outlets have prior restaurant experience, but Food-

One of the earliest Jack in the Box restaurants, constructed in San Diego, California

maker requires all franchisees to reside within a one-hour commute from their restaurants. Of the franchisor's 940 outlets currently operating, about a third are franchise units.

Foodmaker, Inc., P.O. Box 783, San Diego, CA 92112. Telephone: (619) 571-2200

Jani-King Headquartered in Dallas, Texas, a franchisor of interior maintenance services.

Founded in 1969, Jani-King has been franchising since 1974. A typical Jani-King franchisee operates a commercial cleaning service for business and industrial clients, usually under long-term contracts. Of the 1,300 Jani-King outlets currently operating, all except a dozen are franchise units.

Jani-King, 4950 Keller Springs, Ste. 190, Dallas, TX 75248. Telephone: (800) 552-5264

Janimaster International, Inc. Headquartered in Greenville, South Carolina, a franchisor of interior maintenance services.

Founded in 1980, Janimaster has been franchising since 1986. A typical Janimaster franchisee operates a commercial janitorial cleaning service. All of the chain's 80 outlets currently in business are franchise units.

Janimaster International, Inc., 44 Pine Knoll Dr., Ste. B, Greenville, SC 29609. Telephone: (803) 292-0000

Japan Camera Centre 1 Hour Photo Headquartered in Don Mills, Ontario, a franchisor of specialty retail outlets.

Founded in 1959, Japan Camera has been franchising since 1981. A typical Japan Camera franchisee operates a retail photography store devoted to camera and film sales supplemented by one-hour photoprocessing service. Of the franchisor's 150 outlets currently operating, all except 25 are franchise units.

Japan Camera Centre 1 Hour Photo, 150 Lesmill Rd., Don Mills, Ont., Canada M3B 2T5. Telephone: (416) 445-1481

Jazzercise Headquartered in Carlsbad, California, a franchisor of physical-fitness dance studios.

Founded in 1976 by a former jazz dance instructor, Judi Shepard Missett, Jazzercise has been franchising since 1978. The company began in 1972 as a one-woman operation, offering jazz dance instruction at the San Diego YMCA and the Oceanside Parks recreation center. Additional classes were added two years later, for the Carlsbad, California Parks and Recreation Department. Missett conceived the name Jazzercise as the title of a book, *Jazzercise: A Fun Way to Fitness*, published in 1978 by Bantam Books.

In 1977, Missett trained eleven Jazzercise instructors, who were subsequently dispersed to other parts of the country. Expansion began in earnest in 1979, when an international Jazzercise elebration in Medina, Ohio drew a crowd of 1,400 enthusiasts. That same year, Jazzercise went international with classes in Europe, Brazil, and Japan.

By 1981, the number of certified Jazzercise instructors had reached 1,200, and the number of students topped 150,000. Jazzercise record albums, videocassettes, and a nationally syndicated newspaper column penned by Missett further sparked expansion. The company designed and began licensing its own athletic footwear in 1984, and introduced a full line of workout apparel three years later.

The company is currently organized into four divisions — Corporate Operations, Franchise Operations, Marketing, and Finance. The number of Jazzercise franchises worldwide presently exceeds 3,750.

A typical Jazzercise franchisee operates a personal fitness center employing a standardized system of aerobic dance instruction and supervision. Instructors lead clients through predesigned Jazzercise routines to the accompaniment of upbeat dance tunes on records or tapes. All of the 3,800 Jazzercise outlets currently operating are franchise units.

Jazzercise, 2808 Roosevelt St., Carlsbad, CA 92008. Telephone: (619) 434-2101; (800) FIT-IS-IT See Missett, Judi Sheppard.

Jerry's Subs Pizza Headquartered in Gaithersburg, Maryland, a franchisor of fast-food outlets.

Founded in 1954, Jerry's has been franchising since 1979. A typical Jerry's franchisee operates a fast-food operation with a limited menu featuring Eastern submarine-style sandwiches, hot pizza, fresh salads, and beverage service. Of the franchisor's 60 outlets currently operating, all except three are franchise units.

Jerry's Subs Pizza, 15942 Shady Grove Rd., Gaithersburg, MD 20877. Telephone: (301) 921-8777

Jiffy Lube Headquartered in Baltimore, Maryland, a franchisor of automobile service outlets.

Founded in 1972, Jiffy Lube has been franchising since the following year. A typical Jiffy Lube franchisee operates a quick oil-change and lubrication service. Of the franchisor's 920 outlets currently operating, 810 are franchise units.

Jiffy Lube, P.O. Box 17223, Baltimore, MD 21203. Telephone: (301) 298-8200

John Casablanca Modeling and Career Centers Headquartered in New York City, a franchisor of adult vocational schools.

Founded in 1979, John Casablanca has been franchising since 1980. A typical John Casablanca franchisee operates a vocational center specializing in modeling careers and utilizing the franchisor's proprietary curricula and teaching aids. Of the franchisor's 81 outlets currently operating, none are company-owned.

John Casablanca Modeling and Career Centers, 111 E. 22nd St., 4th Floor, New York, NY 10010. Telephone: (212) 420-0655

John Robert Powers Headquartered in Boston, Massachusetts, a franchisor of adult vocational schools. Founded in 1923, JRP has been franchising since 1950.

A typical JRP franchisee operates a private career preparation school conducting curricula in modeling, self-improvement, and finishing. Of the franchisor's 62 outlets currently operating, all except two are franchise units.

John Robert Powers, 9 Newbury St., Boston, MA 02116. Telephone: (617) 267-8781

Johnson, Howard Dearing Patent medicine salesman, restaurateur, hotelier, and franchisor of Howard Johnson lodging establishments and restaurants.

Johnson was an undistinguished patent medicine salesman in 1925, when he borrowed 500 dollars from a friend to swing the purchase of a small retail store in Quincy, Massachusetts. The primary feature of patent medicine stores in the 1920s was a soda fountain for mixing "medicinal" tonics and flavored syrups with carbonated water. In the wake of Prohibition, America was on a patent-medicine binge, consuming stimulant-laced tonic drinks as fast as they could be supplied. Howard Johnson's soda fountain also served soft drinks concocted from flavored syrups, but his real love was ice cream. His store sold three flavors — vanilla, chocolate, and strawberry.

Experimenting with a hand-cranked freezer in the basement of the store, Johnson came up with his own line of ice cream which, within years, made his soda fountain the most popular eatery in town. Adding hamburgers, hot dogs, and sandwiches to the menu, he converted the drugstore into the world's first Howard Johnson's restaurant. In 1929, he opened another outlet with a diversified menu. But with the Great Depression, his plans for bold expansion in the food-service trade began to dim.

In 1935, Johnson convinced the owner of a restaurant in nearby Cape Cod to use the Howard Johnson name in return for a fee and an agreement to buy food and supplies from Johnson. The franchising concept worked for both entrepreneurs. Early "HoJo" outlets specialized in ice cream and sandwiches and bore cartoon interpretations of Simple Simon and his Pie Man on roadside signs. Johnson had franchised 400 restaurants in 1954 when he expanded entered the lodging trade, franchising his first motor lodge in Savannah Georgia.

In 1959, Johnson handed over the reins of his small business empire to his son, Howard Brennan Johnson, who oversaw the chain's operations until 1980, when the company was sold to a British conglomerate, Imperial Group plc. The Johnson family's company-owned restaurants are currently operated by Marriott Corp., under the Big Boy name. The Howard Johnson lodging chain is franchised by Prime Motor Inns, Inc. of Fairfield, New Jersey. See Howard Johnson Company.

Jreck Subs Headquartered in Watertown, New York, a franchisor of fast-food outlets.

Founded in 1969, Jreck Subs has been franchising since 1974. A typical Jreck Subs franchisee operates a fast-food stand devoted to submarine-style sandwiches and beverage service. The chain consists of 41 outlets, all of which are franchise units.

Jreck Subs, P.O. Box 6, Watertown, NY 13601. Telephone: (315) 782-0760

Just Pants Headquartered in Elk Grove Village, Illinois, a franchisor of retail apparel outlets.

Founded in 1969, Just Pants has been franchising since its inception. A typical JP franchisee operates a specialty clothing store devoted to casual trousers, slacks, tops, and sportswear. The outlet is distinguished by a focus on youthful customers. All of the 85 Just Pants outlets currently open and operating are franchise units.

Just Pants, 1030 Bonaventure Dr., Elk Grove Village, IL 60007. Telephone: (312) 894-7500

Kale's Collision
to
Kwik Kopy

Kale's Collision Headquartered in Livonia, Michigan, a franchisor of automotobile refinishing outlets.
Founded in 1977, KC has been franchising since 1983. A typical KC franchisee operates an auto body repairing and painting shop. Kale's opeates 23 franchise units plus one company-owned outlet.
Kale's Collision, 11725 Merriman Rd., Livonia, MI 48150.

Kampgrounds of America Headquartered in Billings, Montana, a franchisor of recreational camping facilities.
Founded in 1961, KOA has been franchising since the following year. A typical KOA franchisee operates a fully developed, commercial campground catering to vacationing families. Of the franchisor's 640 outlets currently operating, all except 16 are franchise units.
KOA, Inc., 550 N. 31st St., Billings, MT 59114. Telephone: (406) 248-7444

Kansas, Franchise Regulations To date, the Kansas legislature has not adopted any generally applicable franchise investment law. However, petroleum, farm machinery, and beer retailers are protected by separate laws.
Kansas law does not require franchisors to register or file disclosures with any state regulatory body. In the absence of such a requirement, the federal Franchise Rule applies, requiring franchisors to furnish a disclosure document prescribed by the Federal Trade Commission to prospective franchisees ten business days before a franchise sale is made.
See Franchise Rule.

Kentucky, Franchise Regulations The Kentucky legislature has not adopted any generally applicable franchise investment law. However, the rights of automobile dealers and liquor store owners under franchise agreements are protected under spearate laws.
Kentucky law does not require franchisors to register or file disclosures with any state regulatory body. In the absence of such a requirement, the federal Franchise Rule applies, requiring franchisors to furnish a disclosure document prescribed by the Federal Trade Commission to prospective franchisees ten business days before a franchise sale is made.

The Motor Vehicles law regulates the relationship between automobile wholesalers and dealers. Beer retailers receive protection from the Malt Beverages law.

See Franchise Rule.

Kentucky Fried Chicken Headquartered in Louisville, Kentucky, a franchisor of fast food outlets.

In 1952, Harlan Sanders, a motel/restaurant operator from Corbin, Kentucky, served his friend Pete Harmon a special fried chicken dinner prepared with 11 "secret" herbs and spices. Harmon owned a hamburger restaurant in Salt Lake City. Within days after obtaining Sander's recipe, "Kentucky Fried Chicken" appeared on his menu. Harmon's restaurant revenues tripled, with most of the new sales attributable to fried chicken orders.

Harmon opened a second restaurant in 1952, with "the Kentucky Colonel," Harlan Sanders, in attendance. With Harmon's encouragement, Sanders launched a national franchising effort for his system of fried chicken preparation. Franchisees received the colonel's "secret recipe" and paid the franchisor five cents for every chicken they prepared and sold.

Harmon and another hamburger operator named Jim Collins, became the first KFC franchisees. Today, both entrepreneurs oversee small business empires with more than 250 outlets.

A typical KFC franchisee operates a convenience reurant specializing in southern fried chicken. Once known as Colonel Sanders, KFC was acquired by Pepsico in 1981. It is estimated that of the franchisor's 7,700 outlets currently operating, almost 90 percent are franchise units.

KFC Corporation, 1441 Gardiner Ln., Louisville, KY 40218. Telephone: (502) 456-8300

Kernels Headquartered in Toronto, Ontario, a franchisor of specialty food outlets.

Founded in 1983, Kernels has been franchising since the following year. A typical Kernels franchisee operates a retail shop devoted entirely to popcorn, popcorn accessories, and related products. Less than half of the 40 outlets currently operating are franchise units.

Kernels, 40 Eglinton Ave. East, Ste. 250, Toronto, Ont.,Canada M4P 3A2. Telephone: (416) 487-4194

Kiddie Kobbler Headquartered in Nepean, Ontario, a franchisor of retail apparel outlets.

Founded in 1951, KK has been franchising since its inception. A typical KK franchisee operates a clothing store specializing in footwear, accessories, and selected fashion items for children. Of the franchisor's 60 outlets currently operating, all except two are franchise units.

Kiddie Kobbler, 68 Robertson Rd., No. 106, Nepean, Ont., Canada K2H 8P5. Telephone: (613) 820-0505

King Bear Headquartered in Merrick, New York, a franchisor of automotive parts and repair outlets.

Founded in 1973, King Bear has been franchising since the following year. A typical King Bear franchisee operates an auto repair business combined with an auto parts supply house. Of the franchisor's 64 outlets currently operating, all are franchise units.

King Bear Auto Service Centers, 1390 Jerusalem Ave., Merrick, NY 11566. Telephone: (516) 483-3500

Kits Cameras Headquartered in Kent, Washington, a franchisor of specialty retail outlets.

Founded in 1975, Kits has been franchising since its inception. A typical Kits franchisee operates a retail store devoted to photographic equipment and supplies, including cameras, lenses, accessories, projectors, film, and photoprocessing service. Of the franchisor's 75 outlets currently operating, 33 are franchise units.

Kits Cameras, 6051 S. 194th St., Kent, WA 98032. Telephone: (206) 872-3688

Koenig Corp. Headquartered in Milford, Connecticut, a franchisor of specialty retail outlets.

Founded in 1948, Koenig has been franchising since 1971. Elliott Koenig traces his company's origins to a small sign shop operated by his parents in 1933. Koenig took over the family business in 1948 and expanded into retail "Art Carts" marketing art supplies to freelance artists. By the 1970s, he had acquired a sizable chain of retail art supply houses and in 1971 began franchising Koenig Art Emporiums.

A typical Koenig franchisee operates a retail art supplies store with a diverse inventory of artist's tools, lamps, desks, drawing boards, equipment, and supplies. Two thirds of the 100 Koenig outlets currently in business are franchise outlets.

Koenig Corp., 1777 Boston Post Rd., Milford, CT 06460. Telephone: (203) 877-4541

Kroc, Ray Entrepreneur, fast food chain operator, and professional baseball team owner.

A high school dropout who trained to play the piano professionally, Kroc was arguably the most famous American figure in franchising, as the prime mover behind the phenomenally successful McDonald's hamburger chain.

At 15, the young Kroc reputedly fibbed about his age to drive an ambulance in Europe during World War I. When the war ended, he returned home to a day job as a paper up salesman, playing the piano at night. In 1927, he joined Lily Cup Company as a commercial sales representative.

While calling on an account in the 1930s, Kroc had the opportunity to see an electric malted milk machine that could mix five malts at once. Fascinated, he bought the rights to market the machine to other soda fountain operators. For 15 years, with little competition, the Multimixer provided Kroc with an ample income. In 1954, a small hamburger stand outside San Berandino, California placed an order for

ten of Kroc's machines, immediately piquing the salesman's curiosity. When he drove out from Chicago to deliver the mixers in person, he found the McDonald brothers, Mac and Dick, systematically turning out hamburgers with assembly-line efficiency.

The idea struck Kroc that, if he could convince the boys to franchise their fast food stand, he could sell two or three malted milk machines to every new restaurant. The first franchised McDonald's drive-through restaurant opened in 1955 in Des Plaines, Illinois. Within four years, Kroc had sold a hundred franchises, drawing no income for himself except sales of his malted milk machine.

The McDonald boys did not share Kroc's enthusiasm for expansion and, in 1961, he bought out their interest in the franchise organization. In the decade that followed, McDonald's Corporation burgeoned into the largest fast food organization in the world, with 3,000 outlets by 1972. With an enormous advertising pool funded by franchisees, lavish television and radio campaigns made the McDonald's trademark the most recognizable in franchising.

In 1981, Kroc purchased the San Diego Padres professional baseball franchise, which his wife continued to manage after his death from a brain lesion in 1984.

Kwik Kopy Headquartered in Cypress, Texas, a franchisor of instant printing shops.

Founded in 1967, Kwik Kopy has been franchising since its inception. A typical Kwik Kopy franchisee operates a retail quick printing and duplication service. All except two of the franchisor's 1,000 outlets are franchise units.

Kwik Kopy, P. O. Box 777, Cypress, YX 77429. Telephone: (713) 373-3535

Langenwalter
to
Louisiana

Langenwalter Dye Concept Headquartered in Anaheim, California, a franchisor of interior maintenance services.

Founded in 1972, Langenwalter has been franchising since 1981. A typical Langenwalter franchisee operates a mobile home-maintenance business devoted to carpet cleaning, dyeing, and restoration, utilizing the franchisor's dyes and equipment. The chain is comprised of 130 units, all of which are owned by independent franchisees.

Langenwalter Dye Concept, 4410 E. LaPalma, Anaheim, CA 92807. Telephone: (714) 526-7610

Larry's Olde Fashioned Ice Cream Parlors Headquartered in Tampa, Florida, a franchisor of specialty fast-food outlets.

Founded in 1981, Larry's has been franchising since the following year. A typical Larry's franchisee operates a retail ice cream parlor based on the franchisor's standardized site design and ice cream. Of the franchisor's 52 outlets currently operating, all except three are franchise units.

Larry's Old Fashioned Ice Cream Parlors, 14550 McCormick Dr., Tampa, FL 33626.

Lawn Doctor Headquartered in Matawan, New Jersey, a franchisor of lawn care services.

Founded in 1967, Lawn Doctor has been franchising since 1970. A typical Lawn Doctor franchisee operates a lawn installation and planning service, including seeding, soil nutrition, irrigation, and weed and pest control. The franchisor's patented "Turf Tamer," a machine which facilitates the application and spray of chemicals, is an integral tool of the franchisee's business. Of the franchisor's 290 outlets currently operating, all except one are franchise units.

Lawn Doctor, 142 Hwy. 34, Matawan, NJ 07747. Telephone: (800) 631-5660

Lazer Maze Headquartered in Newbury Park, California, a franchisor of participatory amusement attractions.

Founded in 1986, Lazer Maze has been franchising since its inception. A typical Lazer Maze franchisee operates an interactive amusement game with a space-age motif in which participants compete using laser "weapons". The chain has eight franchise outlets plus a single company-owned unit.

Lazer Maze, 3809 Old Conejo Rd., Newbury Park, CA 91320.

Le Peep Restaurants Headquartered in Denver, Colorado, a franchisor of food service outlets.

Founded in 1981, Le Peep has been franchising since 1983. A typical Le Peep franchisee operates a family-style restaurant featuring a diverse breakfast, lunch, and dinner menu. Of the franchisor's 60 outlets currently operating, about half are franchise units.

Le Peep Restaurants, Inc., 1777 S. Harrison St., Ste. 802, Denver, CO 80210. Telephone: (303) 691-3770

Lederer, Jules Entrepreneur and franchisor of car rental agencies. The prime mover behind Budget Rent A Car, Lederer transformed a small time used car rental lot in Los Angeles into the world's most prolific rent-a-car chain.

The first Budget rental office was opened in 1958 by Lederer's cousin, who sought out the latter's business and marketing advice. Lederer liked what he saw and invested the money to purchase a hundred new cars for his cousin's rental fleet. Budget's strategy was to rent new automobiles at about half the rates charged by Hertz and Avis, the industry kingpins. The tact paid off and, in 1960, an associate, Kemmons Wilson, founder of the Holiday Inn lodging chain, talked Lederer into franchising.

Over the next two years, Budget surged from two franchises in Chicago and Hawaii to 50 outlets nationwide. Modeling his franchise system after Warren Avis' chain, Lederer opened his 100th rental office in 1964. Four years later, Budget was acquired by the Transamerica conglomerate.

Currently the fourth largest rent-a-car chain in dollar sales, Budget has more outlets worldwide than any of its competitors. The company's orange and black logo can be seen from the jungles of Bora Bora to the streets of Paris. Budget is presently owned by a large investment bank. The company has an aggressive corporate account program and a cooperative business arrangement with Sears Roebuck, the nation's largest retailer. *Consumer Reports* rated Budget second in the car rental industry in overall customer satisfaction, in a dead heat with American International Hertz, and Avis.

Lee Myles Headquartered in Maywood, New Jersey, a franchisor of automobile transmission service outlets.

Founded in 1947, Lee Myles has been franchising since 1964. A typical Lee Myles franchisee operates a retail auto transmission service shop, performing both major repair work and minor servicing on automatic transmissions for all makes and models of passenger cars. The Lee Myles chain consists of 104 outlets, all of which are franchise units.

Lee Myles Transmissions, 25 E. Spring Valley Ave., Maywood, NJ 07607. Telephone: (201) 843-3200

Lee's Famous Recipe Country Chicken Headquartered in Nashville, Tennesee, a franchisor of fast-food outlets.

Founded in 1966, Lee's has been franchising since 1968. A typical Lee's franchisee operates fast-food restaurant devoted to southern-style fried chicken prepared in accordance with the franchisor's specifications. Of the franchisor's 280 outlets currently operating, 235 are franchise units.

Lee's Famous Recipe Country Chicken, 1727 Elm Hill Park, Nashville, TN 37210.

Lemon Tree, The Headquartered in Levittown, New York, a franchisor of haircutting salons.

Founded in 1976, TLT has been franchising since its inception. A typical TLT franchisee operates a retail hair care salon with a family orientation. Of the franchisor's 50 outlets currently operating, all are franchise units.

The Lemon Tree, 3301 Hempstead Turnpike, Levittown, NY 11756. Telephone: (516) 735-2828

Licenses and Permits Before a franchise or any other tupe of business may commence operation, the owner must obtain the licenses, permits, and certificates required by local municipal, county, state, and federal laws and ordinances.

The specific permits required for a particular franchise may vary from one area to another. Franchisees should consult city, county, and state regulatory agencies for a complete list of the licenses and application procedures which apply in their localities.

The following list includes typical licenses and permits commonly required for any type of franchise outlet.

Federal Employment Identification Number

This taxpayer's number is required of all employers. To request a federal employment identification number, franchisees may obtain Form SS-40 from a local office of the Internal Revenue Service.

Business License

Many cities and counties require a special license for the privilege of doing business. Commonly, all revenues of the business will be taxed by the applicable government agency. Franchisees should contact city and country clerks to apply for the business license and obtain the appropriate reporting forms.

Wholesale License

Franchisees who are resellers of goods purchased from wholesale sources may be required to obtain a license for this purpose from the city, county, or state. The "resale number" or "wholesale certificate" entitles the franchisee to obtain products for resale, usually at wholesale prices, without paying state or country sales tax. The resale number must usually be provided to vendors for their permanent wholesale customer records.

Zoning Permits

In many communities, a business license will be granted only if the outlet location is approved by zoning authorities. A special use permit may be required for a retail business in certain areas, particularly residential areas. To obtain a special use permit for the outlet, a franchisee may be required to make an appearance at a zoning hearing or zoning commission meeting, to describe the proposed business and present reasons for locating it in the zoned area. Franchisors normally assist their franchisees in fulfilling local zoning requirements.

Fire, Safety, and Health Permits

Many cities and counties require a fire and safety inspection of the outlet prior to granting of a business permit. A health inspection may also be required.

The local business regulatory agency should be consulted for information and requirements on fire, safety, and health permits.

Fictitious Name Statement (dba)

In most states, business owners are required to obtain a special permit to use a trade name in the conduct of a business. The owner is generally be required to pay a fee, and to publish a notice of his or her intention to use the trade name.

Franchisees must normally secure their franchisor's approval before assuming a trade name.

Liederman, David Bakery operator and franchisor of retail cookie outlets. Founder of David's Cookies, Liederman is generally acknowledged as the "Cookie King" in the specialized bakery goods segment of the food-service franchise trade.

Liederman's dual interests, cooking and law, led him to enroll simultaneously in cooking school and law college. After graduating in 1975, he set out for central France, where he caught on as a cook in the three-star restaurant of Jean and Pierre Troisgrois. Discouraged by a poor outlook for advancement, he returned to New York City to practice law and write a Nouvelle Cuisine cookbook. Chasing a dream of financial independence, Liederman started a private sauce manufacturing business and opened a restaurant, the Manhattan Market.

He opened his first cookie shop in 1979, to the rave reviews of New York food critics. By 1983, he had 84 outlets in 18 states. His product and franchise, both aptly named David's Cookies, benefited from his French-chef training and the fact that he uses only genuine Swiss chocolate from Lindt & Sprungli in Switzerland.

Today, approximately 200 David's Cookies franchise outlets generate a reported $20 million in annual sales. The stores currently feature private label ice cream, yoghurt, sandwiches and beverages, as well as cookies.

Liederman's Manhattan Market restaurant is currently managed by his wife.

Lien Chemical Company Headquartered in Elmhurst, Illinois, a franchisor of building maintenance services.

Founded in 1929, Lien Chemical has been franchising since 1960. A typical Lien Chemical franchisee operates a maintenance service specializing restroom "risk management". Of the franchisor's 46 outlets currently operating, 36 are franchise units.

Lien Chemical Co., 501 W. Lake St., Elmhurst, IL 60126. Telephone: (312) 832-6500

Li'l Peach Food Stores Headquartered in Westford, Massachusetts, a franchisor of retail convenience stores.

Founded in 1971, Li'l Peach has been franchising since 1974. A typical Li'l Peach franchisee operates a convenience food store stocking groceries, dairy products, and self-service fast food. Of the franchisor's 65 outlets currently operating, all except four are franchise units.

Li'l Peach Food Stores, 10 Brookside Rd., Westford, MA 01886.

Little Caesar's Pizza Headquartered in Farmington Hills, Michigan, a franchisor of fast-food outlets.

Founded in 1959, Little Caesar's has been franchising since 1961. A typical Little Caesar's franchisee operates a food-service business devoted to pizza prepared with a variety of toppings. Of the franchisor's estimated 2,000 outlets currently operating, about 1,500 are franchise units.

Little Caesar's Pizza, 24120 Haggerty Rd., Farmington Hills, MI 48024. Telephone: (313) 478-6200

Little King Restaurant Corp. Headquartered in Omaha, Nebraska, a franchisor of fast-food outlets.

Founded in 1968, Little King has been franchising since 1976. A typical Little King franchisee operates a fast)food operation with a limited menu featuring freshly baked pizza, submarine- and delicatessen-style sandwiches, bakery goods, andbeverage service. The outlet also features a 300-calorie "light" menu for the diet conscious. Of the franchisor's 76 outlets currently operating, 36 are franchise units.

Little King Restaurant Corp., 11811 "I" St., Omaha, NE 68137. Telephone: (800) 228-2148

Little Professor Book Centers Headquartered in Ann Arbor, Michigan, a franchisor of retail book outlets.

Founded in 1965, Little Professor has been franchising since 1969. A typical Little Professor franchisee operates a retail book store utilizing the franchisor's inventory, purchasing, and merchandizing systems. The average inventory consists of 2,000 hardcover titles, 5,000 paperback, and 200 magazine titles. Magazine sales account for approximately 18 percent of the outlet's revenues. All but one of the 120 Little Professor outlets currently in business are franchise units.

Little Professor Book Centers, 110 N. 4th Ave., Ann Arbor, MI 48104. Telephone: (313) 994-1212

Living Lighting Headquartered in Toronto, Ontario, a franchisor of specialty furnishings outlets.

Founded in 1968, Living Lighting has been franchising since its inception. A typical LL franchisee operates a retail store specializing in lamps, fixtures, and decorative lighting products. Of the 70 Living Lighting outlets currently operating, all except six are franchise units.

Living Lighting, 39 Orfus Rd. Ste. C, Toronot, Ont., Canada M6A 1L7. Telephone: (416) 789-3251

Long John Silver's Seafood Shoppes Headquartered in Lexington, Kentucky, a franchisor of fast-food outlets.

Founded in 1969, LJS has been franchising since the following year. A typical LJS franchisee operates a fast-food restaurant modeled after an Old English fish and chips shop with a diverse offering of marine regale. The menu features such selections as breaded fish fillets, fried shrimp, clams, oysters, and scallops, cooked with the aid of the franchisor's standardized food-preparation system utilizing computers for timing and inventory control.

LJS is distinguished for its franchisee development programs. The company's management training curriculum received accreditation from the American Council on Education. Of the franchisor's estimated 1,500 outlets currently operating, about one third are franchise units.

Long John Silver's Inc., P.O. Box 11988, Lexington, KY 40579. Telephone: (606) 268-5211

London Fish & Chips Headquartered in South San Francisco, California, a franchisor of fast-food outlets.

Founded in 1967, London Fish & Chips has been franchising since its inception. A typical London

Fish & Chips franchisee operates a fast-food restaurant featuring a limited menu of seafood items served with french fried potatoes. Of the franchisor's 45 outlets currently operating, all are franchise units.

London Fish & Chips, 306 S. Maple Ave., South San Francisco, CA 94080. Telephone: (415) 873-1300

Louisiana, Franchise Regulations The Louisiana legislature has not adopted any generally applicable franchise investment law. However, dealers in the motor vehicle and petroleum industries are protected by separate laws.

Louisiana law does not require franchisors to register or file disclosures with any state regulatory body. In the absence of such a requirement, the federal Franchise Rule applies, requiring franchisors to furnish a disclosure document prescribed by the Federal Trade Commission to prospective franchisees ten business days before a franchise sale is made. *(See Franchise Rule.)*

**MAACO
to
Mundus**

MAACO Headquartered in King of Prussia, Pennsylvania, a franchisor of automobile refinishing outlets.

Founded in 1972, Maaco has been franchising since the following year. The trade name is derived from the initials of its founder, Anthony A. Martino, who also started the AAMCO organization. A typical franchisee operates an auto body repair and painting business, based on a standardized production system and equipment package. All of the 440 Maaco outlets nationwide are operated by franchisees.

Maaco Auto Painting and Bodyworks, 381 Brooks Rd., King of Prussia, PA 19406. Telephone: (800) 523-1180

M.G.M Liquor Warehouse Headquartered in St. Paul, Minnesota, a franchisor of retail liquor, wine, and beer outlets.

Founded in 1971, M.G.M. has been franchising since 1979. A typical M.G.M. franchisee operates a discount liquor supermarket based on the franchisor's site-selection, merchandising, and purchasing systems. Of the franchisor's 30 outlets currently operating, all except four are franchise units.

M.G.M. Liquor Warehouse, 1124 Carpenteur Ave. West, St. Paul, MN 55113. Telephone: (912) 487-1006

Mad Hatter Mufflers Headquartered in St. Petersburg, Florida, a franchisor of muffler and brake outlets.

Founded in 1974, Mad Hatter has been franchising since 1986. A typical Mad Hatter franchisee operates an automotive repair shop focusing on exhaust systems, brakes, suspension systems, and wheel alignment service. Of the franchisor's 42 outlets currently operating, all except one are franchise units.

Mad Hatter Mufflers, 3493 Tyrone Blvd. N, St. Petersburg, FL 33710.

Magicuts Headquartered in Scarborough, Ontario, a franchisor of hair care salons.

Founded in 1980, Magicuts has been franchising since 1982, mostly in Canada. A typical Magicuts franchisee operates a retail hair cutting and styling business. Of the franchisor's 145 outlets currently operating, all except seven are franchise units.

Magicuts, 2105 Midland Ave., Ont., Canada M1P 3E3. Telephone: (416) 299-9099

Maid Brigade USA Headquartered in Liburn, Georgia, a franchisor of residential cleaning services.

Founded in 1978, Maid Brigade has been franchising since the following year. A typical Maid Brigade franchisee operates a maid service for residences. Of the franchisor's 165 outlets currently operating, all but two are franchise units.

Maid Brigade USA, P.O. Box 1901, Liburn, GA 30226

Maids, The Headquartered in Omaha, Nebraska, a franchisor of interior maintenance services.

Founded in 1979, TMI has been franchising since 1981. A typical TMI franchisee operates a full-service housecleaning business providing periodic cleaning in addition to special projects. Of the 165 TMI outlets currently operating in the U.S. and Canada, none are company owned.

The Maids, 4820 Dodge St., Omaha, NE 68132. Telephone: (800) THE-MAID

Mail Boxes Etc. USA Headquartered in San Diego, California, a franchisor of business services outlets.

Founded in 1980, Mail Boxes Etc. has been franchising since its inception. A typical Mail Boxes Etc. franchisee operates a postal receiving center supplemented by personal business services such as telephone answering, document copying, and light secretrarial services. Of the franchisor's 600 outlets currently operating, all except two are franchise units.

Mail Boxes, Etc. USA, 5555 Oberlin Dr., San Diego, CA 92121. Telephone: (619) 452-1553

Maine, Franchise Regulations The Maine legislature has not adopted any generally applicable franchise investment law. However, the franchise rights of automobile dealers and beer retailers are protected by separate laws.

Maine law does not require franchisors to register or file disclosures with any state regulatory body. In the absence of such a requirement, the federal Franchise Rule applies, requiring franchisors to furnish a disclosure document prescribed by the Federal Trade Commission to prospective franchisees ten business days before a franchise sale is made. (See Franchise Rule.)

Business opportunity ventures are regulated by the Department of Business Regulations. To report possible fraudulent or deceptive practices, contact: Department of Business Regulations, Special Opportunities Section, State House Station 35, Augustus, ME 04330. Telephone: (207) 289-3676.

Major Video Headquartered in Las Vegas, Nevada, a franchisor of specialty retail outlets.

Founded in 1984, Major Video has been franchising since since the following year. A typical Major Video franchisee operates a retail store devoted to the rental and sale of videocassette movies, VCRs, and video accessories. Of the chain's 150 outlets currently in business, all except 30 are franchise units.

Major Video, 955 Corier Dr., Las Vegas, NV 89119

Management Recruiters Headquartered in Cleveland, Ohio, a franchisor of executive recruitment agencies.

Founded in 1957, MRI has been franchising since 1965. A typical MRI franchisee operates an executive search business catering to middle-management job candidates, as well as employers with executive openings. The parent company, MRI, operates three other subsidiaries specializing in different fields: Sales Consultants, Office Mates Five, and CompuSearch. All of the 330 Management Recruiters outlets currently operating are franchise units.

Management Recruiters, 1127 Euclid Ave., Cleveland, OH 44115. Telephone: (216) 696-1122

Marco's Pizza Headquartered in Toledo, Ohio, a franchisor of fast-food outlets.

Founded in 1978, Marco's has been franchising since the following year. A typical Marco's franchisee operates a fast-food business devoted to pizza, specialty sandwiches, salads, and beverage service. Of the franchisor's 38 outlets currently operating, 22 are franchise units.

Marco's Pizza, 5254 Monroe St., Toledo, OH 43623. Telephone: (419) 885-4844

Marcoin Business Services Headquartered in Seattle, Washington, a franchisor of accounting support services.

Founded in 1952, Marcoin has been franchising since its inception. The company started out by providing specialized accounting services to the petroleum industry. A typical Marcoin franchisee operates a bookkeeping/accounting service catering to small-to-medium-size businesses. In addition, the outlet may offer computer hardware and software services, tax preparation, and general business and financial counseling. Of the franchisor's 130 outlets currently operating, all except 15 are franchise units.

Marcoin Business Services, 2001 Sixth Ave., Ste. 2501, Seattle, WA 98121

Marie Callender Pie Shops Headquartered in Orange, California, a franchisor of food service outlets.

Founded in 1964, Marie Callender has been franchising since the following year. A typical Marie Callender franchisee operates a family-style restaurant modeled after an Old World pie shop and featuring a diverse breakfast, lunch, and dinner menu. A retail pie and pastry counter greets customers at the entrance. Of the franchisor's 160 outlets currently operating, less than half are franchise units.

Marie Callender Pie Shops, 1100 Town & Country Rd., Ste. 1300, Orange, CA 92668

Marriott, J. Willard Restaurateur, hotelier, and founder of Marriott Corporation, a franchisor of restaurants.

Marriott got his start as a franchisee of A&W Restaurants in Washington, DC. In 1928, Marriott converted his regional chain of root beer stands into Hot Shoppe's, specializing in barbeque beef sandwiches. The outlets grew into a successful chain of eateries that became the foundation of the $5.3 billion Marriott Corp. empire.

The world's second largest hotel chain, Marriott Corp. today franchises both Roy Rogers restaurants and Bob's Big Boy outlets. In addition, the company operates a system of company-owned restaurants acquired from Howard Johnson Company in 1982. Shortly after the acquisition, Marriott sold off the Howard Johnson lodging chain to Prime Motor Inns.

Maryland, Franchise Regulations Franchisors operating in the state of Maryland are governed by the Franchise Registration and Disclosure law, which requires registration and disclosure of pertinent information about the franchisor, franchise business, and franchise agreement. Other state laws protect the rights of automobile dealers and beer retailers.

Before offering or selling a franchise in the state, a franchisor must first prepare a disclosure document prescribed by the statute, then file the information, along with the franchise agreement, financial statements, and related documents, with the Attorney General's Office. The Attorney General must approve the registration before the franchisor may proceed to offer or sell franchises.

In addition to a disclosure document, franchisors are also required to submit the following items:

1. Application for registration of the franchise offering;
2. Salesman disclosure form;
3. Consent to service of process;
4. Auditor's consent to use of audited financial statements;
5. Cross-reference sheet showing the location in the franchise agreement of the key items in the disclosure document.

The *Uniform Franchise Offering Circular* (UFOC), devised by a consortium of midwestern securities commissioners as a uniform method of complying with state franchise investment laws, fulfills the disclosure requirements of the Maryland law. There are minor variations and differences in language required by the Maryland statute, including a different cover page. *(See Uniform Franchise Offering Circular.)*

The disclosure document or UFOC must be furnished to a prospective franchisee at least ten business days before a franchise sale is made.

For information about state franchise laws, regulations, and filing requirements, or to report possible violations, contact: Office of the Attorney General, Securities Division, 26 S. Calvert St., Baltimore, MD 21202. Telephone: (301) 659-4141.

Massachusetts, Franchise Regulations To date, the Massachusetts legislature has not adopted any generally applicable franchise investment law. However, the rights of automobile retailers and beer and wine dealers are protected under separate laws.

Massachusetts law does not require franchisors to register or file disclosures with any state regulatory body. In the absence of such a requirement, the federal Franchise Rule applies, requiring franchisors to furnish a disclosure document prescribed by the Federal Trade Commission to prospective franchisees ten business days before a franchise sale is made.

See Franchise Rule.

Master Host Inns Headquartered in Atlanta, Georgia, a franchisor of lodging outlets.

Founded in 1972, Master Host has been franchising since its inception. The parent company, Hospitality International, also licenses franchisees under the trade names Red Carpet Inns and Scottish Inns. A typical Master Host franchisee operates a full*service resort and convention facility based on the franchisor's specifications for outlet design, size, construction, and decor. Each hotel features recreational and banquet facilities, meeting rooms, and a food and beverage operation.

All of the franchisor's 250 Master Host Inn, Scottish Inn, and Red Carpet Inn outlets all are franchise units.

Hospitality International, 1152 Spring St., Ste. A, Atlanta, GA 30309. Telephone: (800) 251-1962

Mazzio's Pizza Headquartered in Tulsa, Oklahoma, a franchisor of fast-food outlets.

Founded in 1961, Mazzio's has been franchising since 1966. A typical Mazzio's franchisee operates a fast-food pizza restaurant with sit-down, take-out, and drive-up facilities. Of the franchisor's 210 outlets currently operating, 120 are franchise units.

Mazzio's Pizza, 4441 S. 72nd East, Tulsa, OK 74146. Telephone: (918) 663-8880

McDonald, Maurice and Richard Cofounders of McDonald's, the drive-in hamburger stand from which emerged the phenomenally successful restaurant chain bearing their name.

The McDonald brothers, Maurice ("Mac") and Richard ("Dick"), opened their first eatery in Pasadena, California in the late 1930s. A drive-in operation with three uniformed carhops who served customers in their automobiles, the tiny outlet sold not hamburgers, but hot dogs. In 1940, the brothers opened a second, more ambitious outlet in nearby San Bernadino, with twenty carhops and parking for 125 cars. Featuring beef and pork sandwiches and Arkansas-style hickory-smoked ribs, the new restaurant met with astounding success. By 1948, the brothers' wealth had exceeded their dreams. But the headaches of the barbeque business and of operating a congested drive-in facility left them with little time to enjoy their newfound riches.

Exasperated, the enterprising brothers closed the lucrative drive-in and three months later, reopened the restaurant as a streamlined hamburger stand designed for high volume and speedy service. The outlet's advertising symbol was a cartoon cook named Speedy. Almost overnight, the restaurant metamorphosed from a teenage hangout into a respectable eatery that catered to working class families.

The McDonald brothers called their new system of hamburger preparation the "Speedy Service System." By the mid 1950s, the San Bernadino outlet had become a virtual fast-food profit factory.

In 1952, the two brothers sold their first franchise to Neil Fox in Phoenix, Arizona. The cautious restaurant operators sold nine franchises before they began to have second thoughts about the wisdom of creating a multi-outlet restaurant chain. The idea of trekking across the country from one motel to another in search of restaurant managers did not appeal to either. Their hearts were not in franchising, and, predictably, the expansion effort foundered.

In 1954, the San Bernadino outlet was visited by a malted milk machine salesman named Ray Kroc, who was interested in selling franchises for the McDonald brothers' hamburger operation. Kroc formed McDonald's System, Inc. in 1955. In 1961, the McDonalds sold Kroc all their interests in the hamburger business for $2.7 million, enough to pay each brother $1 million after taxes.

McDonald's Founded in 1937, a franchisor of fast-food restaurants and the largest chain of specialty hamburger outlets in the world.

Two brothers, Richard and Maurice McDonald, opened the first McDonald's restaurant in Pasadena, California, as a carhop drive-in specializing in hot dogs. A second drive-in facility opened in San Bernadino in 1940. The new outlet was eventually converted into a hamburger stand, streamlined for high volume and fast sevrice. The new restaurant featured 1.6-ounce hamburgers at a price of fifteen cents and sported a neon sign depicting an animated chef named Speedy.

The new McDonald's concept, dubbed the "Speedy Service System," was based on assembly-line production and service. By the mid 1950s, the San Bernadino outlet had become an enormous success.

In 1952, the first McDonald's franchise was sold to a gasoline dealer named Neil Fox in Phoenix, Arizona. A local neon sign maker, George Dexter, drafted the design for the huge, yellow arches that would become the restaurant's symbol for the succeeding three decades. Fox paid a fee of $1,000 for his franchise.

Expansion began in earnest when Ray Kroc stepped into the picture. Impressed by the assembly-line efficiency of the San Bernadino outlet, Kroc negotiated the rights to sell licenses for the brothers' Speedy Service System. McDonald's System, Inc. was incorporated on March 2, 1955.

Surrounding himself with raw, hungry talent, Kroc guided the franchisor to national prominence.

Although his contract restricted him from altering the Speedy Service System, Kroc began to modify the McDonald's format on his own. As the chain proliferated, the relationship between Ray Kroc and the McDonald brothers began to cool. Kroc acquired all rights to the McDonald's system in 1961.

McDonald's stock first appeared on the New York Stock Exchange on April 15, 1965, at about seventeen times the company's earnings for the prior year. Within weeks, the price had soared from $22.50 to $49.00 a share, sealing the destinies of Ray Kroc and his associates as members of the wealthy elite.

In 1963, the "Speedy" chef logo was replaced by "Archie McDonald," to avoid confusion with "Speedy Alka Seltzer." In December of the same year, Willard Scott, who had previously played Bozo the Clown on television, appeared as another clown, Ronald McDonald, destined to be the hamburger chain's symbol for the next 25 years. In 1988, the company trotted out a new mascot, "McMan-in-the-Moon," in an attempt to appeal to more upscale, cosmopolitan consumers.

Despite numerous challenges by imitators, plaguerizers, and heavily financed competitors, McDonald's success in capturing the loyalty and purse strings of the fast-food consumer remains unparalleled. With 9,500 outlets, including 2,300 overseas, the McDonald's fast food chain is second in size only to Pepsico, which operates Kentucky Fried Chicken, Taco Bell, and Pizza Hut outlets.

McDonald's Corporation, McDonald's Plaza, Oak Brook, IL 60521. Telephone: (312) 575-6196.

See Kroc, Ray; McDonald, Maurice and Richard; McMan-in-the- Moon; and Ronald McDonald.

McMan-in-the-Moon The upscale, cosmopolitan advertising symbol of McDonald's Corporation, the world's largest franchisor of hamburger restaurants.

In August 1988, McDonald's Corporation took a calculated risk when it launched a national television campaign based on a locally produced commercial with a radically different tone than anything the company had previously tried. The commercial featured a tuxedoed, piano-playing character with a crescent-shaped moon for a head. Sporting sunglasses and sitting atop a two-story "Big Mac" hamburger sandwich before the backdrop of a nightlit metropolis, the offbeat "McMan-in-the-Moon" pounded out a McDonaldized version of the Three Penny Opera hit, "Mack the Knife". The original song was popularized by singer Bobby Darin in the late 1950s. The message was "Mac Tonight," an invitation to upscale urbanites to dine at McDonald's. The commercial was created by Davis, Johnson, Mogul & Colombatto, the agency for McDonald's Operators Association of Southern California, representing a departure from the company's traditional use of national advertising agencies. The McMan-in-the-Moon spot was also a deviation from the familiar "Ronald McDonald" motif, which featured the clown character who had served as the franchise chain's advertising symbol for the previous 25 years.

See McDonald's; Ronald McDonald; Kroc, Ray.

Medical Personnel Pool Headquartered in Ft. Lauderdale, Florida, a franchisor of personnel employment agencies.

Founded in 1965 as a division of Personnel Pool of America, Medical Personnel Pool has been franchising since 1968. A typical Medical Personnel Pool franchisee operates a temporary employment agency devoted to health-care personnel, with particular emphasis on home nursqng services. Of the franchisor's 26 outlets currently operating, 190 are franchise units.

Medical Personnel Pool, 303 S. 17th St., Ft. Lauderdale, FL 33316. Telephone: (800) 327-1396

Medicap Pharmacy Headquartered in Des Moines, Iowa, a franchisor of drug stores.

Founded in 1971, Medicap has been franchising since 1974. A typical Medicap franchisee operates a retail pharmacy. Of the franchisor's 70 outlets currently operating, all are franchise units.

Medicap Pharmacies, 10202 Douglas Ave., Des Moines, IA 50322. Telephone: (515) 276-5491

Medicine Shoppe International Headquartered in St. Louis, Missouri, a franchisor of retail drugstores.

Founded in 1970 as a retail vehicle for licensed pharmacists, Medicine Shoppe has been franchising since its inception. A typical Medicine Shoppe franchisee operates a retail drugstore merchandising over-the-counter medications and sundries in conjunction with a prescription pharmacy. The franchisor does not own any of the chain's 740 outlets.

Medicine Shoppe International, 1100 N. Lindbergh Blvd., St.Louis, MO 63132

Meineke Discount Mufflers Headquartered in Charlotte, North Carolina, a franchisor of automotive service outlets.

Founded in 1972, Meineke has been franchising since its inception. A typical Meineke franchisee operates a retail muffler and brake service, marketing the franchisor's proprietary line of replacement parts and equipment. The franchisor's emphasis is on discounting pricing, enabled by high-volume turn-over and assembly-line style efficiency. Of the franchisor's 720 outlets currently operating, all except ten are franchise units.

Meineke Discount Mufflers, 128 S. Tyron, Ste. 900, Charlotte, NC 28202. Telephone: (800) 231-9877

Merle Harmon's Fan Fair Headquartered in Elm Grove, Wisconsin, a franchisor of specialty retail outlets.

Founded in 1977, Fan Fair has been franchising since 1981. A typical Fan Fair franchisee operates a retail store devoted to specialty items and memorabilia related to professional sports. Of the franchisor's 85 outlets currently operating, all but six are franchise units.

Merle Harmon's Fan Fair, 12425 Knoll Rd., Elm Grove, WI 53122

Merlin's Magic Muffler and Brake Headquartered in Barrington, Illinois, a franchisor of automotive service outlets.

Founded in 1975, Merlin's has been franchising since its inception. A typical Merlin's franchisee operates a retail service and repair business specializing in automotive exhaust systems, brake service, suspension systems, and lube jobs. The chain consists of 44 outlets, 30 of which are franchise units.

Merlin's Magic Muffler and Brake, 100 W. Higgins Rd., Ste. 2050, South Barrington, IL 60010. Telephone: (312) 382-2010

Merry Maids Headquartered in Omaha, Nebraska, a franchisor of interior maintenance services.

Founded in 1980, Merry Maids has been franchising since the following year. A typical Merry Maids franchisee operates a house cleaning business based on a standardized system. Of the franchisor's 470 outlets currently operating, all except one are franchise units.

Merry Maids, 11117 Mill Valley Rd., Omaha, NE 68154. Telephone: (800) 345-5535

Michigan, Franchise Regulations Franchisors operating in the state of Michigan are governed by the Franchise Registration, Disclosure, Pyramid Sales law, which requires registration and disclosure of pertinent information about the franchisor, franchise business, and franchise agreement. In addition, the Motor Vehicles Dealers law protects the rights of automobile retailers.

Before offering or selling a franchise in the state, a franchisor must first prepare a disclosure document prescribed by the statute, then file the information, along with the franchise agreement, financial statements, and related documents, with the Michigan Department of Commerce. The deparment must approve the registration before the franchisor may proceed to offer or sell franchises.

In addition to a disclosure document, franchisors are also required to submit the following items:

1. Application for registration of the franchise offering;
2. Salesman disclosure form;
3. Consent to service of process;
4. Auditor's consent to use of audited financial statements;
5. Cross-reference sheet showing the location in the franchise agreement of the key
   items in the disclosure document.

The *Uniform Franchise Offering Circular* (UFOC), devised by a consortium of midwestern securities commissioners as a uniform method of complying with state franchise investment laws, fulfills the disclosure requirements of the Michigan statute. There are minor variations and differences in language required by the Michigan law, including a different cover page. (See *Uniform Franchise Offering Circular*.)

The disclosure document or UFOC must be furnished to a prospective franchisee at least ten business days before a franchise sale is made.

For information about state franchise laws, regulations, and filing requirements, or to report possible violations, contact: Corporation and Securities Bureau, Department of Commerce, 6546 Mercantile Way, Lansing, MI 48823. Telephone: (517) 373-1041.

MicroAge Computer Stores Headquartered in Tempe, Arizona, a franchisor of specialty retail outlets.

Founded in 1976 by two former bank executives, Alan Hald and Jeffrey McKeever, MicroAge has been franchising since 1980. The chain began as a single retail shop operating under the name Byte Shop in a dry riverbed outside the city limits of Phoenix. A year later, the devoted founders and self-styled "visionary futurists" were riding the crest of the computer revolution, opening new sites in upscale shopping centers in Phoenix, Tucson, and Dallas, Texas. Simultaneously, they opened a wholesale warehouse and expanded into the mail-order business, adopting the name Phoenix Group, Inc.

The company-owned retail outlets were converted from Byte Shops to MicroAge Computer Stores in 1979. A typical MicroAge franchisee operates a retail store devoted to personal and business computers, peripheral devices, and software. Outlet owners may qualify individually to market hardware supplied by IBM, Apple, AT&T, and other major manufacturers. In addition, the franchisee may also offer integrated voice-and-data equipment and wide-area network services. Of the franchisor's 200 outlets currently operating, all except six are franchise units.

MicroAge, 2308 S. 55th St., Tempe, AZ 85258. Telephone: (602) 968-3168

Midas Headquartered in Chicago, Illinois, a franchisor of automotive muffler and brake shops.

Founded in 1956, Midas has been franchising since its inception. A typical Midas franchisee operates a retail service outlet devoted to sales and installation of exhaust system parts and equipment. The Midas chain consists of 2,200 outlets, all but 200 of which are franchise units.

Midas International, 225 N. Michigan Ave., Chicago, IL 60601. Telephone: (312) 565-7500

Mifax Headquartered in Waterloo, Iowa, a franchisor of office and computer services.

Founded in 1948, Mifax has been franchising since 1969. A typical Mifax franchisee operates a business support service catering to medical practices. The service mix includes office systems counseling and design, data processing, financial administration, and reporting services. All of the 60 Mifax outlets currently operating are franchise units.

Mifax, P.O. Box 5800, Waterloo, IA 50704. Telephone: (800) 553-2003

Mighty Distributing System Headquartered in Norcross, Georgia, a franchisor of automotive parts outlets.

Founded in 1963, MDS has been franchising since 1970. Atypical MDS franchisee operates markets auto parts, tools, and accessories to customers in a designated territory. Of the franchisor's 200 outlets currently operating, all but six are franchise units.

Mighty Distributing System of America, 50 Technology Park/Atlanta, Norcross, GA 30092. Telephone: (404) 448-3900

Mike's Restaurants Headquartered in Montreal, Quebec, a franchisor of fast-food outlets.

Founded in 1967, Mike's has been franchising since 1972. Atypical Mike's franchisee operates a fast-food restaurant specializing in pizza, submarine sandwiches, salads, and beverage service. All of the franchisor's 95 outlets currently operating are franchise units.

Mike's Restaurants, 8200 Decarie, Ste. 307, Montreal, Que., Canada H4P 2P5. Telephone: (514) 341-5544

Milex Headquartered in Chicago, Illinois, a franchisor of automobile service outlets.

Founded in 1978, Milex has been franchising since the following year. A typical Milex franchisee operates an auto service business specializing in tune-ups, brake service, and oil changes. The Milex chain consists of 26 outlets, all are franchise units.

Milex, 4914 N. Lincoln Ave., Chicago, IL 60625. Telephone: (800) 562-5200

Ming Auto Beauty Centers Headquartered in Overland Park, Kansas, a franchisor of automobile rustproofing and refinishing outlets.

Founded in 1935, Ming has been franchising since 1968. A typical Ming franchisee operates a retail car care business specializing in exterior rustproofing and enhancement. Of the franchisor's 47 outlets currently operating, all but two are franchise units.

Ming Auto Beauty Centers, 7526 Metcalf St., Overland Park, KS 66204. Telephone: (800) 443-2306

Mini Maid Headquartered in Marietta, Georgia, a franchisor of interior maintenance services.

Founded in 1973, Mini Maid has been franchising since 1975. A typical Mini Maid franchisee operates a full-service housecleaning business. All 140 of the Mini Maid outlets currently in business are franchise units.

Mini Maid, 747 Chance Rd., Marietta, GA 30066. Telephone: (404) 973-3271

Minit-Tune Headquartered in Vancouver, British Columbia, a franchisor of automotive service outlets.

Founded in 1976, Minit-Tune has been franchising since its inception. A typical Minit-Tune franchisee operates an auto tune- up and lubrication service. All of the franchisor's 48 outlets currently operating all are franchise units.

Minit-Tune Auto Centers, 497 W. 5th Ave., Vancouver, BC, Canada V5Y 1J9. Telephone: (604) 873-5551

Minnesota, Franchise Regulations Franchisors operating in the state of Minnesota are governed by the Franchise Registration, Disclosure, Pyramid, Unfair Practices Act, which requires registration and disclosure of pertinent information about the franchisor, franchise business, and franchise agreement. The rights of franchise dealers in the automobile, farm equipment, beer retailing, and petroleum industries are protected under separate laws.

Before offering or selling a franchise in the state, a franchisor must first prepare a disclosure document prescribed by the statute, then file the information, along with the franchise agreement, financial statements, and related documents, with the Minnesota Department of Commerce.

In addition to a disclosure document, franchisors are also required to submit the following items:

1. Application for registration of the franchise offering;
2. Salesman disclosure form;
3. Consent to service of process;
4. Auditor's consent to use of audited financial statements;
5. Cross-reference sheet showing the location in the franchise agreement of the key
items in the disclosure document.

The disclosure document devised by a consortium of midwestern securities commissioners as a uniform method of complying with state franchise investment laws, the *Uniform Franchise Offering Circular*, or UFOC, fulfills the disclosure requirements of the Minnesota act. There are minor variations and differences in language required by the Minnesota statute, including a different cover page. (See *Uniform Franchise Offering Circular*.)

The disclosure document or UFOC must be furnished to a prospective franchisee at least ten business days before a franchise sale is made.

For information about state franchise laws, regulations, and filing requirements, or to report possible violations, contact: Department of Commerce, Fifth Floor, Metro Square Blgd., Seventh and Roberts Streets, St. Paul, MN 55101. Telephone: (612) 296- 6328.

Minority Enterprise Small Business Investment Company (MESBIC) A finance, leasing, or investment company licensed by the Small Business Administration to finance or invest in small businesses owned by members of disadvantaged minority groups.

The MESBIC is a hybrid of the Small Business Investment Company, or SBIC. Like a SBIC, a MESBIC provides funding and/or financial assistance to small business owners who might otherwise not qualify for conventional commercial loans. The participaants encompass a diversity of financial and investment groups, including private venture capital management firm, commercial finance companies, equipment leasing companies, insurance companies, employee profit sharing programs, and credit unions.

Any business whose ownership is controlled by a member of a disadvantaged minority group, such as a Black, Hispanic, Asian, or Native American, can qualify for grants, loans, or investments under the MESBIC program.

The Minority Business Development Agency publishes computer lists of licensed MESBICs in various regions of the country. To obtain information about Minority Enterprise Small Business Investment Companies, contact: Minority Business Development Agency, Washington, DC 20230.

Minute Muffler Headquartered in Lethbridge, Alberta, a franchisor of retail muffler shops.

Founded in 1968, Minute has been franchising since 1979. A typical Minute franchisee operates a retail automotive service outlet specializing in the sale, service, and installation of exhaust systems and components. Of the franchisor's 105 outlets currently operating, all except one are franchise units.

Minute Muffler, 1600 Third Ave. South, Lethbridge, Alberta, Canada T1J 0K8. Telephone: (403) 329-1020

Minuteman Press Headquartered in Farmingdale, New York, a franchisor of quick-print outlets.

Founded in 1973, Minuteman has been franchising since 1975. A typical Minuteman franchisee operates a contemporary full-service printing shop offering a broad range of printing, binding, and document reproduction services. Of the franchisor's 830 outlets currently operating, all are franchise units.

Minuteman Press International, 1640 New Hwy., Farmingdale, NY 11735. Telephone: (516) 249-1370

Miracle Auto Painting Headquartered in Foster City, California, a franchisor of automobile refinishing outlets.

Founded in 1953, Miracle has been franchising since 1964. A typical Miracle franchisee operates an auto body repair and painting shop with an emphasis on competitive pricing and high-volume turnover. Of the franchisor's 56 outlets currently operating, all except four are franchise units.

Miracle Auto Painting, 1065 E. Hillsdale Blvd., Foster City, CA 94404. Telephone: (800) 331-0404

Miracle Ear Headquartered in Minneapolis, Minnesota, a franchisor of specialty retail outlets.

Founded in 1948, Miracle has been franchising since 1983. A typical Miracle franchisee operates a retail hearing aid center. Of the franchisor's 445 outlets currently operating, all except one are franchise units.

Miracle Ear, 600 S. City Rd., Ste. 18, Minneapolis, MN 55426

Miracle Method Headquartered in Los Angeles, California, a franchisor of specialty interior remodeling services.

Founded in 1977, Miracle Method has been franchising since 1980. A typical Miracle Method franchisee operates a remodeling business devoted to repair and refinishing of sinks, bathtubs, and bathroom fixtures. All of the franchisor's 107 outlets currently operating are franchise units.

Miracle Method Bathroom Restoration, 3740 Overland Ave., Ste. C, Los Angeles, CA 90034. Telephone: (415) 680-8850

Missett, Judi Sheppard Founder and chief executive of Jazzercise, a franchisor of physical fitness outlets.

Missett attended Northwestern University in Evanston, Illinois, where she earned a bachelor's degree in theatre and radio/television with an emphasis on dance. She performed professionally with a jazz-dance troupe led by master Gus Giordano.

Misset taught her first fitness classs in 1969 in an Evanston, Illinois studio, between dance performances. In 1972, she moved her one-woman operation to California, where she began conducting exercise classes at the San Diego YWCA and, later, for the local Parks and Recreation department. She began offering jazz-dance instruction to the general public in 1974.

Judi Sheppard Missett, founder of Jazzercise

Missett began franchising in 1976; by December, 1977, she had sold eleven franchises. The following year, Bantam Books published her book, *Jazzercise: A Fun Way to Fitness*. In 1980, she signed a contract with Westinghouse Broadcasting to appear on national television on "P.M. Magazine." A year later, she was featured in a five-part syndicated series on ABC-TV.

Misset currently presides over a multimillion-dollar corporation that employs more than 100 people and has franchised nearly 4,000 instructors, who conduct exercise classes for an estimated 400,000 students.

Since the business's inception, Sheppard has choreographed all the Jazzercise routines. She writes a nationally syndicated newspaper column, has been the subject of feature articles in numerous magazines, and appears periodically on television "talk" shows. In 1985, she was named Small Business Person of the Year by the U.S. Small Business Administration. In 1986, she received the Outstanding Business Award from the International Dance Exercise Association and was honored by President Reagan as Top Woman Entrepreneur. Her second book, *The Jazzercise Workout Book*, published by Charles Scribner's Sons, was released the same year.

See Jazzercise.

Mississippi, Franchise Regulations The Mississippi legislature has not adopted any generally applicable franchise investment law. However, the rights of automobile dealers are protected under the Motor Vehicle Commission Act.

Mississippi law does not require franchisors to register or file disclosures with any state regulatory body. In the absence of such a requirement, the federal Franchise Rule applies, requiring franchisors to furnish a disclosure document prescribed by the Federal Trade Commission to prospective franchisees ten business days before a franchise sale is made

See Franchise Rule.

Missouri, Franchise Regulations The Missouri legislature has not adopted any generally applicable franchise investment law. However, the Termination, Renewal, Pyramid Sales Act prohibits franchisors from terminating or refusing to renew a franchise without good cause and reasonable notice.

Missouri law does not require franchisors to register or file disclosures with any state regulatory body. In the absence of such a requirement, the federal Franchise Rule applies, requiring franchisors to furnish a disclosure document prescribed by the Federal Trade Commission to prospective franchisees ten business days before a franchise sale is made.

See Franchise Rule.

Mister Donut of America Headquartered in Minneapolis, Minnesota, a franchisor of fast-food outlets.

Founded in 1955, Mister Donut has been franchising since the following year. A typical Mister Donut franchisee operates a fast-food bakery goods shop specializing in doughnuts and coffee service. Each outlet features 55 varieties of doughnuts and bakery goods which are sold over the counter, served to sit-down patrons in indoor booths, or supplied to drive-up or take-out customers. Of the franchisor's 609 outlets currently operating, all except one are franchise units.

Mister Donut of America, Multifoods Tower, P.O. Box 2942, Minneapolis, MN 55402. Telephone: (800) 328-8304

Mister Transmission Headquartered in Richmond Hill, Ontario, a franchisor of automotive transmission repair and service outlets.

Founded in 1963, MT has been franchising since 1973. A typical MT franchisee operates retail auto transmission service shop, performing major repair work as well as routine servicing and adjustments. Of the franchisor's 102 outlets currently operating, none are company-owned.

Mister Transmission, 30 Wertheim Court, No. 5, Richmond Hill, Ont., Canada L4B 1B9

Molly Maid Headquartered in Ann Arbor, Michigan, a franchisor of interior maintenance services.

Founded in 1978, Molly Maid has been franchising since 1980. A typical Molly Maid franchisee operates a residential cleaning business with a full-time staff of one to five workers. Of the franchisor's 336 outlets currently operating, all are franchise units.

Molly Maid, 3001 S. State St., Ste. 707, Ann Arbor, MI 48108. Telephone: (800) 331-4600

Mom's Cinnamon Roll Shops Headquartered in Englewood, Colorado, a franchisor of specialty bakery goods outlets.

Founded in 1985, Mom's has been franchising since the following year. A typical Mom's franchisee operates a retail bakery goods store devoted to hot cinnamon rolls prepared on the premises. Of the franchisor's 24 outlets currently operating, all except two are franchise units.

Mom's Cinnamon Roll Shops, 8100 S. Quebec St., Ste. B-206, Englewood, CO 80112. Telephone: (303) 721-0797

Monaghan, Thomas Fast food operator, professional sports team owner, and franchisor of pizza delivery restaurants.

An orphan, Monaghan barely made it through high school, enlisting in the Marine Corps as soon as he graduated. An avid reader of self-help books, he finally decided to study architecture at Eastern Michigan University. To finance his education, he scraped together $900 to buy a pizza restaurant named Dominick's, near the Ypsilanti campus. His brother James cosigned for the loan. Monaghan's funds were so sparse he had to sleep on a pizza table in the back of the restaurant. Worse, he found it nearly impossible to turn a profit serving walk-in customers with a wide selection of toppings. His brother wanted out of the business, finally settling for a used Volkswagon in return for his share of the restaurant. In desparation, Monaghan closed the dining room and, to reduce overhead, focused exclusively on home delivery.

Changing the name to Domino's and guaranteeing thirty-minute delivery, Monoghan rapidly expanded into eight restaurants in three years. In 1968, he began selling franchises, mostly to delivery drivers who wanted to be their own bosses. Today, the former architecture student oversees a staggering empire of more than 3,000 pizza outlets and is one of America's wealthiest entrepreneurs.

But Monaghan's road from rags to riches was not entirely free of pitfalls. In 1968, his corporate headquarters was destroyed in a fire, along with the company's records. In the 1970s, he faced bankruptcy on four different occasions. At one point, he was slapped with a multimillion dollar lawsuit over the Domino trade name. Yet, despite Monaghan's financial and legal woes, Domino's sales continued to grow at a phenomenal 40 percent annual rate from 1978 to the present.

In 1984, Monaghan purchased his favorite baseball team, the Detroit Tigers for $50 million, the highest price ever paid for a baseball franchise. The team immediately won the World Series under his ownership. He later constructed his own "Leaning Tower of Pizza" to house the headquarters for his massive business empire. Though he never completed college, his passion for architecture remains unquelled. His experimental Domino's Farms development outside Ann Arbor incorporates innovative designs by the world's leading architects, including the late Frank Lloyd Wright.

Since 1970, the demand for pizza has grown faster than any other segment of the fast food market, thrusting Domino's to the top of the franchise restaurant industry. The chain's success is based on its exclusive dedication to home delivery, with no sit-down service whatsoever. Pizzas en route are kept warm inside delivery vehicles equipped with specially designed ovens. Many of the company's franchisees started out as delivery drivers. The average age of a Domino's franchise owner is 23.

See Domino's Pizza.

Money Mailer Headquartered in Huntington Beach, California, a franchisor of advertising sales services.

Founded in 1979, Money Mailer has been franchising since the following year. A typical Money Mailer franchisee operates a sales territory for direct-mail advertising coupons. The chain consists of 190 outlets, including one company-owned operation.

Money Mailer, 15472 Chemical Lane, Huntington Beach, CA 92649. Telephone: (800) MAILER-1

Montana, Franchise Regulations To date, the Montana legislature has not adopted any generally applicable franchise investment law. However, the rights of automobile retailers and beer and wine dealers are protected under separate laws.

Montana law does not require franchisors to register or file disclosures with any state regulatory body. In the absence of such a requirement, the federal Franchise Rule applies, requiring franchisors to furnish a disclosure document prescribed by the Federal Trade Commission to prospective franchisees ten business days before a franchise sale is made.

See Franchise Rule.

Moto Photo, Inc. Headquartered in Dayton, Ohio, a franchisor of retail photofinishing outlets.

Founded in 1981, Moto Photo has been franchising since the following year. A typical Moto Photo franchisee operates a photofinishing store featuring one-hour film processing and supplemented by reprint, enlargement, and portrait photography services. Of the franchisor's 275 outlets currently operating, 222 are franchise units.

Moto Photo, Inc., 4444 Lake Center Dr., Dayton, OH 45426. Telephone: (800) 333-6686

Motra Transmission Headquartered in Chicago, Illinois, a franchisor of automotive transmission outlets.

Founded in 1980, Motra has been franchising since its inception. A typical Motra franchisee operates a retail transmission installation and repair business. The Motra chain currently consists of 35 outlets, none of which are company-owned.

Motra Transmission, 4912 N. Lincoln Ave., Chicago, IL 60625. Telephone: (800) 562-5200, Ext. 334

Mountain Mike's Pizza, Inc. Headquartered in Sacramento, California, a franchisor of fast-food outlets.

Founded in 1978, Mountain Mike's has been franchising since its inception. A typical Mountain Mike's franchisee operates a fast-food restaurant with a diversified Italian-style menu featuring thick-crust pizza, hot hamburgers, pasta, sandwiches, and fresh salads. Of the franchisor's 60 outlets currently operating, all except one are franchise units.

Mountain Mike's Pizza, Inc., 1608 "I" St., Ste. 102, Sacramento, CA 95814. Telephone: (916) 448-5934

Movieland, USA Headquartered in Ft. Smith, Arkansas, a franchisor of videocassette rental outlets.

Founded in 1981, Movieland has been franchising since 1984. A typical Movieland franchisee operates a retail store devoted to videocassette and VCR rentals and sales. Of the chain's 30 outlets currently in business, all except five are franchise units.

Movieland, USA, 4120 Rogers Ave., Ft. Smith, AR 72903

Mr. Build Headquartered in Windsor, Connecticut, a franchisor of construction and remodeling contractors.

Founded in 1981, Mr. Build has been franchising since its inception. A typical Mr. Build franchisee operates a licensed home improvement and remodeling business, performing one or more contracting services such as plumbing, electrical, roofing, construction, or maintenance. All of the franchisor's 605 outlets are franchise units.

Mr. Build, 1 Univac Lane, Windsor, CT 06095. Telephone: (203) 285-0766

Mr. Gatti's Headquartered in Austin, Texas, a franchisor of food service outlets.

Founded in 1969, Mr. Gatti's has been franchising since 1975. A typical Mr. Gatti's franchisee operates a specialty restaurant devoted to pizza, pasta, and Italian sandwiches, with recreational facilities for children. Of the franchisor's 338 outlets currently operating, 182 are franchise units.

Mr. Gatti's Restaurants, 220 Foremost Dr., Austin, TX 78745. Telephone: (512) 282-5580

Mr. Grocer Headquartered in Kitchener, Ontario, a franchisor of Canadian retail grocery markets.

Founded in 1983, Mr. Grocer has been franchising since its inception. A typical Mr. Grocer franchisee operates a full-service grocery market based on a standarized inventory and purchasing system. Of the franchisor's 60 outlets currently operating, all are franchise units.

Mr. Grocer, 1 Goodrich Dr., Kitchener, Ont., Canada N2C 2E9. Telephone: (519) 894-7434

Mr. Philly Headquartered in Middleburg Heights, Ohio, a franchisor of fast-food outlets.

Founded in 1965, Mr. Philly has been franchising since 1970. A typical Mr. Philly franchisee operates a fast-food restaurant devoted to specialty sandwiches, including the franchisor's trademarked Cheesesteak and Romanburger sandwiches. All but a dozen of the 150 Mr. Philly outlets currently open are franchise units.

Mr. Philly. Telephone: 6902 Pearl Rd., 4th Floor, Middleburg Heights, OH 44130

Mr. Sign Headquartered in Bohemia, New York, a franchisor of sign making outlets.

Founded in 1985, Mr. Sign has been franchising since the following year. A typical Mr. Sign franchisee operates a retail/commercial sign business utilizing a computer-based sign-making system. All 48 Mr. Sign outlets currently open and operating are franchise units.

Mr. Sign, 159 Keyland Court, Bohemia, NY 11716

Mr. Steak Headquartered in Littleton, Colorado, a franchisor of family-style steakhouses.

Founded in 1962, Mr. Steak has been franchising since its inception. A typical Mr. Steak franchisee operates a full-service restaurant featuring a limited menu centered around beef, seafood,and sandwiches. Of the franchisor's 175 outlets currentlyoperating, all except 30 are franchise units.

Mr. Steak, P. O. Box 4006, Littleton, CO 80120. Telephone:(800) 446-4491

Mr. Submarine Headquartered in Toronto, Ontario, a franchisor of fast-food outlets.

Founded in 1968, Mr. Submarine has been franchising since 1972. A typical Mr. Submarine franchisee operates a fast-food operation devoted to submarine)style sandwiches, fresh salads, and beverage service. Of the franchisor's 275 Canadian outlets currently operating, all except 12 are franchise units.

Mr. Submarine, 300-720 Spadina Ave., Toronto, Ont., Canada M5S 2T9. Telephone: (416) 962-6232

Mr. Transmission Headquartered in Nashville, Tennessee, a franchisor of automotive transmission service and repair outlets.

Founded in 1962, Mr. Transmission has been franchising since 1976. A typical Mr. Transmission franchisee operates a retail auto transmission ship offering repair, rebuilding, and reconditioning services. Of the franchisor's 140 outlets currently operating, all except eight are franchise units.

Mr. Transmission, 400 Harding Industrial Dr., Nashville, TN 37211. Telephone: (615) 251-3504

Mrs. Powell's Delicious Cinnamon Rolls Headquartered in Idaho Falls, Idaho, a franchisor of specialty bakery goods outlets.

ounded in 1984, Mrs. Powell's has been franchising since the following year. A typical Mrs. Powell's franchisee operates a retail bakery goods shop featuring the franchisor's proprietary, freshly baked cinnamon rolls. Of the franchisor's 42 outlets currently operating, all except one are franchise units.

Mrs. Powell's Delicious Cinnamon Rolls, 1970 E. 17th St., Ste. 103, Idaho Falls, ID 83401. Telephone: (208) 523-0093

Mrs. Vanelli's Pizza & Italian Foods Headquartered in Mississauga, Ontario, a franchisor of fast-food outlets.

Founded in 1981, Mrs. Vanelli's has been franchising since 1984. A typical Mrs. Vanelli's franchisee operates a fast-food restaurant devoted to Italian cuisine. Of the franchisor's 46 outlets currently operating, 40 are franchise units.

Mrs. Vanelli's Pizza & Italian Foods, 2133 Royal Windsor Dr., Ste. 23, Mississauga, Ont., Canada L5J 1K5. Telephone: (416) 823-8883

Mundus Colleges, Inc. Headquartered in Phoenix, Arizona, a franchisor of adult vocational schools.

Founded in 1979, Mundus has been franchising since 1988. A typical Mundus franchisee operates a proprietary post-secondary school offering curricula in travel career preparation, airline training, law office automation, business computer skills, and hotel/resort training.

Mundus Colleges, Inc. began as an outgrowth of Mundus Travel, Inc., one of the ten largest U.S. travel companies, which was acquired by Ask Mr. Foster Travel in 1987. Mundus Institute was formed in 1980 as a travel college and a year later, began marketing its travel curriculum to other vocational and trade schools. A comprehensive computer-based instructional system provides hands-on training in American Airline SABRE, United Airlines APOLLO, TWA PARS, Eastern System One, and Delta DATAS II/III.

The institute expanded into other computer-oriented curricula in 1986, modifying programs originally developed for in-house corporate training. In 1988, the educational division was acquired by Franchise Associates International. Mundus Colleges, Inc. franchises private vocational schools which utilize the franchisor's computer-based instructional systems, teaching materials, and turn-key curricula. The

Mundus system includes 180 franchise outlets and affiliated schools, none of which are owned by the franchisor.

Mundus Colleges, Inc., 11811 N. Tatum Blvd. Ste. 1050, Phoenix, AZ 85028. Telephone: (602) 996-9831

Naked Furniture
to
NuVision

Naked Furniture Headquartered in Rochester, New York, a franchisor of specialty furnishings outlets.

Founded in 1972, Naked Furniture has been franchising since 1979. A typical Naked Furniture franchisee operates a retail store devoted to unfinished solid wood furniture and stains. The outlet is distinguished by its do-it-yourself orientation and diverse selection of home furnishings. Of the franchisor's 50 outlets currently operating, all except three are franchise units.

Naked Furniture, 845 Maple St., Rochester, NY 14611. Telephone: (716) 436-4060

Namco Headquartered in Milford, Massachusetts, a franchisor of commercial advertising services.

Founded in 1955, Namco has been franchising since 1982. A typical Namco franchisee operates a marketing territory specializing in advertising sales for telephone directory covers. Of the 43 Namco outlets currently operating, 35 are franchise units.

Namco Systems, 47 Summer St., Milford, MA 01757

National Maintenance Contractors Headquartered in Redmond, Washington, a franchisor of interior maintenance services.

Founded in 1970, NMC has been franchising since 1975. A typical NMC franchisee operates a commercial janitorial cleaning service. All 224 of the NMC outlets currently operating are franchise units.

National Maintenance Contractors, 4024 148th St. NE, Bldg.N, Redmond, WA 98052. Telephone: (208) 881-0500

National Video Headquartered in Portland, Oregon, a franchisor of videocasette rental outlets.

Founded in 1980, National Video has been franchising since the following year. Chairman Ron Berger opened the first outlet with a $1,000 investment and the idea of eliminating membership fees that were usually charged to customers. Besides charging a low per-unit fee to rent movies, National was also the first video store to rent VCRs. By marketing multiple outlets, the franchise company,proliferated rapidly, opening its 1,000th store in 1986.

A typical National Video franchisee operates a videocasette rental business supplemented by sales of video-related items such as VCRs, camcorders, and party items. Of the estimated 1,400 National Video outlets currently operating, all except one are franchise units.

National Video, P.O. Box 18220, Portland, OR 97218. Telephone: (800) 547-1310

Nebraska, Franchise Regulations The Nebraska Franchise Practices Act grants franchisees certain rights with respect to termination and renewal of the franchise agreement. Franchisors are prohibited from terminating or refusing to renew a franchise without good cause or in bad faith. In addition, the Business Practices Act forbids misrepresentation in the offer or sale of "seller-assisted marketing plans."

For information about the Franchise Practices Act, or to report possible violations, contact: Division of Securities, P. O. Box 95006, Lincoln, NE 68509. Telephone: (402) 471-2171.

Nebraska law does not require franchisors to register or file disclosures with any state regulatory body. In the absence of such a requirement, the federal Franchise Rule applies, requiring franchisors to furnish a disclosure document prescribed by the Federal Trade Commission to prospective franchisees ten business days before a franchise sale is made.

See Franchise Rule.

Nevada, Franchise Regulations The Nevada legislature has not adopted any generally applicable franchise investment law. However, the rights of automobile retailers, service stations owners, and beer and wine dealers under franchise agreements are protected under separate laws.

Nevada law does not require franchisors to register or file disclosures with any state regulatory body. In the absence of such a requirement, the federal Franchise Rule applies, requiring franchisors to furnish a disclosure document prescribed by the Federal Trade Commission to prospective franchisees ten business days before a franchise sale is made.

See Franchise Rule.

New Hampshire, Franchise Regulations To date, the New Hampshire legislature has not adopted any generally applicable franchise investment law. However, the rights of automobile retailers and service station owners under franchise agreements are protected under separate laws.

New Hampshire law does not require franchisors to register or file disclosures with any state regulatory body. In the absence of such a requirement, the federal Franchise Rule applies, requiring franchisors to furnish a disclosure document prescribed by the Federal Trade Commission to prospective franchisees ten business days before a franchise sale is made.

See Franchise Rule.

New Jersey, Franchise Regulations The New Jersey legislature has not adopted any generally applicable franchise investment law. However, the Franchise Practices Act prohibits franchisors from terminating or refusing to renew a franchise without good cause and reasonable notice.

New Jersey law does not currently require franchisors to register or file disclosures with any state regulatory body. In the absence of such a requirement, the federal Franchise Rule applies, requiring franchisors to furnish a disclosure document prescribed by the Federal Trade Commission to prospective franchisees ten business days before a franchise sale is made.

See Franchise Rule.

New Mexico, Franchise Regulations To date, the New Mexico legislature has not adopted any generally applicable franchise investment law. However, the rights of automobile retailers and beer and liquor dealers are protected under separate laws.

New Mexico law does not require franchisors to register or file disclosures with any state regulatory body. In the absence of such a requirement, the federal Franchise Rule applies, requiring franchisors to furnish a disclosure document prescribed by the Federal Trade Commission to prospective franchisees ten business days before a franchise sale is made.

See Franchise Rule.

New York, Franchise Regulations Franchisors operating in the state of New York are governed by the Franchise Registration/Disclosure law, which requires registration and disclosure of pertinent information about the franchisor, franchise business, and franchise agreement. Other state laws protect the rights of automobile dealers and service station owners operating under franchise agreements.

Before offering or selling a franchise in the state, a franchisor must first prepare a disclosure document prescribed by the statute, then file the information, along with the franchise agreement, financial statements, and related documents, with the New York Department of Law. The department must approve the registration before the franchisor may proceed to offer or sell franchises.

In addition to a disclosure document, franchisors are also required to submit the following items:
1. Application for registration of the franchise offering;
2. Salesman disclosure form;
3. Consent to service of process;
4. Auditor's consent to use of audited financial statements;
5. Cross-reference sheet showing the location in the franchise agreement of the key items in the disclosure document.

The *Uniform Franchise Offering Circular* (UFOC), devised by a consortium of midwestern securities commissioners as a uniform method of complying with state franchise investment laws, fulfills the disclosure requirements of the New York law. There are minor variations and differences in language required by the New York statute, including a different cover page. (See *Uniform Franchise Offering Circular.*)

The disclosure document or UFOC must be furnished to a prospective franchisee at least ten business days before a franchise sale is made.

For information about state franchise laws, regulations, and filing requirements, or to report possible violations, contact: Department of Law, World Trade Center, Room 4874, New York, NY 10047.

NYPD New York Pizza Department Headquartered in San Diego, California, a franchisor of specialty fast-food service outlets.

Founded in 1983, NYPD has been franchising since the following year. A typical NYPD franchisee operates a fast-food restaurant specializing in pizza. The outlet is distinguished by home-delivery service provided by agents dressed in simulated police uniforms and driving vehicles resembling New York City police cars. Of the franchisor's 14 outlets currently operating, ten are franchise units.

NYPD New York Pizza Department, 9449 Balboa Ave., Ste. 212, San Diego, CA 92123. Telephone: (619) 292-9111

Norell Temporary Services Headquartered in Atlanta, Georgia, a franchisor of temporary employment agencies.

Founded in 1961, Norell has been franchising since 1967. A typical Norell franchisee operates a personnel recruitment and placement agency specializing in temporary employment of office, clerical, and data processing workers. The company's service objective is the ability to respond to a personnel request within 45 minutes. The chain consists of 240 outlets, 112 of which are franchise units.

Norell Temporary Services, 3535 Piedmont Rd. NE, Atlanta, GA 30305. Telephone: (800) 334-9694

North Carolina, Franchise Regulations The North Carolina legislature has not adopted any generally applicable franchise investment law. However, the rights of automobile retailers and beer and wine dealers are protected under separate laws.

North Carolina law does not require franchisors to register or file disclosures with any state regulatory body. In the absence of such a requirement, the federal Franchise Rule applies, requiring franchisors to furnish a disclosure document prescribed by the Federal Trade Commission to prospective franchisees ten business days before a franchise sale is made.

See Franchise Rule.

North Dakota, Franchise Regulations Franchisors operating in the state of North Dakota are governed by the Franchise Investment Law, which requires registration and disclosure of pertinent information about the franchisor, franchise business, and franchise agreement. Additional laws protect the rights of farm equipment, automobile, and recreational vehicle dealers.

Before offering or selling a franchise in the state, a franchisor must first prepare a disclosure document prescribed by the statute, then file the information, along with the franchise agreement, financial statements, and related documents, with the Securities Commissioner.

In addition to a disclosure document, franchisors are also required to submit the following items:

1. Application for registration of the franchise offering;
2. Salesman disclosure form;
3. Consent to service of process;
4. Auditor's consent to use of audited financial statements;
5. Cross-reference sheet showing the location in the franchise agreement of the key items in the disclosure document.

The disclosure document devised by a consortium of midwestern securities commissioners as a uniform method of complying with state franchise investment laws, the *Uniform Franchise Offering Circular*, or UFOC, fulfills the disclosure requirements of the North Dakota law. There are minor variations and differences in language required by the North Dakota statute, including a different cover page. (See *Uniform Franchise Offering Circular.*)

The disclosure document or UFOC must be furnished to a prospective franchisee at least ten business days before a franchise sale is made.

For information about state franchise laws, regulations, and filing requirements, or to report possible violations, contact: Securities Commission, Capital Bldg., Third Floor, Bismarck, ND 58505. Telephone: (701) 224-2910.

See Franchise Rule.

Novus Windshield Repair Headquartered in Minneapolis, Minnesota, a franchisor of automotive windshield repair outlets.

Founded in 1972, Novus has been franchising since 1985. A typical Novus franchisee operates windshield repair and replacement service, based on the franchisor's proprietary line of sealant products. Of the franchisor's 685 outlets currently operating, all are franchise units.

Novus Windshield Repair, 10425 Hampshire Ave. S, Minneapolis, MN 55438. Telephone: (800) 328-1117

Numero Uno Headquartered in Panorama City, California, a franchisor of speciality food service outlets.

Founded in 1973, Numero Uno has been franchising since the following year. A typical Numero Uno franchisee operates a specialty restaurant with an Italian motif and a menu devoted to pizza, pasta, and salads. Of the franchisor's 62 outlets currently operating, all except six are franchise units.

Numero Uno Franchise Corp., 8214 Van Nuys Blvd., Panorama City, CA 91402

Nursefinders Headquartered in Arlington, Texas, a franchisor of nursing-care employment agencies.

Founded in 1972, Nursefinders has been franchising since 1978. A typical Nursefinders franchisee operates a temporary employment agency specializing in in-home nursing-care services. Of the 100 Nursefinders outlets currently operating, 69 are franchise units.

Nursefinders, 1400 N. Cooper Rd., Arlington, TX 76011. Telephone: (817) 460-1181

Nutra Bolic Headquartered in Canton, Ohio, a franchisor of weight-loss centers.

Founded in 1982, Nutra Bolic has been franchising since 1984. A typical Nutra Bolic franchisee operates a personal weight-loss center based on an individualized program of diet counseling, nutrition instruction, and supervision. Of the franchisor's 180 outlets currently operating, 160 are owned by franchisees.

Nutra Bolic Weight Reduction System of America, 4790 Douglas Circle NW, Canton, OH 44718. Telephone: (216) 499-3334

Nutri System Headquartered in Willow Grove, Pennsylvania, a franchisor of weight-loss centers.

Founded in 1971, Nutri System has been franchising since the following year. A typical Nutri System franchisee operates a multi-faceted, weight-loss and fitness center employing medically trained counselors, nutrition experts, and exercise facilities. Clients of the center receive a supervised weight-reduction program based on a combined regimen of nutrition education, behavior modification, and exercise. Each center markets the franchisor's own Nu System Cuisine line of diet foods and supplements. Of the franchisor's estimated 1,000 outlets currently operating, approximately 830 are franchise units.

Nutri System, 3901 Commerce Ave., CS 925, Willow Grove, PA 19090. Telephone: (215) 784-5600

NuVision Optical Headquartered in Flint, Michigan, a franchisor of retail optometric outlets.

Founded in 1949, NuVision has been franchising since 1983. A typical NuVision franchisee operates a retail optical dispensing center with on-premises optometric services. Prescriptions are filled by the franchisor's laboratory. Of the franchisor's 220 outlets currently operating, approximately 50 are franchise units.

NuVision Optical, P.O. Box 2600, Flint, MI 48501. Telephone: (313) 767-0900

Ohio
to
Oregon

Ohio, Franchise Regulations To date, the Ohio legislature has not adopted any generally applicable franchise investment law. However, the Business Opportunities Purchasers Protection Act prohibits deception or misrepresentation in the offer or sale of business opportunity ventures. The rights of automobile dealers and beer and liquor retailers are protected by separate laws.

Ohio law does not require franchisors to register or file disclosures with any state regulatory body. In the absence of such a requirement, the federal Franchise Rule applies, requiring franchisors to furnish a disclosure document prescribed by the Federal Trade Commission to prospective franchisees ten business days before a franchise sale is made.

Business opportunity ventures are regulated by the attorney general. To report possible fraudulent or deceptive practices, contact: Assistant Attorney General, Consumer Frauds & Crime Section, State Office Tower, 15th Floor, 30 E. Broad St., Columbus, OH 43215. Telephone: (614) 466-8831.

See Franchise Rule.

Oklahoma, Franchise Regulations The Oklahoma legislature has not adopted any generally applicable franchise investment law. However, the rights of farm equipmemt dealers operating under franchise agreements are protected under a separate law.

Oklahoma law does not require franchisors to register or file disclosures with any state regulatory body. In the absence of such a requirement, the federal Franchise Rule applies, requiring franchisors to furnish a disclosure document prescribed by the Federal Trade Commission to prospective franchisees ten business days before a franchise sale is made.

See Franchise Rule.

Olga's Kitchen Headquartered in Troy, Michigan, a franchisor of family-style restaurants.

Founded in 1975, Olga's Kitchen has been franchising since 1984. A typical Olga's Kitchen franchisee operates a full-service restaurant featuring a traditional, Old-World ambience and a varied menu of hot and cold meals for breakfast, lunch, and dinner. Of the franchisor's 47 outlets currently operating, 10 are franchise units.

Olga's Kitchen, 1940 Northwood Dr., Troy, MI 48084. Telephone: (313) 362-0001

One Hour Martinizing Dry Cleaning Headquartered in Cincinnati, Ohio, a franchisor of dry cleaning outlets.

Founded in 1949, One Hour Martinizing has been franchising since its inception, growing to become the largest dry cleaning chain in North America. A typical One Hour Martinizing franchisee operates a retail dry cleaning business utilizing the franchisor's proprietary dry cleaning process and equipment. The chain presently boasts 1,000 outlets, all operated under franchise licenses.

One Hour Martinizing, 2005 Ross Ave., Cincinnati, OH 45212. Telephone: (513) 351-6211

One Potato Two, Inc. Headquartered in New Hope, Minnesota, a franchisor of fast-food outlets.

Founded in 1977, One Potato Two has been franchising since 1984. A typical One Potato Two franchisee operates a fast-food stand specializing in baked potatoes served with a variety of meat and vegetable toppings. Of the franchisor's 54 outlets currently operating, 14 are franchise units.

One Potato Two, Inc., 5640 International Parkway, New Hope, MN 55428. Telephone: (612) 537-3833

Operating Manual A written guide to operating a business, particularly a franchise outlet, usually containing mandatory and suggested specifications, standards, operating procedures, and rules.

The Guidelines for Preparfor of a Uniform Franchise Offering Circular, issued by the Midwest Securities Commissioners Association and accepted by the Federal Trade Commission, refer to the operating manual in the instructions for completing Section XI-C of the disclosure document:

> *(3) Describe any operating manual provided to the franchisee to assist the franchisee and his employees in the operation of the franchised business and whether the franchisor retains the righ to change the terms of the manual and, if so, under what circumstances.*

The provision of an operating manual to a franchisee fulfills an important condition of the federal definition of a "franchise" relationship. Under the FTC's landmark *Franchise Rule*, a franchise is any commercial relationship involving a licensed trademark, payment of a fee, and "significant control or assistance."

Franchisors normally consider their operating manuals to be trade secrets. Consequently, most franchise agreements obligate the franchisee to keep the contents confidential. A typical operating manual is loaned, not given, to the franchisee for the term of the franchise agreement. Upon expiration of the franchise, all copies of the manual in the franchisee's possession must be returned to the franchisor. Many agreements obligate the managers and employees of the franchisee's outlet to sign confidentiality oaths, preventing disclosure of any portion of the operating manual to unauthorized parties.

A typical franchise agreement gives the franchisor the right to modify the manual periodically, providing that the modifications do not alter any of the franchisee's rights. Franchisees are usually bound to adhere to any mandatory policies, procedures, specifications, and standards published in the operating manual.

Although there is no "standard" franchise operating manual, a good manual touches on virtually aspect of starting, developing, staffing, managing, operating, and promoting the franchise business. The work may be divided into a series of volumes, each devoted to a separate topic, such as marketing or daily operating procedures. It is common for managers and rank-and-file employees to have separate manuals, as well.

The sample table of contents illustrates the organization of a typical franchise operating manual and lists representative topics. Obviously, the actual contents of any manual depends on the industry, business, type and size of the outlet, and franchise business system. The example includes sections from several different operating manuals currently in use.

OPERATING MANUAL
Contents

MARKETING AND SALES PROMOTION

SALES POLICIES AND PROCEDURES

DAILY OPERATING PROCEDURES

Orange Julius of America Headquartered in Bloomington, Minnesota, a franchisor of fast-food outlets.

Founded in 1926, Orange Julius has been franchising since 1963. A typical Orange Julius franchisee operates a specialty fast-food and beverage operation in a retail shopping mall, strip center, or standalone site, distinguished by its orange decor and"red-devil" logo. Outlets range in size from small, open juice bars to freestanding restaurants offering hamburgers, hot dogs, and specialty sandwiches. All Orange Julius outlets mix and serve an assortment of real juice drinks. Of the franchisor's 745 outlets currently operating, all except one are franchise units.

Orange Julius of America, 5701 Green Valley Dr., Bloomington, Minnesota.

Oregon, Franchise Regulations Franchisors operating in the state of Oregon are governed by the Franchise Disclosure law, which requires registration and disclosure of pertinent information about the franchisor, franchise business, and franchise agreement.

Before offering or selling a franchise in the state, a franchisor must first prepare a disclosure document prescribed by the statute, then file the information, along with the franchise agreement, financial statements, and related documents, with the Oregon Corporations Commissioner.

In addition to a disclosure document, franchisors are also required to submit the following items:

1. Application for registration of the franchise offering;
2. Salesman disclosure form;
3. Consent to service of process;
4. Auditor's consent to use of audited financial statements;
5. Cross-reference sheet showing the location in the franchise agreement of the key items in the disclosure document.

The *Uniform Franchise Offering Circular* (UFOC) devised by a consortium of midwestern securities commissioners as a uniform method of complying with state franchise investment laws, fulfills the disclosure requirements of the Oregon statute. There are minor variations and differences in language required by the Oregon statute, including a different cover page.

The disclosure document or UFOC must be furnished to a prospective franchisee at least ten business days before a franchise sale is made.

For information about state franchise laws, regulations, and filing requirements, or to report possible violations, contact: Corporations Commissioner, Department of Commerce, Commerce Bldg., Salem, OR 97310. Telephone: (503) 378-4387.

See Uniform Franchise Offering Circular.

**PCR
to
Quality Inns**

PCR Personal Computer Rentals Headquartered in Coral Gables, Florida, a franchisor of specialty equipment rental outlets.

Founded in 1983, PCR has been franchising since the following year. A typical PCR franchisee operates a rental outlet for small business computer systems, catering to corporate, professional, and industrial clients. Of the franchisor's 37 outlets currently operating, all except one are franchise units.

PCR Personal Computer Rentals, 800 Douglas Entr., North Tower, Ste. 355, Coral Gables, FL 33134. Telephone: (305) 444-9930

PIP Postal Instant Press Headquartered in Los Angeles, California, a franchisor of instant printing shops.

Founded in 1965, PIP has been franchising since 1968. A typical PIP franchisee operates a retail quick printing shop, specializing in offset printing and duplication services. All except two of the franchisor's 1,120 active outlets are franchise units.

PIP, 8201 Beverly Blvd., Los Angeles, CA 90048. Telephone: (800) 292-4747

PKG's Headquartered in Cincinnati, Ohio, a franchisor of packaging and shipping outlets.

Founded in 1983, PKG' has been franchising since its inception. A typical PKG' franchisee operates a service business specializing in custom packaging and freight forwarding. Of the franchisor's 52 outlets currently operating, all except four are franchise units.

PKG's, 5400 Cornell Rd., Cincinnati, OH 45242. Telephone: (800) 543-7547

Pacer Racer Headquartered in Chattanooga, Tennessee, a franchisor of recreational equipment.

Founded in 1977, Pacer has been franchising since its inception. A typical Pacer franchisee operates a miniature race track facility devoted to rentals of the franchisor's proprietary Pacer Racer go-karts. Of the franchisor's 170 outlets currently operating, all except four are franchise units.

Pacer Manufacturing, 5954 Brainerd Rd., Chattanooga, TN 37421-3598. Telephone: (615) 892-7264

Packy the Shipper Headquartered in Racine, Wisconsin, a franchisor of specialty services outlets.

Founded in 1976, PTS has been franchising since 1981. A typical PTS franchisee operates a service business combining custom packaging service with freight forwarding via third—party shippers. All of the 1,120 Packy the Shipper outlets currently in business are operated under franchise licenses.

Packy the Shipper, 409 Main St., Racine, WI 53403. Telephone: (414) 633-9540

Padgett Business Services Headquartered in Athens, Georgia, a franchisor of accounting and consulting outlets.

Founded in 1965, Padgett has been franchising since 1975. A typical Padgett franchisee operates a business support service utilizing the franchisor's accounting system. Outlets offer general business consulting, tax counseling, and accounting/bookkeeping services. Of the franchisor's 80 outlets currently operating, all are franchise units.

Padgett Business Services, 263 W. Clayton St., Athens. GA 30601. Telephone: (404) 548-1040

Pak Mail Centers of America, Inc. Headquartered in Aurora, Colorado, a franchisor of specialty services outlets.

Founded in 1982, Pak Mail has been franchising since 1984. A typical Pak Mail franchisee operates a custom packaging and shipping service. None of the 190 Pak Mail outlets currently operating are company owned.

Pak Mail Centers of America, Inc., 10555 E. Dartmouth Ave., Ste. 360, Aurora, CO 80014. Telephone: (800) 833-2821

Palmer Video Corp. Headquartered in Union, New Jersey, a franchisor of specialty retail outlets.

Founded in 1984, Palmer has been franchising since its inception. A typical Palmer franchisee operates a retail store specializing in videocassette rentals and sales of VCRs, camcorders, and televisions. The chain presently boasts a hundred outlets, 16 of which are company owned with the remainder operated under franchise licenses.

Palmer Video Corp., 1767 Morris Ave., Union, NJ 07083. Telephone: (201) 686-3030

Panhandler Shops Headquartered in Downsview, Ontario, a franchisor of specialty retail outlets.

Founded in 1974, Panhandler has been franchising since its inception. A typical Panhandler franchisee operates a retail gift boutique marketing a selection of collectible items, souvenirs, and memorabilia. Of the franchisor's 80 outlets currently operating, all are franchise units.

Panhandler Shops. 4699 Keele St., Ste. 3, Downsview, Ont., Canada M3J 2N8. Telephone: (416) 6611-9916

Papa Aldo's Pizza Headquartered in Portland, Oregon, a franchisor of specialty food outlets.

Founded in 1984, Papa Aldo's has been franchising since 1986. A typical Papa Aldo's franchisee operates a retail foodshop specializing in "take and bake" pizza, pasta, and pastries. Of the franchisor's 80 outlets currently operating, all except three are franchise units.

Papa Aldo's, 9600 SW Capitol Highway, Portland, OR 97219. Telephone: (604) 683-9688

Parson-Bishop Headquartered in Cincinnati, Ohio, a franchisor of credit collection services. Founded in 1973, Parson-Bishop has been franchising since 1986. A typical Parson-Bishop franchisee operates a commercial collection service for business clients with accounts receivable problems. None of the franchisor's 50 outlets currently operating are company-owned.

Parson-Bishop National Collections, Inc., 7870 Camargo Rd., Cincinnati, OH 45243. Telephone: (513) 561-5560

Party Harty Headquartered in Voorhees, New Jersey, a franchisor of specialty retail outlets.

Founded in 1987, Party Harty has been franchising since its inception. A typical Party Harty franchisee operates a retail store specializing in party goods and supplies. Of the franchisor's 32 outlets currently operating, all except two are franchise units.

Party Harty, 3 Eagle Pl., Rte. 561, Voorhees, NJ 08043

Paul Davis Systems, Inc. Headquartered in Jacksonville, Florida, a franchisor of specialized consulting services.

Founded in 1966, Paul Davis has been franchising since 1970. A typical Paul Davis franchisee operates a consulting business devoted to insurance claims. Franchisees specialize in estimating property damage and managing restoration projects, utilizing the franchisor's computer-based cost control system. None of the chain's 120 outlets are company owned.

Paul Davis Systems, Inc., 1100 Cesery Blvd., Ste. 20, Jacksonville, FL 32211. Telephone: (404) 951-0056

Pay N Play Racquetball Headquartered in Fountain Valley, California, a franchisor of racquetball facilities.

Founded in 1978, Pay N Play has been franchising since 1985. A typical Pay N Play franchisee operates a racquetball center utilizing automated equipment to facilitate play and scorekeeping. Of the franchisor's nine outlets currently operating, all except one are franchise units.

Pay N Play Racquetball of America, Inc., 11770 E. Warner St., Fountain Valley, CA 92708

Payless Car Rental Headquartered in St. Petersburg, Florida, a franchisor of automobile rental outlets.

Founded in 1971, Payless has been franchising since its inception. A typical Payless franchisee operates a discount car rental business, with three fulltime and two parttime employees. All except one of the franchisor's 116 outlets are franchise units.

Payless Car Rental, 5510 Gulfport Blvd., St. Petersburg, FL 33707. Telephone: (813) 381-2758

Pearle Vision Centers Headquartered in Dallas, Texas, a franchisor of retail eye care centers.

Founded in 1962, Pearle Vision has been franchising since 1980. The first outlet was opened by an optometrist, Dr. Stanley Pearle, in 1962. When the company began franchising in 1980, Pearle Vision had already established one of the largest retail chains of its kind, with more than 300 outlets.

A typical Pearle Vision franchisee operates a retail store marketing optometric services and dispensing optical prescriptions. The outlet merchandises frames, lenses, sunglasses, and related optical accessories, and may also provide diagnostic and prescriptive services from a trained optician or optometrist.

The laws of some states do not permit prescriptive services to be performed on the same premises where optical aids are sold. In those localities, a Pearle Vision franchisee may operate a retail optical store without an on-site optometrist. Of the 860 Pearle Vision Centers currently operating, more than half are franchise units.

Pearle Vision Center, Inc., 2534 Royal Lane, Dallas, TX 75229. Telephone: (214) 241-3381

Penguin's Place Frozen Yogurt Stores Headquartered in Thousand Oaks, California, a franchisor of specialty food outlets.

Founded in 1983, Penguin's Place has been franchising since 1985. A typical Penguin's Place franchisee operates a retail shop devoted to frozen yoghurt products. Of the franchisor's 140 outlets currently operating, all except 11 are franchise units.

Penguin's Place, 325 E. Hillcrest, Ste. 130, Thousand Oaks, CA 91360. Telephone: (805) 495-3608

Pennsylvania, Franchise Regulations To date, the Pennsylvania legislature has not adopted any generally applicable franchise investment law. However, the rights of automobile retailers and service station owners operating under franchise agreements are protected by separate laws.

Pennsylvania law does not require franchisors to register or file disclosures with any state regulatory body. In the absence of such a requirement, the federal Franchise Rule applies, requiring franchisors to furnish a disclosure document prescribed by the Federal Trade Commission to prospective franchisees ten business days before a franchise sale is made.

See Franchise Rule.

Pennysaver Headquartered in New York City, a franchisor of specialty publishing outlets.

Founded in 1973, Pennysaver has been franchising since 1979. A typical Pennysaver franchisee operates an advertising sales and publishing business devoted to a weekly shopper's guide containing classified advertising, community services, and bargain merchandise for sale. Of the franchisor's 410 outlets currently operating, none are company owned.

Pennysaver, 80 8th Ave., New York, NY 10011. Telephone: (212) 243-6800

Pepe's Mexican Restaurants Headquartered in Chicago, Illinois, a franchisor of food service outlets.

Founded in 1967, Pepe's has been franchising since its inception. A typical Pepe's franchisee operates a specialty restaurant devoted to Mexican-style cuisine, with table service in addition to take-out facilities. Depending on the locality, the outlet may have a full-service cocktail lounge. Of the 65 Pepe's outlets currently in business, all except three are franchise units.

Pepe's Mexican Restaurants, 1325 W. 15th St., Chicago, IL 60608. Telephone: (312) 733-2500

Perkins, Inc. Headquartered in Memphis, Tennessee, a franchisor of food service outlets.

Founded in 1960, Perkins has been franchising since 1962. In 1979, the chain was acquired by Holiday Inns. A typical Perkins franchisee operates a family-style restaurant and coffee shop with a diversified menu featuring pancakes, omelettes, hamburgers, and dinners. Of the franchisor's 330 outlets currently operating, about two thirds are franchise units.

Perkins Restaurants, 6075 Polar Ave., Memphis, TN 38119. Telephone: (901) 766-6412

Perma Ceram International Headquartered in Waldwick, New Jersey, a franchisor of specialized interior remodeling services.

Founded in 1975, Perma Ceram has been franchising since its inception. A typical Perma Ceram franchisee operates a remodeling business devoted to repair and refinishing of ceramic surfaces and fixtures. Of the franchisor's 130 outlets currently operating, all except one are franchise units.

Perma Ceram International, 39 Mackay Ave., Waldwick, NJ 07463. Telephone: (800) 564-5039

Perma-Glaze Headquartered in Tucson, Arizona, a franchisor of specialty interior remodeling services.

Founded in 1978, Perma-Glaze has been franchising since 1981. A typical Perma-Glaze franchisee operates a remodeling business specializing in repair and resurfacing of porcelain and fiberglas fixtures, such as bathtubs, shower stalls, and sinks. Of the franchisor's 65 outlets currently operating, all except two are franchise units.

Perma-Glaze, 132 S. Sherwood Village Dr., Tucson, AZ 85710

Perma-Guard Car Care Centers Headquartered in Oakville, Ontario, a franchisor of automobile rustproofing and detailing outlets.

Founded in 1974, Perma-Guard has been franchising since 1976. A typical Perma-Guard franchisee operates a retail car care business marketing the franchisor's proprietary line of rustproofing and refinishing products. All of the franchisor's 45 Canadian outlets are franchise units.

Perma-Guard, 1380 Speers Rd., Oakville, Ont., Canada L6L 5V3. Telephone: (416) 827-7266

Personnel Pool Headquartered in Ft. Lauderdale, Florida, a franchisor of temporary employment agencies.

Founded in 1946, Personnel Pool has been franchising since 1961. A typical Personnel Pool franchisee operates a recruitment and placement business specializing in temporary employment of technical and semi-skilled workers, including clerical workers, word processing operators, paralegal specialists, and light industrial personnel. A separate division, Medical Personnel Pool, supplies nurses, physical therapists, and home-care specialists, handling calls around the clock. Of the franchisor's 200 outlets currently operating, 130 are franchise units.

Personnel Pool of America, 303 SE 17th St., Ft. Lauderdale, FL 33316. Telephone: (800) 531-2121

Petland Headquartered in Chillicothe, Ohio, a franchisor of retail pet outlets.

Founded in 1967, Petland has been franchising since 1972. A typical Petland franchisee operates a retail store devoted to sales of household pets, pet care products, cages, toys, bedding, and accessories. Of the franchisor's 162 outlets currently operating, all except five are franchise units.

Petland, 195 N. Hickory St., Chillicothe, OH 45601. Telephone: (614) 775-2464

Pet Valu Headquartered in Toronto, Ontario, a franchisor of retail pet supplies outlets.

Founded in 1976, Pet Valu has been franchising since 1987. A typical Pet Valu franchisee operates a retail store devoted to discount pet food and supplies. Of the franchisor's 85 outlets currently operating, 15 are franchise units.

Pet Valu, 720 Tapscott Rd., Ste. 103, Toronto, Ont., Canada M1X 1C6

Physicians Weight Loss Centers Headquartered in Akron, Ohio, a franchisor of weight-loss centers.

Founded in 1979, PWL has been franchising since its inception. A typical PWL franchisee operates a personal weight-loss center based on the "Futra-Loss" diet, a medically supervised regimen of diet counseling and nutrition. Each center employs a licensed physician and a registered or practical nurse on-site. The outlet markets a proprietary line of vitamins and diet foods to enrollees and graduates of the weight-loss program. Of the franchisor's 350 outlets currently operating, all except 24 are franchise units.

Physician's Weight Loss Centers of America, 30 Springside Dr., Akron, OH 44313. Telephone: (800) 322-7952

Pinnacle 1 Headquartered in Charleston, South Carolina, a franchisor of business service outlets.

Founded in 1981, Pinncale 1 has been franchising since its inception. A typical Pinncale 1 franchisee operates a bookkeeping service for small-to-medium size businesses and self-employed individuals. Outlets also offer tax counseling and preparation services. Of the franchisor's 40 outlets currently operating, all except four are franchise units.

Pinnacle 1, 3350 Lenape St., Charleston, SC 29405. Telephone: (803) 744-5861

Pioneer Take-Out Corp. Headquartered in Los Angeles, California, a franchisor of fast-food outlets.

Founded in 1961, Pioneer has been franchising since 1964. A typical Pioneer franchisee operates a fried-chicken restaurant based on the franchisor's standardized food preparation system. Of the franchisor's 226 outlets currently operating, 200 are franchise units.

Pioneer Take-Out Corp., 3663 W. 6th St., Los Angeles, CA 90020. Telephone: (213) 738-0646

Pizza Delight Headquartered in Moncton, New Brunswick, a franchisor of fastfood outlets.

Founded in 1969, Pizza Delight has been franchising since 1971. A typical Pizza Delight franchisee operates a food service operation specializing in fast food items with a continental flair, including pizza and pasta. Of the franchisor's 190 outlets currently operating, all except four are franchise units.

Pizza Delight, P.O. Box 2070, Station A, Moncton, NB, Canada E1C 8H7. Telephone: (506) 853-0990

Pizza Factory Headquartered in Oakhurst, California, a franchisor of fast food outlets.

Founded in 1982, Pizza Factory has been franchising since 1985. A typical Pizza Factory franchisee operates a fast food restaurant featuring pizza, pasta, and sandwiches. Of the franchisor's 40 outlets currently operating, all except three are franchise units.

Pizza Factory, P.O. Box 989, Oakhurst, CA 93644

Pizza Hut Headquartered in Wichita, Kansas, a franchisor of fast-food outlets.

Founded in 1958, Pizza Hut has been franchising since the following year. The franchise company is currently a subsidiary of Pepsico, which does not actively solicit new Pizza Hut franchisees, although existing outlets are occasionally resold or leased.

A typical Pizza Hut franchisee operates a family-style pizza restaurant supplemented by sandwich, salad, pasta, and beverage service. Of the franchisor's estimated 6,000 outlets currently operating, less than half are franchise units.

Pizza Hut, P.O. Box 428, Wichita, KS 67201. Telephone: (316) 681-9000

Pizza Inn Headquartered in Dallas, Texas, a franchisor of fast-food outlets. Founded in 1960, Pizza Inn has been franchising since 1963. A typical Pizza Inn franchisee operates a fast-food restaurant specializing in pizza, Italian-style cuisine, and beverage service. Of the franchisor's 690 outlets currently operating, 460 are franchise units.

Pizza Inn, 2930 Stemmons Fwy., Dallas, TX 75247. Telephone: (800) 527-9405

Pizza Man "He Delivers" Headquartered in North Hollywood, California, a franchisor of fast-food outlets.

Founded in 1972, Pizza Man has been franchising since its inception. A typical Pizza Man franchisee operates a fast-food restaurant specializing in pizza, fried chicken, and barbeque spare ribs, with both sit-down and home-delivery service. All of the franchisor's 56 outlets currently operating are franchise units.

Pizza Man "He Delivers", 6930 1/2 Tujunga Ave., North Hollwood, CA 91605. Telephone: (818) 766-4395

Pizza Movers Headquartered in Landover, Maryland, a franchisor of fast-food outlets.

Founded in 1985, Pizza Movers has been franchising since the following year. A typical Pizza Movers franchisee operates a fast-food pizza restaurant specializing in home-delivery service. Of the franchisor's 70 outlets currently operating, all except nine are franchise units.

Pizza Movers, 1300 Mercantile Lane, Ste. 198, Landover, MD 20785

Pizza Pizza Headquartered in Toronto, Ontario, a franchisor of fast-food outlets.

Founded in 1968, Pizza Pizza has been franchising since 1975. A typical Pizza Pizza franchisee operates a fast-food pizza restaurant specializing in take-out and home-delivery service. Of the franchisor's 160 Canadian outlets currently operating, all except three are franchise units.

Pizza Pizza, 580 Jarvis St., Toronto, Ont., Canada M4Y 2H9. Telephone: (416) 967-0177

Pizzeria Uno Headquartered in Boston, Massachusetts, a franchisor of food service outlets.

Founded in 1943, Pizzeria Uno has been franchising since 1979. A typical Pizzeria Uno franchisee operates a full-service restaurant and cocktail lounge, specializing in deep-dish pizza prepared with a variety of meat and vegetable toppings. Of the franchisor's 45 outlets currently operating, all except 20 are franchise units.

Pizzeria Uno, 100 Charles Rd., Boston, MA 02132

Playorena Headquartered in Roslyn Heights, New York, a franchisor of recreational centers for children.

Founded in 1981, Playorena has been franchising since 1984. A typical Playorena franchisee operates an exercise-play center where parents and children participate in structured, child-development programs. Of the franchisor's 63 outlets currently operating, 24 are franchise units.

Playorena, 125 Mineola Ave., Roslyn Heights, NY 11577. Telephone: (516) 621-7529

Pofolks, Inc. Headquartered in Nashville, Tennessee, a franchisor of food service outlets.

Founded in 1975, Pofolks has been franchising since 1983. A typical Pofolks franchisee operates a family-style restaurant with a Southern ambience and menu. Of the franchisor's 150 outlets currently operating, all except 36 are franchise units.

Pofolks, Inc., 301 S. Perimeter Park Dr., Ste. 201, Nashville, TN 37211

Ponderosa, Inc. Headquartered in Dayton, Ohio, a franchisor of food service outlets.

Founded in 1965, Ponderosa has been franchising since the following year. A typical Ponderosa franchisee operates a cafeteria-style steakhouse with a diversified menu devoted to steaks, hamburgers, chicken, seafood, salads, and desserts. Of the franchisor's 700 outlets currently operating, 300 are franchise units.

Ponderosa, Inc., P.O. Box 578, Dayton, OH 45401. Telephone: (800) 543-9670

Popeye's Famous Fried Chicken & Biscuits Headquartered in Jefferson, Louisiana, a franchisor of fast-food restaurants.

Founded in 1972 by fried-chicken maven Alvin Copeland, Popeye's has been franchising since 1976. A former grocery clerk and doughnut cook, Copeland had previously tried and failed with two different chicken restaurants, before opening Popeye's Mighty Good Fried Chicken. The chain was originally named after a character in a motion picture titled *The French Connection*. In 1976, Copeland developed an association with the Popeye cartoon character under an agreement with King Features.

A typical Popeye's franchisee operates a fast-food restaurant specializing in Cajun-style fried chicken prepared according to the franchisor's recipe and specifications. Meals are accompanied by spicy rice, red beans, home-style biscuits, or other options. Some outlets also feature expanded menus and salad bars.

The Popeye's chain currently consists of 715 outlets, of which 620 are franchise units. Popeye's, Inc. is a wholly-owned subsidiary of A. Copeland Enterprises.

Popeye's Famous Fried Chicken & Biscuits, One Popeye Plaza, 1333 S. Clearview Parkway, Jefferson, LA 70121. Telephone: (504) 733-4300

See Copeland, Alvin

Port of Subs Headquartered in Reno, Nevada, a franchisor of fast-food outlets.

Founded in 1975, Port of Subs has been franchising since 1986. A typical Port of Subs franchisee operates a fast-food operation specializing in freshly prepared submarine-style sandwiches. Of the franchisor's 30 outlets currently operating, all except five are franchise units.

Port of Subs, 100 Washington St., Ste. 200, Reno, NV 89503. Telephone: (702) 322-7901

Precision Tune Headquartered in Sterling, Virginia, a franchisor of automobile tune-up centers.

Founded in 1975, Precision has been franchising since 1978. A typical Precision franchisee operates a specialty auto tune-up business, from a standalone service facility or in conjunction with an existing service station. Of the franchisor's 417 outlets currently operating, all are franchise units.

Precision Tune, 1319 Shepard Dr., Sterling, VA 22170

Price Fixing An illegal attempt or practice to restrain prices. Price fixing is one of the first earliest business practices to be declared *per se* illegal by the U.S. Supreme Court, under the provisions of the Sherman Antitrust Act. (See *antitrust*.) A franchisor engages in price fixing when it encourages, coerces, or forces its franchisees to abide by suggested or mandatory retail prices.

Under the Sherman Act, no instance or form of price fixing is allowable or justifiable, even though the practice may be considered reasonable, necessary, or harmless. Any attempt by a wholesaler or franchisor to raise, lower, or maintain prices is illegal, according to the Supreme Court; any minimum, maximum, or fixed price violates the law. The most famous case involving an attempt to set a minimum price for the resale of a product involved the Adolph Coors Company in 1974. In *Coors v. FTC*, the court ruled that a contract establishing a minimum retail price is illegal under the provisions of the Sherman Act. The brewery argued that the fixed minimum price was reasonable in terms of the business and its market, and was in no way anticompetitive. The circuit court countered that "the power to fix prices, whether reasonably exercised or not, involves power to control the market and to fix arbitrary and unreasonable prices."

Another landmark case, *U.S. v. Parke Davis & Co.*, involved "suggested retail price" lists announced by a company policy bulletin. Parke Davis & Co. instituted a policy not to sell to wholesalers who distributed the company's products to dealers who refused to comply with the suggested prices. The Supreme Court found this practice to be "an unlawful combination" of influences to restrain pricing.

In this case, and in similar trials involving Shell Oil Co., Toyota Motor Sales, Inc., and Tandy Corp., the courts have declared that suggested prices are legal only to the extent that dealers are free to ignore them. If any punitive action or other "meaningful effect" results from noncompliance with any suggested price list, the practice constitutes illegal price fixing.

Thus, a franchisor can only suggest, but not stipulate, the price at which its franchisees offer products and services to their customers.

Print Masters Headquartered in Torrance, California, a franchisor of document duplication outlets.

Founded in 1977, Print Masters has been franchising sinceits inception. A typical Print Masters franchisee operates a retail printing center offering on-premises offset printing, supportive graphic services, and high-speed document copying. None of the 80 Print Masters outlets presently in business are company owned.

Print Masters, 370 S. Crenshaw Blvd., Torrance, CA 90053. Telephone: (800) 221-8945

Print Shack Headquartered in Tampa, Florida, a franchisor of document duplication outlets.

Founded in 1982, Print Shack has been franchising since the following year. A typical Print Shack franchisee operates a retail printing center specializing in on-premises quick-print services and self-service document copying. The chain has 116 outlets, none of which are company owned.

Print Shack, 500 N. Westshore Blvd., Ste. 610, Tampa, FL 33609. Telephone: (800) 237-5167

Print Three Headquartered in Scarborough, Ontario, a franchisor of document duplication outlets.

Founded in 1970, Print Three has been franchising since 1982. A typical Print Three franchisee operates a retail printing service utilizing electronic desktop publishing equipment and laser-based printers. All of the franchisor's 125 outlets are franchise units.

Print Three, 156 Shorting Rd., Scarborough, Ont., Canada M1S 3S6. Telephone: (800) 268-4177

Priority Management Systems Headquartered in Irving, Texas, a franchisor of executive training services.

Founded in 1984, PMS has been franchising since its inception. A typical PMS franchisee operates a consulting business specializing in "productivity training" for management personnel. The outlet's clients may include Fortune 500 corporations as well as small and mid-sized companies. The PMS chain currently consists of 145 outlets, all of which are franchise units.

Priority Management Systems, 2401 Gateway Dr., Ste. 155, Irving, TX 75063. Telephone: (800) 221-9031

Pro Image, The Headquartered in Bountiful, Utah, a franchisor of specialty retail outlets.

Founded in 1985 by two brothers, Kevin and Chad Olson, ProImage has been franchising since its inception. A typical ProImage franchisee operates a retail store devoted to sports apparel and gifts bearing the trademarks of professional sports franchises. The inventory consists of team caps, jackets, jerseys, sweatshirts, mascot dolls, pins, and other sports-related novelties. The Pro Image chain consists today of 98 outlets, all of which are operated under franchise licenses.

The Pro Image, 380 N. 200 West, Ste. 203, Bountiful, UT 84010. Telephone: (801) 292-8777

Professional Carpet Systems Headquartered in Forest Park, Georgia, a franchisor of interior maintenance services.

Founded in 1978, PCS has been franchising since 1980. A typical PCS franchisee operates a mobile home-maintenance business specializing in the cleaning, dyeing, and restoration of carpet fabrics. Of the franchisor's 180 outlets currently operating, all except two are franchise units.

Professional Carpet Systems, 5250 Old Dixie Hwy., Forest Park, GA 30050. Telephone: (800) 235-3170

ProForma, Inc. Headquartered in Cleveland, Ohio, a franchisor of business supply outlets.

Founded in 1978, ProForma has been franchising since 1985. A typical ProForma franchisee operates a retail outlet devoted to business forms and office and computer supplies. Of the franchisor's 80 outlets currently operating, all except one are franchise units.

ProForma, Inc., 4705 Van Epps Rd., Cleveland, OH 44131. Telephone: (800) 825-1525

ProFusion Systems Headquartered in Aurora, Colorado, a franchisor of vinyl repair outlets.

Founded in 1980, ProFusion has been franchising since 1983. A typical ProFusion franchisee operates a service business based on the franchisor's system of thermo-plastic repair. All of the 120 ProFusion outlets currently in business are franchise units.

ProFusion Systems, 2851 S. Parker Rd., Ste. 650, Aurora, CO 80014

proVenture Headquartered in Quincy, Massachusetts, a franchisor of commercial brokerage services.

Founded in 1984, proVenture has been franchising since the following year. A typical proVenture franchisee operates a business brokerage office for sale-minded companies and prospective investors. Of the franchisor's ten outlets currently operating, all except one are franchise units.

proVenture Business Group, 79 Parkingway, Quincy, MA 02169. Telephone: (617) 773-0530

Putt-Putt Headquartered in Fayetteville, North Carolina, a franchisor of miniature-golf and electronic game outlets.

Founded in 1954, Putt-Putt has been franchising since the following year. Founder Donald Clayton opened the first outlet after having been forced into semi-retirement by an ailing heart. A typical Putt-Putt franchisee operates an amusement facility centered around a miniature-golf course. Optional packages include an electronic game room and an ice cream snack bar. Of the franchisor's 325 outlets currently operating, all except eight are franchise units.

Putt-Putt Golf and Games, 3007 Ft. Bragg Rd., Fayetteville, NC 28303. Telephone: (919) 485-7131

Quaker State Minit-Lube Headquartered in Salt Lake City, Utah, a franchisor of automotive service outlets.

Founded in 1977, Quaker State has been franchising since its inception. A typical Quaker State franchisee operates a quick oil change and lubrication service. Of the franchisor's 300 outlets currently operating, about a third are franchise units.

Quaker State Minit-Lube, Inc., 1385 W. 2200 S, Salt Lake City, UT 84119. Telephone: (801) 972-6667

Quality Inns Headquartered in Silver Spring, Maryland, a franchisor of lodging outlets.

Founded in 1941. The company also franchises Comfort Innsand Clarion Resorts, Quality has been franchising since its inception. A typical Quality franchisee operates an economy-priced motel offering clean, attractively furnished accommodations and traditional hotel amenities at economical rates. The premises may include a swimming pool, meeting rooms, and food and beverage service. Of the franchisor's 950 Quality Inn, Comfort Inn, and Clarion Resort outlets currently operating, all except 11 are franchise units.

Quality Inns, 10750 Columbia Pk., Silver Spring, MD 20901. Telephone: (301) 236-5080

Rainbow
to
Runza

Rainbow International Headquartered in Waco, Texas, a franchisor of interior maintenance services.

Founded in 1981, Rainbow International has been franchising since its inception. A typical Rainbow International franchisee operates a mobile home-maintenance business devoted to carpet protection, cleaning, dyeing, repair, and restoration services, utilizing the franchisor's standardized techniques, chemicals, and equipment. All except five of the 1,450 Rainbow International outlets currently in business are franchise units.

Rainbow International Carpet Dyeing & Cleaning Co., 1010 N. University Parks Dr., Waco, TX 76707. Telephone: (800) 624-7613

RainSoft Water Conditioning Company Headquartered in Elk Grove Village, Illinois, a franchisor of water treatment services.

Founded in 1953, RainSoft has been franchising since 1968. A typical RainSoft franchisee operates a residential and commercial water-treatment business devoted to installing and servicing the franchisor's line of water-softening systems, filters, and purification devices. Of the franchisor's 305 outlets currently operating, all except one are franchise units.

RainSoft Water Conditioning Co., 2080 E. Lunt Ave., Elk Grove Village, IL 60007. Telephone: (312) 437-9400

Rally's Hamburgers Headquartered in Louisville, Kentucky, a franchisor of fast-food outlets.

Founded in 1984, Rally's has been franchising since 1986. A typical Rally's franchisee operates a fast-food restaurant specializing in hamburgers, sandwiches, fried potatoes, soft drinks, and milk shakes. Of the franchisor's 80 outlets currently operating, all except one are franchise units.

Rally's Hamburgers, 10002 Shelbyville Rd., Ste. 150, Louisville, KY 40223

Ramada Inn System Headquartered in Phoenix, Arizona, a franchisor of lodging outlets.

Founded in 1954, Ramada has been franchising since 1959. The company also owns the Tropicana casino hotels in Las Vegas and Atlantic City, from which Ramada derives approximately half of its annual income. Chief executive Richard Snell has called for an aggressive expansion program, including the establishment of new upscale hotels catering to the convention trade. With more than 100,000 rooms in 590 properties, Ramada is presently the fourth largest hotel operator in the United States.

A typical Ramada franchisee operates a mid-priced full-service hotel with on-premises food and beverage service, swimming pool, and banquet and convention facilities. Besides tourist-class Ramada Inn prototypes, the chain also franchises a more upscale excutive-class hotel under the trade name Renaissance Inn. The Ramada chain consists of 590 outlets, including 40 franchise units.

Ramada Inn System, P.O. Box 29004, Phoenix, AZ 85006. Telephone: (602) 273-4000

Rax Restaurants Headquartered in Columbus, Ohio, a franchisor of fast-food outlets.

Founded in 1967, Rax has been franchising since 1978. A typical Rax franchisee operates a family-style restaurant featuring a varied menu of hot and cold fast-food items, including roast beef, turkey, chicken, and ham sandwiches; fresh salads; baked potatoes served with various toppings; and specialty items for diners on low-salt diets. The outlet is distinguised by its emphasis on nutrition, as reflected in entrees that meet American Heart Association dietary criteria. Of the franchisor's 520 outlets currently operating, 370 are franchise units.

Rax Restaurants, 1266 Dublin Rd., Columbus, OH 43215. Telephone: (614) 486-3669

Realty Executives Headquartered in Phoenix, Arizona, a franchisor of real estate sales offices.

Founded in 1964, Realty Executives has been franchising since 1978. A typical Realty Executives franchisee operates a real estate brokerage for commercial and residential property listed for sale. The outlet rents desk space, telephones, and business services to brokers and sales representatives with whom the agency shares commissions. Of the franchisor's 70 outlets currently operating, all except 23 are franchise units.

Realty Executives, 4427 N. 36th St., Phoenix, AZ 85018. Telephone: (800) 528-0365

Realty World Corp. Headquartered in Fairfax, Virginia, a franchisor of independent real estate sales offices.

Founded in 1974, Realty World has been franchising since its inception. A typical Realty World franchisee operates a real estate brokerage under the franchisor's trademark. The outlet offers residential and commercial real estate, including sale, leasing, and, in some cases, financial assistance. All of the 1,760 Realty World outlets currently operating are independent franchise units.

Realty World Corp., 12500 Fair Lakes Circle, Fairfax, VA 22033. Telephone: (703) 631-9300

Recognition Express Headquartered in San Juan Capistrano, California, a franchisor of employee recognition products.

Founded in 1972, Recognition Express has been franchising since 1974. A typical Recognition Express franchisee operates a commercial sales business specializing in awards, plaques, trophies, and related "recognition" products. The chain consists of 96 outlets, all of which are franchise units.

Recognition Express, 31726 Rancho Vieho Rd., Ste. 115, San Juan Capistrano, CA 92675. Telephone: (714) 493-3666

Red Carpet Inns Headquartered in Atlanta, Georgia, a franchisor of lodging outlets.

Founded in 1972, Red Carpet Inns has been franchising since its inception. The parent company, Hospitality International, also licenses franchisees under the trade names Scottish Inns and Master Host Inns. A typical Red Carpet Inns franchisee operates a full-service, mid-price hotel with on-premises food and beverage service, recreational facilities, and uniformed bell service, based on the franchisor's specifications and standards.

All of the franchisor's 250 Red Carpet Inn, Scottish Inn, and Master Host Inn outlets are franchise units.

Hospitality International, 1152 Spring St., Ste. A, Atlanta, GA 30309. Telephone: (800) 251-1962

Red Carpet Real Estate Headquartered in San Diego, California, a franchisor of independent real estate sales offices.

Founded in 1966, Red Carpet has been franchising since the following year. Northern California realtor Anthony Yniguez opened the first Red Carpet office in Contra Costa County, across the bay from San Francisco. His idea was to form a council of local brokers to join forces to generate referrals and fund cooperative advertising. In 1986, the chain formed an agreement with Guild Mortgage Co. of San Diego to integrate mortgage services with the Red Carpet sales network.

A typical Red Carpet franchisee operates a residential and commercial real estate business under the franchisor's trademark. The outlet focuses on sales, leases, and rentals, primarily of residential property. The Red Carpet network currently has 460 members, none of which are owned by the franchisor.

Red Carpet Real Estate Services, Inc., P.O. Box 85660, San Diego, CA 92138. Telephone: (619) 571-7181

Red Robin Burger & Spirits Emporium Headquartered in Irvine, California, a franchisor of food and beverage service outlets.

Founded in 1969, Red Robin has been franchising since 1979. A typical Red Robin franchisee operates a specialty restaurant and cocktail lounge, featuring a menu devoted to "gourmet" hamburger sandwiches. Of the franchisor's 48 outlets currently operating, 31 are franchise units.

Red Robin, 9 Executive Circle, Irvine, CA 92714

Registration In franchising, the act of submitting an application with a state authority responsible for overseeing franchise practices, to offer or sell franchises in that state.

In 1971, California became the first state to enact a franchise investment law requiring registration by franchisors. The law requires that, before offering franchises in the state, a franchisor must file an application with the Department of Corporations and await approval. Section 31114 declares:

> *The application for registration shall be accompanied by a proposed offering pro-*
> *spectus, which shall contain the material information set forth in the application...*

The referenced "offering prospectus" was subsequently adopted by a consortium of midwestern securities commissioners as the Uniform Franchise Offering Circular, or UFOC, a standardized document designed to fulfill the requirements of various state franchise investment laws. In brief, the document discloses pertinent information about the franchisor, franchise business, and franchise agreement, emphasizing areas which might have a negative impact on franchisees.

Fourteen other states, commonly called the registration states, have since enacted similar laws calling for the registration of franchise offerings and the filing of disclosures.

The application for registration consists of four basic parts: (1) a facing page, (2) a supplemental information page, (3) a salesman disclosure form, and (4) a copy of the proposed offering circular (UFOC). The prescribed forms used by the 15 registration states are shown in the examples.

Some states, including California, also require franchisors to submit copies of any proposed advertising materials to be used to promote franchise opportunities. In most instances, both the registration and the advertisements must be approved by the regulatory agency before the franchisor may proceed. The state franchise investment laws also stipulate a waiting period, usually ten business days, after the UFOC is furnished to a prospective franchisee and before a sale is made.

Failure to register can result in criminal as well as civil penalties. In 1988, an Illinois court ruled that the executives of a franchise organization can be held personally liable for registration and disclosure violations under that state's Franchise Disclosure Act.

Approval of a registration by a state agency does not in any way constitute approval or endorsement of a franchisor's offering.

See Registration States.

Registration States The fifteen U.S. states which have enacted franchise registration and disclosure laws.

The following states currently have such laws on their books:

California
Hawaii
Illinois
Indiana
Maryland
Michigan
Minnesota
New York
North Dakota
Oregon
Rhode Island
South Dakota
Virginia
Washington
Wisconsin

Franchisors operating in these states must register with a state regulatory authority and file disclosures regarding the franchise business and agreeement. The Uniform Franchise Offering Circular (UFOC), with minor variations, modifications, and additions, satisfies the disclosure obligations imposed by the registration states.

See Registration, Uniform Franchise Offering Circular, and individual state listings.

UNIFORM FRANCHISE REGISTRATION APPLICATION

FILE NO.

FEE: _____

Date of Application: _____

APPLICATION FOR:

_____ REGISTRATION OF AN OFFER OR SALE OF FRANCHISES

_____ REGISTRATION RENEWAL STATEMENT OR ANNUAL REPORT

AMENDMENT NUMBER _____ TO APPLICATION

_____ POST-EFFECTIVE

FILED UNDER SECTION _____

_____ PRE-EFFECTIVE

DATED _____

1. Name of Franchisor.

   Name under which Franchisor is doing or intends to do business.

2. Franchisor's principal business address.

   Name and address of Franchisor's agent authorized to receive process in this state.

3. Name, address, and telephone number of subfranchisors, if any, for this state.

4. Name, address, and telephone number of person to whom communications regarding this application should be directed.

SUPPLEMENTAL INFORMATION

1.

    A. States in which this proposed registration is effective.

    B. States in which this proposed registration is or will be shortly filed.

    C. The states, if any, which have refuses, by order or otherwise, to register these franchises.

    D. The states, if any, which have revoked or suspended the right to offer these franchises.

    E. The states, if any in which the proposed registration of these franchises have been withdrawn.

2.   The following sets forth in budget form the total projected financing required by franchisor to fulfill the franchisor's obligations to provide real estate, improvement, equipment, inventory, training and all other items included in the offering. Show separately the sources of all of the required funds including any proposed loans or contributions to capital.

    I certify under penalty of law that I have read this application and the exhibits attached hereto and incorporated herein by reference, and know the contents thereof and that the statements therein are true and correct.

SALESMAN DISCLOSURE FORM

1. As required by this state's statute, list the persons who will engage in the offer or sale of franchises in this state and for each person list the following information:

    A. Name;
    B. Business address and telephone number;
    C. Home address and telephone number;
    D. Present employer;
    E. Present title;
    F. Social security number;
    G. Birthdate; and
    H. Employment or occupation during the past 5 years. For each such employment state the name of the employer, position held, and beginning and ending dates.

2. State whether any person identified in 1, above:

    A. has any administrative or civil action pending against him alleging a violation of any franchise law, fraud, embezzlement, fraudulent conversion, restraint of trade, unfair or deceptive business practices, misappropriation of property, or comparable allegations?

             YES ___   NO ___

    B. Has during the 10-year period immediately preceding the date of the offering circular:

        (1) been convicted of a felony or pleaded nolo contendere to any felony charge or been held liable in any other civil action by final action if such felony or civil action involved violation of any franchise law, fraud, embezzlement, fraudulent conversion, restraint of trade, unfair or deceptive practices, misappropriation of property or any comparable violations of law?

                 YES ___   NO ___

        (2) entered into or been named in any consent judgment, decree, order or assurance under any federal or state franchise, securities, antitrust, monopoly, trade practice, or trade regulation law?

                 YES ___   NO ___

RE/MAX Headquartered in Englewood, Colorado, a franchisor of independent real estate sales offices.

Founded in 1973, RE/MAX has been franchising since 1976. A typical RE/MAX franchisee operates a real estate listing and sales business utilizing the franchisor's trademark, signage, and advertising. All of the franchisor's 1,400 outlets currently operating are owned by independent franchisees.

RE/MAX, P.O. Box 3907, Englewood, CO 80155. Telephone: (800) 525-7452

Rent A Wreck Headquartered in Los Angeles, California, a franchisor of automobile rental outlets.

Founded in 1969, Rent A Wreck has been franchising since 1980. A typical Rent A Wreck franchisee operates a used-car rental business, either as a standalone operation or as an adjunct to a related automotive sales or service business. Of the franchisor's 355 outlets currently operating, all except one are franchise units.

Rent A Wreck, 10889 Wilshire Blvd., Ste. 12960, Los Angeles, CA 90024. Telephone: (800) 421-7253

Rent-A-Dent Headquartered in Seattle, Washington, a franchisor of automobile rental outlets.

Founded in 1976, Rent-A-Dent has been franchising since 1980. A typical Rent-A-Dent franchisee operates a car rental lot featuring used vehicles offered at discount rates. Of the franchisor's 100 outlets currently operating, all except ten are franchise units.

Rent-A-Dent Car Rental System, 19415 Pacific Hwy. South,Ste. 413, Seattle, WA 98188. Telephone: (800) 426-5243

Residence Inn, The Headquartered in Wichita, Kansas, a franchisor of residential hotels.

Founded in 1975, The Residence Inn has been franchising since 1981. A typical The Residence Inn franchisee operates a condominium-style lodging establishment catering to extended-stay occupants. Of the franchisor's 90 outlets currently operating, all except 23 are franchise units.

The Residence Inn, 257 N. Broadway, Wichita, KS 67202. Telephone: (316) 267-6767

Rhode Island, Franchise Regulations Franchisors operating in the state of Rhode Island are governed by the Franchise and Distributorship Investment Regulation Act, which requires registration and disclosure of pertinent information about the franchisor, franchise business, and franchise agreement.

Before offering or selling a franchise in the state, a franchisor must first prepare a disclosure document prescribed by the statute, then file the information, along with the franchise agreement, financial statements, and related documents, with the Department of Business Regulation.

In addition to a disclosure document, franchisors are also required to submit the following items:

1. Application for registration of the franchise offering;
2. Salesman disclosure form;
3. Consent to service of process;
4. Auditor's consent to use of audited financial statements;
5. Cross-reference sheet showing the location in the franchise agreement of the key items in the disclosure document.

The *Uniform Franchise Offering Circular* (UFOC) devised by a consortium of midwestern securities commissioners as a uniform method of complying with state franchise investment laws, fulfills the disclosure requirements of the Rhode Island statute. There are minor variations and differences in language required by the Rhode Island statute, including a different cover page. (See *Uniform Franchise Offering Circular.*)

The disclosure document or UFOC must be furnished to a prospective franchisee at least ten business days before a franchise sale is made.

For information about state franchise laws, regulations, and filing requirements, or to report possible violations, contact: Chief Securities Examiner, Department of Business Regulation, 100 N. Maine St., Providence, RI 02903. Telephone: (401) 277-2405.

Ritzy's Headquartered in Columbus, Ohio, a franchisor of fast-food outlets.

Founded in 1980, Ritzy's has been franchising since 1983. A typical Ritzy's franchisee operates a fast-food restaurant with a family-style motif and a classic menu featuring hamburgers, hot dogs, ice cream, and soft drinks. Of the franchisor's 75 outlets currently operating, all except 17 are franchise units.

Ritzy's, 1496 Old Henderson Rd., Columbus, OH 43220. Telephone: (614) 459-3250

Robin's Donuts Headquartered in Thunder Bay, Ontario, a franchisor of fast-food outlets.

Founded in 1975, Robin's has been franchising since 1977. A typical Robin's franchisee operates a specialty bakery goods shop specializing in freshly prepared doughnuts, muffins, and coffee service. Of the franchisor's 124 outlets currently operating, all except two are franchise units.

Robin's Donuts, 906 E. Victoria Ave., Thunder Bay, Ont., Canada P7C 1B4. Telephone: (807) 623-4453

Rockefeller, John Davison (1839-1937) Industrialist, philanthropist, and originator of the petroleum franchise. Born on July 8, 1839 in Richford, New York, Rockefeller went to work for a Cleveland mercantile firm at the tender age of 16. Four years later, he entered into a partnership, Clark and Rockefeller, a commodities trading firm which prospered during the Civil War. With four partners, he organized a new enterprise in Cleveland, to build an oil refinery.

Within months, Rockefeller and Andrews had become the largest refinery in the United States. With his brother William and an investor named Henry Flagler, Rockefeller constructed a second refinery and, in 1870, incorporated Standard Oil of Ohio. By 1878, Rockefeller was the dominant power of the entire worldwide oil industry.

In 1882, he entrusted Standard Oil to a nine-man directorate, one of the trusts that inspired the passage of the Sherman Antitrust Act of 1890. Rockefeller's trust controlled 95 percent of the petroleum industry in the United States, with additional holdings in mining, manufacturing, and transportation.

Standard Oil spawned the proliferation of franchised Standard and Chevron service stations in the twentieth century, and, by the 1960s, the petroleum and automobile industries represented more than 60 percent of all U.S. franchise outlets.

The Rockefeller Institute for Medical Research, now Rockefeller University, was founded in 1901. The Rockefeller Foundation, dedicated to humanitarianism and the arts, was established in 1913. In all, Rockefeller's philanthropic legacy totalled $500 million. His autobiography, *Random Reminiscences of Men and Events,* appeared in 1909.

Rocky Mountain Chocolate Factory Headquartered in Durango, Colorado, a franchisor of retail confection outlets.

Founded in 1981, Rocky Mountain has been franchising since 1982. A typical Rocky Mountain franchisee operates a retail food service specializing in chocolates, nuts, and candies. Of the franchisor's 60 outlets currently operating, all except five are franchise units.

Rocky Mountain Chocolate Factory, P.O. Box 2408, Durango, CO 81302. Telephone: (303) 259-0554

Rodeway Inns International Headquartered in Dallas, Texas, a franchisor of lodging outlets.

Founded in 1961, Rodeway has been franchising since its inception. A typical Rodeway franchisee operates a full-service lodging establishment in the medium rate category, with 100 rooms, swimming pool, and modest food and beverage operations. Besides licensing new franchise outlets, the chain also has a "conversion" program by which independent property owners can join the Rodeway Inn system. The Rodeway Inn chain presently consists of 160 franchise outlets.

Rodeway Inns International, 8585 N. Stemmons Fwy., Ste. 400-S, Dallas, TX 75247. Telephone: (800) 345-3453

Romac Headquartered in Portland, Maine, a franchisor of commercial accounting services.

Founded in 1966, Romac has been franchising since 1978. A typical Romac franchisee operates a diversified business support service offering accounting, data processing, banking, and executive recruitment services. Of the franchisor's 40 outlets currently operating, all except one are franchise units.

Romac, P.O. Box 7469, Portland, ME 04112. Telephone: (800) 341-0263

Ronald McDonald Long-tenured advertising symbol for McDonald's, the largest operator of hamburger restaurants.

Ronald McDonald is probably the first advertising character ever to become a national celebrity strictly as part of an advertising campaign. From his inception, the stereotype red-wigged harlequin bore more than a casual resemblence to the famous Bozo the Clown character which had been immortalized on 33-RPM recordings and, later, on daily television. Ronald McDonald appeared only in commercials characterized by a soft-sell approach that often included a short story or children's safety message. The ads were aimed directly at children, rather than their parents, in a subtle campaign to influence the buying behavior of families.

In his most successful commercial, the clown landed at a McDonald's drive-in on a flying saucer shaped like a hamburger. The ad later served as an inspiration for a float unveiled at Macy's Thanksgiving Day Parade in 1965. McDonald's executives attributed the float with an eight-percent increase in winter profits.

Ronald McDonald was the stepchild of two Washington entrepreneurs, John Gibson and Oscar "Goldy" Goldstein, who obtained a franchise for the Washington metropolitan area in 1956. Operating under the name the Gee Gee Corporation, the franchisees expanded to five outlets within four years. Searching for high exposure media advertising, Goldstein pushed for sponsorship of a new show called Bozo's Circus. Goldstein saw the children's audience as the key to influencing the purchasing behavior of the nation's burgeoning parent population.

Sponsoring Bozo proved to be an enormous huge success for the Washington-based franchisees. The renowned clown's personal appearances at the restaurants attracted thousands of excited children and stopped traffic for miles. When Bozo's Circus was suddenly canceled by the network, Goldstein came up with the idea of creating an exclusive McDonald's clown similar to Bozo.

Ronald Mcdonald was first played by Willard Scott, the same performer who had played Bozo the Clown on television (and later caught on as a weatherman with NBC). The imitation Bozo made his television debut in Washington on December 1963 and was a smashing success. By the mid 1960s, Gee Gee had expanded to 25 stores and was spending half a million dollars a year on advertising, mostly on Ronald McDonald spots.

The commercial clown was catapulted into the national limelight by D'Arcy's Advertising in Chicago, the agency hired by McDonald's Corporation to direct national advertising efforts. For the "big time" Ronald McDonald, the agency chose another internationally known harlequin, Coco the Clown. Since Coco only spoke Hungarian, his first commercials featured the theme song "McDonald's is your kind of place," put to the melody of "Down by the Riverside."

Over its 25-year tenure as the hamburger chain's primary advertising symbol, the Ronald McDonald character came to perfuse almost every aspect of the chain's promotional activities. Ronald McDonald Houses, conceived by Elkman Advertising, Philadelphia, are located adjacent to children's hospitals and provide free or low-cost room and board for families with children requiring extended hospital care. Thirty percent of McDonald's outlets have on-premises McDonald Playlands, children's playgrounds with equipment bearing resemblences to Ronald McDonald characters.

Roth Young Personnel Service Headquartered in New York City, a franchisor of personnel recruitment agencies.

Founded in 1962, Roth Young has been franchising since 1977. A typical Roth Young franchisee operates an executive search and employment agency. Of the franchisor's 31 outlets currently operating, none are company-owned.

Roth Young Personnel Service, 1500 Broadway, New York, NY 10036. Telephone: (212) 869-0937

Roto-Rooter Headquartered in Des Moines, Iowa, a franchisor of plumbing maintenance services.

Founded in 1935, Roto-Rooter has been franchising since its inception, becoming one of the most recognizable trademarks in franchising. A typical Roto-Rooter franchisee operates a drain and sewer cleaning service catering to households. All except 25 of the franchisor's 750 active outlets are franchise units.

Roto-Rooter, 300 Ashworth Rd., West Des Moines, IA 50265. Telephone: (515) 223-1343

Roto-Static International Headquartered in Mississauga, Ontario, a franchisor of interior maintenance services.

Founded in 1977, Roto-Static has been franchising since its inception. A typical Roto-Static franchisee operates a mobile home-care business specializing in carpet and upholstery cleaning and restoration.

Roto-Static International, 6810-I Kitimat Rd., Mississauga, Ont., Canada L5N 5M2

Round Table Franchise Corp. Headquartered in San Francisco, California, a franchisor of fast-food outlets.

Founded in 1959, Round Table has been franchising since 1962. A typical Round Table franchisee operates a pizza restaurant with a standardized exterior and interior design. Pizzas are prepared with a variety of meat, vegetable, seafood, or fruit toppings. The outlet may also sell wine, beer, and soft drinks. All 550 Round Table outlets currently in operation are franchise units.

Round Table Franchise Corp., 655 Montgomery St., 7th Floor, San Francisco, CA 94111. Telephone: (415) 392-7500

Roy Rogers Restaurants Headquartered in Rockville, Maryland, a franchisor of family-style restaurants.

Founded in 1968, Roy Rogers has been franchising since its inception. The chain that bears the name of America's most famous retired singing cowboy is actually a subsidiary of Marriott Corp. Once devoted primarily to roast beef, today's Roy Rogers menu also features such traditional fast-food fare as fried chicken and hamburgers.

A typical Roy Rogers franchisee operates a fast-food restaurant based on a standardized menu, food preparation system, and site design. Of the franchisor's 570 outlets currently operating, 224 are franchise units.

Roy Rogers Restaurants, 1803 Research Blvd., Ste. 101, Rockville, MD 20850. Telephone: (800) 423-2409, Ext. 6128

Runza Drive-Inns Headquartered in Lincoln, Nebraska, a franchisor of fast-food outlets.

Founded in 1960, Runza has been franchising since 1980. A typical Runza franchisee operates a drive-in fast-food restaurant, serving hamburgers and other specialty sandwiches to customers in their automobiles. Of the franchisor's 50 outlets currently operating, all except 14 are franchise units.

Runza Drive-Inns, P.O. Box 6042, Lincoln, NE 68516. Telephone: (402) 423-2394

St. Clair
to
Silvan

St. Clair Paint and Wallpaper Headquartered in Toronto, Ontario, a franchisor of specialty home decoration outlets.

Founded in 1939, St. Clair has been franchising since 1970. A typical St. Clair franchisee operates a retail store devoted to paints, decorative wall and window coverings, and accent products. Of the franchisor's 175 outlets currently operating, 125 are franchise units.

St. Clair Paint & Wallpaper, 36 Dufflaw Rd., Toronto, Ont., Canada M6A 2W1. Telephone: (416) 789-0561

St. Hubert Bar-B-Q Headquartered in Laval, Quebec, a franchisor of specialty restaurants.

Founded in 1951, St. Hubert has been franchising since 1979. A typical St. Hubert franchisee operates a family-style restaurant specializing in barbequed ribs and chicken. Of the franchisor's 110 outlets currently operating, about 75 are franchise units.

St. Hubert Bar-B-Q, 2 Pl. Laval, Laval, Que., Canadfa H7N 5N6

Sales Consultants International Headquartered in Cleveland, Ohio, a franchisor of executive recruitment agencies.

Founded in 1957 as a subsidiary of Management Recruiters, Inc., SCI has been franchising since 1965. A typical SCI franchisee operates an executive search, recruitment, and placement business specializing in sales and marketing professionals. Customers of the outlet include employers as well as job candidates. Of the franchisor's 133 outlets currently operating, 107 are franchise units.

Sales Consultants International, 1127 Euclid Ave., Cleveland, OH 44115. Telephone: (216) 696-1122

Sanders, Harlan Former restaurant chain operator and spokesperson for the Kentucky Fried Chicken franchise organization.

Born in Henryville, Indiana on September 9, 1890, Sanders was widely known as the "Kentucky Colonel" who devised the secret recipe for fried chicken based on 11 "secret" herbs and spices. The Kentucky Fried Chicken chain, today owned and operated by Pepsico, was spawned by from Sander's original recipe.

A high-school dropout, Sanders married Claudia Ledington in 1948. He operated a gasoline service station and a small roadside eatery, Sander's Cafe, in Corbin, Kentucky, from 1929 until 1956. In 1954, he happened to cook a special fried chicken dinner for his friend, Pete Harmon, who operated a hamburger stand in Salt Lake City. Inspired by Sander's recipe, Harmon began offering fried chicken at his own restaurant and, after tripling his revenues, convinced the Kentucky colonel to franchise.

Colonel Sanders' Kentucky Fried Chicken began operations in 1956. Sanders ran his own outlet until 1964, and served as a director of the franchising corporation from 1964 until 1970. He later became part owner of the Cape Codder restaurant chain and operated the Colonel Sanders Kentucky Inn in Shelbyville, Kentucky.

In 1965, Sanders received the Horatio Alger Award for his enterpreneurial achievements and charitable contributions.

Sandler Systems Headquartered in Stevenson, Maryland, a franchisor of executive training services.

Founded in 1983, Sandler has been franchising since the following year. A typical Sandler franchisee operates an educational service devoted to sales and marketing professionals. All of the franchisor's 60 outlets currently operating are franchise units.

Sandler Systems, 10411 Stevenson Rd., Stevenson, MD 21153. Telephone: (301) 653-9056

Sandwich Tree, The Headquartered in Vancouver, British Columbia, a franchisor of fast-food outlets.

Founded in 1977, The Sandwich Tree has been franchising since 1981. A typical The Sandwich Tree franchisee operates a fast-food restaurant specializing in specialty sandwiches, salads, and soups, all prepared with fresh ingredients. Of the franchisor's 70 outlets currently operating, all except seven are franchise units.

The Sandwich Tree, 1740-885 W. Georgia St., Vancouver, B.C., Canada V6C 3E8. Telephone: (604) 682-5253

Sanford Rose Associates Headquartered in Akron, Ohio, a franchisor of management recruitment agencies.

Founded in 1959, Sanford Rose has been franchising since 1970. A typical Sanford Rose franchisee operates a personnel recruitment agency specializing in job candidates and positions in management, sales, and marketing positions. Of the franchisor's 85 outlets currently operating, all except one are franchise units.

Sanford Rose Associates, 265 S. Main St., Akron, OH 44308. Telephone: (800) 321-2174

Saucy's Pizza Headquartered in Everett, Washington, a franchisor of specialty food outlets.

Founded in 1982, Saucy's has been franchising since the following year. A typical Saucy's franchisee operates a retail fast)food shop devoted to "We Make/You Bake" pizza and pasta. Of the franchisor's 77 outlets currently operating, all except three are franchise units.

Saucy's Pizza, 2930 Wetmore Ave., Ste. 908, Everett, WA 98201

Sbarro, Inc. Headquartered in Commack, New York, a franchisor of fast-food outlets.
Founded in 1977, Sbarro has been franchising since its inception. A typical Sbarro franchisee operates a cafeteria-style food service business, specializing in Italian cuisine, usually in a shopping mall or strip center. The outlet is distinguished by its decorative display of hanging salamis and cheeses and a red, white, and green sign reminiscent of the Italian flag. Customers choose from a buffet of pizza, pasta, specialty sandwiches, salads, and desserts. Of the franchisor's 275 outlets currently operating, 75 are franchise units.
Sbarro, Inc., 763 Larkfield Rd., Commack, NY 11725. Telephone: (516) 864-0200

Scandia Down Shops Headquartered in Seattle, Washington, a franchisor of specialty retail outlets.
Founded in 1970, Scandia has been franchising since its inception. A typical Scandia franchisee operates a retail boutique devoted to bedding products and furnishings. Of the franchisor's 80 outlets currently operating, none are company-owned.
Scandia Down Shops, P.O. Box 88819, Seattle, WA 98188. Telephone: (800) 237-5337

Schlotzsky's Headquartered in Austin, Texas, a franchisor of fast-food outlets.
Founded in 1971, Schlotzsky's has been franchising since 1976. A typical Schlotzsky's franchisee operates a delicatessen-style restaurant featuring specialty sandwiches, fresh salads, soup, hot entrees, and beverage service. Of the franchisor's 222 outlets currently operating, all except nine are franchise units.
Schlotzsky's, 200 W. 4th St., Austin, TX 78701. Telephone: (512) 480-9871

Scottish Inns Headquartered in Atlanta, Georgia, a franchisor of lodging outlets.
Founded in 1972, Scottish Inns has been franchising since its inception. The parent company, Hospitality International, also licenses franchisees under the trade names Red Carpet Inns and Master Host Inns. A typical Scottish Inns franchisee operates an economy-class motel emphasizing attractive accommodations at a reasonable price, based on the franchisor's specifications for outlet design, size, construction, and decor.
All of the franchisor's 250 Scottish Inn, Red Carpet Inn, and Master Host Inn are franchise units.
Hospitality International, 1152 Spring St., Ste. A, Atlanta, GA 30309. Telephone: (800) 251-1962

Seafood America Headquartered in Warminster, Pennsylvania, a franchisor of specialty food outlets.
Founded in 1976, Seafood America has been franchising since 1978. A typical Seafood America franchisee operates a retail store specializing in seafood, sold either cooked or fresh. Of the franchisor's 30 outlets currently operating, all except four are franchise units.
Seafood America, 645 Meams Rd., Warminster, PA 18974. Telephone: (215) 672-2211

Second Cup, The Headquartered in Oakville, Ontario, a franchisor of specialty food outlets.
Founded in 1972, The Second Cup has been franchising since 1975. A typical The Second Cup franchisee operates a retail shop devoted to exotic coffees, teas, and related gift items and accessories. Of the franchisor's 132 outlets currently operating, all except four are franchise units.
The Second Cup, 293 Church St., Oakville, Ont., Canada L6J 1N9. Telephone: (416) 842-5050

Second Sole Headquartered in San Diego, California, a franchisor of specialty shoe stores.

Founded in 1976, Second Sole has been franchising since its inception. A typical Second Sole franchisee operates a specialty apparel outlet devoted to athletic footwear and accessories. Of the franchisor's 60 outlets currently operating, all except one are franchise units.

Second Sole, 9605 Scranton Rd., Suite 840, San Diego, CA 92121. Telephone: (619) 458-0761

Service America Corp. Headquartered in Atlanta, Georgia, a franchisor of building maintenance services.

Founded in 1965, Service America has been franchising since 1985. A typical Service America franchisee operates a maintenance service specializing in HVAC (Heating, Ventillation, and Air Conditioning) systems. All 86 of the Service America outlets currently operating are franchise units.

Service America Corp., 223 Perimeter Center Pkwy., Ste. 510, Atlanta, GA 30346

ServiceMaster Residential and Commercial Services Headquartered in Downers Grove, Illinois, a franchisor of interior maintenance services.

Founded in 1948, ServiceMaster has been franchising since 1952. A typical ServiceMaster franchisee operates a mobile residential and commercial cleaning service. The chain is comprised of 3,875 outlets, all of which are franchise units.

ServiceMaster, 2300 Warrenville Rd., Downers Grove, IL 60515. Telephone: (800) 338-6833

ServPro Headquartered in Rancho Cordova, California, a franchisor of interior maintenance services.

Founded in 1967, ServPro has been franchising since the following year. A typical ServPro franchisee operates a maintenance service catering to residential and commercial clients, with an emphasis on carpet, floor, drapery, and surface care and restoration. All of the 650 ServPro outlets currently operating are franchise units.

ServPro Industries, Inc., 11357 Pyrites Way, Rancho Cordova, CA 95670. Telephone: (800) 826-9586

7-Eleven Stores Headquartered in Dallas, Texas, a franchisor of retail convenience stores.

7-Eleven has been franchising since 1964, when its parent company, The Southland Corpation, acquired a chain of franchised stores in California. Long recognized as one of the most successful retailers in North America, Southland began in 1927 as an ice vending business. It started the convenience retailing industry that same year when one of the company's ice dock managers began offering customers bread, milk, and eggs in addition to ice. Southland remains remains the dominant force in convenience retailing, with 7,000 7-Eleven stores in the United States and Canada. In addition, almost 5,000 7-Eleven stores are operated by licensees or affiliates in 16 foreign countries.

A typical 7-Eleven franchisee stocks about 3,000 grocery and fast food items, and many outlets also sell self-serve gasoline. Personal services, such as money orders, video rentals, and automatic teller machines, are becoming increasingly important to the stores' product mix. Approximately 3,400 of the 7-Eleven outlets, located in 20 states, are franchised or are available for franhise.

7-Eleven Stores, The Southland Corporation, 2711 N. Haskell Ave., Box 719, Dallas, TX 75221. Telephone: (214) 828-7763

The Southland Corporation, parent to 7-Eleven Stores, invented the convenience market by adding milk, eggs, and a few groceries to the ice vending outlet pictured above.

Seven-Up Popular soft drink and franchise tradename.

Seven-Up was concocted by Charles Grigg, a St. Louis soft drink bottler, in 1929. Griggs began marketing the new lemon-lime soda as a means of diversifying his product line, which previously had been devoted exclusively to orange soda. The name Seven-Up was derived from the seven-ounce bottles in which the soda was originally marketed. The classic Seven-Up trademark was registered in 1935.

In 1985, the Philip Morris tobacco company obtained the marketing rights to Seven-Up in a $5.75 billion acquisition of General Foods Company. A year later, Pepsico, the second-largest soft drink franchisor, offered $380 million for the Seven-Up subsidiary, at the same time that industry leader Coca-Cola made a bid to take over Dr. Pepper. The proposed mergers were blocked by the Federal Trade Commission. The acquisitions would have left Coca-Cola, Inc. and Pepsico with a combined 80 percent of the worldwide soft drink market.

In October, 1986, two Dallas financiers, Thomas O. Hicks and Robert B. Haas, acquired Seven-Up in a leveraged buyout for $240 million. In the five months prior, Hicks and Haas had obtained Dr. Pepper and A&W in similar takeover deals. Although under common ownership, the companies continue to operate under independent management.

Seven-Up remains the third-largest soft-drink franchisor, with an estimated seven percent share of industry sales.

Shakey's, Inc. Headquartered in Irving, Texas, a franchisor of fast-food outlets.

Founded in 1954, Shakey's has been franchising since 1958. A typical Shakey's franchisee operates a family-style pizza restaurant supplemented by salad, pasta, and beverage service. Of the franchisor's 360 outlets currently operating, 350 are franchise units.

Shakey's, Inc., 1320 Greenway Dr., Ste. 600, Irving, TX 75038. Telephone: (800) 527-9268

Shefield & Sons Headquartered in Abbotsford, British Columbia, a franchisor of specialty retail outlets.

Founded in 1976, Shefield has been franchising since its inception. A typical Shefield franchisee operates a retail tobacco store supplemented by sales of pipes and gift items. All 60 of the Shefield & Sons outlets currently in business are operated under franchise licenses.

Shefield & Sons, P.O. Box 490, Abbotsford, B.C., Canada V2S 5Z5. Telephone: (604) 859-1014

Sheraton Inns, Inc. dquartered in Boston, Massachusetts, a franchisor of lodging outlets.

Founded in 1937, Sheraton has been franchising since 1962. The chain was acquired by ITT Corp. in 1968. A typical Sheraton franchisee operates an upscale lodging establishment designed, constructed, and managed according to the franchisor's specifications. The average outlet has 100 rooms with a restaurant, cocktail lounge, meeting rooms, and recreational facilities. Larger resort properties may include additional facilities such as multiple restaurants, condominium-style accommodations, convention services, and banquet facilities. Seventy percent of the approximately 500 Sheraton Inns currently operating are franchise units.

Sheraton Inns, Inc., 60 State St., Boston, MA 02109. Telephone: (617) 367-5300

Shine Factory, The Headquartered in Calgary, Alberta, a franchisor of automobile detailing outlets.

Founded in 1979, TSF has been franchising since its inception. A typical TSF franchisee operates a car appearance service specializing in detailing, polishing, and exterior refurbishing of passenger cars and light trucks. All of the 24 Shine Factory outlets currently open are franchise units.

The Shine Factory, 116 Monument Pl. SE, Calgary, Alberta, Canada T2A 1X3

Shoney's Restaurants Headquartered in Nashville, Tennessee, a franchisor of family-style restaurants.

Founded in 1959, Shoney's has been franchising since 1971. A typical Shoney's franchisee operates a full-service restaurant with a family orientation. The Shoney's, Inc. chain includes Lee's Famous Recipe Country Fried Chicken and Captain D's Seafood Restaurants.. Of the franchisor's 625 outlets currently operating, about two thirds are franchise units.

Shoney's Restaurants, 1727 Elm Hill Pike, Nashville, TN 37210. Telephone: (615) 361-5201.
See Captain D's, Lee's Famous Recipe Country Fried Chicken

Showbiz Pizza Time Headquartered in Irving, Texas, a franchisor of food service outlets.

Founded in 1980 by Robert L. Brock, Showbiz Pizza has been franchising since the following year. Previously, Brock had purchased one of the first Holiday Inn franchises in 1955 and later organized his own franchise hotel chain, Park Inns.

A typical Showbiz Pizza franchisee operates a specialty restaurant featuring a pizza menu and an automated "theater" with animated robots playing the leading roles. The outlet also houses a variety of electronic games and rides to occupy family members before and after food service. Of the franchisor's 265 outlets currently operating, about half are franchise units.

Showbiz Pizza Time, 4441 W. Airport Fwy., Irving, TX 75015. Telephone: (214) 258-8507

Silk Plants, Etc. Headquartered in Libertyville, Illinois, a franchisor of specialty retail outlets.

Founded in 1985, SPE has been franchising since its inception. A typical SPE franchisee operates a retail store devoted to custom silk plants, flowers, and related accessories for interior decoration. Of the franchisor's 160 outlets currently operating, 50 are franchise units.

Silk Plants, Etc., 1755 Butterfield Rd., Libertyville, IL 60048

Singer, Isaac Merrit (1811-1875) Inventor, manufacturer, pioneering franchisor of sewing machine distributorships.

Born on October 27, 1811 in Rensselaer County, New York of German immigrants, Singer is commonly believed to be the first American entrepreneur to have applied the franchise method of distributorship on a national scale. He attended public school in Oswego until the age of 12, when he ran away from home. He took a job as an apprentice in a machine ship in Rochester until 1830, when he began a 20-year career as a roving actor and sometimes mechanic.

In 1851, he happened to see a working model of a sewing machine and was immediately inspired to engineer an improved version. In 11 days, he built the first modern sewing machine powered by a foot treadle and with a horizontal table. Unlike previous models, Singer's machine enabled continuous sewing, in a straight line or curved.

In 1851, Singer formed a partnership with an attorney, Edward Clark, and, within ten years, the new enterprise had become the world's foremost manufacturer of sewing machines. Clark oversaw marketing, introducing such innovative concepts as trade-in allowances and installment buying. Clark and Singer sold territories for their sewing machines to independent, roving marketing representatives, thus inventing two important business concepts: traveling salesman and franchises.

In 1863, the partners incorporated their enterprise as Sewing Manufacturing Company. Singer retired to England to spend his last days in a personal palace constructed in Torquay. One of the most recognizable trade names in America, Singer Sewing Machines is generally acknowledged as the first franchise trademark.

Sir Goony Headquartered in Chattanooga Tennessee, a franchisor of miniature-golf outlets.

Founded in 1960, Sir Goony has been franchising since its inception. A typical Sir Goony franchisee operates a miniature-golf facility based on a standardized layout, equipment package, and design scheme. Of the franchisor's 45 outlets currently operating, all except five are franchise units.

Sir Goony, 5954 Brainerd Rd., Chattanooga, TN 37421-3598. Telephone: (615) 892-7264

Sirloin Stockade Headquartered in Hutchinson, Kansas, a franchisor of family-style restaurants.

Founded in 1984, Sirloin Stockade has been franchising since its inception. A typical Sirloin Stockade franchisee operates a full-service restaurant with a steakhouse motif and a diversified menu featuring steak, seafood, and chicken. Of the franchisor's 65 outlets currently operating, all except six are franchise units.

Sirloin Stockade, 9 Compound Dr., Hutchinson, KS 67502

Sir Speedy Headquartered in Laguna Hills, California, a franchisor of instant printing shops.

Founded in 1968, Sir Speedy has been franchising since its inception. A typical Sir Speedy franchisee operates a retail quick printing shop, with emphasis on letterhead, business cards, and duplicating. All of the franchisor's 720 outlets are franchise units.

Sir Speedy, 23131 Verdugo Dr., Laguna Hills, CA 92653. Telephone: (800) 854-3321

Site Selection The selection of a site for a franchise outlet is usually one of the first decisions faced by a business-format franchisee. A principal business address must be secured before certain licenses or permits required to conduct the business may be obtained. Moreover, location may have a bearing on the outlet's success or failure.

Some franchisors select the sites for their franchisees' outlets, or offer an optional service to do so. Others, though they may not actively assist with securing a site, may reserve the right to approve the franchisee's selection. In such cases, the franchisee may be required to submit from three to five potential sites for the franchisor's review and approval.

The following considerations influence the selection of a site for a typical retail or commercial franchise outlet:

Zoning

As with other businesses, the outlet must comply with local zoning laws, statutes, and ordinances. Among other considerations, zoning may affect fire inspections, health inspections, business permits, and other licenses or permits relating to the site.

Security

The outlet's files and records are confidential. All information, correspondence, records, and customer lists dealing with the franchise business should be adequately safeguarded against potential abuse, including theft. Security from loss by fire, flood, etc. should also be a consideration, in that insurance alone will not compensate a franchisee adequately for the devastating effects of the destruction of the outlet's business records and files.

Space requirements

The franchisor may require the outlet to be situated in a particular type of facility, such as a shopping mall, business park, high rise complex, strip center, or standalone retail site. The new franchisee must anticipate both interior and exterior space requirements. If a long-term lease is required, future expansion needs should also be taken into consideration.

Franchisees should allow for ample parking for both customers and employees. Employee parking should be situated away from the entrance to the place of business, providing maximum parking convenience for customers.

Franchisees should allow for ample parking for both customers and employees. Employee parking should be situated away from the entrance to the place of business, providing maximum parking convenience for customers.

Fixtures and improvements

As franchisees evaluate potential sites, they often seek the answers to the following questions: What are the existing provisions for lighting, heating, ventilating, air conditioning, and parking? What share of these costs will the franchisee be required to undertake?

The outlet's exterior sign is one of the franchisee's principal advertising media. Where applicable, the site should allow the sign to be prominently displayed and easily visible to passing traffic in both directions. For retail outlets, sites located away from a main thoroughfare, e.g., in the back of a business park where the exterior sign is hidden from passing traffic, should be avoided.

Conducive environment

It is important in most franchise businesses, to select an attractive building surrounded by other businesses which project a favorable image on the outlet as well as the franchise. Even though a franchisor may not require the outlet to be situated in the most expensive and presitigious building complex in a given locality, the franchisee is responsible for maintaining the high standard of image and quality of the franchise organization.

The site should be professional in appearance, clean, attractive, and preferably, located in a well maintained area. On a personal note, franchisees should also consider that they will be spending the majority of their waking hours in their franchise outlet. Will the location provide a comfortable environment for the business's employees? Will customers will feel comfortable?

Surrounding area

The overall image of the surroundings, the proximity to major customer groups, accessibility of major traffic arteries, and visibility, all also may influence the outlet's success. The franchisee's own personal image is derived, in part, from the company he or she keepts. Similarly, the business's image will be derived, in part, from the surrounding businesses. A location in a modern shopping mall or business park projects a professional, success-oriented image. Conversely, a business located in a run-down strip center or warehouse area presents a poor image.

Proximity to customers

In most businesses, location determines to some extent the makeup of the outlet's primary customers. For example, a business located near upper-income residential areas is more likely to attract consumers who have ample disposable income. A business located in an industrial park or high rise complex caters to business customers. A franchisee who selects a strip center or shopping mall for the outlet will be perceived as catering to housewives and shoppers.

Access to thoroughfares

One important attribute of the outlet site is accessibility to major thoroughfares. Convenience is a key factor in the consumer's decision to patronize retail establishments. Access to major arteries and thoroughfares is a substantial advantage, particularly in a large metropolitan area.

Most franchisors have a profile of the ideal outlet site, with specifications for space requirements, lease provisions, visibility and access from major thoroughfares, and other considerations. Many franchisors rely on local realtors or property managers to select sites in geographical markets where the franchisors may have limited prior experience.

Because site selection often has a profound influence on the outlet's viability, the matter of who chooses the location, and how, may become an issue in future litigation between franchisor and franchisee. When, for whatever reason, a franchise outlet fails, one of the first argument that the franchisee's attorney is likely to raise is that the franchisor selected or approved a poor location. Yet, the franchisor's know-how and experience are integral components of the franchise relationship, and, reasonably, no franchisee should be expected to assume the responsibility of site selection without some form of guidance or assistance.

60 Minute Tune/10 Minute Lube Headquartered in Bellevue, Washington, a franchisor of automotive service outlets.

Founded in 1979, 60 Minute has been franchising since its inception. A typical 60 Minute franchisee operates an auto service business specializing in "while-you-wait" engine tune-ups and oil changes. Of the franchisor's 51 outlets currently operating, all except one are franchise units.

60 Minute Tune/10 Minute Lube, 11811 NE 1st St., Ste. 208, Bellevue, WA 98005. Telephone: (206) 453-8078

Sizzler Restaurants International, Inc. Headquartered in Los Angeles, California, a franchisor of food service outlets.

Founded in 1959, Sizzler has been franchising since 1961. A typical Sizzler franchisee operates a cafeteria-style steakhouse featuring steaks, seafood, and fresh salads at reasonable prices. Of the franchisor's 600 outlets currently operating, about two thirds are franchise units.

Sizzler Restaurants International, Inc., 5400 Alta Rd., Los Angeles, CA 90066. Telephone: (213) 827-2300

Skipper's Headquartered in Bellevue, Washington, a franchisor of fast-food outlets.

Founded in 1969, Skipper's has been franchising since 1978. A typical Skipper's franchisee operates fast-food restaurants featuring a limited menu of freshly prepared specialty seafood items. Of the franchisor's 215 outlets currently operating, 30 are franchise units.

Skipper's, 14450 NE 29th Pl., Ste. 200, Bellevue, WA 98007. Telephone: (206) 885-2116

Skyline Chili Restaurants Headquartered in Cincinnati, Ohio, a franchisor of fast-food outlets.

Founded in 1949, Skyline has been franchising since 1965. A typical Skyline franchisee operates a fast-food restaurant with a menu oriented to chili and chili-prepared dishes. Of the franchisor's 78 outlets currently operating, 60 are franchise units.

Skyline Chili Restaurants, 109 Illinois Ave., Cincinnati, OH 45215. Telephone: (513) 761-4371

Sleepy Bear The advertising symbol of the California-based Travelodge franchise lodging chain.

The Sleepy Bear symbol first appeared in April of 1954, when the Travelodge Coordinating Council elected by the chain's hotel managers approved the logo to appear on hotel signs and advertisements. The original logo portrayed a sleepy-eyed furry bear with one paw and leg extended in a state of sleepwalking.

At the time, Travelodge was a California chain, and the ursine sleepwalker was a satirical takeoff of the state flag, which depicted a Golden Bear. No gender has ever been associated with the bear, who sports a long-sleeved nightshirt and an old-fashioned nightcap with the name Sleepy embroidered on its brim.

The first Travelodge to display the Sleepy Bear image opened in Bishop, California in May, 1954. The mascot became an integral part of the chain's image and began to be incorporated into the room decor. In 1956, a costumed Sleepy Bear character began making personal appearances at Travelodge properties around the company. Fuzzy Sleepy Bear dolls became coveted toys in the 1950s, and Travelodge properties grew to be synonymous with "Sleepy Bear motels."

In 1971, the sleepwalking bear was transformed into an orange silhouette and incorporated into the company's corporate logo. The following year, Sleepy Bear was immortalized in genuine regal china as a Jim Beam whiskey bottle figurine. The fuzzy mascot has two separate fan clubs — the Cuddly Bear Club for secretaries of traveling executives and the Sleepy Bear Club for children. Membership is free to Travelodge guests and their relatives.

The Sleepy Bear doll, complete with night shirt and night cap, is manufactured by Beaver Enterprises, which continues to sell thousands of the furry toy every year.

The sleepwalking bear's silhouette continues to grace refurbished Travelodge hotels today.
See Travelodge.

Slye, Leonard (Roy Rogers) Cowboy singer, songwriter, actor, and public figure whose name appears on Roy Rogers restaurants.

Born in Cincinnati, Ohio, on November 5, 1911, Slye, better known by his stage name, Roy Rogers, became America's most famous singing cowboy during a decade-long tenure on the NBC TV network. His credits include 91 feature motion pictures, numerous recordings on RCA, Decca, and Capitol, and more than 6,000 personal appearances on behalf of charity organizations.

His popular television series, The Roy Rogers Show, featured himself and his wife, Dale Evans, along with a youthful, trouble-prone sidekick, Tim Spencer.

Roger's most popular recordings included *Happy Trails, My Heart Went Thataway, Dusty, No Bed of Roses,* and *Down Along the Sleepy Rio Grande.*

The family-style restaurants bearing his name are franchised by Marriott Corporation. Roy Rogers Restaurants feature roast beef sandwiches, hamburgers, fried chicken, and fresh salads. Franchisees receive a trademark license entitling them to use the singing cowboy's name on their restaurant signs.
See Roy Rogers Restaurants.

Slumberland International Headquartered in St. Paul, Minnesota, a franchisor of specialty retail outlets.

Founded in 1967, Slumberland has been franchising since 1977. A typical Slumberland franchisee operates a retail hard- goods store specializing in mattresses, beds, and bedroom furnishings. Of the franchisor's 21 outlets currently operating, a dozen are franchise units.

Slumberland International, 630 Pierce Butler Rte., St. Paul, MN 55104. Telephone: (612) 487-2081

Small Business Administration (SBA) Federal agency established by law and empowered to assist small businesses through the dissemination of information and the extension of direct and guaranteed financial assistance.

The SBA has long been regarded by many Americans as a kind of "economic equalizer," helping to preserve the entrepreneurial spirit of the free enterprise system. The agency serves as a federal clearinghouse for information for and about small businesses, and also as a source of financial assistance to small business owners.

Financial Assistance for Franchisees

The SBA is best known for offering financial assistance in the form of direct loans, grants, and guaranteed third-party loans to small business owners. Franchised businesses not only qualify for SBA assistance under the agency's guidelines, but may actually receive special favor. Whereas two thirds of all small businesses fail, most in the first year of operation, approximately 95 percent of franchise outlets survive at least five years, according to statistics compiled by the Department of Commerce.

The SBA makes direct and guaranteed loans to franchise buyers who cannot borrow on reasonable terms from conventional lenders. According to the agency, the SBA program includes about 1,000 private lenders who offer business loans to borrowers who might otherwise not qualify. Although the loan is extended by a third-financial institution, such as a bank, savings and loan, or finance company, the SBA guarantees to fulfill the borrower's obligations.

To qualify for a SBA loan, the borrower must first be turned down by at least three conventional lenders. When SBA funding is available, the rates are reasonable, usually lower than conventional commercial loan rates. In addition, the amount of a SBA may be higher than the maximum that a private lender may be willing to extend.

The SBA also licenses independent investors, including venture capital pools, to finance small business enterprises, including franchise operations. *Small Business Investment Companies*, or SBICs, are licensed to arrange leases for equipment and property; finance land, equipment, and buildings; or make equity investments. An offshoot of the SBIC program is the *Minority Enterprise Small Business Investment Company*, or MESBIC, licensed by the SBA to finance or invest in small businesses owned by members of officially recognized minority groups.

Because the SBA is funded by Congress, funding is not always available to underwrite or guarantee small business loans. For information about participating lenders and SBA-guaranteed loans, contact the nearest regional office of the Small Business Administration, or write to the following address to request the publication, *SBA Business Loans*: Small Business Administration, Washington, DC 20416.

Information for Small Business Owners

In addition to financial assistance, the SBA also disseminates information to help small business owners make intelligent planning and financial decisions. Two publications, *Franchise Index/Profile* and *Are You Ready for Franchising?*, may be of interest to prospective franchise buyers.

For a complete list of SBA publications, write to: Small Business Administration, Office of Management Assistance, 1441 L Street, Washington, DC 20416.

Small Business Investment Company (SBIC) A finance, leasing, or investment company licensed by the Small Business Administration to finance or invest in small businesses.

The SBIC is an alternative source of funding and/or financial assistance for small business owners who might otherwise not qualify for a conventional commercial loan. Whereas the SBA makes direct or guaranteed loans to businesses, including franchise operations, a licensed SBIC may provide financial assistance through other methods. For example, a typical SBIC may make a direct equity investment in a small business, with participation of from five percent to 50 percent. Others may arrange for leases of land, buildings or equipment, or offer direct financing.

Most SBICs specialize in a particular industry or field, such as electronics, restaurants, convenience stores, or lodging establishments. A special type of SBIC, the *Minority Enterprise Small Business Investment Company*, or *MESBIC*, is licensed to invest in small businesses owned by members of acknowledge minority groups.

SBICs encompass a diversity of financial and investment groups, including private venture capital management firm, commercial finance companies, equipment leasing companies, insurance companies, employee profit sharing programs, and credit unions.

The National Association of SBICs publishes computer lists of member SBICs in various regions of the country. To obtain information about licensed Small Business Investment Companies, contact: National Association of SBICs, 512 Washington Bldg., Washington, DC 20005. The association's telephone number is: (202) 638-3411.

Snelling and Snelling Headquartered in Sarasota, Florida, a franchisor of personnel employment agencies.

Founded in 1951 by Robert and Anne Snelling, the Snelling and Snelling organization has been franchising since 1955. A typical franchisee operates a personnel recruitment and placement business focusing on clerical, administrative, engineering, technical, and sales positions. The organization is distinguished by its motivational employee recognition program. A separate division, Snelling Temporaries, specializes in temporary employment services.

All of the 385 outlets currently operating all are franchise units.

Snelling and Snelling, 4000 S. Tamiami Triangle, Sarasota, FL 33581. Telephone: (800) 237-9475

Robert Snelling (left); Anne Snelling (right)

Snelling, Robert O. Franchisor of permanent and temporary employment services.

Robert Snelling joined his father's employment service in 1952, after receiving his bachelor's degree in chemical engineering from Pennsylvania State University, and was soon managing the staff and handling training. His brother Ray worked for the company from 1954 until his retirement in 1969. Robert served in the Army Adjutant General Corps from 1953 to 1954.

In 1957, he assumed the head of the company, which then consisted of 27 employment counselors and seven franchise outlets.

Snelling is presently chairman of the board of Snelling and Snelling, Inc., whose affiliated companies and franchise systems include the Snelling and Snelling chain, Snelling Temporaries, Bryant Bureau, Plan Maintenance, Inc., and Creative Communications. He serves on the board of regents of CBN University and is on the advisory board of the Southeast National Bank. He received an honorary doctorate from Albright College in 1970.

Snelling has been active in public service since 1972, serving on various committes and advisory boards, including the White House Committee on Small Business in 1986 and an advisory committee to Labor Secretary William E. Brock in 1989.

He wrote *The Opportunity Explosion*, published by MacMillan in 1969. With his wife, Anne, he wrote *Jobs! What They Are - Where They Are - What They Pay*, published by Simon Schuster in 1985, and *The Right Job*, published by Viking Penguin in 1987.

See Snelling and Snelling

Soap Opera Washateria Headquartered in Shreveport, Louisiana, a franchisor of self-service laundromats.

Founded in 1981, Soap Opera has been franchising since 1984. A typical Soap Opera franchisee operates a self-service laundry and dry cleaning facility. Of the franchisor's 25 outlets currently operating, all except one are franchise units.

Soap Opera Washateria and Dry Cleaning, P.O. Box 78328, Shreveport, LA 71137-8328. Telephone: (800) 247-SOAP

Softwaire Centres International Headquartered in San Ramon, California, across the bay from San Francisco, a franchisor of specialty retail outlets.

Founded in 1981, SCI has been franchising since its inception. A typical SCI franchisee operates a retail store merchandising computer software, accessories, and a limited selection of hardware. All of 40 Softwaire Centers currently operating are franchise units.

Softwaire Centers International, 210 Porter Dr., Ste. 220, San Ramon, CA 94583. Telephone: (415) 820-5050

Software City Headquartered in Teaneck, New Jersey, a franchisor of specialty retail outlets.

Founded in 1980, Software City has been franchising since 1982. A typical Software City franchisee operates a retail boutique devoted to computer software, books, and accessories. The outlet also markets a limited selection of computer hardware, primarily for home and desktop use. Of the franchisor's 90 outlets currently operating, all except one are franchise units.

Software City, 1415 Queen Anne Rd., Teaneck, NJ 07666. Telephone: (201) 833-8510

Sonic Drive-Ins Headquartered in Oklahoma City, a franchisor of fast-food outlets.

Founded in 1959, Sonic has been franchising since its inception. The first Sonic outlet was opened by founder Troy Smith in 1953, in Shawnee, Oklahoma, under the name Top Hat Drive-In. Top Hat is attributed with such drive-in innovations as the canopied car stall, intercoms for placing orders, and uniformed carhops.

In 1955, a former grocery store manager, Charles Pappe, happened to stop at Smith's Top Hat Drive-In while on the way to opening his own restaurant in nearby Woodward, Oklahoma. Pappe ended up opening a Top Hat outlet, using equipment and supplies on loan from Troy Smith. Pappe and Smith adopted the Sonic name to intimate "service with the speed of sound." When Pappe died in 1967, 41 Sonic Drive-Ins had already been franchised.

Sonic Industries, Inc. was organized in 1973. C. Stephen Lynn completed a leveraged buyout of the company in April, 1986. With nationwide sales of $341 million, Sonic is the fifth largest hamburger chain.

A typical Sonic franchisee operates a drive-in restaurant featuring 1950s-style "car hops" serving customers who order by intercom from their cars. The menu features such fast-food classics as hamburgers, Coney Island hot dogs, onion rings, milkshakes, and soft drinks. Of the franchisor's 985 outlets currently operating, 910 are franchise units. In an effort to capitalize on the company's 1950s motif and image, teen idol Frankie Avalon has been retained as company spokesperson.

Sonic Drive-Ins, 120 Robert S. Kerr, Oklahoma City, OK 73102. Telephone: (800) 458-8778

An early Sonic Drive-In, circa 1959, in Stillwater, Oklahoma;

Sonitrol Security Systems Headquartered in Alexandria, Virginia, a franchisor of building security services.

Founded in 1964, Sonitrol has been franchising since the following year. A typical Sonitrol franchisee operates a sales and installation business for the franchisor's patented audio security alarms and control systems. All except 13 of the 170 Sonitrol outlets currently in business are franchise units.

Sonitrol, 424 N. Washington St., Alexandria, VA 22314. Telephone: (703) 549-3900

Sonny's Real Pit BarBQ Headquartered in Gainesville, Florida, a franchisor of food service outlets.

Founded in 1968, Sonny's has been franchising since 1975. A typical Sonny's franchisee operates a specialty restaurant featuring the franchisor's barbecue-style beef, ribs, and chicken. The franchise chain consists of 75 outlets, none of which are owned by the franchisor.

Sonny's Real Pit BarBQ, 3631 SW Archer Rd., Gainesville, FL 32608. Telephone: (904) 376-9721

South Carolina, Franchise Regulations To date, the South Carolina legislature has not adopted any generally applicable franchise investment law.

South Carolina law does not require franchisors to register or file disclosures with any state regulatory body. In the absence of such a requirement, the federal Franchise Rule applies, requiring franchisors to furnish a disclosure document prescribed by the Federal Trade Commission to prospective franchisees ten business days before a franchise sale is made.

The relationship between automobile wholesalers and retailers under franchise agreements are regulated by the Motor Vehicle Dealers law.

See Franchise Rule.

South Dakota, Franchise Regulations Franchisors operating in the state of South Dakota are governed by the South Dakota Franchise Law, which requires registration and disclosure of pertinent information about the franchisor, franchise business, and franchise agreement.

Before offering or selling a franchise in the state, a franchisor must first prepare a disclosure document prescribed by the statute, then file the information, along with the franchise agreement, financial statements, and related documents, with the Division of Securities.

In addition to a disclosure document, franchisors are also required to submit the following items:

1. Application for registration of the franchise offering;
2. Salesman disclosure form;
3. Consent to service of process;
4. Auditor's consent to use of audited financial statements;
5. Cross-reference sheet showing the location in the franchise agreement of the key items in the disclosure document.

The disclosure document devised by a consortium of midwestern securities commissioners as a uniform method of complying with state franchise investment laws, the *Uniform Franchise Offering Circular*, or UFOC, fulfills the disclosure requirements of the South Dakota law. There are minor variations and differences in language required by the South Dakota statute, including a different cover page. (*See Uniform Franchise Offering Circular.*)

The disclosure document or UFOC must be furnished to a prospective franchisee at least ten business days before a franchise sale is made.

For information about state franchise laws, regulations, and filing requirements, or to report possible violations, contact: Franchise Administrator, Division of Securities, State Capital Bldg., Pierre, SD 57501. Telephone: (605) 773-3241.

Sparkle Wash International Headquartered in Cleveland, Ohio, a franchisor of exterior building maintenance services.

Founded in 1965, Sparkie Wash has been franchising since 1967. A typical Sparkie Wash franchisee operates a commercial exterior cleaning and restoration service. Of the franchisor's 176 outlets currently operating, all except four are franchise units.

Sparkie Wash International, 26851 Richmond Rd., Cleveland, OH 44146. Telephone: (800) 321-0770

Sparks Tune-Up Headquartered in King of Prussia, Pennsylvania, a franchisor of automotive tune-up centers.

Founded in 1980, Sparks, a subsidiary of Maaco Auto Painting and Bodyworks, has been franchising since 1983. A typical Sparks franchisee operates an auto service outlet devoted primarily to tune-ups and light maintenance. The Sparks chain consists of 160 outlets, all of which are franchise units.

Sparks Tune-Up Centers, 381 Brooks Rd., King of Prussia, PA 19406. Telephone: (800) 523-1190

Sparky Coin-Op Washmobile Headquartered in Longboat Key, Florida, a franchisor of self-service car wash outlets.

Founded in 1948, Sparky Coin-Op has been franchising since its inception. A typical Sparky Coin-Op franchisee operates a coin-operated carwash facility based on a standardized site design and equipment package. The chain consists of 270 outlets, all of which are franchise units.

Sparky Coin-Op Washmobile, P.O. Box 543, Longboat Key, FL 33548. Telephone: (813) 377-8320

Speedy Muffler King Headquartered in Chicago, Illinois, a franchisor of automotive muffler shops.

Founded in 1956, SMK has been franchising since 1986. A typical SMK franchisee operates a retail auto service and repair facility, specializing in exhaust systems. Secondary emphasis is placed on suspension and brake systems. Of the franchisor's 560 outlets currently operating, five are franchise units.

Speedy Muffler King, 8430 W. Bryn Mawr, Ste. 400, Chicago, IL 60631

Speedy Transmission Centers Headquartered in Deerfield Beach, Florida, a franchisor of automotive transmission outlets.

Founded in 1983, Speedy has been franchising since the following year. A typical Speedy franchisee operates a retail transmission installation and repair business. Of the franchisor's 23 outlets currently operating, all except one are franchise units.

Speedy Transmission Centers, 1239 E. Newport Center Dr., Ste. 115, Deerfield Beach, FL 33442. Telephone: (305) 428-0077

Sport-About Headquartered in Minneapolis, Minnesota, a franchisor of sporting goods stores.

Founded in 1978, Sport-About has been franchising since its inception. A typical Sport-About franchisee operates a retail outlet devoted to athletic apparel and footwear, sports and camping equipment, and accessory items. All but one of the franchisor's 61 outlets are franchise units.

Sport-About, Inc., 1557 Coon Rapids Rd., Minneapolis, MN 55419. Telephone: (612) 757-8414

Sport Shack Headquartered in St. Paul, Minnesota, a franchisor of sporting goods outlets.

Founded in 1974, Sport Shack has been franchising since the following year. A typical Sport Shack franchisee operates a retail store specializing in sporting goods, athletic apparel, shoes, accessories, and equipment. Of the franchisor's 40 outlets currently operating, all except one are franchise units.

Sport Shack, 3450 E. Lexington Ave., Ste. 100, St. Paul, MN 55126. Telephone: (612) 426-0072

Sports Fantasy Headquartered in Columbus, Georgia, a franchisor of specialty retail outlets.

Founded in 1986, Sports Fantasy has been franchising since its inception. A typical Sports Fantasy franchisee operates a retail store devoted to sports wear, gift items, and memorabilia bearing professional team logos. Of the franchisor's 25 outlets currently operating, about a third are franchise units.

Sports Fantasy, P.O. Box 1847, Columbus, GA 31902. Telephone: (404) 327-0257

Spotless Office Services Headquartered in Vancouver, British Columbia, a franchisor of interior building maintenance services.

Founded in 1970, SOS has been franchising since 1982. A typical SOS franchisee operates a commercial janitorial cleaning service. Of the franchisor's 118 outlets currently operating, all except one are franchise units.

Spotless Office Services, 4040 Brockton Cr., North Vancouver, B.C., Canada V7G 1E6. Telephone: (604) 929-4432

Spring Crest Drapery Centers Headquartered in Brea, California, a franchisor of specialty home decoration outlets.

Founded in 1955, Spring Crest has been franchising since 1968. A typical Spring Crest franchisee operates a window covering sales and installation business, based on the franchisor's selected lines of draperies, blinds, and accessories. Of the franchisor's 315 outlets currently operating, all except one are franchise units.

Spring Crest Drapery Centers, 505 W. Lambert Rd., Brea, CA 92621. Telephone: (800) 552-5523

Spring-Green Lawn Care Headquartered in Naperville, Illinois, a franchisor of grounds maintenance services.

Founded in 1977, Spring-Green has been franchising since its inception. A typical Spring-Green franchisee operates a service business devoted to lawn and tree care for residential and commercial properties. Of the franchisor's 140 outlets currently operating, all except three are franchise units.

Spring-Green Lawn Care, P.O. Box 908, Naperville, IL 60566. Telephone: (815) 436-8777

Staff Builders, Inc. Headquartered in Lake Success, New York, a franchisor of personnel employment agencies.

Founded in 1961, SBI has been franchising since 1965. A typical SBI franchisee operates an employment agency handling both temporary and permanent placement. Of the franchisor's 132 outlets currently operating, 25 are franchise units.

Staff Builders, Inc., 1981 Marcus Ave., Lake Success, New York 11042

Stained Glass Overlay Headquartered in Irvine, California, a franchisor of specialty home decoration outlets.

Founded in 1974, SGO has been franchising since 1981. Expansion began in earnest when the chain was acquired by a partnership headed by Barry Rupp in 1983. A typical SGO franchisee operates a window decorating business utilizing the franchisor's patented process for producing stained-glass designs. Of the franchisor's 325 outlets currently operating, all except one are franchise units.

Stained Glass Overlay, Inc., 2392 Morse Ave., Irvine, CA 92714. Telephone: (800) 654-7666

Stanley Steemer Carpet Cleaner Headquartered in Dublin, Ohio, a franchisor of interior maintenance services.

Founded in 1947, Stanley Steemer has been franchising since 1972. A typical Stanley Steemer franchisee operates a mobile home-service business specializing in carpet and upholstery care. Of the franchisor's 225 outlets currently operating, all except 24 are franchise units.

Stanley Steemer, 5500 Stanley Steemer Pky., Dublin, OH 43017. Telephone: (800) 848-7496

Statutory Law Original laws which have been enacted by a body authorized to pass laws; as opposed to case law, which is derived from decisions rendered by federal and state appellate judges.

Statutory laws are enacted on four levels: (1) federal, (2) state, (3) county, and (4) city.

Federal laws are statutory laws passed by the United States Congress. *State* laws are typically enacted by a state legislature. *County ordinances* are a type of statutory law enacted by a body with authority over a county, such as a board of supervisors. City laws, commonly referred to as *municipal ordinances*, are passed by a body with authority over a municipality, such as a city council.

In addition to statutory laws, there are also so-called "quasi-statutory" laws which are written by agencies that have authority to make rules and regulations. As an example, the United States Federal Trade Commission has the authority to write rules pertaining to the offer and sale of franchises. As another example, the California Department of Corporations and the New York Attorney General's Office have the authority to write and enforce rules pertaining to business and franchise practices in their respective states.

Agencies that write rules and regulations derive their authority from laws enacted by a legislative body or, in some cases, from an executive order issued by the President, a governor, or city manager. A set of books containing statutory laws is called a "set of statutes." Together, organized in a systematic fashion, the statutes make up a "code."

A series of publications containing quasi-statutory law (rules and regulations) is called a "register."

To date, fifteen states have enacted statutes regulating the offer and sale of franchises. Most of the remaining states have statutory laws protecting the rights of franchises in certain industries, such as petroleum, automotive sales, and farm equipment.

The most important quasi-statutory law governing franchising in the United States is the Federal Trade Commission's sweeping Franchise Rule, requiring franchisors to furnish prospective franchisees with certain disclosures before any franchise sale is made.

See *Registration States, Case Law, Federal Trade Commission, Franchise Rule,* and individual state listings.

Steak Escape, The Headquartered in Columbus, Ohio, a franchisor of fast-food outlets.

Founded in 1982, Steak Escape has been franchising since the following year. A typical Steak Escape franchisee operates a fast-food operation specializing in hot, Philadelphia-style "cheesesteak" sandwiches.

Of the franchisor's 40 outlets currently operating, all except one are franchise units.

The Steak Escape, 392 E. Town St., Columbus, OH 43215. Telephone: (614) 461-1711

Steamatic, Inc. Headquartered in Grand Prairie, Texas, a franchisor of interior maintenance services.

Founded in 1948, Steamatic has been franchising since 1967. A typical Steamatic franchisee operates a residential/commercial maintenance business devoted to carpet and upholstery cleaning and restoration. Of the franchisor's 240 outlets currently operating, all except ten are franchise units.

Steamatic, Inc., 1601 109th St., Grand Prairie, TX 75050. Telephone: (800) 527-1295

Sterling Optical Headquartered in Woodbury, New York, a franchisor of retail optical stores.

Founded in 1912, Sterling has been franchising since 1986. A typical Sterling franchisee operates an optical dispensing outlet merchandising lenses and frames for prescription eyeglasses, sunglasses, and specialty optical aids. Of the franchisor's 235 outlets currently operating, 34 are franchise units.

Sterling Optical, 357 Crossways Park Dr., Woodbury, NY 11797. Telephone: (516) 364-2600

Steve's Ice Cream Headquartered in Lindenhurst, New York, a franchisor of specialty fast-food outlets.

Founded in 1972, Steve's Ice Cream has been franchising since 1981. A typical franchisee operates an ice cream parlor devoted to the franchisor's premium line of "gourmet" ice cream products. The Steve's Ice Cream chain is comprised of 52 outlets, none of which are company-owned.

Steve's Ice Cream, 424 E. John St., Lindenhurst, NY 11757. Telephone: (516) 884-5656

Sub Station II Headquartered in Sumter, South Carolina, a franchisor of fast-food outlets.

Founded in 1975, Sub Station has been franchising since 1976. A typical Sub Station franchisee operates a fast-food operation specializing in submarine sandwiches. Of the franchisor's 125 outlets currently operating, all except six are franchise units.

Sub Station II, P.O. Drawer 2260, Sumter, SC 29150. Telephone: (803) 773-4711

SUBWAY Sandwiches and Salads Headquartered in Milford, Connecticut, a franchisor of fast-food outlets.

Founded in 1965 by Fred DeLuca and Peter Buck, SUBWAY has been franchising since 1974. DeLuca opened his first sandwich shop in Bridgeport, Connecticut with $1,000 borrowed from nuclear physicist Buck, a family friend. After six months of sluggish sales, the partners opened their second outlet across town in the hope of increasing the business's visibility. Over the last decade, SUBWAY has enjoyed the status of the fastest growing fast-food franchise chain in North America.

A typical SUBWAY franchisee operates a fast-food restaurant specializing in submarine sandwiches, salads, and beverage service. The menu includes at least fifteen varieties of the traditional Eastern submarine sandwich, based on a combination of meats, cheeses, and vegetables on a long Italian roll. Salads are prepared from essentially the same ingredients as sandwiches. Of the estimated 2,400 SUBWAY outlets currently operating, all except 25 are franchise units.

SUBWAY Sandwiches and Salads, 25 High St., Milford, CT 06460. Telephone: (800) 243-9741

Subway store #3, Pete's Submarines, the oldest Subway outlet still in existence.

Suddenly Slender Headquartered in Denver, Colorado, a franchisor of personal body-care centers.

Founded in 1969, Suddenly Slender has been franchising since 1981. A typical Suddenly Slender franchisee operates a personal weight-control and beauty outlet based on the franchisor's proprietary body-wrap system. Of the franchisor's 280 outlets currently operating, all are franchise units.

Suddenly Slender, 3255 S. Parker Rd., Ste. 105, Denver, CO 80231. Telephone: (303) 753-6337

Sunshine Polishing Systems Headquartered in San Diego, California, a franchisor of mobile automotive detailing services.

Founded in 1982, SPS has been franchising since the following year. A typical SPS franchisee operates a mobile auto polishing business based on the franchisor's proprietary products and refinishing techniques. Of the franchisor's 335 outlets currently operating, none are company-owned.

Sunshine Polishing Systems, 4560 Alvarado Canyon, Ste. 2A, San Diego, CA 92120. Telephone: (619) 285-9222

Supercuts Headquartered in San Rafael, California, a franchisor of hair care salons.

Founded in 1976, Supercuts has been franchising since 1979. A typical Supercuts franchisee operates a retail hair care salon situated in a shopping mall or strip center, employing a standardized haircutting process. The "unisex" outlet caters to men, women, and children. Nearly 95 percent of the chain's 510 outlets are operated by independent franchisees.

Supercuts, 555 Northgate Dr., San Rafael, CA 94903. Telephone: (415) 472-1170

Super 8 Motels Headquartered in Aberdeen, South Dakota, a franchisor of lodging outlets.

Founded in 1972, Super 8 has been franchising since 1974. A typical Super 8 franchisee operates an economy-class lodging establishment offering full-size, attractively furnished accommodations at highly competitive rates. Room prices are minimized by eliminating such traditional hotel services as uniformed bell service and food and beverage operations. Super 8 outlets are distinctive among budget motels for equipping rooms with color televisions and direct-dial telephone service. Of the 430 Super 8 outlets currently operating, all except six are franchise units.

Super 8 Motels, P.O. Box 4090, Aberdeen, SD 57401. Telephone: (605) 225-2272

Swensen's Ice Cream Company Headquartered in Andover, Massachusetts, a franchisor of specialty fast-food outlets.

Founded in 1948, Swensen's has been franchising since 1963. Earle Swensen's original Ice Cream Factory remains a familiar landmark atop Russian Hill in San Francisco. According to the franchisor, "Earle was so particular about the quality of his ice cream that he developed his own premium mix." His ice cream has received numerous awards throughout California and the U.S.

Swensen's now serves Earle's ice cream in three distinctive types of outlets: ice cream-only store, specialty retail outlets, and full-service parlor-restaurants. Each type of outlet mimicks the turn-of-the-century motif on which the franchisor's success was originally based.

Ice cream-only locations primarily offer a take-out menu featuring cones, shakes, sodas, and other fountain specialties. Ice cream manufacturing facilities have been removed from specialty retail outlets, which operate as satellites of full-service locations. Swensen's freestanding parlor-restaurants incorporate an upscale interior decor highlighted by Tiffany- style lamps, ceiling fans, hand-etched glass, and marble-topped tables.

In May, 1988, Steve's Ice Cream completed acquisition of the Swensen's chain.

A typical Swensen's franchisee operates a fast-food restaurant featuring a nostalgic ambience and the franchisor's proprietary line of "old-fashioned" ice cream. Each outlet has a turn-of-the-century motif and a wholesome soup-and-sandwich menu. Ice cream is churned on the premises from fresh ingredients. Of the franchisor's 245 outlets currently operating, all except four are franchise units.

Swensen's Ice Cream Company, 200 Andover Park Dr., Ste. 1000, Andover, MA 01810

See Steve's Ice Cream.

Swiss Colony Stores, Inc. Headquartered in Monroe, Wisconsin, a franchisor of specialty food and gift outlets.

The Swiss Colony, Inc., from which Swiss Colony Stores, Inc. holds a license to franchise, was founded in 1926 by Raymond R. Kubly, Sr., as a mail order company selling cheese products for holiday occasions. It has remained a family-owned business throughout its history, but has grown substanially since 1926.

The original Swiss Colony Store was established in 1949 in downtown Monroe, Wisconsin. Two additional outlet were opened in 1962. The first franchise was sold a year later.

A typical Swiss Colony franchisee operates a retail outlet featuring a diverse assortment of gift foods and confections. The inventory consists of a variety of packaged cheeses, sausages, delicatessen products, candy, preserves, and bakery goods. Each outlet also offers gift-mailing service and, in some cases, on-premises food service.

The Swiss Colony retail outlet is based on the premise that snacking is an inherent American trait. Recently, in response to increased public health consciousness, the company introduced a new "nutritionally beneficial" product line. Dick Cope, president of Swiss Colony Stores, Inc., foresees continued expansion of the franchise chain.

All except five of the 100 Swiss Colony outlets currently operating are franchise units.

Swiss Colony Stores, Inc., 1 Alpine Lane, Monroe, WI 53566. Telephone: (608) 328-8803

Sylvan Learning Centers Headquartered in Montgomery, Alabama, a franchisor of educational service outlets.

Founded in 1979 in response to a rising public demand for supplemental learning resources, SLC has been franchising since 1980. The chain is currently operated by Kinder-Care, a diversified company specializing in children-oriented industries, including life insurance, publishing, and apparel. A typical SLC franchisee operates a "teaching store" tutoring children in reading and math in the after-school hours.

Diagnostic testing is used to determine the appropriate curriculum level of each enrollee, and to detect any potential learning disabilities. Students are typically enrolled for individualized tutoring sessions twice a week over an 18-week course. A merit system of positive rewards is used to motivate achievement. Of the franchisor's 460 outlets currently operating, all except 40 are franchise units.

Syvlan Learning Corp., 2400 Presidents Dr., Montgomery, AL 36116. Telephone: (800) 545-5060

The Swiss Colony open-facade architecture, maximizing visibility of the outlet's stock of gift and specialty foods, is a familiar fixture in enclosed shopping malls

T

TCBY
to
Twistee Treat

TCBY 'The Country's Best Yogurt' Headquartered in Little Rock, Arkansas, a franchisor of specialty fast-food outlets.

Founded in 1981, TCBY has been franchising since the following year. A typical TCBY franchisee operates a fast-food service devoted to the franchisor's line of soft frozen yoghurt. Of the franchisor's 1,075 outlets currently operating, 972 are franchise units.

TCBY, 11300 TCBY Tower, 245 Capitol Ave., Little Rock, AR 72201

TGI Friday's Headquartered in Dallas, Texas, a franchisor of food and beverage service outlets.

Founded in 1965, TGI Friday's has been franchising since 1970. A typical TGI Friday's franchisee operates a full-service restaurant and cocktail lounge with an upscale, California-style motif and a singles-scene ambience. The menu has a diverse orientation ranging from "gourmet" hamburgers to seafood. Of the 130 TGI Friday's outlets currently operating, fewer than ten percent are franchise units.

TGI Friday's, P.O. Box 809062, Dallas, TX 75380. Telephone: (214) 450-5400

T.J. Cinnamons Headquartered in Kansas City, Missouri, a franchisor of specialty bakery goods outlets.

Founded in 1985, TJC has been franchising since its inception. A typical TJC franchisee operates a retail bakery goods store specializing in cinnamon rolls prepared by hand from the franchisor's "secret" dough. Of the franchisor's 220 outlets currently operating, all except eight are franchise units.

T.J. Cinnamons, Ltd., 800 W. 47th St., Ste. 555, Kansas City, MO 64112. Telephone: (816) 931-9341

TRC Temporary Services Headquartered in Atlanta, Georgia, a franchisor of temporary employment agencies.

Founded in 1980, TRC has been franchising since 1984. A typical TRC franchisee operates a personnel services agency devoted to temporary employment of office and industrial personnel. Of the 40 TRC outlets currently operating, 25 are franchise units.

TRC, 100 Ashford Center N, Ste. 500, Atlanta, GA 30338. Telephone: (404) 392-1411

TV Focus Headquartered in Fairvew, New Jersey, a franchisor of advertising services.

Founded in 1980, TV Focus has been franchising since its inception. A typical TV Focus franchisee operates an advertising service centered on local editions of the franchisor's TV Focus television and shopping guide. All of 215 outlets currently operating are franchise units.

TV Focus, One Anderson Ave., Fairview, NJ 07022. Telephone: (201) 945-2800

TV Tempo Headquartered in Athens, Georgia, a franchisor of specialty publishing outlets.

Founded in 1974, TV Tempo has been franchising since its inception. A typical TV Tempo franchisee operates an advertising sales business centered on a free television viewing guide. All 85 TV Tempo outlets currently operating are franchise units.

TV Tempo, 3131 Atlanta Hwy., Athens, GA 30606. Telephone: (404) 546-6001

Taco Bell Headquartered in Irvine, California, a franchisor of fast-food outlets.

Founded in 1962, Taco Bell has been franchising since 1965. A typical Taco Bell franchisee operates a retail fast-food restaurant with a Mexican decor and menu. The chain was acquired in 1978 by Pepsico, Inc., which immediately invested $200 million to upgrade the image of the nation's largest Mexican food retailer. The chain's controversial logo, which depicted a sleepy Mexican lounging under an oversized sombrero, was replaced with an illuminated mission bell. Of the franchisor's 2,760 outlets currently operating, 1,120 are franchise units.

Taco Bell, 17901 Von Karman, Irvine, CA 92714. Telephone: (714) 863-4595

Taco John's International Headquartered in Cheyenne, Wyoming, a franchisor of fast-food outlets.

Founded in 1969, TJ has been franchising since its inception. A typical TJ franchisee operates a retail fast-food restaurant specializing in Mexican-style cuisine. Of the franchisor's 440 outlets currently operating, all except six are franchise units.

Taco John's International, 808 W. 20th St., Cheyenne, WY 82001. Telephone: (307) 635-0101

TacoTime Headquartered in Eugene, Oregon, a franchisor of fast-food outlets.

Founded in 1959, TacoTime has been franchising since 1961. A typical TacoTime franchisee operates a retail fast-food restaurant devoted to Mexican food, with sit-down, take-out, and drive-through facilities. Of the franchisor's 275 outlets currently operating, 250 are franchise units.

TacoTime, 3880 W. 11th Ave., Eugene, OR 97402. Telephone: (800) 547-8907

Taco Villa/Del Taco Headquartered in Dallas, Texas, a franchisor of fast food outlets.

Founded in 1977, Del Taco has been franchising since 1984. A typical Del Taco franchisee operates a food service business devoted to a diversity of Mexican-style menu items, including tacos, tostadas, burros, and enchiladas. Of the franchisor's 150 outlets currently operating, less than half are franchise units.

Taco Villa/Del Taco, 1801 Royal Ln., Ste. 902, Dallas, TX 75229. Telephone: (214) 556-0771

Tastee Freeze International Headquartered in Utica, Michigan, a franchisor of fast-food outlets.

Founded in 1950, Tastee Freeze has been franchising since its inception. Tastee Freeze was founded in 1950 by Harry Axene, who had previously cofounded Dairy Queen, in a partnership with Leo Moranz. Moranz had developed an ice cream freezer which improved on the original, free-flowing dispenser used by Dairy Queen outlets. By the end of the decade, Tastee Freeze boasted more than 500 outlets.

A typical Tastee Freeze franchisee operates a fast-food business devoted to the franchisor's proprietary soft ice cream, in addition to hamburgers, sandwiches, and soft drinks. The chain presently consists of 490 outlets, all of which are franchise units.

Tastee Freeze International, 8345 Hall Rd., Utica, MI 48087. Telephone: (313) 739-5520

Taylor Rental Centers Headquartered in New Britain, Connecticut, a franchisor of general equipment rental outlets.

Founded in 1945, Taylor has been franchising since 1962. A typical Taylor franchisee operates an equipment rental business stocking a diverse inventory of tools and appliances, ranging from light industrial equipment to furniture for wedding receptions and parties. Of the chain's 360 outlets currently operating, 250 are franchise units.

Taylor Rental Centers, P.O. Box 8000, New Britain, CT 06050. Telephone: (203) 229-9100

Temp Force, Inc. Headquartered in Westbury, New York, a franchisor of temporary employment agencies.

Founded in 1959, Temp Force has been franchising since 1975. A typical Temp Force franchisee operates a recruitment agency devoted to temporary employment of clerical and industrial personnel. Of the 74 Temp Force outlets currently operating, 67 are franchise units.

Temp Force, Inc., 1600 Stewart Ave., Ste. 700, Westbury, NY 11590

Temps & Co. Headquartered in Atlanta, Georgia, a franchisor of temporary employment agencies.

Founded in 1968, Temps has been franchising since 1988. A typical Temps franchisee operates a personnel services business specializing in temporary employment of skilled office workers. The chain consists of 16 outlets, two of which are franchise units.

Temps & Co., 245 Peachtree Center, Ste. 2500, Atlanta, GA 30303. Telephone: (800) 438-6086

Tender Sender Headquartered in Portland, Oregon, a franchisor of specialty services outlets.

Founded in 1982 by a paper salesman named Michale Hanna, Tender Sender has been selling franchises since 1983. A typical Tender Sender franchisee operates a custom gift wrapping, packaging, and shipping service. Slightly less than half of the 90 Tender Sender outlets currently in business are operated under franchise licenses.

Tender Sender, 7370 SW Durham Rd., Portland, OR 97224. Telephone: (503) 684-1426

Tennessee, Franchise Regulations The Tennessee legislature has not adopted any generally applicable franchise investment law. However, the rights of farm equipmemt dealers and automobile retailers operating under franchise agreements are protected under separate laws.

Tennessee law does not require franchisors to register or file disclosures with any state regulatory body. In the absence of such a requirement, the federal Franchise Rule applies, requiring franchisors to furnish a disclosure document prescribed by the Federal Trade Commission to prospective franchisees ten business days before a franchise sale is made.

See Franchise Rule.

Texas, Franchise Regulations The Texas legislature has not yet enacted any generally applicable franchise investment law. However, automobile dealers operating under franchise agreements are protected by the Motor Vehicle Code.

Texas law does not require franchisors to register or file disclosures with any state regulatory body. In the absence of such a requirement, the federal Franchise Rule applies, requiring franchisors to furnish a disclosure document prescribed by the Federal Trade Commission to prospective franchisees ten business days before a franchise sale is made.

See Franchise Rule.

Texas State Optical Headquartered in Dallas, Texas, a franchisor of eye care centers.

Founded in 1935, TSO has been franchising under its own identity since 1972 and currently also operates the 850-outlet Pearle Vision chain. A typical TSO franchisee operates a retail optical supply outlet in association with an optometric practice, usually in a shopping mall or strip center. Of the estimated 170 Texas State Optical outlets currently operating, about 140 are franchise units.

Texas State Optical, 2534 Royal Lane, Dallas, TX 75229. Telephone: (214) 241-3381

That Muffler & Brake Place Headquartered in Redmond, Washington, a franchisor of automotive service outlets.

Founded in 1987, That Muffler has been franchising since its inception. A typical franchisee operates a retail service shop specializing in exhaust and brake system sales and installation. All ten That Muffler outlets currently open and operating are franchise units.

That Muffler & Brake Place, 2601 151 Pl. NE, Redmond, WA 98052

Three-Star Muffler Headquartered in Memphis, Tennessee, a franchisor of automobile service outlets.

Founded in 1977, Three-Star has been franchising since 1980. A typical Three-Star franchisee operates an service shop specializing in exhaust system components, service, and installation. The Three-Star chain consists of ten outlets, all of which are franchise units.

Three-Star Muffler, 5050 Poplar Ave., Memphis, TN 38157. Telephone: (901) 761-3085

Thrifty Rent-A-Car Headquartered in Tulsa, Oklahoma, a franchisor of automobile rental outlets.

Founded in 1962, Thrifty has been franchising since 1964. A typical Thrifty franchisee operates a discount car rental business, usually "off-premises" (near, but not at, a major airport). Outlets are distinguished by complimentary airport transportation provided by chaufeur-driven limousines. Of the franchisor's 668 outlets currently operating, all except 21 are franchise units.

Thrifty Rent-A-Car System, P.O. Box 35250, Tulsa, OK 74153. Telephone: (918) 665-9219

Tidy Car Headquartered in Boca Raton, Florida, a franchisor of specialty service outlets.

Founded in 1976, Tidy Car has been franchising since the following year. A typical Tidy Car franchisee operates a service business devoted to on-site automotive detailing and care. Of the franchisor's 300 outlets currently operating, all are franchise units.

Tidy Car, 1515 N. Federal Hwy., Ste. 411, Boca Raton, FL 33432

Tie-In Arrangement An illegal franchise practice of requiring franchisees to purchase products, equipment, supplies, or other items from a designated supplier, usually an affiliate or other benefactor of the franchisor.

An illegal tie-in arrangement exists when a franchise contract unjusitifiably obligates the franchisee to buy something from the franchisor or a third party which provides kick backs to the franchisor. Early franchise agreements sometimes required franchisees to purchase equipment or fixtures from stipulated sources, often at prices higher than those available for the same or comparable products from others. Upon investigation, it was often found that the franchisors were receiving "finder's fees" or other forms of illegal compensation from the suppliers named in the franchise agreements.

The landmark legal case which decided the legality of tie-in arrangements was the 1971 suit, *Siegal v. Chicken Delight*. In that case, a Chicken Delight franchisee pressed for the right to buy restaurant equipment and supplies from third party suppliers, at better terms than those that were available from the franchisor's wholesale subsidiary. The Supreme Court ruled that the franchisor's obligation to purchase from a designated supplier, which was actually the franchisor doing business under another name, was unlawful.

As a result of the Chicken Delight decision, franchisors began requiring franchisees to purchase items not from a mandatory supplier, but rather in accordance with reasonable specifications and standards. In 1977, a circuit court ruling in *Kentucky Fried Chicken v. Diversified Packaging* upheld the rights of franchisors to approve the suppliers from whom franchisees purchase supplies, as a reasonable measure to maintain quality control.

In the 1982 case of *Krehl v. Baskin Robbins*, a federal court further upheld franchisors' rights to require franchisees to purchase products that are unique or trademarked. According to the court, because the Baskin-Robbins franchise serves only to distribute a private brand of ice cream, the company's franchisees can be contractually obligated to sell no other brands.

As in other aspects of the franchise relationship, the courts consider the reasonableness of a tie-in arrangement in determinings its legality. From the franchisor's standpoint, the ability to control quality standards is an integral component of the franchise relationship. From the franchisee's perspective, outlet owners deserve the right to acquire fixtures and supplies which are generally available and not unique at the most favorable terms possible.

See Antitrust.

Tim Horton Donuts Headquartered in Oakville, Ontario, a franchisor of specialty bakery goods outlets.

Founded in 1964, Tim Horton has been franchising since the following year. A typical Tim Horton franchisee operates a fast-food bakery goods store selling a diverse selection of doughnuts, muffins, cakes, and pies. Of the franchisor's 370 outlets currently operating, all except 19 are franchise units.

Five Canadian franchisor's outlets are located in the U.S. Tim Horton Donuts, 874 Sinclair Rd., Oakville, Ont., Canada L6K 2Y1. Telephone: (416) 845-6511

Tinder Box International Headquartered in Houston, Texas, a franchisor of retail tobacconists.

Founded in 1928 in Santa Monica, California, Tinder Box has been franchising since 1965. The franchise company was acquired from Imasco U.S.A by a group of investors headed by Gary Blumenthal, the chain's present chief executive. A typical Tinder Box franchisee operates a retail tobacco shop with a tobacco bar, walk-in humidor, and an inventory of pipes, ceramics, leather and brass goods, curiosities, games, and "collectibles". Of the franchisor's 186 outlets currently operating, 150 are franchise units.

Tinder Box International, 16945 Northchase Dr., Ste. 1590, Houston, TX 77060. Telephone: (800) 322-4TBI; Texas: (713) 876- 2824

Togo's Eatery Headquartered in Campbell, California, a franchisor of fast-food outlets.

Founded in 1972, Togo's has been franchising since 1977. A typical Togo's franchisee operates a fast-food restaurant devoted to specialty sandwiches, salads, soups, and beverage service. The menu features over a hundred different varieties of salads and delicatessen-style cold and hot sandwiches, prepared to order in ample portions by an engaging service staff. Where permissible, outlets also sell beer and wine. Of the franchisor's 120 outlets currently operating, all except eight are franchise units.

Togo's Eateries, 900 E. Campbell Ave., Ste. 1, Campbell, CA 95008. Telephone: (408) 377-1754

Tony Roma's A Place for Ribs Headquartered in Dallas, Texas, a franchisor of food and beverage service outlets.

Founded in 1972, Tony Roma's has been franchising since 1979. A typical Tony Roma's franchisee operates a specialty restaurant and cocktail lounge. The menu features the franchisor's private-recipe barbecued spare ribs and chicken. Of the franchisor's 102 outlets currently operating, all except 16 are franchise units.

Tony Roma's A Place for Ribs, 10000 N. Central Expwy., Ste. 900, Dallas, TX 75231. Telephone: (214) 891-7600

Tool Shack Headquartered in Agoura, California, a franchisor of specialty retail outlets.

Founded in 1979, Tool Shack has been franchising since 1981. A typical Tool Shack franchisee operates a retail store devoted to tools for carpentry, electrical work, automotive repair, construction, carpentry, landscaping, and other uses. Of the 40 Tool Shack outlets currently operating, all except one are franchise units.

Tool Shack, 5236 Colony Dr., Agoura, CA 91301. Telephone: (818) 991-0755

Trademark A distinctive name, figure, word, design, logo, or mark adopted and used by a company to designate its company and/or its goods or services.

Franchise Trademarks

A trademark license is a hallmark of a franchise, which entitles a franchisee to use the franchisor's trademark, as well as business format and products. Trademarks are protected on both federal and local levels. Federal protection is secured by registering a trademark with the Registrar of Patents and Trademarks.

A section of the Uniform Franchise Offering Circular (UFOC) is devoted to trademarks and trade names. The UFOC is a prospectus that all franchisors are required to provide to prospective franchise holders, disclosing pertinent information about the franchisor, the franchise business, and the franchise agreement. In Section 13 of the UFOC, franchisors are required to describe "any trademark, service mark, trade name, logotype or other commercial symbols to be licensed to the franchisee." Each mark, name, logo, or symbol which the franchisee will be entitled to use must be identified. In addition, the UFOC must state whether any of the trademarks and service marks have been registered with the United States Patent and Trademark Office, or whether an application for registration is pending.

Trademark Registration

Before a trademark is registered at the federal level, a search is first conducted to ascertain whether the same trademark has been previously registered by another party. If no prior registration is found, the trademark recieves "applied for" status, permitting the applicant to use the symbol "TM" in association with the trademark. A one-year waiting period, in which the trademark may be contested by others, is required before the trademark is officially "registered," and the owner may use the ® symbol in conjunction with the trademark.

Trademarks are often registered at the state or county level, as well. In disputes over trademark rights, the earliest registration, whether local or federal, generally applies in a particular locality.

For example, even though a trademark may be registered at the federal level, another party who obtained a local registration for the same trademark on an earlier date may be entitled to trademark in his or her locality. Any state registration of a franchise trademark or service mark must also be disclosed in Section 13 of the franchisor's UFOC. Moreover, any rulings or challenges to the franchisor's trademark which may limit a franchisee's license or rights must also be described in that section, along with any known infringements. Specifically, franchisors must provide the following information:

> . . . a description of any presently effective determinations of the patent office, the trademark administrator of this state or any court, any pending interference, opposition or cancellation proceeding and any pending material litigation involving such trademarks, service marks, trade names, logotypes, or other commercial symbols . . .

A common practice among franchisors is to require franchisees to help police the exclusive use of a trademark. Typically, the franchisee will be obligated by the franchise agreement to notify the franchisor of any apparent infringements or challenges. Conversely, a franchisee may seek to obligate the franchisor to participate in the defense of the franchisee in the event of a lawsuit brought by some other party over the use of the franchise trademark.

Leading U.S. Trademarks

A 1987 survey by SRI Research Center in Lincoln, Nebraska determined the ten most recognizable trademarks, as follows:

1. McDonald's
2. Coca-Cola
3. California Raisins
4. Budweiser

5. Miller Beer
6. Pepsi-Cola
7. Ford
8. Tide
9. Bartles and James
10. Burger King

Five of the top ten trademarks are franchised products: McDonald's, Coca-Cola, Pepsi-Cola, Ford, and Burger King.

Travel Agents International Headquartered in Seminole, Florida, a franchisor of travel agencies.

Founded in 1980, TAI has been franchising since the following year. A typical TAI franchisee operates a retail travel agency devoted to airline reservations, cruise bookings, vacation and trip planning, and related travel services. Of the 330 TAI outlets currently in business, all except three are franchise units.

Travel Agents International, Inc., 8640 Seminole Blvd., Seminole, FL 33542. Telephone: (813) 397-0434

Travelodge Headquartered in El Cajon, California, a franchisor of lodging outlets.

Founded in Travelodge, 1946, Travelodge has been franchising since 1966. Over its 40-year history, the chain has survived periodic episodes of economic turmoil and occasional problems with its image, but remains one of the most recognizable names in roadside lodging. Since its inception, the Travelodge chain was confined to California for nearly eight years, and the company's logo depicted a golden bear (the California state symbol) on the verge of falling asleep.

The first out-of-state Travelodge opened in Tacoma, Washington in March, 1956. Within a year, the chain had expanded into the midwest, opening its 62nd motel in Toledo, Ohio — the first Travelodge east of the Mississippi. The first franchise property was sold nearly ten years later.

The Travelodge chain was since acquired by Trusthouse Forte, a British conglomerate, which immediately launched an aggressive program to revitalize the historic lodging chain. The traditional budget motor inns were supplanted by full-service Travelodge Hotels that feature restaurants, cocktail lounges, gift shops, convention facilities and banquet rooms. The company's older economy motels were refurbished under a new sign and logo to upgrade the chain's image. The recognizable 'Sleepy Bear' mascot was changed from a sleepy-eyed brown bear to a more contemporary, orange silhouette.

A typical Travelodge franchisee operates a mid-market lodging establishment providing comfortable accommodations with color televisions and in-room telephones, at competitive rates. The Travelodge chain presently consists of 470 outlets, about half of which are franchise units.

Travelodge, 1973 Friendship Dr., El Cajon, CA 92041. Telephone: (619) 448-1884

See Trusthouse Forte Hotels; Sleepy Bear.

Travel Travel Headquartered in San Diego, California, a franchisor of travel agencies.

Founded in 1979, Travel Travel has been franchising since its inception. A typical Travel Travel franchisee operates an upscale, retail travel agency offering travel planning, airline ticketing, and tour and cruise arrangements to the general public. All but one of the 240 Travel Travel outlets currently operating are owned by independent franchisees.

Travel Travel, 4350 La Jolla Village Dr., San Diego, CA 92122. Telephone: (619) 546-4350

Treadway Inns Headquartered in Saddle Brook, New Jersey, a franchisor of lodging establishments.

Founded in 1912, Treadway began franchising in 1961. A typical Treadway franchisee operates a mid-price hotel. Of the franchisor's 100 outlets, all except four are franchise units.

Treadway Inns, 50 Kenney Pl., Saddle Brook, NJ 07662

Treats Headquartered in Toronto, Ontario, a franchisor of specialty bakery goods outlets.

Founded in 1977, Treats has been franchising since 1979. A typical Treats franchisee operates a retail bakery goods shop featuring freshly baked muffins, cookies and pastries prepared on the premises. Of the franchisor's 125 outlets currently operating, all except six are franchise units.

Treats, 121 Bloor St. E, Ste. 810, Toronto, Ont., Canada M4W 3M5. Telephone: (416) 968-0311

Trendy Tidy's Maid Service Headquartered in Markham, Ontario, a franchisor of domestic service outlets.

Founded in 1978, Trendy Tidy's has been franchising since 1981. A typical Trendy Tidy's franchisee operates a maid service specializing in residential cleaning. Of the franchisor's 50 outlets currently operating, all are franchise units.

Trendy Tidy's Maid Service, 380 Esna Park Dr., Markham, Ont., Canada L3R 1H5

TriMark Headquartered in Wilmington, Delaware, a franchisor of direct-mail advertising services.

Founded in 1969, TriMark has been franchising since 1978. A typical TriMark franchisee operates a direct-mail sales operation utilizing promotional coupons and co-op advertising. All of the franchisor's 105 outlets are franchise units.

TriMark, P.O. Box 10530, Wilmington, DE 19850. Telephone: (800) TRIMARK

Triple Check Income Tax Service Headquartered in Burbank, California, a franchisor of tax preparation outlets.

Founded in 1941, Triple Check has been franchising since 1977. A typical Triple Check franchisee operates a personal service business specializing in preparation of federal and state income tax forms for individuals and very small businesses. The chain presently consists of 250 outlets, all of which are franchise units.

Triple Check Income Tax Service, 727 S. Main St., Burbank, CA 91506. Telephone: (213) 849-2273

Trusthouse Forte Hotels British hotel conglomerate and parent company of the Travelodge chain, a franchisor of mid-market and luxury lodging establishments.

Trusthouse Forte originated as a merger between two longstanding British hospitality enterprises, Trust Houses Group Ltd. and Forte Holdings Ltd. The first Trust Houses began opening in 1903, in an attempt to restore the standards of the old English coaching inns, many of which had fallen into decline after the advent of the railroad. Forte Holdings was founded by Lord Forte of Ripley in 1935, who built or acquired hotels, restaurants, catering businesses, and transportation companies in Britain and North America.

In 1970, with 41 hotels, Forte's company merged with the Trust Houses Group to form one of the world's largest hospitality organizations. Lord Forte's son Rocco is presently the chief executive for the 800-hotel chain. Trusthouse Forte has over 200 properties in Great Britain, including a number of historical luxury establishments, among them the Hyde Park Hotel, Grosvenor House, Westbury, Cumberland, and Waldorff. The hotel group also operates the Ritz in Madrid, George V and Plaza Athenee in Paris, Hotel des Bergues in Geneva, and Beach Plaza in Monte Carlo.

Trusthouse Forte properties in the U.S. include the Westbury and Plaza Athenee in New York, Viscount Hotels, Thriftlodge motels, and the recently revitalized Travelodge chain. With 470 outlets, about half of which are franchise units, Travelodge is currently undergoing a systemwide program to upgrade its image and standards.

The Trusthouse Forte conglomerate employs 72,000 people worldwide at 34 principal subsidiaries. Trusthouse Forte Hotels, Inc., 1973 Friendship Dr., El Cajon, CA 92020. Telephone: (619) 448-1884 *See Travelodge.*

T-Shirts Plus Headquartered in Waco, Texas, a franchisor of specialty apparel outlets.

Founded in 1975, T-Shirts Plus has been franchising since its inception. A typical T-Shirts Plus franchisee operates a retail boutique devoted to T-shirts and sports wear, featuring on-site, customized imprinting service. Of the franchisor's 176 outlets currently operating, all except one are franchise units.

T-Shirts Plus, P.O. Box 20608, Waco, TX 76702. Telephone: (800) 433-3307

Tuff-Kote Dinol Headquartered in Troy, Michigan, a franchisor of automobile rustproofing and refinishing outlets.

Founded in 1967, TKD has been franchising since the following year. The franchise organization originated as a joint franchising effort between a manufacturer of sealing products, Tuff-Kote, and a Swedish chemical firm, Astra-Dinol. A typical TKD franchisee operates an auto detailing service based on the franchisor's proprietary line of chemical sealants. The TKD rustproofing system incorporates a rust penetrant developed by Astra-Dinol and an aluminized sealant first marketed by Tuff-Kote. Franchisees also market automobile trim accessories, sunroofs, and fabric protection aids. Of the franchisor's 131 outlets currently operating, all except seven are franchise units.

TKD North America, 1441 E. Maple Rd., Ste. 304,, Troy, MI 48083. Telephone: (313) 867-4700

Tuffy Service Centers Headquartered in Toledo, Ohio, a franchisor of automobile service centers.

Founded in 1970, Tuffy has been franchising since the following year. A typical Tuffy franchisee operates a retail auto service business specializing in exhaust systems, brake service, and wheel alignment. Of the franchisor's 114 outlets currently operating, 90 are franchise units.

Tuffy Service Centers, 1414 Baronial Plaza Dr., Toledo, OH 43615. Telephone: (800) 228-8339

Twistee Treat Headquartered in North Ft. Myers, Florida, a franchisor of fast-food outlets.

Founded in 1982, Twistee Treat has been franchising since 1984. A typical Twistee Treat franchisee operates a fast-food ice cream stand specializing in hand-dipped ice cream and low-calorie nondairy items. Of the franchisor's 38 outlets currently operating, 17 are franchise units.

Twistee Treat, 3434 Hancock Bridge Pkwy., North Ft. Myers, FL 33903. Telephone: (813) 997-8800

**UBI
to
UTAH**

UBI Business Brokers Headquartered in Los Angeles, California, a franchisor of business brokerage services.

Founded in 1966, UBI has been franchising since 1983. A typical UBI franchisee operates a brokerage operation for businesses and prospective investors. Of an estimated 100 UBI outlets currently open and operating, all are franchise units.

UBI Business Brokers, 11965 Venice Blvd., Los Angeles, CA 90066. Telephone: (213) 390-8635

U&R Tax Services Headquartered in Winnipeg, Manitoba, a franchisor of tax preparation outlets in Canada.

Founded in 1972, U&R has been franchising since the following year. A typical U&R franchisee operates a tax counseling business offering income-tax preparation and educational services. Of the franchisor's 100 outlets currently operating, 65 are franchise units.

U&R Tax Services, 201-1345 Pembina Hwy., Winnipeg, Man., Canada R3T 2B6. Telephone: (204) 284-1806

USA Baby Headquartered in Elmhurst, Illinois, a franchisor of retail furniture outlets.

Founded in 1975, USA Baby has been franchising since 1986. A typical USA Baby franchisee operates a retail hard-goods store specializing in juvenile furniture and accessories. Of the franchisor's 27 outlets currently operating, 17 are franchise units.

USA Baby, 725. N. Larch Ave., Elmhurst, IL 60126. Telephone: (800) 323-4108

Ugly Duckling Headquartered in Tucson, Arizona, a franchisor of used-car rental outlets.

Founded in 1977, Ugly Duckling has been franchising since the following year. A typical Ugly Duckling franchisee operates a discount car rental business featuring a fleet of "pre-driven" vehicles presumably in sound mechanical condition. Of the franchisor's 475 outlets currently operating, all except two are franchise units.

Ugly Duckling Rent A Car Systen, Inc., 7750 E. Broadway, Tucson, AZ 85710. Telephone: (800) 843-3825

Uniclean Systems, Inc. Headquartered in Vancouver, British Columbia, a franchisor of interior maintenance services.

Founded in 1976, Uniclean has been franchising since 1981. A typical Uniclean franchisee operates a commercial janitorial cleaning service.

Uniclean Systems, Inc., 642 W. 29th St., North Vancouver, B.C., V7N 2K2. Telephone: (604) 986-4750

Uniforce Temporary Services Headquartered in New Hyde Park, New York, a franchisor of temporary employment agencies.

Founded in 1961, Uniforce has been franchising since 1976. A typical Uniforce franchisee operates a personnel recruitment and placement agency specializing in temporary employment. Of the franchisor's 75 outlets currently operating, 70 are franchise units.

Uniforce, 1335 Jericho Turnpike, New Hyde Park, NY 11040. Telephone: (516) 437-3300

Uniform Franchise Offering Circular A prospectus which all U.S. franchisors are required to provide to prospective franchisees prior to the signing of a franchise agreement, or any related agreement, or prior to the payment of any franchise fees. The requirements for a Uniform Franchise Offering Circular, or *UFOC*, were prepared and adopted by a consortium of the Midwest Securities Commissioner's Association in 1977. The guidelines were amended in 1981, resulting in the form of disclosure required today by the Federal Trade Commission.

The objective of this so-called "disclosure document" was to create a uniform format for disclosing to prospective franchisees important information about franchisors and franchise agreements, particularly information which might have a negative impact on franchisees. The first attempt to create a uniform disclosure document was aimed at fulfilling the requirements of the franchise investment laws of individual states. To date, the legislatures of thirteen states have passed laws requiring franchisors to prepare some form of disclosure similar or identical to the UFOC. The particular requirements vary slightly among these states, but the overall format in which the disclosures must be made does not differ substantially from the one originally devised by the securities commissioners.

Federal Requirement

When the Federal Trade Commission introduced its sweeping federal franchise regulations in October, 1979, the UFOC became a standard requirement for the offer or sale of any franchise in states which do not have franchise investment laws. FTC Rule 436.1 made it a crime to "'fail to furnish any prospective franchisee with (a UFOC) at the earlier of the 'time for making of disclosure' or the first 'personal meeting'." The rule further defined the "time for making of disclosure" as ten business days before the signing of any franchise agreement, or related agreement, or the payment of a franchise fee, or any other fees related to the franchise. (See *Federal Trade Commission Rule, franchise regulations*.)

Simply stated, federal law requires a franchisor to furnish a UFOC to every prospective franchisee, then wait ten business days before executing any agreement or accepting any payment. A "prospective franchisee" is anyone to whom a franchisor offers or sells a franchise. When a prospective franchisee and a representative of the franchisor meet face to face for the first time, the prospective franchisee must receive the franchisor's UFOC at that time. In any event, both parties must wait at least ten business days before signing the franchise agreement. The prescribed waiting period is designed to allow the prospective franchisee ample time to study the document and share the information with an adviser, such as an attorney or accountant. A franchisor is in violation of the rules if it strikes a franchise agreement or accepts any payment without first furnishing a UFOC and allowing the waiting period to lapse.

Although the federal requirement affects all companies that offer or sell franchises in the United States, it does not supplant the disclosure requirements of the thirteen states which have their own franchise investment laws. (See disclosure requirements under individual state headings.)

Preparation of the UFOC

The UFOC, or simply, the "offering circular," must be written in narrative form, clearly and concisely. The form and content are prescribed in detail by the FTC rules and by the individual state laws. Each item required to be disclosed must appear in a specific order, with appropriate positive or negative comments. The securities commissioners, in their guidelines for preparation of a UFOC, require the disclosures to be "readable and understandable," free of technical language or unnecessary detail.

When the offering circular is prepared to fulfill the requirements of a state law, additional documents may be required, as well. For example, in some states, a franchisor must file the UFOC with a regulatory agency, along with an *application for registration* and a *consent to service of process* signed by the franchisor's officers or principals. A *salesman disclosure form* may also be required, providing personal data about the franchisor's sales representatives and brokers. Some states also require a *supplemental information page* detailing the amount of funds needed by the franchisor to complete his obligations with respect to all franchisees to be established in the one-year period after the effective date of the offering circular. A *cross reference sheet* may also be required, showing where each item referred to in the offering circular is located in the franchise agreement.

Cover Page

Every UFOC must have a cover page bearing a title, certain prescribed language, and an effective date. The language which appears on the cover page differs among the individually regulated states, but for other states, the cover page must contain the following precautions:

INFORMATION FOR PROSPECTIVE FRANCHISEE

REQUIRED BY

FEDERAL TRADE COMMISSION

To protect you, we've required your franchisor to give you this information.

We haven't checked it, and don't know if it's correct.

It should help you make up your mind. Study it carefully. While it includes some information about your contract, don't rely on it alone to understand your contract. Read all of your contract carefully.

Buying a franchise is a complicated investment. Take your time to decide. If possible, show your contract and this information to an advisor, like a lawyer or accountant.

If you find anything you think may be wrong or anything important that's been left out, you should let us know about it. It may be against the law.

There may also be laws on franchising in your state. Ask your state agencies about them.

FEDERAL TRADE COMMISSION

Washington, D.C.

Effective date of offering circular:

In addition to an effective date, some states also require the name and address of the franchisor's registered agent authorized to receive a court summons in the respective state, and the name and address of any subfranchisors or brokers.

Table of Contents

A table of contents must be included in every offering circular, showing the page numbers where each required item appears. The prescribed table of contents is shown in the following example.

TABLE OF CONTENTS

The following information is condensed from the *Guidelines for Preparation of the Uniform Franchise Offering Circular and Related Documents*, prepared by Midwest Securities Commissioners Assn., Committee on Uniform Franchise Regulation, and amended by North American Securities Administrators Assn.

The Franchisor and Any Predecessor

The first item required to be disclosed is pertinent information about the franchisor and any predecessor. In the context of the UFOC, the term "predecessor" refers to any prior owner of the franchising company or its assets. The following information must be disclosed:

A. The complete name of the franchisor and any predecessors to the franchisor's business;

B. The name under which the franchisor does business, if different from above;

C. The franchisor's principal address and the principal addresses of any predecessors to the franchisor's business;

D. The form of organization of the franchisor's business; i.e., corporation, partnership, or other form of organization;

E. A general description of the franchisor's business and of the business in which franchisees are engaged, including the market for the goods and services to be sold by the franchisee and a general description of the businesses with which the franchisee will have to compete;

F. The prior business experience of the franchisor and any predecessors to the franchisor's business, including:

    1. The length of time the franchisor has conducted a business of the type to be operated by the franchisee;

    2. The length of time each predecessor conducted a business of the type to be operated by the franchisee;

    3. The length of time the franchisor has offered franchises for such business;

    4. The length of time each predecessor offered franchises for such business;

    5. Whether the franchisor has offered franchises in other lines of business, and, if so, the nature, number sold, and length of time offered;

    6. Whether each predecessor offered franchises in other lines of business, and if so, the nature, number sold, and length of time offered.

Identity and Business Experience of Persons Affiliated with the Franchisor; Franchise Brokers

In this section, the franchisor must list by name and position the directors, trustees, general partners, principal officers (including the chief executive and chief operating officer, financial, franchise marketing, training and service officers) and other executives or subfranchisor. For each person listed, the franchisor must disclose the principal occupations, title, and employers during the five-year period prior to the effective date of the offering circular.

Litigation

In this section, the following information must be disclosed about each person named in the item above:

A. Whether each person has any pending administrative, criminal or material civil action alleging a violation of any franchise law, fraud, embezzlement, fraudulent conversion, restraint of trade, unfair or deceptive practices, misappropriation of property or comparable allegations;

B. During the 10-year period prior to the effective date of the offering circular, whether each person has been convicted of a felony or pleaded nolo contendere to a felony charge, or been held liable in a legal proceeding involving any of the charges named above;

C. Whether each person is subject to any current court order relating to the franchise, or under any federal, state or Canadian franchise, securities, antitrust, trade regulation, or trade practice law.

Bankruptcy

This section must disclose whether the franchisor or any predecessor, officer, or general partner has been declared bankrupt or filed for reorgnization due to insolvency during the 15-year period prior to the effective date of the circular. If so, the pertinent details must also be disclosed.

Franchisee's Initial Franchise Fee or Other Initial Payment

The amount of the initial franchise fee is disclosed in this section of the offering circular. The following information must also be stated:
1. Whether the initial fee is payable as a lump sum or in installments;
2. The manner in which the franchisor will use or apply the payment;
3. Whether the fee is refundable and, if so, under what circumstances.
If the initial fee charged by the franchisor varies from one agreement to another, the formula for determining the actual amount must be disclosed.

Other Fees

The franchisor must describe in detail any other separate or recurring fees or payments for which the franchisee will be obligated. The following information is required to be disclosed:
1. A detailed description of any fees or charges payable to the franchisor or to an affiliate or designate of the franchisor, including:
    (a) Periodic royalties or service fees;
    (b) Fees for negotiating a lease for the franchisee's site;
    (c) Fees or payments for construction, remodeling, decoration, or equipment;
    (d) Training fees;
    (e) Rent or lease payments for the premises, equipment, or fixtures of the franchisee's outlet;
    (f) Fees or charges for advertising and promotion of the franchisee's outlet;
    (g) Fees or charges for cooperative advertising with other franchisees;
    (h) Fees for operating assistance or supervision;
    (i) Fees for inspections or audits;
    (j) Payments of insurance premiums;
    (k) Payments for goods or supplies, in excess of actual wholesale cost;
    (l) Bookkeeping, accounting, or inventory fees;
    (m) Assignment or transfer fees;
2. Whether each fee is payable to the franchisor or to an affiliate of the franchisor;
3. Whether any fee is imposed or collected on behalf of a third party;
4. The date on which a recurring fee, such as an ongoing royalty, is due;
5. The formula used to compute each fee or payment;
6. Whether each fee or payment is refundable and, if so, under what circumstances.

Franchisee's Initial Investment

This section of the UFOC is used to detail the franchisee's estimated initial cash investment. If the specific amount is not known, a high-low range may be stated, based on the franchisor's experience. The following expenditures must be disclosed:
A. Real property, whether not financed by contract, installment, purchase, or lease;
B. Equipment, fixtures, other fixed assets, construction, remodeling, leasehold improvements and decorating costs;
C. Inventory required to open the business;
D. Security deposits, other prepaid expenses, and working capital required to open the business;
E. Any other expenditures which the franchisee will have to make in order to open the business.
The franchisor must also state whether any part of the franchisee's initial investment may be financed and, if so, the estimated loan repayments and interest must be disclosed.
    The estimated initial investment breakdown must conclude with the following statement:
THERE ARE NO OTHER DIRECT OR INDIRECT PAYMENTS IN CONJUNCTION WITH THE PURCHASE OF THE FRANCHISE.

Obligations of Franchisee to Purchase or Lease from Designated Sources

In this section, the UFOC should list those items that the franchisee is obligated to purchase from designated sources, such as merchandise, services, supplies, fixtures, equipment, inventory, or real estate. This item refers to purchases or leases which are obligatory on the part of the franchisee as a condition of obtaining or retaining the franchise. Items included as part of the franchise at no additional charge to the franchisee do not have to be listed.

The following information must be disclosed:

A. The general category of each article or service required to be purchased or leased from the franchisor or his designated suppliers;

B. Whether the franchisor will or may derive income as a result of any such required purchases or leases;

C. The approximate percentage of the franchisee's total purchases or leases represented by the goods and services required to be purchased or leased from the franchisor.

Obligations of Franchisee to Purchase or Lease in Accordance with Specifications or from Approved Suppliers

In this section, the franchisor must identify any products or services which the franchisee is required to purchase or lease in accordance with specifications prescribed by the franchisor. The following information must be disclosed:

A. The categories of goods, services, supplies, fixtures, equipment, inventory, or real estate required to be so purchased;

B. The manner in which the franchisor formulates and modifies the specifications and standards, including the methods by which suppliers are evaluated and approved or disapproved.

C. Whether the franchisor or an affiliate of the franchisor is himself one of the approved suppliers, or the only approved supplier;

D. Whether the franchisor or its affiliate will or may derive income from such purchases.

Financing Arrangements

This section of the offering circular is devoted to any financing arrangements offered directly or indirectly by the franchisor. The information should include the exact terms of any lease arrangements and any financing covering:

(a) The initial franchise fee;

(b) The purchase of land and the construction or remodeling of the premises;

(c) The purchase of equipment, fixtures, opening inventory, and supplies;

(d) The purchase of inventory and supplies;

(e) Replacement of equipment or fixtures;

(f) Any other continuing expense incurred by the franchisee.

The terms of the financing must also be disclosed, including the identity of the lender, the annual interest rate charged, the term for which the financing is available, the nature of any security which must be given, requirements for a personal guarantee, any prepayment penalty, and any other material terms.

The franchisor must state whether it, its agent, or its affiliate now sells, assigns, or discounts any note, contract, lease or other financial instrument executed by franchisees; has done so in the past; or intends to do so in the future.

Obligations of the Franchisor; Other Supervision, Assistance, or Services

This section lists the obligations to be met by the franchisor, both prior to the opening of the franchisee's outlet and during the operation of the franchisee's business. For each obligation relating to the franchise agreement, the corresponding section and page of the contract must be cited. The following information should appear in the offering circular:

A. Before the outlet opens, the agreement may obligate the franchisor to provide such services as: selecting a site or negotiating a lease for the premises; securing licenses and permits for the business; acquiring and installing equipment, signs, and fixtures; acquiring opening inventory and supplies; hiring and training employees; or conducting a pre-opening advertising campaign in the franchisee's area.

B. Any other services to be provided by the franchisor prior to the opening of the franchisee's business must also be disclosed, even though they are not prescribed by the franchise agreement.

C. During the operation of the franchisee's business, the agreement may obligate the franchisor to provide ongoing assistance, such as: advising the franchisee about products or services to be offered by the franchisee; assisting with hiring and training of employees; conducting advertising campaigns; offering improvements and new developments; establishing administrative, bookkeeping, accounting, inventory control, and general operating procedures; and troubleshooting operating problems encountered by the franchisee. The circular should include a description of any operating manual provided to the franchisee to assist the franchisee and his employees in the operation of the business.

D. Other ongoing supervision, assistance, or services must also be disclosed, even though they are not prescribed by the franchise agreement.

E. If the franchisor selects the site for the franchisee's outlet, the methods and criteria must be disclosed. The circular should describe such factors as the general location and neighborhood, traffic patterns, parking, size, layout, and other physical characteristics of the premises.

F. The approximate length of time between the signing of the franchise agreement and the opening of the franchisee's outlet must be disclosed.

G. The circular must also include a description of the franchisor's training program, including the location, duration, and content. Any charges for training or materials and transportation and living expenses incurred by attendees must also be disclosed.

Exclusive Area or Territory

This section of the circular is devoted to the exclusive area or territory, if any, granted to the franchisee. The disclosure should include a description of the boundaries or a map of the designated territory. The franchisee's rights relative to the territory should be explained in detail. For example, it should be stated whether the franchisor agrees not to operate a company-owned outlet or grant a franchise to another party in the territory in competition with the franchisee's outlet. It should also be stated whether or not the franchisee or other franchisees are restricted in any manner from soliciting sales or accepting orders outside their defined territories.

Any conditions for the continuance of the franchisee's territorial rights must be disclosed in this section. For example, if the franchisee must meet a sales quota or open additional outlets in order to retain his territory, the requirements and quotas must be described in detail. Any circumstances which might allow the franchisor to modify the franchisee's territory must be clearly explained.

Trademarks, Service Marks, Trade Names, Logotypes, and Commercial Symbols

In this section, the franchisor must describe any trademarks, names, logos, or other commercial symbols licensed to the franchisee. A reproduction of any logo or other commercial symbol may be included as part of the disclosure. The circular should identify which, if any, of the trademarks has been registered or applied for registration with the U.S. Patent and Trademark Office. A list of state registrations and applications, if any, should also be included.

If the franchisor's trademark rights are limited in any way, the reason and circumstances must be disclosed. Any determination, petition, claim, or litigation which might affect the franchisor's right to use any trademark, name, or symbol must be listed and summarized.

The circular must state whether the franchisee is obligated to notify the franchisor of any apparent infringements on the trademarks, and if the franchisor is obligated to protect the franchisee's right to use them.

Patents and Copyrights

This section is devoted to any special patents or copyrights owned by the franchisor. For each patent listed, the patent number, issue date, and title should be shown. Copyrights should be identified by registration number and date. If the franchisor has no patents or copyrights, a statement to that effect should appear in the offering circular.

If any of the franchisee's rights to use the patents or copyrights are rectricted or threatened, for example, by another contract or by an infringement or challenge, the reason and circumstances must be explained.

Obligation of the Franchisee to Participate in the Actual Operation of the Franchise Business

In this section, the franchisor must disclose whether the franchisee must actively manage the outlet in person. If the franchisee s permitted to hire a manager for the outlet, the offering circular should provide the following additional information:
(a) Whether the franchisor recommends on-premises supervision by the franchisee;
(b) Who the franchisee can or cannot hire to manage the outlet;
(c) Whether the manager must attend the franchisor's training program;
(d) Whether the franchisor must be informed of the manager's identity.

Restriction on Goods and Services Offered by Franchisee

The offering circular must describe any obligations of the franchisee to sell or provide only those goods and services approved by the franchisor, or to sell to only those customers stipulated by the franchisor. The restrictions and conditions must be explained in detail.

Renewal, Termination, Repurchase, Modification and Assignment of the Franchise Agreement and Related Information

In this section, the franchisor must disclose the term of the franchise, the conditions under which the franchise may be renewed, terminated, or assigned. The following information must be provided:
A. The length of the initial term, and whether the term is affected by any other agreement;
B. The conditions under which the franchisee may renew or extend the agreement;
C. The conditions under which the franchisor may refuse to renew or extend the agreement;
D. The conditions under which the franchisee may terminate the agreement;
E. The conditions under which the franchisor may terminate the agreement;
F. The obligations of the franchisee after termination or expiration of the franchise;
G. The franchisee's interest upon termination or expiration of the franchise;
H. The conditions under which the franchisor may repurchase the franchise, including any right of first refusal;
I. The conditions under which the franchisee may sell or assign all or any interest in the ownership of the franchise or the assets of the business;

J. The conditions under which the franchisor may sell or assign its rights and obligations under the franchise agreement;

K. The conditions under which the franchisee may modify the agreement;

L. The conditions under which the franchisor may modify the agreement;

M. The rights of the franchisee's heirs upon his death or disability;

N. The provisions of any covenant not to compete.

Arrangements with Public Figures

A "public figure" is a person whose name or image is recognizable by the general public in the area where the franchise will be sold. Athletes, entertainers, or fictional personalities, such as cartoon characters, are often associated with franchise offerings. The UFOC must describe any compensation or benefits given or promised to a public figure or, in the case of a cartoon character, its owner.

The disclosure should include a description of the franchisee's rights to use the public figure's name to advertise the outlet, and any charges for those rights. The UFOC should also explain whether the public figure is actually involved in the management or ownership of the franchising company. The total investment of the public figure in the franchise operation, if any, must be disclosed.

Actual, Average, Projected, or Forecasted Franchise Sales, Profits, or Earnings

A. If the franchisor makes any claim to a prospective franchisee regarding actual or average sales, profits, or earnings of franchisees, an exact copy must be included as an exhibit to the offering circular. This earnings claim must bear the following legend in bold-face type:

THESE SALES, PROFITS OR EARNINGS ARE (AVERAGES) OF (A) SPECIFIC FRANCHISE(S) AND SHOULD NOT BE CONSIDERED THE ACTUAL OR POTENTIAL SALES, PROFITS, OR EARNINGS THAT WILL BE REALIZED BY ANY OTHER FRANCHISE. THE FRANCHISOR DOES NOT REPRESENT THAT ANY FRANCHISEE CAN EXPECT TO ATTAIN THESE SALES, PROFITS, OR EARNINGS.

B. Where projected or forecasted franchisee sales, profits, or earnings are proposed to be used, an exact copy must be included in the offering circular, along with this legend in bold-face type:

THESE PROJECTIONS (FORECASTS) OF SALES, PROFITS, OR EARNINGS ARE MERELY ESTIMATES AND SHOULD NOT BE CONSIDERED AS THE ACTUAL OR POTENTIAL SALES, PROFITS OR EARNINGS THAT WILL BE REALIZED BY ANY SPECIFIC FRANCHISEE. THE FRANCHISOR DOES NOT REPRESENT THAT ANY FRANCHISEE CAN EXPECT TO ATTAIN THESE SALES, PROFITS, OR EARNINGS.

C. The basis and assumptions for any earnings claim, whether actual or projected, must be disclosed in detail. Any statement of actual earnings must be based on a substantial number of franchisees during the same period of time, and must be prepared in accordance with generally accepted accounting principles. The locations of the outlets used in the earnings claim must be identified by address, number of years in operation, whether substantially similar to the franchises offered, whether managed by the owner, whether they received any services not generally available to other franchises, and whether such sales, profits, or earnings have been audited.

If the franchisor chooses not to make an earnings claim, a statement to that effect should be included in the offering circular. No other information bearing upon actual or projected sales, income, profits, or earnings is allowable. In a survey of franchisors published by the FTC in January, 1985, only eight percent of the respondents included an earnings claim in their offering circulars.

Information Regarding Franchises of the Franchisor

The following information must be disclosed about the franchisor's existing franchise outlets, current to the close of the franchisor's most recent fiscal year:

A. The total number of franchises, not including company-owned stores, similar to the ones offered, open and operational;

B. The total number of franchises sold but not yet open;

C. The names, addresses, and telephone numbers of all franchises under franchise agreements;

D. The total number of franchises to be sold or granted during the one-year period following the date of the offering circular;

E. The number of franchises that have been canceled, terminated, refused renewal, or repurchased by the franchisor. The circular may include individual breakdowns by state, either for an individual state or for all states in which the franchisor now has or intends to open franchises.

Financial Statements

The UFOC must contain a set of the franchisor's most recent audited financial statements, prepared in accordance with generally accepted accounting principles. Unaudited statements may be used during interim periods.

Agreements

A copy of all franchise and other related agreements should accompany the offering circular. In addition to the franchise agreement, a license agreement, equipment lease, lease for premises, and/or loan agreement may also be attached.

Acknowledgement of Receipt by Prospective Franchisee

The receipt form should be the final and separate page to the offering circular and should not contain any disclosure items.

Sample Uniform Franchise Offering Circular (UFOC)

1. THE FRANCHISOR AND ANY PREDECESSOR

The Franchisor

Franchisor is a [state of incorporation] corporation organized on [date], under the name [corporate name]. Its predecessor was [predecessor name], which was organized as an Arizona corporation on [date].

The franchisor maintains its principal business offices at [address].

Franchisor's Business

Franchisor is a franchising company which grants franchises and trains, advises, and assists franchisees in the establishment and operation of [type of outlet] businesses known as [trade name] outlets. Franchisor's primary activities are education, market planning, advertising, consulting, and coordination for its franchisees.

Franchisor's predecessor, [predecessor name] does business under the name [trade name] and is engaged in the business of [description of predecessor's business].

The Franchise Business

The franchise business is [description of franchise business], utilizing the franchisor's curricula, teaching materials, systems, procedures, and trade marks. The primary customers for the outlet are [description of primary customers]. The franchisee will have to compete with [primary competitors].

2. PRIOR BUSINESS EXPERIENCE OF THE FRANCHISOR AND PREDECESSORS

Franchisor's predecessor, [predecessor name], has operated a business similar to the business to be operated by the franchisee since [date].

Neither the franchisor, its affiliate, nor any other principals have offered any other franchises in any line of business.

PRIOR BUSINESS EXPERIENCE OF PERSONS AFFILIATED WITH FRANCHISOR; FRANCHISE BROKERS

The following table summarizes the prior business experience of the persons affiliated with the franchisor for the five-year period prior to the date of this offering circular.

[Description of prior experience of persons associated with the franchisor]

3. LITIGATION

Neither the franchisor nor any other person identified in Item 2 above has any administrative or material civil action (or a significant number of civil actions irrespective of materiality) pending against them alleging a violation of any franchise law, fraud, embezzlement, fraudulent conversion, restraint of trade, unfair or deceptive business practices, misappropriation of property, or comparable allegations, other than a pending proceeding involving the arrest of such a person.

Neither the franchisor nor any person identified in Item 2 above has during the 10-year period immediately preceding the date of this offering circular been convicted of a felony or pleaded nolo contendere to any felony charge or been held liable in any other civil action or other legal proceeding where such felony, civil action, complaint, or other legal proceeding involved violation of any franchise law, fraud, embezzlement, fraudulent conversion, restraint of trade, unfair or deceptive practices, misappropriation of property or comparable allegations.

Neither the franchisor nor any person identified in Item 2 above is subject to any currently effective injunctive or restrictive order or decree relating to the franchise or under any federal, state, or Canadian franchise, securities, antitrust, trade regulation or trade practice law as a result of a concluded or pending action or proceeding brought by a public agency; nor is subject to any currently effective order of any national securities association or national securities exchange (as defined in the Securities and Exchange Act of 1934) suspending or expelling such persons from membership in such association or exchange.

4. BANKRUPTCY

During the 15-year period immediately preceding the date of the offering circular, neither the franchisor nor any predecessor, current officer or general partner of the franchisor has been adjudged bankrupt or reorganized due to insolvency or been a principal officer of a company or a general partner of a partnership within one year of the time that such company or partnership was adjudged bankrupt or reorganized due to insolvency or is otherwise subject to any pending bankrupcty or reorganization proceeding.

5. FRANCHISEE'S INITIAL FRANCHISE FEE OR OTHER PAYMENT

The full franchise fee is payable to franchisor upon execution of the franchise agreement. The franchise fee is placed with the other general funds of the franchisor and is non-refundable.

The initial franchise fee is $_____.

6. OTHER FEES

Franchisee is obligated to purchase [products required to be purchased by franchisee]. The initial cost to the franchisee is $_____.

Under the franchise agreement, franchisee is obligated to pay to franchisor an ongoing royalty of _____ percent (___%) of gross revenues of the franchise outlet.

There are no other franchise fees or royalties connected with the franchise.

7. FRANCHISEE'S INITIAL INVESTMENT

The initial investment may vary according to franchisee's choice of site, method of business organization, equipment requirements, and improvements. Following is a summary of estimated initial investment requirements for a low and high investment:

Estimated Initial Investment

ITEM	HOW PAID	LOW(1)	HIGH(2)	WHEN DUE	PAID TO
Initial Fee	Lump sum	_____	_____	Signing of Agreement	Franchisor
Equipment	As ordered	_____	_____	As ordered	Suppliers
Lease Deposits	As agreed	_____	_____	As agreed	Lessor
Furnishings	As agreed	_____	_____	As ordered	Vendors
Licenses & Permits	As incurred	_____	_____	As agreed	Licensing Body
Working Capital (3)	As incurred	_____	_____	As incurred	Various
Totals		_____	_____		

NOTES TO ESTIMATED INITIAL INVESTMENT BREAKDOWN

(1) Low investment is based on _____.
(2) High investment is based on _____.

Fixed costs such as rents and salaries will vary, depending upon geographic location.

(3) The estimate for working capital includes _____.

Franchisor does not offer either direct or indirect financing to franchisee for any other item. Franchisee must obtain his own financing, if needed, and should be aware that the availability and terms of financing will depend on factors such as the availability of financing in general, the credit-worthiness of the franchisee, other security the franchisee may have, policies of lending institutions regarding the type of business to be operated by the franchisee, and so forth.

There are no other direct or indirect payments in conjunction with the purchase of the franchise.

8. OBLIGATIONS OF FRANCHISEE TO PURCHASE OR LEASE FROM DESIGNATED SUPPLIERS

Franchisee is obligated to purchase [description of obligatory purchases] from the franchisor's affiliate, [affiliate name], or from another approved supplier. Franchisee is not obligated to purchase any other equipment or supplies from designated suppliers.

9. OBLIGATIONS OF FRANCHISEE TO PURCHASE OR LEASE IN ACCORDANCE WITH SPECIFICATIONS OR FROM APPROVED SUPPLIERS

Franchisee is required to purchase all of the furnishings and initial supplies specified in franchisor's operating manual, in conformance with franchisor's specifications relating to quality, design, image, or other standards.

Franchisee is required to purchase or cause to be printed certain advertising literature for use in promotion of the franchise outlet. These items may be purchased in printed form from franchisor at a price equal to franchisor's actual printing cost plus ten percent (10%). If franchisee elects to have these materials printed by another source, the printed materials must be of equal quality to those offered by franchisor and must contain only the art, photographs, and wording approved by franchisor.

Franchisee is obligated by the Franchise Agreement to purchase business liability, comprehensive and fire/damage insurace in the amount of One Million Dollars ($1,000,000) combined single limit and Three Million Dollars ($3,000,000) per occurrence for business liability, and fire/damage coverage sufficient to repair or replace all equipment, tools, inventory, and supplies essential to the operation of the franchise business. Neither the franchisor nor its affiliate will or may derive profits from the required purchase of equipment or supplies except for equipment or supplies made available by franchisor.

10. FINANCING ARRANGEMENTS

Neither the franchisor nor its affiliates offer any financing directly or indirectly, or arrange or guarantee financing for franchisees. There are no payments received by franhcisor or its affiliate from any person, lending institution, or other source for its placement of financing with such person, lending institution or other source.

There is no past or present practice of the franchisor to sell, assign, or discount to a third party any note, contract, or other obligation of the franchisee in whole or in part.

11. OBLIGATIONS OF THE FRANCHISOR; OTHER SUPERVISION, ASSISTANCE OR SERVICES

Upon execution of the franchise agreement and prior to the opening of the franchise business, it is the obligation of the franchisor to:

1. designate an exclusive territory;

2. provide a training program at a time and location designated by franchisor prior to the opening of the business;

3. provide a list of specifications, standards, and suppliers for inventory, equipment, and supplies;

4. provide guidance in methods, procedures, techniques and operations in the form of an operating manual and other printed materials;

5. provide camera-ready artwork for printed materials to be used by franchisee in the conduct of the franchise business.

There is no other supervision, assistance, or service to be provided by the franchisor prior to the opening of the franchise business pursuant to the franchise agreement or otherwise.

Upon commencement of the franchise business by franchisee, franchisor is obligated to:

1. protect the exclusive territory by assuring that no other franchises or company-owned outlets are granted or established therein;

2. modify the operating manual, as required, to improve or update the systems and procedures;

3. provide ongoing assistance and guidance by personal visits to the franchise outlet by authorized personnel of the franchisor;

4. administer a cooperative advertising fund to conduct advertising and promotions in selected media as the franchisor may deem appropriate, and

5. provide on-site training and assistance in opening and operating the outlet for at least [number of days] business days prior to the opening of the franchise outlet. The training program consists of industry background, business operations, personnel hiring and training, business management, expansion strategies, and [other training topics].

There is no other supervision, assistance, or service to be provided by the franchisor during the operation of the franchise business pursuant to the franchise agreement or otherwise.

Franchisor does not select the location of the franchisee's business, but must approve the location prior to the franchisee's commencement of the business. Franchisor, at no charge, provides guidelines for site selection. Pursuant to the franchise agreement, franchisee is obligated to complete all of the required tasks necessary to commence the franchise business within ninety (90) days after execution of the agreement.

12. EXCLUSIVE AREA OR TERRITORY

Franchisor grants to franchisee during the term of the franchise an exclusive area (franchised territory). Neither the franchisor nor its affiliate will establish other franchises or company-owned outlets using the franchisor's trade marks in the designated territory.

A designated territory is exclusive to the franchisee for the length of the franchise and is not altered by the achievement of a certain sales volume, market penetration or other contingency. Other than the territory granted by the agreement, franchisee may obtain another territory only by executing a separate franchise agreement.

A franchisee shall have no sub-franchising rights whatsoever.

13. TRADE MARKS, SERVICE MARKS, TRADE NAMES, LOGOTYPES AND COMMERCIAL SYMBOLS

Franchisor has applied for a trade mark registration on the Principal Register of the U.S. Patent and Trademark Office for the following:

[trademark registration data]

14. PATENTS AND COPYRIGHTS

Franchisor owns no special patents that pertain to the offering.

Franchisor and its principals possess proprietary know-how in the form of trade secrets, operating methods, specifications, technique, information and systems in the operation of [type of business] outlets. The know-how is disclosed in part in the copyrighted operating manual which franchisee receives solely for the purpose of developing the franchise and for the term of the franchise agreement.

15. OBLIGATION OF THE FRANCHISEE TO PARTICIPATE IN THE ACTUAL OPERATION OF THE FRANCHISE BUSINESS

Franchisee is not obligated to participate fulltime in the operation of the franchise business, provided, however, that if franchisee opts not to participate fulltime, a qualified manager must be in the employ of the franchise business.

16. RESTRICTIONS ON GOODS AND SERVICES OFFERED BY FRANCHISEE

Pursuant to the franchise agreement, the franchisee may not offer any classes or products or services not approved by franchisor. Franchisor will not unreasonably withhold its approval for any products or services which franchisee desires to offer.

Franchisee may not own an interest in, perform any business activity on behalf of, or be in the employ of another [type of business] business without franchisor's permission. Franchisee is not limited in the customers whom he may solicit.

17. RENEWAL, TERMINATION, REPURCHASE, MODIFICATION AND ASSIGNMENT OF THE FRANCHISE AGREEMENT AND RELATED INFORMATION

The term of the franchise agreement is ten years and is not affected by any agreement other than the franchise agreement.

Upon expiration of the initial term, if the franchisee is in compliance with all the provisions of the agreement, franchisee shall have the option to renew for an additional term by notifying the franchisor of its intention to renew six months prior to the expiration of the franchise and by executing a new franchise agreement and supportive agreements as are then customarily used by the franchisor. No fee is charged for renewal of the franchise.

If, upon expiration, the franchisee is in default of the agreement or fails to renew the franchise agreement within thirty (30) days following the expiration, the franchise shall be deemed terminated.

The franchisee may terminate the franchise if franchisor does not fulfill its obligations under the agreement. Franchisee may terminate by exercising its option to sell the franchise to a fully disclosed and approved purchaser.

Franchisor may terminate the franchise if franchisee fails to open the business within 90 days following the signing of the agreement, or if franchisee is in default of the agreement and fails to cure such default within thirty (30) days of notice. Further, the franchisor may terminate the franchise if franchisee abandons the franchise, becomes insolvent or bankrupt (to the extent permitted by the Federal Bankruptcy Law), is convicted or pleads no contest to a felony or crime involving moral turpitude, or makes an un authorized assignment of the franchise, discloses any trade secrets of the franchisor, or has an interest in or engages in a business activity competitive with the franchise (except to the extent permitted by the California Franchise Relations Act, if franchisee is located in California).

Upon termination or expiration, franchisee is obligated to pay franchisor within 15 days any amounts that are due and unpaid for products, services, cease to identify himself as a franchisee, return all advertising materials, forms, stationery, or other printed matter bearing franchisor's trade marks, cancel all fictitious name permits, business licenses or other permits relating to the franchise, notify the telephone company and other listing agencies of the termination, honor the non-compete covenant and return all manual and written communications to the franchisor. Franchisee would thereafter have no interest in or rights to the franchise business.

If franchisee notifies franchisor that it desires to sell any interest in the franchise, franchisor has the right at its sole discretion to repurchase the franchise. Further, should the franchisee obtain a bona fide written offer from a responsible and fully disclosed purchaser, franchisor owuld have the right at its discretion to purchase the interest for the same price and on the same terms and conditions as contained in the offer. Franchisor shall have 30 days to exercise its right of first refusal to repurchase the franchise.

With prior approval of franchisor, franchisee may assign its assets and liabilities to a newly formed corproation that conducts no other business than the franchise and in which franchisee owns and controls not less than sixty percent (60%) of the equity and voting power, and for which franchisee personally guarantees all performance, obligations, and debts created by the franchise agreement.

Except as set forth in the above paragraph, none of the ownership of the franchise may be voluntarily, involuntarily, directly or indirectly assigned, sold, subdivided, or otherwise transferred by franchisee without prior written approval of franchisor. In the event of an approved assignment, other than to a corporation controlled by franchisee, assignee must pay to franchisor a transfer and retaining fee equal to fifty percent (50%) of the initial franchise fee. The approved assignee must execute the then-current franchise agreement.

The agreement may not be modified or amended except by mutual consent and execution of a written instrument. Franchisor is not restricted from transferring the franchise agreement or from designating any subsidiary, affiliate or agent to perform any and all acts franchisor is obligated to perform. Franchisor has the right to modify the operating procedures and specifications of the franchise, but has no right to modify the terms of the agreement subsequent to its signing. Upon death or disability of the franchisee or the principal owner, the executor, administrator, or other personal representative must assign the franchise to a fully disclosed and approved person who meets the standard qualifications for franchisees of the franchisor. If such assignment is not made within 90 days after the death or disability, the failure to transfer the interest in the franchise would constitute a breach. Notwithstanding the above, at any time subsequent to the death or disability of the franchisee or principal owner, franchisor may obtain an interim manager to run the business until such assignment is made.

Franchisee agrees by signing the franchise agreement that it will not engage in any business activity competitive with the franchise for a period of one year from the date of termination or expiration of the franchise. However, such a covenant may or may not be enforceable in the State of California, under the laws of California.

18. ARRANGEMENTS WITH PUBLIC FIGURES

Franchisor does not give or promise any compensation or other benefit to any public figure arising in whole or in part from the use of any public figure in the name or symbol of the franchise or the endoresement or recommendation of the franchise by any public figure in advertisements.

No arrangements have been made by franchisor under which franchisee may use a public figure. Franchisee is wholly unrestricted in its use of public figures in its advertisements and promotions, with the exception that, pursuant to the franchise agreement, printed materials, including endorsements, must be approved in advance by franchisor.

19. ACTUAL, AVERAGE, PROJECTED OR FORECASTED FRANCHISE SALES, PROFITS, OR EARNINGS

Franchisor does not make any statement regarding actual, average, projected, or forecasted franchise sales, profits, or earnings.

20. INFORMATION REGARDING FRANCHISES OF THE FRANCHISOR

As these are the first franchises offered by franchisor, franchisor does not currently have any outlets open or operating.

No franchises have been canceled, terminated, refused renewal, or re-acquired by repurchase or otherwise by franchisor.

Franchisor estimates it will grant franchises as follows during the one-year period following the date of this offering circular:

State   Number of Outlets
[State names]   [outlets to be sold in each state]

21. FRANCHISOR'S FINANCIAL STATEMENTS

Attached are the most recent audited financial statements of the franchisor.

22. AGREEMENTS

Attached is a copy of the franchisor's franchise agreement and all related contracts and agreements.

Uniglobe Travel Headquartered in Vancouver, British Columbia, a franchisor of travel agencies.

Founded in 1979, Uniglobe has been franchising since the following year. Uniglobe was founded by U. Gary Charlwood, cofounder of the Canadian Century 21 real estate network. The first Uniglobe territory was franchised in Canada in 1980 and, three years later, the region was subdivided into three sections: Western Canada, Ontario, and Quebec. Uniglobe expanded into the United States in 1981, operating under a master franchising plan whereby subfranchisors purchased the rights to develop large geographic regions.

Uniglobe International is presently organized into 19 regions in North America, all of which have been sold to subfranchisors headquartered in Columbus, Ohio; Miami, Florida; Salem, New Hampshire; Atlanta, Georgia; Tornto, Ontario; St. Louis, Missouri; Montreal, Quebec; Dallas and Houston, Texas; Denver, Colorado; Detroit, Michigan; Orange County, California; Minneapolis, Minnesota; San Francisco, California; Washington, D.C.; Chicago, Illinois; Seattle, Washington; New York City; and Vancouver, British Columbia.

A typical Uniglobe franchisee operates a retail travel agency offering travel consultation and reservation services for both commercial and leisure travelers. At the end of 1988, the chain boasted 750 outlets in the U.S. and Canada, all operated under franchise licenses.

Uniglobe, 1199 W. Pender St., Ste. 900, Vancouver, B.C., Canada V6E 2R1. Telephone: (604) 662-3800

Uniroyal Goodrich Headquartered in Akron, Ohio, a manufacturer of automotible tires and franchisor of retail tire outlets.

Founded in 1900, the company's predecessor, B. F. Goodrich began franchising independent tire dealers in 1925. Dr. B. F. Goodrich was a Civil War surgeon who formed a manufacturing company in 1870 to produce rubber fire hoses, raincoats, and fireman's boots. In 1900, Goodrich's firm became the first company to begin regular production of automobile tires. In 1983, B. F. Goodrich merged with Uniroyal to form the largest U.S. chain of retail tire centers. A typical Uniroyal Goodrich dealer operates a retail outlet marketing tires and related merchandise for passenger autos, trucks, farm equipment, and industrial vehicles. The Uniroyal Goodrich chain consists of 2,200 outlets, none of which are company-owned.

Uniroyal Goodrich, 600 S. Main St., Akron, OH 44318. Telephone: (800) 321-1800

United Chiropractic Headquartered in Metairie, Louisiana, a franchisor of chiropractic outlets.

Founded in 1983, UC has been franchising since 1986. A typical UC franchisee operates a chiropractic clinic utilizing the franchisor's trademarks and promotional assistance. Of the franchisor's 190 outlets currently operating, over 150 are franchise units.

United Chiropractic, 3900 N. Causeway Rd., Ste. 1295, Metairie, LA 70002

United Consumers Club Headquartered in Merrillville, Indiana, a franchisor of thrift shopping clubs.

Founded in 1971, United Consumers has been franchising since the following year. A typical United Consumers franchisee operates a discount purchasing association which thrives on membership fees. Of the franchisor's 70 outlets currently operating, all except five are franchise units.

United Consumers Club Franchising Corp., 8450 Broadway, Merrillville, IN 46410. Telephone: (219) 736-1100

Utah, Franchise Regulations The Utah legislature has not yet enacted any generally applicable franchise investment law. However, the rights of automobile dealers and service station owners operating under franchise agreements are protected by separate laws.

Utah law does not require franchisors to register or file disclosures with any state regulatory body. In the absence of such a requirement, the federal Franchise Rule applies, requiring franchisors to furnish a disclosure document prescribed by the Federal Trade Commission to prospective franchisees ten business days before a franchise sale is made.

See Franchise Rule.

VR
to
VIRGINIA

VR Business Brokers Headquartered in Boston, Massachusetts, a franchisor of business brokerage services.

Founded in 1979, VR has been franchising since its inception, growing into the largest network of professional business brokers in the United States. In 1988, the value of VR's brokered sales was reported at approximately $2.7 billion. VR is currently owned by The Christie Group, plc, a large brokerage organization in Great Britain. CEO Kevin Eakin joined Christie subsidiary RCC in 1978, becoming a director and general manager in 1984. In November, 1985, Eakin was appointed chief executive of RCC and and, in March, 1988, became the head of VR Business Brokers. The franchisor's chief operating officer is a former franchisee, Brad Bueermann, who still serves as chairman of the board of Omnivest, Inc., a Portland, Oregon based VR franchise. Bueermann is a graduate of Stanford University who previously worked for Citicorp's international banking group in Milan, Italy.

A typical VR franchisee operates a brokerage office listing small-to-medium size businesses for sale, acquisition, or merger. Each office acts as a clearinghouse and resource center for entrepreneurs and small business communities. VR services include preparation of computerized business evaluations, marketing services, and a nationwide database of businesses for sale. Franchisees also assist buyers in obtaining financing and handling negotiations with sellers, landlords, attorneys, accountants, and bankers. Of the franchisor's 205 outlets currently operating, all are franchise units.

VR Business Brokers, 230 Western Ave., Boston, MA 02134. Telephone: (800) 343-4416

ValCom Computer Centers Headquartered in Omaha, Nebraska, a franchisor of specialty computer stores.

Founded in 1983, ValCom has been franchising since its inception. A typical ValCom franchisee operates a retail outlet devoted to computer hardware and software. The chain was originally conceived to sell integrated data processing systems to farming businesses. The company has since adopted a broad base of commercial, industrial, and agricultural clientele, with a focus on small office systems. Of the franchisor's 180 outlets currently operating, all except 20 are franchise units.

ValCom, Inc., 10810 Farnam Dr., Omaha, NE 68154. Telephone: (402) 392-3900

Vermont, Franchise Regulations To date, the Vermont legislature has not enacted any generally applicable franchise investment law. However, the rights of automobile dealers, service station owners, and beer and liquor retailers operating under franchise agreements are protected by separate laws.

Vermont law does not require franchisors to register or file disclosures with any state regulatory body. In the absence of such a requirement, the federal Franchise Rule applies, requiring franchisors to furnish a disclosure document prescribed by the Federal Trade Commission to prospective franchisees ten business days before a franchise sale is made.

See Franchise Rule.

Via de France Headquartered in food service outlets, a franchisor of food-service outlets.

Founded in 1978, Via de France has been franchising since 1988. A typical Via de France franchisee operates a cafe-style restaurant featuring sandwiches, soups, coffees, and fresh bakery goods prepared on the premises. Of the franchisor's 88 outlets currently operating, all except three are franchise units.

Via de France, 8201 Greensboro Dr., McLean, VA 22102

Video Biz Headquartered in Longwood, Florida, a franchisor of videocassette rental outlets.

Founded in 1981, Video Biz has been franchising since 1983. A typical Video Biz franchisee operates a retail store devoted to rental and sale of videotaped movies. Of the franchisor's 170 outlets currently operating, all except two are franchise units.

Video Bizx, 2981 W. State Rd. 434, Ste. 100, Longwood, FL 32779. Telephone: (800) 582-7347

Video Data Services Headquartered in Pittsford, New York, a franchisor of video production services.

Founded in 1982, Video Data has been franchising since 1984. A typical Video Data franchisee operates a video photography business for personal and commercial applications such as weddings, business seminars, speeches, sporting events, and training programs. Of the franchisor's 237 outlets currently operating, all except one are franchise units.

Video Data Services, 24 Grove St., Pittsford, NY 14534. Telephone: (716) 385-4773

Video Galaxy Headquartered in Vernon, Connecticut, a franchisor of videocassette rental outlets.

Founded in 1981, Video Galaxy has been franchising since 1986. A typical Video Galaxy franchisee operates a specialty retail store devoted to videocassette and VCR rentals and sales. All of the franchisor's 38 outlets are franchise units.

Video Galaxy, 101 West St., Vernon, CT 06066

Village Inn Restaurants Headquartered in Denver, Colorado, a franchisor of food service outlets.

Founded in 1958, Village Inn has been franchising since 1961. A typical Village Inn franchisee operates a family-style restaurant and coffee shop. Once devoted primarily to pancakes and waffles, outlets currently feature a diverse breakfast, lunch, and dinner menu. About half of the 270 Village Inn outlets currently open are franchise units.

Village Inn Restaurants, P.O. Box 16601, Denver, CO 80216. Telephone: (303) 296-2121

Virginia, Franchise Regulations Franchisors operating in the state of Virginia are governed by the Retail Franchising Act, which requires registration and disclosure of pertinent information about the franchisor, franchise business, and franchise agreement. Other state laws protect the rights of service station owners, automobile dealers and liquor retailers operating under franchise agreements.

Before offering or selling a franchise in the state, a franchisor must first prepare a disclosure document prescribed by the statute, then file the information, along with the franchise agreement, financial statements, and related documents, with the Division of Securities and Retail Franchising. The examiner must approve the registration before the franchisor may proceed to offer or sell franchises.

In addition to a disclosure document, franchisors are also required to submit the following items:
1. Application for registration of the franchise offering;
2. Salesman disclosure form;
3. Consent to service of process;
4. Auditor's consent to use of audited financial statements;
5. Cross-reference sheet showing the location in the franchise agreement of the key items in the disclosure document.

The disclosure document devised by a consortium of midwestern securities commissioners as a uniform method of complying with state franchise investment laws, the *Uniform Franchise Offering Circular*, or UFOC, fulfills the disclosure requirements of the Virginia law. There are minor variations and differences in language required by the Virginia statute, including a different cover page.

The disclosure document or UFOC must be furnished to a prospective franchisee at least ten business days before a franchise sale is made. For information about state franchise laws, regulations, and filing requirements, or to report possible violations, contact: Examination Coordinator, Franchise Section, Division of Securities and Retail Franchising, 11 S. 12th St., Richmond, VA 23219. Telephone: (804) 786-7751.

See Uniform Franchise Offering Circular.

WXYZ

**Wallpapers to Go
to
Zippy Print**

Wallpapers To Go Headquartered in Houston, Texas, a franchisor of specialty retail outlets.

Founded in 1977, WTG has been franchising since 1986. A typical WTG franchisee operates a retail store devoted to interior decorating products, with an emphasis on wallpaper, window blinds, and accent items. Of the franchisor's 100 outlets currently operating, 70 are franchise units.

Wallpapers To Go, P.O. Box 4586, Houston, TX 77210-4586. Telephone: (800) 843-7094

Washington, Franchise Regulations Franchisors operating in the state of Washington are governed by the Franchise Investment Protection Act, which requires registration and disclosure of pertinent information about the franchisor, franchise business, and franchise agreement.

Before offering or selling a franchise in the state, a franchisor must first prepare a disclosure document prescribed by the statute, then file the information, along with the franchise agreement, financial statements, and related documents, with the Washington Securities Division.

In addition to a disclosure document, franchisors are also required to submit the following items:

1. Application for registration of the franchise offering;
2. Salesman disclosure form;
3. Consent to service of process;
4. Auditor's consent to use of audited financial statements;
5. Cross-reference sheet showing the location in the franchise agreement of the key items in the disclosure document.

The *Uniform Franchise Offering Circular* (UFOC) devised by a consortium of midwestern securities commissioners as a uniform method of complying with state franchise investment laws, fulfills the disclosure requirements of the Washington statute. There are minor variations and differences in language required by the Washington statute, including a different cover page.

The disclosure document or UFOC must be furnished to a prospective franchisee at least ten business days before a franchise sale is made.

For information about state franchise laws, regulations, and filing requirements, or to report possible violations, contact: Registration Attorney, Securities Division, Business and Professional Administration, P. O. Box 648, Olympia, WA 98504. Telephone: (206) 753-6928.

See Uniform Franchise Offering Circular.

Wash on Wheels, Inc. Headquartered in Sanford, Florida, a franchisor of exterior maintenance services.

Founded in 1964, WOW has been franchising since 1987. A typical WOW franchisee operates a commercial exterior cleaning and restoration service. The chain consists of 120 outlets, all of which are franchise units.

WOW, Inc., 5401 S. Bryant Ave., Sanford, FL 32771. Telephone: (800) 345-1969

Weed Man, The Headquartered in Mississauga, Ontario, a franchisor of lawn care services.

Founded in 1970, TWM has been franchising since 1975. A typical TWM franchisee operates an exterior maintenance service devoted to lawn planning, installation, and chemical-based weed control. Of the franchisor's 100 outlets currently operating, all except one are franchise units.

The Weed Man, 2399 Royal Windsor Dr., Mississauga, Ont., Canada L5J 3G4. Telephone: (416) 823-8550

Wendy's International, Inc. Headquartered in Dublin, Ohio, a franchisor of fast-food outlets.

Founded in 1969 by R. David Thomas, Wendy's has been franchising since 1971. Unlike its predecessors in the hamburger trade, the Wendy's chain eschewed assembly-line-style food preparation systems and concentrated on hamburgers prepared to order. The company also boosted the size of it beef patties and initiated a self-service salad bar for sit-down patrons. With aggressive television, radio, and newspaper advertising, Wendy's leaped to national prominence, prompting an era of fierce competition which Fortune magazine dubbed the "Burger Wars." In 1984, a successful ad campaign featuring an elderly spinster crying "Where's the beef?" seized the public imagination.

A typical Wendy's franchisee operates a limited-menu fast-food restaurant specializing in the franchisor's distinctive "char-broiled" hamburgers, other specialty sandwiches, salads, and in some outlets, cafeteria-style Italian and Mexican buffets. Of the franchisor's 3,650 outlets currently operating, about 2,500 are franchise units.

Wendy's International, Inc., 4288 Dublin Granville Rd., Dublin, OH 43017. Telephone: (614) 764-3100

Wesray Corporation An investment company run by former U.S. Treasury Secretary William E. Simon and which owns a diversity of independently managed companies.

Wesray has bought 14 companies since 1981, including two major franchise organizations. In April, 1986, Wesray acquired the Avis Rent A Car system for $250 million. In June, 1985, the company purchased Western Auto from Beneficial Corporation, parent to the Beneficial retail finance chain.

See Avis, Western Auto.

West Coast Video Headquartered in Philadelphia, Pennsylvania, a franchisor of videocassette rental outlets.

Founded in 1983, West Coast has been franchising since 1985. A typical West Coast franchisee operates a rental business devoted to videocassette movies, VCRs, and video accessories. Of the chain's 220 outlets currently in business, all except 60 are franchise units.

West Coast Video, 990 Global Rd., Philadelphia, PA 19115.

West Virginia, Franchise Regulations The West Virginia legislature has not yet enacted any generally applicable franchise investment law. However, automobile dealers operating under franchise agreements are protected by the Motor Vehicle Manufacturers and Dealers law. In addition, the rights of beer retailers and service station owners are also protected by separate laws.

West Virginia law does not require franchisors to register or file disclosures with any state regulatory body. In the absence of such a requirement, the federal Franchise Rule applies, requiring franchisors to furnish a disclosure document prescribed by the Federal Trade Commission to prospective franchisees ten business days before a franchise sale is made.

See Franchise Rule.

Western Auto Headquartered in Kansas City, Missouri, a franchisor of retail automotive parts and hard goods.

Founded in 1909, Western Auto has been franchising since 1935. A typical Western Auto franchisee operates a retail business, merchandising auto parts, tools, and selected hardware and household goods. Of the franchisor's 1,800 outlets currently operating, approximately 1,500 are franchise units.

Western Auto, 2107 Grand Ave., Kansas City, MO 64108. Telephone: (816) 346-4212

Western Medical Services Headquartered in Walnut Creek, California, a franchisor of personnel placement agencies.

Founded in 1948, Western has been franchising since 1984. A typical Western franchisee operates an employment agency devoted to health-care specialists. Of the 66 outlets currently operating, roughly a third are franchise units.

Western Medical Services, 301 Lennon Lane, Walnut Creek, CA 95498. Telephone: (800) WMS-STAT

Western Sizzlin Headquartered in Augusta, Georgia, a franchisor of family-style restaurants.

Founded in 1962, Western Sizzlin has been franchising since 1966. A typical Western Sizzlin franchisee operates a full-service restaurant with a steakhouse motif. Of the franchisor's 580 outlets currently operating, all except three are franchise units.

Western Sizzlin, 1537 Walton Way, Augusta, GA 30904. Telephone: (404) 722-7748

Whataburger, Inc. Headquartered in Corpus Christi, Texas, a franchisor of fast-food outlets.

Founded in 1950, Whataburger has been franchising since 1953. A typical Whataburger franchisee operates a fast-food restaurant specializing in grilled hamburgers, specialty sandwiches, and breakfast service. Each outlet features both drive-up and sit-down facilities. Of the franchisor's 405 outlets currently operating, 144 are franchise units.

Whataburger, Inc., 4600 Parkdale Dr., Corpus Christi, TX 78411. Telephone: (512) 851-0650

White Hen Pantry Headquartered in Elmhurst, Illinois, a franchisor of retail convenience stores.

Founded in 1965, White Hen has been franchising since its inception. A typical White Hen franchisee operates a convenience food store maintaining a limited inventory of selected grocery items and

household goods. Of the franchisor's 350 outlets currently operating, all except ten are franchise units.
White Hen Pantry, 660 Industrial Dr., Elmhurst, IL 60126. Telephone: (312) 833-3100

Wicks 'N' Sticks Headquartered in Houston, Texas, a franchisor of specialty retail outlets.
Founded in 1968, WNS has been franchising since its inception. A typical WNS franchisee operates a retail store specializing in perfumed candles, incense, and related home decorating products. Of the franchisor's 312 outlets currently operating, all except 19 are franchise units.
Wicks 'N' Sticks, P.O. Box 4586, Houston, TX 77210. Telephone: (800) 231-6337

Wienerschnitzel Headquartered in Newport Beach, California, a franchisor of fast-food outlets.
Founded in 1961, Wienerschnitzel has been franchising since 1965. Over the last two decades, the chain's red-caped puppy logo has flown over more than 275 outlets, most of them in the west. A typical Wienerschnitzel franchisee operates a fast-food restaurant devoted to hot dog sandwiches, with drive-through facilities as well as enclosed or patio seating for up to 20 patrons. The menu features a selection of hot dogs, including Polish sausage sandwiches, served with chili or cheese toppings; traditional hamburgers; and chicken. Of the franchisor's 276 outlets currently operating, 201 are franchise units.
Wienerschnitzel, 4440 Von Karman, Newport Beach, CA 92660. Telephone: (714) 752-5800

Wild Birds Unlimited Headquartered in Indianapolis, Indiana, a franchisor of specialty retail outlets.
Founded in 1981, Wild Birds has been franchising since 1983. A typical Wild Birds franchisee operates a retail store devoted to bird-feeding products and supplies, nature books, and related specialty items. All of the franchisor's 27 outlets currently operating are franchise units.
Wild Birds Unlimited, 1430 Broad Ripple Ave., Indianapolis, IN 46220. Telephone: (317) 251-5904

Wilson, Kemmons American hotelier and pioneering franchisor of lodging establishments. A high school dropout and former popcorn vendor, Kemmons is the founder of Holiday Inns, the first and most prolific franchised lodging organization in the world.
Wilson grew up during the Great Depression, forced to leave high school when his widowed mother lost her job. He acquired a popcorn vending machine on installments and rented space in the lobby of the local *Bijou*. When he sold the concession to the theater a year later, he reinvested his profits in a variety of vending machines, eventually acquiring a house, a jukebox distributorship, and several theaters of his own.
After serving in the Air Transport Command during World War II, Wilson failed with a soft drink franchise, before finally succeeding in the construction trade. In 1951, driving with his family on vacation from Tennessee to Washington, DC, he was disgruntled at his inability to find even a single motor inn with sanitary, comfortable accommodations suitable for a vacationing family. Soon afterwards, Wilson opened his own hotel just outside Memphis. Catering to vacationing families, Wilson called his new establishment the Holiday Inn, after the 1942 motion picture starring Bing Crosby.
In sharp contrast to other motor inns of the early 1950s, the Holiday Inn included a ample parking, televisions, phones, a swimming pool for guests, and soft drink dispensers. Over the next two years, Wilson built three more hotels and with an entrepreneur named Wallace Johnson, began franchising Holiday Inns nationwide.
By 1959, the chain boasted a hundred hotels, most owned by doctors, lawyers, and other financially

capable investors. The 1,000th Holiday Inn broke ground in 1969. After a period of economic instability and wavering vacation travel in the 1970s, the company set out to capture a share of the lucrative business travel market, emphasizing a more upscale image to attract executives.

Wilson retired as chief executive of the franchise chain in 1979, after suffering a mild heart attack. Today, Holiday Inns remains the world's largest lodging organization and one of the most recognizable franchise trademarks. The company estimates that 90 percent of the nation's travelers have spent at least one night in a Holiday Inn.

See Holiday Inn.

Winchell's Donut House Headquartered in La Mirada, California, a franchisor of fast-food outlets.

Founded in 1948, Winchell's has been franchising since 1985. A typical Winchell's franchisee operates a fast-food restaurant and bakery goods shop specializing in doughnuts and coffee service, utilizing the franchisor's standardized equipment and specifications. Only ten percent of the 680 Winchell's outlets currently operating are franchise units.

Winchell's Donut Houses, 16424 Valley View Ave., La Mirada, CA 90637. Telephone: (714) 670-5300

Window Man, The Headquartered in Durham, North Carolina, a franchisor of specialty home improvement outlets.

Founded in 1983, Window Man has been franchising since its inception. A typical Window Man franchisee operates a sales business devoted to the franchisor's proprietary line of vinyl windows and space enclosures. All 30 of the Window Man outlets currently operating are franchise units.

The Window Man, 711 Rigsbee Ave., Durham, NC 27701. Telephone: (800) 672-5736

Window Works International Headquartered in Pompano Beach, Florida, a franchisor of specialty home decoration outlets.

Founded in 1978, Window Works has been franchising since its inception. A typical Window Works franchisee operates a retail store devoted to custom window treatments and related decorative products. The chain consists of 90 outlets, all of which are franchise units.

Window Works International, 2101 NW 33rd St., Pompano Beach, FL 33069. Telephone: (305) 977-4800

Wisconsin, Franchise Regulations Franchisors operating in the state of Wisconsin are governed by the Franchise Investment law, which requires registration and disclosure of pertinent information about the franchisor, franchise business, and franchise agreement. The rights of automobile dealers are protected under a separate law.

Before offering or selling a franchise in the state, a franchisor must first prepare a disclosure document prescribed by the statute, then file the information, along with the franchise agreement, financial statements, and related documents, with the Securities Commissioner. The registration must be approved before the franchisor may proceed to offer or sell franchises.

In addition to a disclosure document, franchisors are also required to submit the following items:

1. Application for registration of the franchise offering;
2. Salesman disclosure form;

3. Consent to service of process;

4. Auditor's consent to use of audited financial statements;

5. Cross-reference sheet showing the location in the franchise agreement of the key items in the disclosure document.

The disclosure document devised by a consortium of midwestern securities commissioners as a uniform method of complying with state franchise investment laws, the *Uniform Franchise Offering Circular*, or UFOC, fulfills the disclosure requirements of the Wisconsin law. There are minor variations and differences in language required by the Wisconsin statute, including a different cover page.

The disclosure document or UFOC must be furnished to a prospective franchisee at least ten business days before a franchise sale is made.

For information about state franchise laws, regulations, and filing requirements, or to report possible violations, contact: Securities Commission, P. O. Box 1768, Madison, WI 53701. Telephone: (608) 266-3414.

See Uniform Franchise Offering Circular.

World Bazaar Headquartered in East Point, Georgia, a franchisor of specialty retail outlets.

Founded in 1965, World Bazaar has been franchising since 1968. A typical World Bazaar franchisee operates a retail store devoted to imported goods, household furnishings, home decoration supplies, and gift items. About half of the 300 World Bazaar outlets in North America are franchise units.

World Bazaar, 2110 Lawrence St., East Point, GA 30344. Telephone: (404) 766-5300

Worldwide Refinishing Systems Headquartered in Round Rock, Texas, a franchisor of specialty interior remodeling services.

Founded in 1971, Wordlwide has been franchising since its inception. A typical Wordlwide franchisee operates a remodeling business devoted to refurbishing bathroom and kitchen fixtures and surfaces. Of the franchisor's 48 outlets currently operating, all except one are franchise units.

Worldwide Refinishing Systems, 2001 N. Mays Rd., Round Rock, TX 78680. Telephone: (817) 756-2282

Wyoming, Franchise Regulations The Wyoming legislature has not adopted any generally applicable franchise investment law. However, the rights of automobile retailers are protected by the Motor Vehicle Franchise Act.

Wyoming law does not require franchisors to register or file disclosures with any state regulatory body. In the absence of such a requirement, the federal Franchise Rule applies, requiring franchisors to furnish a disclosure document prescribed by the Federal Trade Commission to prospective franchisees ten business days before a franchise sale is made.

See Franchise Rule.

Yniguez, Anthony Real estate operator and franchisor. Founder of Red Carpet Realty, Yniguez was the first and, arguably, the most successful franchisor of independent real estate sales offices.

A successful real estate salesman, Yniguez retired from business in 1962 at the age of 39. However, his enthusiasm for the real estate trade did not retire and, four years later, Yniguez put together a network of six realtors in Contra Costa county, across the bay from San Francisco. His idea was to link independent realtors together in a local council to share referrals and fund cooperative advertising. He called the organization Red Carpet Realty.

Yniguez sold the first Red Carpet franchise for $500. Some of the early sales offices have since been resold at a profit of nearly 10,000 percent. Today, the realty chain boasts more than 1,300 outlets, accounting for an estimated 1.5 percent of all home sales in America. The organization was acquired in 1983 by the Guild Mortgage Company, based in San Diego.

Yogi Bear Jellystone Camp-Resorts Headquartered in Bushkill, Pennsylvania, a franchisor of outdoor camping resorts.

Founded in 1968, Yogi Bear has been franchising since its inception, under the original name, Yogi Bear Jellystone Park. A typical Yogi Bear franchisee operates a recreational campground catering to vacationing families. The outlet's motif incorporates site designs, signage, and playground equipment bearing the resemblance of Yogi Bear cartoon characters. The franchise chain consists of 105 outlets, none of which are company-owned.

Yogi Bear Jellystone Camp-Resorts, Route 209, Bushkill, PA 18324. Telephone: (717) 588-6661

Zack's Famous Frozen Yogurt, Inc. Headquartered in Metairie, Louisiana, a franchisor of specialty fast-food outlets.

Founded in 1977, Zack's has been franchising since the following year. A typical Zack's franchisee operates a fast-food business specializing in items prepared with the franchisor's proprietary line of frozen yoghurt products. Each outlet offers a broad selection of frozen-dessert items designed to mimick popular ice-cream orders, including cones, shakes, and sundaes. Of the franchisor's 210 outlets currently operating, 184 are franchise units.

Zack's Famous Frozen Yogurt, Inc., P.O. Box 8522, Metairie, LA 70011. Telephone: (504) 836-7080

Ziebart Car Improvement Specialists Headquartered in Troy, Michigan, a franchisor of automobile rustproofing outlets.

Founded in 1954, Ziebart has been franchising since 1963. A typical Ziebart franchisee operates a car finishing, detailing, and rustproofing service based on a standardized product line and marketing system. Of the franchisor's 575 outlets currently operating, all except 22 are franchise units.

Ziebart Corp., 1290 E. Maple Rd., Troy, MI 48007. Telephone: (313) 588-4100

Zippy Print Headquartered in Vancouver, British Columbia, a franchisor of document duplication outlets.

Founded in 1979, Zippy Print has been franchising since 1981. A typical Zippy Print franchisee operates a retail copying center offering on-premises quick-print service and document copying. Of the franchisor's 80 outlets currently operating, 67 are franchise units.

Zippy Print Franchise Canada, Ltd., 308-260 W. Esplanade, North Vancouver, B.C., Canada V7M 3G7

Appendix A
Investment Data

A&W Restaurants

Year company founded: 1919
Franchise fee or other initial payment: $15,000
Franchise royalty or other ongoing payment: 4 percent of sales
Advertising royalty or fee: 4 percent of sales
Estimated initial investment required: $150,000
Total outlets: 525

AAA Employment

Year company founded: 1957
Franchise fee or other initial payment: $10,000
Franchise royalty or other ongoing payment: 10 percent of sales
Advertising royalty or fee: None
Estimated initial investment required: $4,000
Total outlets: 130

AAMCO Transmission

Year company founded: 1963
Franchise fee or other initial payment: $25,000
Franchise royalty or other ongoing payment: 9 percent of sales
Advertising royalty or fee: May vary
Estimated initial investment required: $80,000
Total outlets: 920

ABC Seamless

Year company founded: 1973
Franchise fee or other initial payment: $12,000
Franchise royalty or other ongoing payment: May vary
Advertising royalty or fee: .5 percent of sales
Estimated initial investment required: $40,000
Total outlets: 280

ACA Joe

Year company founded: 1983
Franchise fee or other initial payment: $30,000
Franchise royalty or other ongoing payment: None
Advertising royalty or fee: 3 percent of sales
Estimated initial investment required: $200,000
Total outlets: 170

Acc-U-Tune

Year company founded: 1975
Franchise fee or other initial payment: $18,000
Franchise royalty or other ongoing payment: 7 percent of sales
Advertising royalty or fee: 7 percent of sales
Estimated initial investment required: $68,000
Total outlets: 18

Adia Personnel

Year company founded: 1957
Franchise fee or other initial payment: $17,500
Franchise royalty or other ongoing payment: 35 percent of sales
Advertising royalty or fee: None
Estimated initial investment required: $52,500
Total outlets: 460

Advantage Payroll

Year company founded: 1967
Franchise fee or other initial payment: $10,000
Franchise royalty or other ongoing payment: None
Advertising royalty or fee: None
Estimated initial investment required: $5,000
Total outlets: 17

Adventureland

Year company founded: 1981
Franchise fee or other initial payment: $15,500
Franchise royalty or other ongoing payment: 4.5 percent of sales
Advertising royalty or fee: 3 percent of sales
Estimated initial investment required: $70,000
Total outlets: 800

Aerowest

Year company founded: 1943
Franchise fee or other initial payment: $1,000
Franchise royalty or other ongoing payment: 50 percent of sales
Advertising royalty or fee: None
Estimated initial investment required: $3,000
Total outlets: 25

Affordable Used Car

Year company founded: 1981
Franchise fee or other initial payment: $3,500
Franchise royalty or other ongoing payment: Mayvary
Advertising royalty or fee: None
Estimated initial investment required: $30,000
Total outlets: 140

Affordable

Year company founded: 1981
Franchise fee or other initial payment: $3,500
Franchise royalty or other ongoing payment: Mayvary
Advertising royalty or fee: None
Estimated initial investment required: $30,000
Total outlets: 140

Aid Auto

Year company founded: 1951
Franchise fee or other initial payment: $15,000
Franchise royalty or other ongoing payment: $400per month
Advertising royalty or fee: $600 per month
Estimated initial investment required: $135,000
Total outlets: 86

Air Brook Limousine

Year company founded: 1969
Franchise fee or other initial payment: $7,000
Franchise royalty or other ongoing payment: 40 percent of sales
Advertising royalty or fee: None
Estimated initial investment required: $2,100
Total outlets: 120

Ajax Rent a Car

Year company founded: 1969
Franchise fee or other initial payment: $15,000
Franchise royalty or other ongoing payment: 7 percent of sales
Advertising royalty or fee: None
Estimated initial investment required: $50,000
Total outlets: 190

All American Hero

Year company founded: 1981
Franchise fee or other initial payment: $20,000
Franchise royalty or other ongoing payment: 6 percent of sales
Advertising royalty or fee: 3 percent of sales
Estimated initial investment required: $60,000
Total outlets: 50

All My Muffins

Year company founded: 1984
Franchise fee or other initial payment: $20,000
Franchise royalty or other ongoing payment: 6 percent of sales
Advertising royalty or fee: 2 percent of sales
Estimated initial investment required: $85,000
Total outlets: 5

Allison's Place

Year company founded: 1980
Franchise fee or other initial payment: $99,500
Franchise royalty or other ongoing payment: 3.5 percent of sales
Advertising royalty or fee: 2 percent of sales
Estimated initial investment required: $99,500
Total outlets: 230

Almost Heaven Hot Tubs

Year company founded: 1971
Franchise fee or other initial payment: None
Franchise royalty or other ongoing payment: None
Advertising royalty or fee: None
Estimated initial investment required: $10,000
Total outlets: 975

Aloette Cosmetics

Year company founded: 1978
Franchise fee or other initial payment: $60,000
Franchise royalty or other ongoing payment: 5 percent of sales
Advertising royalty or fee: None
Estimated initial investment required: $15,000
Total outlets: 108

Alphagraphics

Year company founded: 1970
Franchise fee or other initial payment: $47,000
Franchise royalty or other ongoing payment: 3 percent of sales
Advertising royalty or fee: 1 percent of sales
Estimated initial investment required: $200,000
Total outlets: 230

am/pm Mini-Markets

Year company founded: 1980
Franchise fee or other initial payment: $30,000
Franchise royalty or other ongoing payment: 4 percent of sales
Advertising royalty or fee: 2 percent of sales
Estimated initial investment required: $450,000
Total outlets: 550

American Advertising Distributors

Year company founded: 1976
Franchise fee or other initial payment: $19,500
Franchise royalty or other ongoing payment: Mayvary
Advertising royalty or fee: None
Estimated initial investment required: $10,000
Total outlets: 115

American International Rent-A-Car

Year company founded: 1969
Franchise fee or other initial payment: $25,000
Franchise royalty or other ongoing payment: 8 percent of sales
Advertising royalty or fee: None
Estimated initial investment required: $30,000
Total outlets: 1500

American Leak Detection

Year company founded: 1974
Franchise fee or other initial payment: $40,000
Franchise royalty or other ongoing payment: 8 percent of sales
Advertising royalty or fee: None
Estimated initial investment required: $10,000
Total outlets: 95

American Speedy Printing

Year company founded: 1976
Franchise fee or other initial payment: $39,500
Franchise royalty or other ongoing payment: 4 percent of sales
Advertising royalty or fee: 2 percent of sales
Estimated initial investment required: $87,400
Total outlets: 508

American Wholesale Therm

Year company founded: 1980
Franchise fee or other initial payment: $38,500
Franchise royalty or other ongoing payment: 5 percent of sales
Advertising royalty or fee: None
Estimated initial investment required: $145,000
Total outlets: 20

Americlean

Year company founded: 1985
Franchise fee or other initial payment: $15,000
Franchise royalty or other ongoing payment: 4 percent of sales
Advertising royalty or fee: 2 percent of sales
Estimated initial investment required: $15,000
Total outlets: 90

Annie's Book Stop

Year company founded: 1974
Franchise fee or other initial payment: $17,500
Franchise royalty or other ongoing payment: 3.5 percent of sales
Advertising royalty or fee: 1 percent of sales
Estimated initial investment required: $18,000
Total outlets: 100

Applause Video

Year company founded: 1983
Franchise fee or other initial payment: $15,000
Franchise royalty or other ongoing payment: 5 percent of sales
Advertising royalty or fee: 1 percent of sales
Estimated initial investment required: $150,000
Total outlets: 48

Arby's

Year company founded: 1964
Franchise fee or other initial payment: $25,000
Franchise royalty or other ongoing payment: 3.5 percent of sales
Advertising royalty or fee: .07 percent of sales
Estimated initial investment required: $115,000
Total outlets: 2000

Armstrong World Ind.

Year company founded: 1867
Franchise fee or other initial payment: $8,000
Franchise royalty or other ongoing payment: None
Advertising royalty or fee: None
Estimated initial investment required: May vary
Total outlets: 275

Arthur Murray

Year company founded: 1912
Franchise fee or other initial payment: None
Franchise royalty or other ongoing payment: 5 percent of sales
Advertising royalty or fee: 2 percent of sales
Estimated initial investment required: $25,000
Total outlets: 225

ASI Sign Systems

Year company founded: 1977
Franchise fee or other initial payment: $50,000
Franchise royalty or other ongoing payment: 5 percent of sales
Advertising royalty or fee: 1 percent of sales
Estimated initial investment required: $100,000
Total outlets: 34

Athlete's Foot, The

Year company founded: 1972
Franchise fee or other initial payment: $15,000
Franchise royalty or other ongoing payment: 3 percent of sales
Advertising royalty or fee: .5 percent of sales
Estimated initial investment required: $117,000
Total outlets: 500

Athletic Attic

Year company founded: 1973
Franchise fee or other initial payment: $7,500
Franchise royalty or other ongoing payment: 3 percent of sales
Advertising royalty or fee: None
Estimated initial investment required: $150,000
Total outlets: 175

Athletic Training Equipment

Year company founded: 1971
Franchise fee or other initial payment: $6,000
Franchise royalty or other ongoing payment: 6 percent of sales
Advertising royalty or fee: None
Estimated initial investment required: $150,000
Total outlets: 55

Atlantic Personnel

Year company founded: 1983
Franchise fee or other initial payment: $8,500
Franchise royalty or other ongoing payment: 7 percent of sales
Advertising royalty or fee: None
Estimated initial investment required: $3,500
Total outlets: 36

AutoSpa

Year company founded: 1980
Franchise fee or other initial payment: $25,000
Franchise royalty or other ongoing payment: 7 percent of sales
Advertising royalty or fee: 4 percent of sales
Estimated initial investment required: $55,000
Total outlets: 50

Bailey Employment

Year company founded: 1960
Franchise fee or other initial payment: $40,000
Franchise royalty or other ongoing payment: 8 percent of sales
Advertising royalty or fee: None
Estimated initial investment required: $15,000
Total outlets: 20

Barter Exchange

Year company founded: 1983
Franchise fee or other initial payment: $30,000
Franchise royalty or other ongoing payment: None
Advertising royalty or fee: None
Estimated initial investment required: $50,000
Total outlets: 18

Baskin-Robbins/Silicorp

Year company founded: 1945
Franchise fee or other initial payment: $25,000
Franchise royalty or other ongoing payment: .055 percent of sales
Advertising royalty or fee: 4 percent of sales
Estimated initial investment required: $135,000
Total outlets: 200

Baskin-Robbins

Year company founded: 1945
Franchise fee or other initial payment: None
Franchise royalty or other ongoing payment: .5 percent of sales
Advertising royalty or fee: 1.5 percent of sales
Estimated initial investment required: $130,000
Total outlets: 3450

Bath Genie

Year company founded: 1976
Franchise fee or other initial payment: None
Franchise royalty or other ongoing payment: None
Advertising royalty or fee: None
Estimated initial investment required: $19,500
Total outlets: 32

Bathcrest

Year company founded: 1979
Franchise fee or other initial payment: $3,500
Franchise royalty or other ongoing payment: None
Advertising royalty or fee: None
Estimated initial investment required: $27,600
Total outlets: 135

Bathtique

Year company founded: 1969
Franchise fee or other initial payment: $25,000
Franchise royalty or other ongoing payment: 5 percent of sales
Advertising royalty or fee: None
Estimated initial investment required: $40,000
Total outlets: 80

Becker Milk Co.

Year company founded: 1957
Franchise fee or other initial payment: $25,000
Franchise royalty or other ongoing payment: 5 percent of sales
Advertising royalty or fee: None
Estimated initial investment required: $100,000
Total outlets: 784

Beefsteak Charlie's

Year company founded: 1972
Franchise fee or other initial payment: $25,000
Franchise royalty or other ongoing payment: 5 percent of sales
Advertising royalty or fee: 3 percent of sales
Estimated initial investment required: $50,000
Total outlets: 48

Bellini Juvenile

Year company founded: 1975
Franchise fee or other initial payment: $25,000
Franchise royalty or other ongoing payment: 50 percent of sales
Advertising royalty or fee: None
Estimated initial investment required: $90,000
Total outlets: 40

Ben & Jerry's

Year company founded: 1978
Franchise fee or other initial payment: $21,000
Franchise royalty or other ongoing payment: None
Advertising royalty or fee: 4 percent of sales
Estimated initial investment required: $120,000
Total outlets: 70

Ben Franklin Stores

Year company founded: 1877
Franchise fee or other initial payment: $245,000
Franchise royalty or other ongoing payment: None
Advertising royalty or fee: None
Estimated initial investment required: $310,000
Total outlets: 1100

Benihana of Tokyo

Year company founded: 1964
Franchise fee or other initial payment: $50,000
Franchise royalty or other ongoing payment: 5 percent of sales
Advertising royalty or fee: .5 percent of sales
Estimated initial investment required: $375,000
Total outlets: 50

Best Inns

Year company founded: 1970
Franchise fee or other initial payment: $10,000
Franchise royalty or other ongoing payment: 2 percent of sales
Advertising royalty or fee: 1 percent of sales
Estimated initial investment required: $75,000
Total outlets: 25

Better Homes Realty

Year company founded: 1964
Franchise fee or other initial payment: $7,950
Franchise royalty or other ongoing payment: 6 percent of sales
Advertising royalty or fee: None
Estimated initial investment required: $10,000
Total outlets: 100

Big O Tires

Year company founded: 1962
Franchise fee or other initial payment: $10,000
Franchise royalty or other ongoing payment: 2 percent of sales
Advertising royalty or fee: 4 percent of sales
Estimated initial investment required: $75,000
Total outlets: 300

Bighorn Sheepskin Co.

Year company founded: 1984
Franchise fee or other initial payment: None
Franchise royalty or other ongoing payment: None
Advertising royalty or fee: None
Estimated initial investment required: $6,000
Total outlets: 60

Binex

Year company founded: 1965
Franchise fee or other initial payment: $11,500
Franchise royalty or other ongoing payment: None
Advertising royalty or fee: None
Estimated initial investment required: $8,000
Total outlets: 60

Blue Chip Cookies

Year company founded: 1983
Franchise fee or other initial payment: $33,000
Franchise royalty or other ongoing payment: 6 percent of sales
Advertising royalty or fee: 3 percent of sales
Estimated initial investment required: $85,000
Total outlets: 47

Boardwalk Fries

Year company founded: 1981
Franchise fee or other initial payment: $25,000
Franchise royalty or other ongoing payment: 7 percent of sales
Advertising royalty or fee: 2 percent of sales
Estimated initial investment required: $105,000
Total outlets: 65

Bob's Big Boy

Year company founded: 1936
Franchise fee or other initial payment: $25,000
Franchise royalty or other ongoing payment: 3 percent of sales
Advertising royalty or fee: 4 percent of sales
Estimated initial investment required: $100,000
Total outlets: 780

Bojangles

Year company founded: 1976
Franchise fee or other initial payment: $25,000
Franchise royalty or other ongoing payment: 4 percent of sales
Advertising royalty or fee: 1 percent of sales
Estimated initial investment required: $200,000
Total outlets: 380

Bonanza

Year company founded: 1963
Franchise fee or other initial payment: $30,000
Franchise royalty or other ongoing payment: 4.8 percent of sales
Advertising royalty or fee: 3 percent of sales
Estimated initial investment required: $125,000
Total outlets: 610

Boston Pizza

Year company founded: 1963
Franchise fee or other initial payment: $30,000
Franchise royalty or other ongoing payment: 7 percent of sales
Advertising royalty or fee: 2.5 percent of sales
Estimated initial investment required: $500,000
Total outlets: 76

Breadeaux Pisa

Year company founded: 1985
Franchise fee or other initial payment: $15,000
Franchise royalty or other ongoing payment: 5 percent of sales
Advertising royalty or fee: 2 percent of sales
Estimated initial investment required: $35,000
Total outlets: 85

Bresler's

Year company founded: 1930
Franchise fee or other initial payment: $10,000
Franchise royalty or other ongoing payment: 6 percent of sales
Advertising royalty or fee: 3 percent of sales
Estimated initial investment required: $35,000
Total outlets: 300

Brigham's

Year company founded: 1914
Franchise fee or other initial payment: $31,500
Franchise royalty or other ongoing payment: 5 percent of sales
Advertising royalty or fee: 1 percent of sales
Estimated initial investment required: $136,200
Total outlets: 70

Bryant Bureau

Year company founded: 1951
Franchise fee or other initial payment: $10,000
Franchise royalty or other ongoing payment: 5 percent of sales
Advertising royalty or fee: 1 percent of sales
Estimated initial investment required: $30,000
Total outlets: 30

Budget Rent a Car

Year company founded: 1960
Franchise fee or other initial payment: $15,000
Franchise royalty or other ongoing payment: 5 percent of sales
Advertising royalty or fee: 2.5 percent of sales
Estimated initial investment required: $150,000
Total outlets: 3600

Budgetel

Year company founded: 1973
Franchise fee or other initial payment: $20,000
Franchise royalty or other ongoing payment: 5 percent of sales
Advertising royalty or fee: 1 percent of sales
Estimated initial investment required: $250,000
Total outlets: 63

Building Inspector, The

Year company founded: 1985
Franchise fee or other initial payment: $15,000
Franchise royalty or other ongoing payment: 6 percent of sales
Advertising royalty or fee: 3 percent of sales
Estimated initial investment required: $4,000
Total outlets: 41

California Smoothie

Year company founded: 1973
Franchise fee or other initial payment: $25,000
Franchise royalty or other ongoing payment: 5 percent of sales
Advertising royalty or fee: 2 percent of sales
Estimated initial investment required: $125,000
Total outlets: 38

California Closet Co.

Year company founded: 1979
Franchise fee or other initial payment: $25,000
Franchise royalty or other ongoing payment: 5 percent of sales
Advertising royalty or fee: None
Estimated initial investment required: $100,000
Total outlets: 87

Camera America

Year company founded: 1974
Franchise fee or other initial payment: $18,000
Franchise royalty or other ongoing payment: 3.5 percent of sales
Advertising royalty or fee: 2 percent of sales
Estimated initial investment required: $117,000
Total outlets: 95

Canterbury New Zealand

Year company founded: 1904
Franchise fee or other initial payment: $18,000
Franchise royalty or other ongoing payment: 2 percent of sales
Advertising royalty or fee: 2 percent of sales
Estimated initial investment required: $150,000
Total outlets: 70

Caps Nursing Service

Year company founded: 1976
Franchise fee or other initial payment: $25,000
Franchise royalty or other ongoing payment: 6 percent of sales
Advertising royalty or fee: None
Estimated initial investment required: $10,000
Total outlets: 11

Captain D's

Year company founded: 1969
Franchise fee or other initial payment: $10,000
Franchise royalty or other ongoing payment: 3 percent of sales
Advertising royalty or fee: 6 percent of sales
Estimated initial investment required: $50,000
Total outlets: 590

Car-X Muffler

Year company founded: 1971
Franchise fee or other initial payment: $18,500
Franchise royalty or other ongoing payment: 5 percent of sales
Advertising royalty or fee: 5 percent of sales
Estimated initial investment required: $135,000
Total outlets: 120

Carbone's Pizzeria

Year company founded: 1953
Franchise fee or other initial payment: $10,000
Franchise royalty or other ongoing payment: 3 percent of sales
Advertising royalty or fee: 1 percent of sales
Estimated initial investment required: $65,000
Total outlets: 32

Career Blazers

Year company founded: 1949
Franchise fee or other initial payment: $15,000
Franchise royalty or other ongoing payment: Mayvary
Advertising royalty or fee: May vary
Estimated initial investment required: $79,900
Total outlets: 5

Carl's Jr.

Year company founded: 1941
Franchise fee or other initial payment: $35,000
Franchise royalty or other ongoing payment: 4 percent of sales
Advertising royalty or fee: 4 percent of sales
Estimated initial investment required: $180,000
Total outlets: 460

Carline Muffler

Year company founded: 1981
Franchise fee or other initial payment: None
Franchise royalty or other ongoing payment: None
Advertising royalty or fee: None
Estimated initial investment required: $60,000
Total outlets: 90

Carpet Town

Year company founded: 1954
Franchise fee or other initial payment: May vary
Franchise royalty or other ongoing payment: None
Advertising royalty or fee: May vary
Estimated initial investment required: $75,000
Total outlets: 26

Carpeteria

Year company founded: 1960
Franchise fee or other initial payment: $50,000
Franchise royalty or other ongoing payment: 4 percent of sales
Advertising royalty or fee: .25 percent of sales
Estimated initial investment required: $100,000
Total outlets: 70

Carvel

Year company founded: 1934
Franchise fee or other initial payment: $25,000
Franchise royalty or other ongoing payment: May vary
Advertising royalty or fee: May vary
Estimated initial investment required: $65,000
Total outlets: 750

Ceiling Doctor

Year company founded: 1984
Franchise fee or other initial payment: $10,000
Franchise royalty or other ongoing payment: 6 percent of sales
Advertising royalty or fee: 2 percent of sales
Estimated initial investment required: $10,000
Total outlets: 25

Celluland

Year company founded: 1985
Franchise fee or other initial payment: $25,000
Franchise royalty or other ongoing payment: 3.5 percent of sales
Advertising royalty or fee: 1 percent of sales
Estimated initial investment required: $125,000
Total outlets: 21

Century 21

Year company founded: 1972
Franchise fee or other initial payment: $10,500
Franchise royalty or other ongoing payment: 6 percent of sales
Advertising royalty or fee: 2 percent of sales
Estimated initial investment required: $15,000
Total outlets: 7000

Chad's Rainbow

Year company founded: 1981
Franchise fee or other initial payment: $35,000
Franchise royalty or other ongoing payment: 5 percent of sales
Advertising royalty or fee: 2 percent of sales
Estimated initial investment required: $115,000
Total outlets: 30

Champion Auto

Year company founded: 1956
Franchise fee or other initial payment: None
Franchise royalty or other ongoing payment: None
Advertising royalty or fee: None
Estimated initial investment required: $50,000
Total outlets: 130

Check-X-Change

Year company founded: 1982
Franchise fee or other initial payment: $19,700
Franchise royalty or other ongoing payment: $815 per month
Advertising royalty or fee: May vary
Estimated initial investment required: $50,000
Total outlets: 58

Chem-Clean

Year company founded: 1967
Franchise fee or other initial payment: $18,000
Franchise royalty or other ongoing payment: None
Advertising royalty or fee: None
Estimated initial investment required: May vary
Total outlets: 62

Chem-Dry

Year company founded: 1977
Franchise fee or other initial payment: $1,350
Franchise royalty or other ongoing payment: $100per month
Advertising royalty or fee: None
Estimated initial investment required: $4,900
Total outlets: 1840

Chez Chocolat

Year company founded: 1986
Franchise fee or other initial payment: May vary
Franchise royalty or other ongoing payment: 5 percent of sales
Advertising royalty or fee: None
Estimated initial investment required: $30,000
Total outlets: 52

Chicken Delight

Year company founded: 1952
Franchise fee or other initial payment: $15,000
Franchise royalty or other ongoing payment: 5 percent of sales
Advertising royalty or fee: 2 percent of sales
Estimated initial investment required: $125,000
Total outlets: 90

Children's Orchard

Year company founded: 1980
Franchise fee or other initial payment: $13,500
Franchise royalty or other ongoing payment: 6 percent of sales
Advertising royalty or fee: 1 percent of sales
Estimated initial investment required: $18,500
Total outlets: 16

Church's Fried Chicken

Year company founded: 1953
Franchise fee or other initial payment: $15,000
Franchise royalty or other ongoing payment: 4 percent of sales
Advertising royalty or fee: 5 percent of sales
Estimated initial investment required: $300,000
Total outlets: 1500

Cindy's Cinnamon Rolls

Year company founded: 1985
Franchise fee or other initial payment: $25,000
Franchise royalty or other ongoing payment: 5 percent of sales
Advertising royalty or fee: None
Estimated initial investment required: $43,500
Total outlets: 41

Cinnamon Sam's

Year company founded: 1985
Franchise fee or other initial payment: $25,000
Franchise royalty or other ongoing payment: 5 percent of sales
Advertising royalty or fee: 2 percent of sales
Estimated initial investment required: $110,000
Total outlets: 36

Classy Maids

Year company founded: 1980
Franchise fee or other initial payment: $5,900
Franchise royalty or other ongoing payment: 6 percent of sales
Advertising royalty or fee: None
Estimated initial investment required: $3,000
Total outlets: 30

Club Nautico

Year company founded: 1981
Franchise fee or other initial payment: $15,000
Franchise royalty or other ongoing payment: 10 percent of sales
Advertising royalty or fee: 2 percent of sales
Estimated initial investment required: $75,000
Total outlets: 55

Coast to Coast Stores

Year company founded: 1928
Franchise fee or other initial payment: $5,000
Franchise royalty or other ongoing payment: $100per month
Advertising royalty or fee: May vary
Estimated initial investment required: $90,000
Total outlets: 965

Coffee Beanery

Year company founded: 1976
Franchise fee or other initial payment: $17,500
Franchise royalty or other ongoing payment: 4 percent of sales
Advertising royalty or fee: 2 percent of sales
Estimated initial investment required: $130,000
Total outlets: 20

Color-Glo

Year company founded: 1970
Franchise fee or other initial payment: May vary
Franchise royalty or other ongoing payment: 5 percent of sales
Advertising royalty or fee: $60 per montho
Estimated initial investment required: May vary
Total outlets: 240

Colt Drapery

Year company founded: 1979
Franchise fee or other initial payment: $5,000
Franchise royalty or other ongoing payment: 5 percent of sales
Advertising royalty or fee: None
Estimated initial investment required: $10,000
Total outlets: 63

Command Performance

Year company founded: 1976
Franchise fee or other initial payment: $21,500
Franchise royalty or other ongoing payment: 6 percent of sales
Advertising royalty or fee: None
Estimated initial investment required: May vary
Total outlets: 267

Communications World

Year company founded: 1979
Franchise fee or other initial payment: $10,000
Franchise royalty or other ongoing payment: 4 percent of sales
Advertising royalty or fee: 1 percent of sales
Estimated initial investment required: $5,000
Total outlets: 65

Comprehensive Accounting

Year company founded: 1949
Franchise fee or other initial payment: $30,000
Franchise royalty or other ongoing payment: May vary
Advertising royalty or fee: None
Estimated initial investment required: $10,000
Total outlets: 340

Compufund Network

Year company founded: 1983
Franchise fee or other initial payment: $1,790
Franchise royalty or other ongoing payment: $350 per month
Advertising royalty or fee: $500 per month
Estimated initial investment required: $3,500
Total outlets: 120

Computerland

Year company founded: 1976
Franchise fee or other initial payment: $15,000
Franchise royalty or other ongoing payment: 5 percent of sales
Advertising royalty or fee: 1 percent of sales
Estimated initial investment required: $150,000
Total outlets: 800

Conroy's

Year company founded: 1960
Franchise fee or other initial payment: $75,000
Franchise royalty or other ongoing payment: 7.75 percent of sales
Advertising royalty or fee: 3 percent of sales
Estimated initial investment required: May vary
Total outlets: 75

Cookie Factory

Year company founded: 1974
Franchise fee or other initial payment: $20,000
Franchise royalty or other ongoing payment: 5 percent of sales
Advertising royalty or fee: 1 percent of sales
Estimated initial investment required: $70,000
Total outlets: 46

Copy Mat

Year company founded: 1973
Franchise fee or other initial payment: $40,000
Franchise royalty or other ongoing payment: 7 percent of sales
Advertising royalty or fee: 1 percent of sales
Estimated initial investment required: $193,500
Total outlets: 50

Cost Cutters

Year company founded: 1982
Franchise fee or other initial payment: $12,500
Franchise royalty or other ongoing payment: 4 percent of sales
Advertising royalty or fee: 4 percent of sales
Estimated initial investment required: $15,500
Total outlets: 290

Cottman Transmission

Year company founded: 1962
Franchise fee or other initial payment: $22,500
Franchise royalty or other ongoing payment: 7.5 percent of sales
Advertising royalty or fee: 13 percent of sales
Estimated initial investment required: $75,000
Total outlets: 150

Coustic-Glo

Year company founded: 1970
Franchise fee or other initial payment: $9,750
Franchise royalty or other ongoing payment: 5 percent of sales
Advertising royalty or fee: 1 percent of sales
Estimated initial investment required: $3,000
Total outlets: 240

Coverall

Year company founded: 1979
Franchise fee or other initial payment: $3,250
Franchise royalty or other ongoing payment: 10 percent of sales
Advertising royalty or fee: 1 percent of sales
Estimated initial investment required: $1,500
Total outlets: 900

Crossland Furniture Restoration

Year company founded: 1944
Franchise fee or other initial payment: None
Franchise royalty or other ongoing payment: 5 percent of sales
Advertising royalty or fee: 3 percent of sales
Estimated initial investment required: $85,000
Total outlets: 110

Crusty's Pizza

Year company founded: 1957
Franchise fee or other initial payment: $15,000
Franchise royalty or other ongoing payment: 5 percent of sales
Advertising royalty or fee: 5 percent of sales
Estimated initial investment required: $35,000
Total outlets: 200

Culligan Water Conditioning

Year company founded: 1936
Franchise fee or other initial payment: None
Franchise royalty or other ongoing payment: May vary
Advertising royalty or fee: May vary
Estimated initial investment required: $68,000
Total outlets: 806

Cultures Fresh Food

Year company founded: 1977
Franchise fee or other initial payment: $30,000
Franchise royalty or other ongoing payment: 5 percent of sales
Advertising royalty or fee: 2 percent of sales
Estimated initial investment required: $225,000
Total outlets: 60

Cutlery World

Year company founded: 1966
Franchise fee or other initial payment: $20,000
Franchise royalty or other ongoing payment: 6.5 percent of sales
Advertising royalty or fee: 1 percent of sales
Estimated initial investment required: $50,000
Total outlets: 185

Dairy Queen

Year company founded: 1940
Franchise fee or other initial payment: $30,000
Franchise royalty or other ongoing payment: 4 percent of sales
Advertising royalty or fee: 3.5 percent of sales
Estimated initial investment required: $385,000
Total outlets: 5000

Dan Hanna Auto Wash

Year company founded: 1985
Franchise fee or other initial payment: $24,000
Franchise royalty or other ongoing payment: 3 percent of sales
Advertising royalty or fee: 2 percent of sales
Estimated initial investment required: $350,000
Total outlets: 50

David's Cookies

Year company founded: 1979
Franchise fee or other initial payment: $25,000
Franchise royalty or other ongoing payment: None
Advertising royalty or fee: None
Estimated initial investment required: $125,000
Total outlets: 200

Dawn Donut

Year company founded: 1956
Franchise fee or other initial payment: $15,000
Franchise royalty or other ongoing payment: 4.5 percent of sales
Advertising royalty or fee: 4.5 percent of sales
Estimated initial investment required: $111,500
Total outlets: 65

Days Inn

Year company founded: 1971
Franchise fee or other initial payment: May vary
Franchise royalty or other ongoing payment: 6.5 percent of sales
Advertising royalty or fee: None
Estimated initial investment required: $500,000
Total outlets: 700

Debit One

Year company founded: 1983
Franchise fee or other initial payment: $20,000
Franchise royalty or other ongoing payment: 8 percent of sales
Advertising royalty or fee: 1 percent of sales
Estimated initial investment required: $35,500
Total outlets: 77

Deck the Walls

Year company founded: 1979
Franchise fee or other initial payment: $35,000
Franchise royalty or other ongoing payment: 6 percent of sales
Advertising royalty or fee: 2 percent of sales
Estimated initial investment required: $145,000
Total outlets: 254

Decorating Den

Year company founded: 1970
Franchise fee or other initial payment: $6,900
Franchise royalty or other ongoing payment: 6 percent of sales
Advertising royalty or fee: 2 percent of sales
Estimated initial investment required: $5,000
Total outlets: 720

Denny's

Year company founded: 1953
Franchise fee or other initial payment: $35,000
Franchise royalty or other ongoing payment: 4 percent of sales
Advertising royalty or fee: 2 percent of sales
Estimated initial investment required: $750,000
Total outlets: 1390

Descamps

Year company founded: 1888
Franchise fee or other initial payment: None
Franchise royalty or other ongoing payment: None
Advertising royalty or fee: None
Estimated initial investment required: $100,000
Total outlets: 195

Dial-a-Gift

Year company founded: 1980
Franchise fee or other initial payment: $10,000
Franchise royalty or other ongoing payment: 4 percent of sales
Advertising royalty or fee: $100 per month
Estimated initial investment required: $10,000
Total outlets: 130

Dictograph

Year company founded: 1902
Franchise fee or other initial payment: $15,000
Franchise royalty or other ongoing payment: 6 percent of sales
Advertising royalty or fee: None
Estimated initial investment required: $100,000
Total outlets: 72

Diet Center Inc.

Year company founded: 1970
Franchise fee or other initial payment: $12,000
Franchise royalty or other ongoing payment: May vary
Advertising royalty or fee: None
Estimated initial investment required: $15,000
Total outlets: 2330

Dip N Strip

Year company founded: 1970
Franchise fee or other initial payment: None
Franchise royalty or other ongoing payment: 6 percent of sales
Advertising royalty or fee: None
Estimated initial investment required: $15,000
Total outlets: 280

Dipper Dan

Year company founded: 1963
Franchise fee or other initial payment: None
Franchise royalty or other ongoing payment: None
Advertising royalty or fee: None
Estimated initial investment required: $70,000
Total outlets: 250

Docktor Pet

Year company founded: 1967
Franchise fee or other initial payment: $15,000
Franchise royalty or other ongoing payment: 4.5 percent of sales
Advertising royalty or fee: None
Estimated initial investment required: $134,800
Total outlets: 270

Dollar Rent a Car

Year company founded: 1966
Franchise fee or other initial payment: $7,500
Franchise royalty or other ongoing payment: 9 percent of sales
Advertising royalty or fee: None
Estimated initial investment required: $50,000
Total outlets: 1600

Domestic Aide

Year company founded: 1976
Franchise fee or other initial payment: $7,500
Franchise royalty or other ongoing payment: 7 percent of sales
Advertising royalty or fee: 2 percent of sales
Estimated initial investment required: $12,000
Total outlets: 30

Domino's Pizza

Year company founded: 1960
Franchise fee or other initial payment: $1,300
Franchise royalty or other ongoing payment: 5.5 percent of sales
Advertising royalty or fee: 3 percent of sales
Estimated initial investment required: $75,000
Total outlets: 4600

Dr. Nick's Transmissions

Year company founded: 1971
Franchise fee or other initial payment: $21,500
Franchise royalty or other ongoing payment: 7 percent of sales
Advertising royalty or fee: $1,200
Estimated initial investment required: $25,000
Total outlets: 30

Dr. Vinyl

Year company founded: 1972
Franchise fee or other initial payment: $20,000
Franchise royalty or other ongoing payment: 4 percent of sales
Advertising royalty or fee: 1 percent of sales
Estimated initial investment required: $1,000
Total outlets: 80

Drake Personnel

Year company founded: 1951
Franchise fee or other initial payment: $15,000
Franchise royalty or other ongoing payment: 7 percent of sales
Advertising royalty or fee: None
Estimated initial investment required: $20,000
Total outlets: 235

Drug Emporium

Year company founded: 1977
Franchise fee or other initial payment: $25,000
Franchise royalty or other ongoing payment: 1 percent of sales
Advertising royalty or fee: .1 percent of sales
Estimated initial investment required: $700,000
Total outlets: 150

Dry Clean USA

Year company founded: 1961
Franchise fee or other initial payment: $25,000
Franchise royalty or other ongoing payment: 5 percent of sales
Advertising royalty or fee: 2 percent of sales
Estimated initial investment required: $220,000
Total outlets: 245

Duds N Suds

Year company founded: 1983
Franchise fee or other initial payment: $25,000
Franchise royalty or other ongoing payment: 4 percent of sales
Advertising royalty or fee: 1 percent of sales
Estimated initial investment required: $130,000
Total outlets: 80

Dunhill Personnel

Year company founded: 1952
Franchise fee or other initial payment: $15,000
Franchise royalty or other ongoing payment: 3 percent of sales
Advertising royalty or fee: 1 percent of sales
Estimated initial investment required: $50,000
Total outlets: 340

Dunkin' Donuts

Year company founded: 1950
Franchise fee or other initial payment: $30,000
Franchise royalty or other ongoing payment: 4.9 percent of sales
Advertising royalty or fee: 5 percent of sales
Estimated initial investment required: $25,000
Total outlets: 1735

Duraclean

Year company founded: 1930
Franchise fee or other initial payment: $9,500
Franchise royalty or other ongoing payment: 2 percent of sales
Advertising royalty or fee: None
Estimated initial investment required: $15,000
Total outlets: 615

Earl Keim Realty

Year company founded: 1958
Franchise fee or other initial payment: $7,000
Franchise royalty or other ongoing payment: 5 percent of sales
Advertising royalty or fee: 1 percent of sales
Estimated initial investment required: $30,000
Total outlets: 90

Econo Lodge

Year company founded: 1969
Franchise fee or other initial payment: $20,000
Franchise royalty or other ongoing payment: 4 percent of sales
Advertising royalty or fee: 2.5 percent of sales
Estimated initial investment required: $250,000
Total outlets: 440

Econo Lube N Tune

Year company founded: 1973
Franchise fee or other initial payment: $79,500
Franchise royalty or other ongoing payment: 6 percent of sales
Advertising royalty or fee: 8 percent of sales
Estimated initial investment required: $80,000
Total outlets: 115

El Chico

Year company founded: 1940
Franchise fee or other initial payment: $35,000
Franchise royalty or other ongoing payment: 4 percent of sales
Advertising royalty or fee: 1 percent of sales
Estimated initial investment required: $750,000
Total outlets: 96

El Pollo Asado

Year company founded: 1983
Franchise fee or other initial payment: $25,000
Franchise royalty or other ongoing payment: 4 percent of sales
Advertising royalty or fee: 3 percent of sales
Estimated initial investment required: $150,000
Total outlets: 47

Eldorado Stone

Year company founded: 1969
Franchise fee or other initial payment: $3,400
Franchise royalty or other ongoing payment: 4 percent of sales
Advertising royalty or fee: None
Estimated initial investment required: $50,000
Total outlets: 26

Electronic Realty Associates

Year company founded: 1971
Franchise fee or other initial payment: $13,900
Franchise royalty or other ongoing payment: Mayvary
Advertising royalty or fee: May vary
Estimated initial investment required: $10,000
Total outlets: 2840

ELS International

Year company founded: 1961
Franchise fee or other initial payment: $20,000
Franchise royalty or other ongoing payment: 5 percent of sales
Advertising royalty or fee: None
Estimated initial investment required: $150,000
Total outlets: 34

Employers Overload

Year company founded: 1947
Franchise fee or other initial payment: $15,000
Franchise royalty or other ongoing payment: 5 percent of sales
Advertising royalty or fee: .5 percent of sales
Estimated initial investment required: $35,000
Total outlets: 72

Empress Travel

Year company founded: 1957
Franchise fee or other initial payment: $35,000
Franchise royalty or other ongoing payment: Mayvary
Advertising royalty or fee: May vary
Estimated initial investment required: $50,000
Total outlets: 60

Endrust

Year company founded: 1975
Franchise fee or other initial payment: $30,000
Franchise royalty or other ongoing payment: None
Advertising royalty or fee: None
Estimated initial investment required: $50,000
Total outlets: 85

Entre Computer Centers

Year company founded: 1981
Franchise fee or other initial payment: $15,000
Franchise royalty or other ongoing payment: 5.5 percent of sales
Advertising royalty or fee: .5 percent of sales
Estimated initial investment required: $150,000
Total outlets: 195

Ernie's Wine & Liquors

Year company founded: 1938
Franchise fee or other initial payment: $10,000
Franchise royalty or other ongoing payment: 1 percent of sales
Advertising royalty or fee: None
Estimated initial investment required: $125,000
Total outlets: 40

European Tanspa

Year company founded: 1982
Franchise fee or other initial payment: $5,000
Franchise royalty or other ongoing payment: Mayvary
Advertising royalty or fee: None
Estimated initial investment required: $35,000
Total outlets: 125

Everything Yogurt

Year company founded: 1976
Franchise fee or other initial payment: $30,000
Franchise royalty or other ongoing payment: 5 percent of sales
Advertising royalty or fee: 1 percent of sales
Estimated initial investment required: $150,000
Total outlets: 185

Express Services

Year company founded: 1983
Franchise fee or other initial payment: $9,000
Franchise royalty or other ongoing payment: 6 percent of sales
Advertising royalty or fee: 2 percent of sales
Estimated initial investment required: $28,250
Total outlets: 105

F·O·R·T·U·N·E

Year company founded: 1959
Franchise fee or other initial payment: $30,000
Franchise royalty or other ongoing payment: 7 percent of sales
Advertising royalty or fee: 1 percent of sales
Estimated initial investment required: $22,000
Total outlets: 50

Famous Amos

Year company founded: 1975
Franchise fee or other initial payment: $25,000
Franchise royalty or other ongoing payment: 4 percent of sales
Advertising royalty or fee: 3 percent of sales
Estimated initial investment required: $50,000
Total outlets: 70

Foremost Liquors

Year company founded: 1949
Franchise fee or other initial payment: May vary
Franchise royalty or other ongoing payment: 1.5 percent of sales
Advertising royalty or fee: 1 percent of sales
Estimated initial investment required: $200,000
Total outlets: 76

Fortunate Life

Year company founded: 1986
Franchise fee or other initial payment: $9,000
Franchise royalty or other ongoing payment: 10 percent of sales
Advertising royalty or fee: May vary
Estimated initial investment required: $8,000
Total outlets: 45

Foster's Donuts

Year company founded: 1970
Franchise fee or other initial payment: $35,000
Franchise royalty or other ongoing payment: 5 percent of sales
Advertising royalty or fee: .5 percent of sales
Estimated initial investment required: $25,000
Total outlets: 55

Foster's Freeze

Year company founded: 1946
Franchise fee or other initial payment: $25,000
Franchise royalty or other ongoing payment: 4 percent of sales
Advertising royalty or fee: 3 percent of sales
Estimated initial investment required: $400,000
Total outlets: 200

Four Seasons Greenhouse

Year company founded: 1978
Franchise fee or other initial payment: $5,000
Franchise royalty or other ongoing payment: None
Advertising royalty or fee: None
Estimated initial investment required: $8,250
Total outlets: 250

Four Star Pizza

Year company founded: 1981
Franchise fee or other initial payment: $9,000
Franchise royalty or other ongoing payment: 5 percent of sales
Advertising royalty or fee: 1 percent of sales
Estimated initial investment required: $25,000
Total outlets: 85

Fox's Pizza Den

Year company founded: 1971
Franchise fee or other initial payment: $8,000
Franchise royalty or other ongoing payment: $200per month
Advertising royalty or fee: None
Estimated initial investment required: $43,000
Total outlets: 115

Framing Experience

Year company founded: 1975
Franchise fee or other initial payment: $16,000
Franchise royalty or other ongoing payment: 5 percent of sales
Advertising royalty or fee: None
Estimated initial investment required: $64,000
Total outlets: 30

Franklin's

Year company founded: 1971
Franchise fee or other initial payment: $25,000
Franchise royalty or other ongoing payment: 5 percent of sales
Advertising royalty or fee: 1.5 percent of sales
Estimated initial investment required: $150,000
Total outlets: 92

Freedom Rent-A-Car

Year company founded: 1981
Franchise fee or other initial payment: $5,000
Franchise royalty or other ongoing payment: 3.5 percent of sales
Advertising royalty or fee: 1 percent of sales
Estimated initial investment required: $25,000
Total outlets: 160

Freshens

Year company founded: 1985
Franchise fee or other initial payment: $19.500
Franchise royalty or other ongoing payment: 4 percent of sales
Advertising royalty or fee: 4 percent of sales
Estimated initial investment required: $105,000
Total outlets: 80

Friendship Inn

Year company founded: 1960
Franchise fee or other initial payment: $12,500
Franchise royalty or other ongoing payment: Mayvary
Advertising royalty or fee: None
Estimated initial investment required: May vary
Total outlets: 135

Frontier Fruit & Nut

Year company founded: 1976
Franchise fee or other initial payment: $15,000
Franchise royalty or other ongoing payment: 6 percent of sales
Advertising royalty or fee: None
Estimated initial investment required: $35,000
Total outlets: 260

Frusen Gladje

Year company founded: 1980
Franchise fee or other initial payment: $25,000
Franchise royalty or other ongoing payment: None
Advertising royalty or fee: 1.5 percent of sales
Estimated initial investment required: $115,000
Total outlets: 35

Fuddruckers

Year company founded: 1980
Franchise fee or other initial payment: $50,000
Franchise royalty or other ongoing payment: 5 percent of sales
Advertising royalty or fee: None
Estimated initial investment required: $750,000
Total outlets: 106

G. Fried Carpetland

Year company founded: 1889
Franchise fee or other initial payment: None
Franchise royalty or other ongoing payment: 2 percent of sales
Advertising royalty or fee: None
Estimated initial investment required: $50,000
Total outlets: 26

Gallery of Homes

Year company founded: 1950
Franchise fee or other initial payment: $13,900
Franchise royalty or other ongoing payment: 4 percent of sales
Advertising royalty or fee: 2 percent of sales
Estimated initial investment required: $12,000
Total outlets: 260

Gelato Classico

Year company founded: 1976
Franchise fee or other initial payment: $25,000
Franchise royalty or other ongoing payment: None
Advertising royalty or fee: None
Estimated initial investment required: $50,000
Total outlets: 30

General Business Service

Year company founded: 1962
Franchise fee or other initial payment: $25,000
Franchise royalty or other ongoing payment: 7 percent of sales
Advertising royalty or fee: None
Estimated initial investment required: May vary
Total outlets: 600

Gibraltar Transmissions

Year company founded: 1977
Franchise fee or other initial payment: $30,000
Franchise royalty or other ongoing payment: 7 percent of sales
Advertising royalty or fee: None
Estimated initial investment required: $90,000
Total outlets: 80

Gingess Formalwear

Year company founded: 1936
Franchise fee or other initial payment: $15,000
Franchise royalty or other ongoing payment: 6 percent of sales
Advertising royalty or fee: 1 percent of sales
Estimated initial investment required: $145,000
Total outlets: 235

Giorgio

Year company founded: 1978
Franchise fee or other initial payment: $30,000
Franchise royalty or other ongoing payment: 5 percent of sales
Advertising royalty or fee: 4 percent of sales
Estimated initial investment required: $300,000
Total outlets: 30

Gloria Jean's Coffee Beans

Year company founded: 1979
Franchise fee or other initial payment: $19,500
Franchise royalty or other ongoing payment: 6 percent of sales
Advertising royalty or fee: 1 percent of sales
Estimated initial investment required: $100,000
Total outlets: 37

Godfather's Pizza

Year company founded: 1973
Franchise fee or other initial payment: $15,000
Franchise royalty or other ongoing payment: 5 percent of sales
Advertising royalty or fee: 5 percent of sales
Estimated initial investment required: $125,000
Total outlets: 810

Goodyear Tire Centers

Year company founded: 1896
Franchise fee or other initial payment: May vary
Franchise royalty or other ongoing payment: None
Advertising royalty or fee: None
Estimated initial investment required: $50,000
Total outlets: 1570

Gourmet Cup

Year company founded: 1985
Franchise fee or other initial payment: $25,000
Franchise royalty or other ongoing payment: 6 percent of sales
Advertising royalty or fee: 2 percent of sales
Estimated initial investment required: $90,000
Total outlets: 20

Grand Slam USA

Year company founded: 1976
Franchise fee or other initial payment: $6,000
Franchise royalty or other ongoing payment: 6 percent of sales
Advertising royalty or fee: None
Estimated initial investment required: $130,000
Total outlets: 57

Grandy's

Year company founded: 1973
Franchise fee or other initial payment: $15,000
Franchise royalty or other ongoing payment: 4 percent of sales
Advertising royalty or fee: .8 percent of sales
Estimated initial investment required: $850,000
Total outlets: 205

Grease Monkey

Year company founded: 1978
Franchise fee or other initial payment: $25,000
Franchise royalty or other ongoing payment: 5 percent of sales
Advertising royalty or fee: 6 percent of sales
Estimated initial investment required: $75,000
Total outlets: 131

Great Clips

Year company founded: 1982
Franchise fee or other initial payment: $12,500
Franchise royalty or other ongoing payment: 6 percent of sales
Advertising royalty or fee: 5 percent of sales
Estimated initial investment required: $37,500
Total outlets: 160

Great Expectations

Year company founded: 1955
Franchise fee or other initial payment: $18,000
Franchise royalty or other ongoing payment: 6 percent of sales
Advertising royalty or fee: 2 percent of sales
Estimated initial investment required: $80,000
Total outlets: 300

Great Frame Up

Year company founded: 1970
Franchise fee or other initial payment: $19,500
Franchise royalty or other ongoing payment: 6 percent of sales
Advertising royalty or fee: 2 percent of sales
Estimated initial investment required: $145,000
Total outlets: 95

Ground Round, The

Year company founded: 1969
Franchise fee or other initial payment: $30,000
Franchise royalty or other ongoing payment: 3 percent of sales
Advertising royalty or fee: 2 percent of sales
Estimated initial investment required: $1,300,000
Total outlets: 200

Gymboree

Year company founded: 1976
Franchise fee or other initial payment: $8,000
Franchise royalty or other ongoing payment: 6 percent of sales
Advertising royalty or fee: 2 percent of sales
Estimated initial investment required: $12,000
Total outlets: 350

H&R Block

Year company founded: 1955
Franchise fee or other initial payment: $600
Franchise royalty or other ongoing payment: May vary
Advertising royalty or fee: None
Estimated initial investment required: $2,000
Total outlets: 8800

Hair Performers

Year company founded: 1967
Franchise fee or other initial payment: $15,000
Franchise royalty or other ongoing payment: 6 percent of sales
Advertising royalty or fee: 2 percent of sales
Estimated initial investment required: $55,000
Total outlets: 290

Haircrafters

Year company founded: 1955
Franchise fee or other initial payment: $20,000
Franchise royalty or other ongoing payment: 6 percent of sales
Advertising royalty or fee: None
Estimated initial investment required: $53,000
Total outlets: 400

Hampton Inns

Year company founded: 1983
Franchise fee or other initial payment: $35,000
Franchise royalty or other ongoing payment: 4 percent of sales
Advertising royalty or fee: 2.5 percent of sales
Estimated initial investment required: $2,500,000
Total outlets: 180

Handle With Care

Year company founded: 1980
Franchise fee or other initial payment: $12,500
Franchise royalty or other ongoing payment: 5 percent of sales
Advertising royalty or fee: 1 percent of sales
Estimated initial investment required: $25,0000
Total outlets: 190

Hardee's

Year company founded: 1961
Franchise fee or other initial payment: $15,000
Franchise royalty or other ongoing payment: 3.5 percent of sales
Advertising royalty or fee: 5 percent of sales
Estimated initial investment required: $671,180
Total outlets: 3000

Hasty Markets

Year company founded: 1981
Franchise fee or other initial payment: $32,500
Franchise royalty or other ongoing payment: 6 percent of sales
Advertising royalty or fee: .05 percent of sales
Estimated initial investment required: $200,000
Total outlets: 135

Headquarters Company

Year company founded: 1967
Franchise fee or other initial payment: $30,000
Franchise royalty or other ongoing payment: 1 percent of sales
Advertising royalty or fee: May vary
Estimated initial investment required: $250,000
Total outlets: 72

Health Force

Year company founded: 1960
Franchise fee or other initial payment: $39,500
Franchise royalty or other ongoing payment: 8.5 percent of sales
Advertising royalty or fee: .05 percent of sales
Estimated initial investment required: $60,000
Total outlets: 50

Health Mart

Year company founded: 1980
Franchise fee or other initial payment: None
Franchise royalty or other ongoing payment: None
Advertising royalty or fee: None
Estimated initial investment required: $5,000
Total outlets: 466

Healthcare Recruiters

Year company founded: 1977
Franchise fee or other initial payment: $25,000
Franchise royalty or other ongoing payment: 10 percent of sales
Advertising royalty or fee: 1 percent of sales
Estimated initial investment required: $50,000
Total outlets: 36

Heavenly Ham

Year company founded: 1982
Franchise fee or other initial payment: $25,000
Franchise royalty or other ongoing payment: 4 percent of sales
Advertising royalty or fee: 1 percent of sales
Estimated initial investment required: $80,000
Total outlets: 25

Heidi's

Year company founded: 1982
Franchise fee or other initial payment: $22,000
Franchise royalty or other ongoing payment: 4 percent of sales
Advertising royalty or fee: 4 percent of sales
Estimated initial investment required: $100,000
Total outlets: 90

Help U-Sell

Year company founded: 1976
Franchise fee or other initial payment: May vary
Franchise royalty or other ongoing payment: 7 percent of sales
Advertising royalty or fee: 7 percent of sales
Estimated initial investment required: $25,000
Total outlets: 353

Hickory Farms of Ohio

Year company founded: 1956
Franchise fee or other initial payment: $20,000
Franchise royalty or other ongoing payment: 6 percent of sales
Advertising royalty or fee: 2 percent of sales
Estimated initial investment required: $150,000
Total outlets: 340

Hillary's

Year company founded: 1976
Franchise fee or other initial payment: $28,000
Franchise royalty or other ongoing payment: 5 percent of sales
Advertising royalty or fee: $500 per year
Estimated initial investment required: $10,000
Total outlets: 25

Hilton Inn

Year company founded: 1947
Franchise fee or other initial payment: $25,000
Franchise royalty or other ongoing payment: 5 percent of sales
Advertising royalty or fee: None
Estimated initial investment required: $5,000,000
Total outlets: 275

Holiday Inn

Year company founded: 1952
Franchise fee or other initial payment: May vary
Franchise royalty or other ongoing payment: 4 percent of sales
Advertising royalty or fee: 1.5 percent of sales
Estimated initial investment required: $5,500,000
Total outlets: 1600

Homes & Land Magazine

Year company founded: 1982
Franchise fee or other initial payment: $1,500
Franchise royalty or other ongoing payment: May vary
Advertising royalty or fee: None
Estimated initial investment required: $100
Total outlets: 264

Hometrend

Year company founded: 1981
Franchise fee or other initial payment: May vary
Franchise royalty or other ongoing payment: .5 percent of sales
Advertising royalty or fee: .5 percent of sales
Estimated initial investment required: $104,000
Total outlets: 50

House of Almonds

Year company founded: 1968
Franchise fee or other initial payment: $15,000
Franchise royalty or other ongoing payment: 5 percent of sales
Advertising royalty or fee: 2 percent of sales
Estimated initial investment required: $130,000
Total outlets: 68

HouseMaster

Year company founded: 1971
Franchise fee or other initial payment: $17,000
Franchise royalty or other ongoing payment: 6 percent of sales
Advertising royalty or fee: 4 percent of sales
Estimated initial investment required: $10,000
Total outlets: 100

Howard Johnson

Year company founded: 1954
Franchise fee or other initial payment: $30,000
Franchise royalty or other ongoing payment: 5 percent of sales
Advertising royalty or fee: May vary
Estimated initial investment required: $2,500,000
Total outlets: 450

Huntington Learning Center

Year company founded: 1977
Franchise fee or other initial payment: $10,000
Franchise royalty or other ongoing payment: 6 percent of sales
Advertising royalty or fee: 2 percent of sales
Estimated initial investment required: $45,000
Total outlets: 90

I Can't Believe It's Yogurt

Year company founded: 1977
Franchise fee or other initial payment: $20,000
Franchise royalty or other ongoing payment: 5 percent of sales
Advertising royalty or fee: 2 percent of sales
Estimated initial investment required: $94,000
Total outlets: 175

Ice Cream Churn

Year company founded: 1974
Franchise fee or other initial payment: $7,500
Franchise royalty or other ongoing payment: Mayvary
Advertising royalty or fee: May vary
Estimated initial investment required: $2,500
Total outlets: 530

In N Out Food Stores

Year company founded: 1976
Franchise fee or other initial payment: $15,000
Franchise royalty or other ongoing payment: 3.75 percent of sales
Advertising royalty or fee: 1.75 percent of sales
Estimated initial investment required: $60,000
Total outlets: 50

Inacomp

Year company founded: 1976
Franchise fee or other initial payment: $5,000
Franchise royalty or other ongoing payment: 5 percent of sales
Advertising royalty or fee: None
Estimated initial investment required: $200,000
Total outlets: 80

Ink Well, The

Year company founded: 1972
Franchise fee or other initial payment: $20,000
Franchise royalty or other ongoing payment: 5 percent of sales
Advertising royalty or fee: 2.5 percent of sales
Estimated initial investment required: $40,000
Total outlets: 50

Insty Prints

Year company founded: 1965
Franchise fee or other initial payment: $40,000
Franchise royalty or other ongoing payment: 3 percent of sales
Advertising royalty or fee: 2 percent of sales
Estimated initial investment required: $50,000
Total outlets: 360

International Blimpie

Year company founded: 1964
Franchise fee or other initial payment: $15,000
Franchise royalty or other ongoing payment: 6 percent of sales
Advertising royalty or fee: 3 percent of sales
Estimated initial investment required: $60,000
Total outlets: 320

International House of Pancakes

Year company founded: 1958
Franchise fee or other initial payment: $50,000
Franchise royalty or other ongoing payment: 4.5 percent of sales
Advertising royalty or fee: 3 percent of sales
Estimated initial investment required: May vary
Total outlets: 458

International Mergers & Acquisitions

Year company founded: 1970
Franchise fee or other initial payment: $10,000
Franchise royalty or other ongoing payment: 3 percent of sales
Advertising royalty or fee: 1 percent of sales
Estimated initial investment required: $15,000
Total outlets: 40

Island Water Sports

Year company founded: 1978
Franchise fee or other initial payment: $25,000
Franchise royalty or other ongoing payment: None
Advertising royalty or fee: May vary
Estimated initial investment required: $55,000
Total outlets: 25

Jack in the Box

Year company founded: 1951
Franchise fee or other initial payment: $25,000
Franchise royalty or other ongoing payment: 4 percent of sales
Advertising royalty or fee: 5 percent of sales
Estimated initial investment required: $285,000
Total outlets: 940

Jackson Hewitt

Year company founded: 1960
Franchise fee or other initial payment: $3,000
Franchise royalty or other ongoing payment: Mayvary
Advertising royalty or fee: May vary
Estimated initial investment required: $13,000
Total outlets: 50

Jani-King

Year company founded: 1969
Franchise fee or other initial payment: $6,500
Franchise royalty or other ongoing payment: 10 percent of sales
Advertising royalty or fee: .5 percent of sales
Estimated initial investment required: $34,000
Total outlets: 1300

Janimaster International

Year company founded: 1980
Franchise fee or other initial payment: $7,995
Franchise royalty or other ongoing payment: 6 percent of sales
Advertising royalty or fee: None
Estimated initial investment required: $2,000
Total outlets: 80

Japan Camera

Year company founded: 1959
Franchise fee or other initial payment: $40,000
Franchise royalty or other ongoing payment: 8 percent of sales
Advertising royalty or fee: 3.5 percent of sales
Estimated initial investment required: $40,000
Total outlets: 150

Jazzercise

Year company founded: 1972
Franchise fee or other initial payment: $500
Franchise royalty or other ongoing payment: May vary
Advertising royalty or fee: None
Estimated initial investment required: $2,000
Total outlets: 3800

Jerry's Subs

Year company founded: 1954
Franchise fee or other initial payment: $30,000
Franchise royalty or other ongoing payment: 5 percent of sales
Advertising royalty or fee: 3 percent of sales
Estimated initial investment required: $250,000
Total outlets: 60

Jiffy Lube

Year company founded: 1979
Franchise fee or other initial payment: $25,000
Franchise royalty or other ongoing payment: 5 percent of sales
Advertising royalty or fee: 8 percent of sales
Estimated initial investment required: $95,000
Total outlets: 920

John Casablanca

Year company founded: 1979
Franchise fee or other initial payment: $6,500
Franchise royalty or other ongoing payment: 7 percent of sales
Advertising royalty or fee: 3 percent of sales
Estimated initial investment required: $7,000
Total outlets: 81

John Robert Powers

Year company founded: 1923
Franchise fee or other initial payment: $30,000
Franchise royalty or other ongoing payment: 10 percent of sales
Advertising royalty or fee: $150 per month
Estimated initial investment required: $20,000
Total outlets: 62

Jreck Subs

Year company founded: 1968
Franchise fee or other initial payment: $10,000
Franchise royalty or other ongoing payment: 5 percent of sales
Advertising royalty or fee: 2 percent of sales
Estimated initial investment required: $76,000
Total outlets: 41

Just Pants

Year company founded: 1969
Franchise fee or other initial payment: $15,000
Franchise royalty or other ongoing payment: 5 percent of sales
Advertising royalty or fee: 3 percent of sales
Estimated initial investment required: $133,500
Total outlets: 85

K&W Tax Service

Year company founded: 1979
Franchise fee or other initial payment: $8,500
Franchise royalty or other ongoing payment: 50 percent of sales
Advertising royalty or fee: 8 percent of sales
Estimated initial investment required: $10,000
Total outlets: 30

Kale's Collision

Year company founded: 1977
Franchise fee or other initial payment: $15,000
Franchise royalty or other ongoing payment: 6 percent of sales
Advertising royalty or fee: $1,000
Estimated initial investment required: $12,000
Total outlets: 24

Kampgrounds of America

Year company founded: 1961
Franchise fee or other initial payment: $20,000
Franchise royalty or other ongoing payment: 8 percent of sales
Advertising royalty or fee: 2 percent of sales
Estimated initial investment required: $85,000
Total outlets: 640

Kentucky Fried Chicken

Year company founded: 1972
Franchise fee or other initial payment: $20,000
Franchise royalty or other ongoing payment: 4 percent of sales
Advertising royalty or fee: 5 percent of sales
Estimated initial investment required: $150,000
Total outlets: 7700

Kernels

Year company founded: 1983
Franchise fee or other initial payment: $25,000
Franchise royalty or other ongoing payment: 8 percent of sales
Advertising royalty or fee: None
Estimated initial investment required: $75,000
Total outlets: 40

Kiddie Kobbler

Year company founded: 1951
Franchise fee or other initial payment: $20,000
Franchise royalty or other ongoing payment: 4 percent of sales
Advertising royalty or fee: 1 percent of sales
Estimated initial investment required: $120,000
Total outlets: 60

King Bear

Year company founded: 1973
Franchise fee or other initial payment: $19,900
Franchise royalty or other ongoing payment: $150 per month
Advertising royalty or fee: $300 per month
Estimated initial investment required: $65,000
Total outlets: 64

Kits Camera

Year company founded: 1975
Franchise fee or other initial payment: $19,500
Franchise royalty or other ongoing payment: 6 percent of sales
Advertising royalty or fee: 1.5 percent of sales
Estimated initial investment required: $100,000
Total outlets: 75

Koenig Art Emporium

Year company founded: 1971
Franchise fee or other initial payment: $25,000
Franchise royalty or other ongoing payment: 6 percent of sales
Advertising royalty or fee: None
Estimated initial investment required: $155,000
Total outlets: 100

Kwik Kopy

Year company founded: 1967
Franchise fee or other initial payment: $22,000
Franchise royalty or other ongoing payment: 4 percent of sales
Advertising royalty or fee: None
Estimated initial investment required: $110,000
Total outlets: 1000

L'il Peach

Year company founded: 1971
Franchise fee or other initial payment: $10,000
Franchise royalty or other ongoing payment: 15 percent of sales
Advertising royalty or fee: None
Estimated initial investment required: $35,000
Total outlets: 65

Langenwalter Dye Concept

Year company founded: 1972
Franchise fee or other initial payment: $14,500
Franchise royalty or other ongoing payment: None
Advertising royalty or fee: $100 per month
Estimated initial investment required: $3,000
Total outlets: 130

Larry's

Year company founded: 1981
Franchise fee or other initial payment: $15,000
Franchise royalty or other ongoing payment: 1 percent of sales
Advertising royalty or fee: 3 percent of sales
Estimated initial investment required: $60,000
Total outlets: 52

Lawn Doctor

Year company founded: 1967
Franchise fee or other initial payment: None
Franchise royalty or other ongoing payment: 10 percent of sales
Advertising royalty or fee: May vary
Estimated initial investment required: $25,500
Total outlets: 290

Lazer Mase

Year company founded: 1986
Franchise fee or other initial payment: $15,000
Franchise royalty or other ongoing payment: 5 percent of sales
Advertising royalty or fee: 2 percent of sales
Estimated initial investment required: $255,000
Total outlets: 9

Le Peep

Year company founded: 1981
Franchise fee or other initial payment: $30,000
Franchise royalty or other ongoing payment: 5 percent of sales
Advertising royalty or fee: 1 percent of sales
Estimated initial investment required: $300,000
Total outlets: 60

Lee Myles Transmission

Year company founded: 1947
Franchise fee or other initial payment: $20,000
Franchise royalty or other ongoing payment: 6 percent of sales
Advertising royalty or fee: 4.5 percent of sales
Estimated initial investment required: $70,000
Total outlets: 104

Lee's

Year company founded: 1966
Franchise fee or other initial payment: $10,000
Franchise royalty or other ongoing payment: 3 percent of sales
Advertising royalty or fee: 1 percent of sales
Estimated initial investment required: $76,000
Total outlets: 280

Lemon Tree

Year company founded: 1976
Franchise fee or other initial payment: $7,500
Franchise royalty or other ongoing payment: 6 percent of sales
Advertising royalty or fee: $400 per month
Estimated initial investment required: $19,100
Total outlets: 50

Lien Chemical

Year company founded: 1929
Franchise fee or other initial payment: $9,000
Franchise royalty or other ongoing payment: 5 percent of sales
Advertising royalty or fee: None
Estimated initial investment required: $16,500
Total outlets: 46

Little Caesar's

Year company founded: 1959
Franchise fee or other initial payment: $15,000
Franchise royalty or other ongoing payment: 5 percent of sales
Advertising royalty or fee: May vary
Estimated initial investment required: $120,000
Total outlets: 2000

Little King

Year company founded: 1968
Franchise fee or other initial payment: $19,500
Franchise royalty or other ongoing payment: 5 percent of sales
Advertising royalty or fee: None
Estimated initial investment required: $85,000
Total outlets: 76

Little Professor

Year company founded: 1965
Franchise fee or other initial payment: $21,000
Franchise royalty or other ongoing payment: 2.75 percent of
    sales
Advertising royalty or fee: .5 percent of sales
Estimated initial investment required: $90,000
Total outlets: 120

Living Lighting

Year company founded: 1968
Franchise fee or other initial payment: $25,000
Franchise royalty or other ongoing payment: 7 percent of sales
Advertising royalty or fee: 5 percent of sales
Estimated initial investment required: $90,000
Total outlets: 70

London Fish & Chips

Year company founded: 1967
Franchise fee or other initial payment: $7,500
Franchise royalty or other ongoing payment: 6 percent of sales
Advertising royalty or fee: None
Estimated initial investment required: $35,000
Total outlets: 45

Long John Silver's

Year company founded: 1969
Franchise fee or other initial payment: $20,000
Franchise royalty or other ongoing payment: 4 percent of sales
Advertising royalty or fee: 5 percent of sales
Estimated initial investment required: $380,000
Total outlets: 1500

M.G.M. Liquor Warehouse

Year company founded: 1971
Franchise fee or other initial payment: $25,000
Franchise royalty or other ongoing payment: May vary
Advertising royalty or fee: 1 percent of sales
Estimated initial investment required: $350,000
Total outlets: 30

MAACO

Year company founded: 1972
Franchise fee or other initial payment: $25,000
Franchise royalty or other ongoing payment: 8 percent of sales
Advertising royalty or fee: $2,000
Estimated initial investment required: $155,000
Total outlets: 440

Mad Hatter Mufflers

Year company founded: 1975
Franchise fee or other initial payment: $17,500
Franchise royalty or other ongoing payment: 8 percent of sales
Advertising royalty or fee: 4 percent of sales
Estimated initial investment required: $81,000
Total outlets: 42

MagiCuts

Year company founded: 1981
Franchise fee or other initial payment: $18,000
Franchise royalty or other ongoing payment: 7 percent of sales
Advertising royalty or fee: 2 percent of sales
Estimated initial investment required: $70,000
Total outlets: 145

Maid Brigade

Year company founded: 1978
Franchise fee or other initial payment: $15,000
Franchise royalty or other ongoing payment: 6 percent of sales
Advertising royalty or fee: 2 percent of sales
Estimated initial investment required: $10,000
Total outlets: 50

Maids, The

Year company founded: 1979
Franchise fee or other initial payment: $12,900
Franchise royalty or other ongoing payment: 4.5 percent of sales
Advertising royalty or fee: 2 percent of sales
Estimated initial investment required: $20,000
Total outlets: 165

Mail Boxes Etc. USA

Year company founded: 1980
Franchise fee or other initial payment: $19,500
Franchise royalty or other ongoing payment: 5 percent of sales
Advertising royalty or fee: 2 percent of sales
Estimated initial investment required: $40,000
Total outlets: 600

Major Video

Year company founded: 1984
Franchise fee or other initial payment: $25,000
Franchise royalty or other ongoing payment: 4 percent of sales
Advertising royalty or fee: 1 percent of sales
Estimated initial investment required: $325,000
Total outlets: 150

Management Recruiters

Year company founded: 1957
Franchise fee or other initial payment: $20,000
Franchise royalty or other ongoing payment: 5 percent of sales
Advertising royalty or fee: ,5 percent of sales
Estimated initial investment required: $15,000
Total outlets: 330

Marco's Pizza

Year company founded: 1978
Franchise fee or other initial payment: $12,000
Franchise royalty or other ongoing payment: 4.5 percent of sales
Advertising royalty or fee: 2.5 percent of sales
Estimated initial investment required: $80,000
Total outlets: 38

Marcoin

Year company founded: 1952
Franchise fee or other initial payment: $30,000
Franchise royalty or other ongoing payment: 8.5 percent of sales
Advertising royalty or fee: .5 percent of sales
Estimated initial investment required: $7,000
Total outlets: 130

Marie Callender

Year company founded: 1964
Franchise fee or other initial payment: $25,000
Franchise royalty or other ongoing payment: 3 percent of sales
Advertising royalty or fee: 2 percent of sales
Estimated initial investment required: $300,000
Total outlets: 160

Mazzio's Pizza

Year company founded: 1961
Franchise fee or other initial payment: $20,000
Franchise royalty or other ongoing payment: 3 percent of sales
Advertising royalty or fee: 1 percent of sales
Estimated initial investment required: $450,000
Total outlets: 210

McDonald's

Year company founded: 1955
Franchise fee or other initial payment: $22,500
Franchise royalty or other ongoing payment: 12 percent of sales
Advertising royalty or fee: 4 percent of sales
Estimated initial investment required: $325,000
Total outlets: 13900

Medical Personnel

Year company founded: 1965
Franchise fee or other initial payment: $15,000
Franchise royalty or other ongoing payment: 5 percent of sales
Advertising royalty or fee: None
Estimated initial investment required: $35,000
Total outlets: 265

Medicap Pharmacy

Year company founded: 1971
Franchise fee or other initial payment: $15,000
Franchise royalty or other ongoing payment: 4 percent of sales
Advertising royalty or fee: 1 percent of sales
Estimated initial investment required: $75,000
Total outlets: 70

Medicine Shoppe

Year company founded: 1970
Franchise fee or other initial payment: $18,000
Franchise royalty or other ongoing payment: 5.5 percent of sales
Advertising royalty or fee: 2 percent of sales
Estimated initial investment required: $60,000
Total outlets: 740

Meineke Discount Muffler

Year company founded: 1972
Franchise fee or other initial payment: $22,500
Franchise royalty or other ongoing payment: 7 percent of sales
Advertising royalty or fee: 10 percent of sales
Estimated initial investment required: $67,500
Total outlets: 720

Merle Harmon's Fan Fair

Year company founded: 1977
Franchise fee or other initial payment: $15,000
Franchise royalty or other ongoing payment: 5 percent of sales
Advertising royalty or fee: 1 percent of sales
Estimated initial investment required: $85,000
Total outlets: 85

Merlin's Magic Muffler

Year company founded: 1975
Franchise fee or other initial payment: $22,000
Franchise royalty or other ongoing payment: 4.9 percent of sales
Advertising royalty or fee: 5 percent of sales
Estimated initial investment required: $30,000
Total outlets: 44

Merry Maids

Year company founded: 1980
Franchise fee or other initial payment: $17,000
Franchise royalty or other ongoing payment: 7 percent of sales
Advertising royalty or fee: None
Estimated initial investment required: $12,500
Total outlets: 470

MicroAge Computer Stores

Year company founded: 1976
Franchise fee or other initial payment: $15,000
Franchise royalty or other ongoing payment: 4 percent of sales
Advertising royalty or fee: 1 percent of sales
Estimated initial investment required: $76,000
Total outlets: 200

Midas

Year company founded: 1956
Franchise fee or other initial payment: $10,000
Franchise royalty or other ongoing payment: 5 percent of sales
Advertising royalty or fee: 5 percent of sales
Estimated initial investment required: $140,000
Total outlets: 2200

Mifax

Year company founded: 1969
Franchise fee or other initial payment: $13,800
Franchise royalty or other ongoing payment: None
Advertising royalty or fee: None
Estimated initial investment required: $13,840
Total outlets: 60

Mighty Distributing

Year company founded: 1963
Franchise fee or other initial payment: $15,000
Franchise royalty or other ongoing payment: 5 percent of sales
Advertising royalty or fee: .5 percent of sales
Estimated initial investment required: $75,000
Total outlets: 200

Mike's

Year company founded: 1967
Franchise fee or other initial payment: $40,000
Franchise royalty or other ongoing payment: 5 percent of sales
Advertising royalty or fee: 3 percent of sales
Estimated initial investment required: $100,000
Total outlets: 95

Milex Tune-Up

Year company founded: 1978
Franchise fee or other initial payment: $17,500
Franchise royalty or other ongoing payment: 5 percent of sales
Advertising royalty or fee: 5 percent of sales
Estimated initial investment required: $35,000
Total outlets: 26

Ming Auto Beauty

Year company founded: 1935
Franchise fee or other initial payment: $25,000
Franchise royalty or other ongoing payment: 5 percent of sales
Advertising royalty or fee: 4 percent of sales
Estimated initial investment required: $45,000
Total outlets: 47

Mini Maid

Year company founded: 1973
Franchise fee or other initial payment: $8,900
Franchise royalty or other ongoing payment: $350 per month
Advertising royalty or fee: None
Estimated initial investment required: $6,700
Total outlets: 140

Minut-Tune

Year company founded: 1976
Franchise fee or other initial payment: $20,000
Franchise royalty or other ongoing payment: 5 percent of sales
Advertising royalty or fee: 5 percent of sales
Estimated initial investment required: $75,000
Total outlets: 48

Minute Muffler

Year company founded: 1968
Franchise fee or other initial payment: $10,000
Franchise royalty or other ongoing payment: None
Advertising royalty or fee: None
Estimated initial investment required: May vary
Total outlets: 105

Minuteman Press

Year company founded: 1973
Franchise fee or other initial payment: $24,500
Franchise royalty or other ongoing payment: 6 percent of sales
Advertising royalty or fee: None
Estimated initial investment required: $24,500
Total outlets: 820

Miracle Auto Painting

Year company founded: 1953
Franchise fee or other initial payment: $35,000
Franchise royalty or other ongoing payment: 5 percent of sales
Advertising royalty or fee: 5 percent of sales
Estimated initial investment required: $48,100
Total outlets: 56

Miracle Ear

Year company founded: 1948
Franchise fee or other initial payment: $12,500
Franchise royalty or other ongoing payment: May vary
Advertising royalty or fee: None
Estimated initial investment required: $75,000
Total outlets: 445

Miracle Method

Year company founded: 1977
Franchise fee or other initial payment: $19,950
Franchise royalty or other ongoing payment: 7.5 percent of sales
Advertising royalty or fee: 3 percent of sales
Estimated initial investment required: $15,000
Total outlets: 107

Mister Donut

Year company founded: 1955
Franchise fee or other initial payment: $25,000
Franchise royalty or other ongoing payment: 4.9 percent of sales
Advertising royalty or fee: 3.5 percent of sales
Estimated initial investment required: $275,000
Total outlets: 610

Mister Transmission

Year company founded: 1963
Franchise fee or other initial payment: $20,000
Franchise royalty or other ongoing payment: 7 percent of sales
Advertising royalty or fee: May vary
Estimated initial investment required: $45,000
Total outlets: 100

Molly Maid

Year company founded: 1978
Franchise fee or other initial payment: $16,900
Franchise royalty or other ongoing payment: 4 percent of sales
Advertising royalty or fee: 2 percent of sales
Estimated initial investment required: $8,000
Total outlets: 336

Mom's Cinnamon Rolls

Year company founded: 1985
Franchise fee or other initial payment: $20,000
Franchise royalty or other ongoing payment: 5 percent of sales
Advertising royalty or fee: 3 percent of sales
Estimated initial investment required: $65,000
Total outlets: 25

Money Mailer

Year company founded: 1979
Franchise fee or other initial payment: May vary
Franchise royalty or other ongoing payment: None
Advertising royalty or fee: None
Estimated initial investment required: May vary
Total outlets: 190

Moto Photo

Year company founded: 1981
Franchise fee or other initial payment: $35,000
Franchise royalty or other ongoing payment: 6 percent of sales
Advertising royalty or fee: .5 percent of sales
Estimated initial investment required: $125,500
Total outlets: 275

Motra Transmission

Year company founded: 1980
Franchise fee or other initial payment: $17,500
Franchise royalty or other ongoing payment: 7 percent of sales
Advertising royalty or fee: May vary
Estimated initial investment required: $25,000
Total outlets: 35

Mountain Mike's

Year company founded: 1978
Franchise fee or other initial payment: $12,500
Franchise royalty or other ongoing payment: 4 percent of sales
Advertising royalty or fee: 2 percent of sales
Estimated initial investment required: $60,000
Total outlets: 60

Movieland USA

Year company founded: 1984
Franchise fee or other initial payment: $10,000
Franchise royalty or other ongoing payment: 4 percent of sales
Advertising royalty or fee: 1 percent of sales
Estimated initial investment required: $40,000
Total outlets: 30

Mr. Build

Year company founded: 1981
Franchise fee or other initial payment: $6,000
Franchise royalty or other ongoing payment: May vary
Advertising royalty or fee: $300 per month
Estimated initial investment required: $20,000
Total outlets: 605

Mr. Gatti's

Year company founded: 1969
Franchise fee or other initial payment: $10,000
Franchise royalty or other ongoing payment: 4 percent of sales
Advertising royalty or fee: 1 percent of sales
Estimated initial investment required: $60,000
Total outlets: 338

Mr. Grocer

Year company founded: 1983
Franchise fee or other initial payment: None
Franchise royalty or other ongoing payment: 3.85 percent of
 sales
Advertising royalty or fee: .75 percent of sales
Estimated initial investment required: $100,000
Total outlets: 60

Mr. Philly

Year company founded: 1965
Franchise fee or other initial payment: $21,500
Franchise royalty or other ongoing payment: 4 percent of sales
Advertising royalty or fee: 6 percent of sales
Estimated initial investment required: $130,000
Total outlets: 150

Mr. Sign

Year company founded: 1985
Franchise fee or other initial payment: $17,500
Franchise royalty or other ongoing payment: 5 percent of sales
Advertising royalty or fee: 2 percent of sales
Estimated initial investment required: $37,000
Total outlets: 48

Mr. Steak

Year company founded: 1962
Franchise fee or other initial payment: $16,000
Franchise royalty or other ongoing payment: 3 percent of sales
Advertising royalty or fee: 1 percent of sales
Estimated initial investment required: $750,000
Total outlets: 175

Mr. Submarine

Year company founded: 1968
Franchise fee or other initial payment: $15,000
Franchise royalty or other ongoing payment: 5 percent of sales
Advertising royalty or fee: 3 percent of sales
Estimated initial investment required: $35,000
Total outlets: 275

Mr. Transmission

Year company founded: 1962
Franchise fee or other initial payment: $19,500
Franchise royalty or other ongoing payment: 8 percent of sales
Advertising royalty or fee: 10 percent of sales
Estimated initial investment required: $103,000
Total outlets: 140

Mrs. Powell's

Year company founded: 1984
Franchise fee or other initial payment: $25,000
Franchise royalty or other ongoing payment: 5 percent of sales
Advertising royalty or fee: 2 percent of sales
Estimated initial investment required: $75,000
Total outlets: 42

Mrs. Vanelli's Pizza

Year company founded: 1981
Franchise fee or other initial payment: $25,000
Franchise royalty or other ongoing payment: 6 percent of sales
Advertising royalty or fee: 2 percent of sales
Estimated initial investment required: $115,000
Total outlets: 46

Mundus Colleges

Year company founded: 1977
Franchise fee or other initial payment: $15,000
Franchise royalty or other ongoing payment: None
Advertising royalty or fee: None
Estimated initial investment required: $26,500
Total outlets: 63

Naked Furniture

Year company founded: 1972
Franchise fee or other initial payment: $16,500
Franchise royalty or other ongoing payment: 4 percent of sales
Advertising royalty or fee: None
Estimated initial investment required: $100,000
Total outlets: 50

Namco

Year company founded: 1954
Franchise fee or other initial payment: $25,000
Franchise royalty or other ongoing payment: 15 percent of sales
Advertising royalty or fee: None
Estimated initial investment required: $5,000
Total outlets: 43

National Maintenance Contractors

Year company founded: 1979
Franchise fee or other initial payment: $2,500
Franchise royalty or other ongoing payment: 20 percent of sales
Advertising royalty or fee: None
Estimated initial investment required: $1,500
Total outlets: 224

National Video

Year company founded: 1980
Franchise fee or other initial payment: $29,900
Franchise royalty or other ongoing payment: 4.9 percent of sales
Advertising royalty or fee: 3 percent of sales
Estimated initial investment required: $150,000
Total outlets: 1400

New York Pizza Department

Year company founded: 1984
Franchise fee or other initial payment: $10,000
Franchise royalty or other ongoing payment: 5 percent of sales
Advertising royalty or fee: 3 percent of sales
Estimated initial investment required: $100,000
Total outlets: 14

Norell Temporary

Year company founded: 1961
Franchise fee or other initial payment: $15,000
Franchise royalty or other ongoing payment: May vary
Advertising royalty or fee: None
Estimated initial investment required: $50,000
Total outlets: 240

Novus Windshield Repair

Year company founded: 1972
Franchise fee or other initial payment: $2,900
Franchise royalty or other ongoing payment: 6 percent of sales
Advertising royalty or fee: 2 percent of sales
Estimated initial investment required: $2,000
Total outlets: 685

Numero Uno

Year company founded: 1973
Franchise fee or other initial payment: $25,000
Franchise royalty or other ongoing payment: 5.5 percent of sales
Advertising royalty or fee: 4.5 percent of sales
Estimated initial investment required: $210,000
Total outlets: 62

Nursefinders

Year company founded: 1975
Franchise fee or other initial payment: $15,000
Franchise royalty or other ongoing payment: 5 percent of sales
Advertising royalty or fee: None
Estimated initial investment required: $70,000
Total outlets: 100

Nutra Bolic

Year company founded: 1982
Franchise fee or other initial payment: $17,900
Franchise royalty or other ongoing payment: 5 percent of sales
Advertising royalty or fee: None
Estimated initial investment required: $10,000
Total outlets: 180

Nutri System

Year company founded: 1971
Franchise fee or other initial payment: $13,000
Franchise royalty or other ongoing payment: 7 percent of sales
Advertising royalty or fee: None
Estimated initial investment required: $60,000
Total outlets: 1000

NuVision Optical

Year company founded: 1949
Franchise fee or other initial payment: $10,000
Franchise royalty or other ongoing payment: 8.5 percent of sales
Advertising royalty or fee: 7 percent of sales
Estimated initial investment required: $17,000
Total outlets: 220

Olga's Kitchen

Year company founded: 1975
Franchise fee or other initial payment: $25,000
Franchise royalty or other ongoing payment: 5 percent of sales
Advertising royalty or fee: 3 percent of sales
Estimated initial investment required: $300,000
Total outlets: 47

One Hour Martinizing

Year company founded: 1949
Franchise fee or other initial payment: $20,000
Franchise royalty or other ongoing payment: 2.4 percent of sales
Advertising royalty or fee: 4 percent of sales
Estimated initial investment required: $135,000
Total outlets: 1000

1 Potato 2

Year company founded: 1978
Franchise fee or other initial payment: $20,000
Franchise royalty or other ongoing payment: 6 percent of sales
Advertising royalty or fee: 2 percent of sales
Estimated initial investment required: $65,000
Total outlets: 54

Orange Julius

Year company founded: 1926
Franchise fee or other initial payment: $30,000
Franchise royalty or other ongoing payment: 6 percent of sales
Advertising royalty or fee: 3.5 percent of sales
Estimated initial investment required: $150,000
Total outlets: 745

Pacer Racer

Year company founded: 1977
Franchise fee or other initial payment: None
Franchise royalty or other ongoing payment: None
Advertising royalty or fee: None
Estimated initial investment required: $10,000
Total outlets: 170

Packy the Shipper

Year company founded: 1976
Franchise fee or other initial payment: $995
Franchise royalty or other ongoing payment: May vary
Advertising royalty or fee: None
Estimated initial investment required: $995
Total outlets: 1120

Padgett Business Service

Year company founded: 1965
Franchise fee or other initial payment: $14,500
Franchise royalty or other ongoing payment: 9 percent of sales
Advertising royalty or fee: None
Estimated initial investment required: $27,000
Total outlets: 80

Pak Mail

Year company founded: 1983
Franchise fee or other initial payment: $15,500
Franchise royalty or other ongoing payment: 5 percent of sales
Advertising royalty or fee: 1 percent of sales
Estimated initial investment required: $35,000
Total outlets: 190

Palmer Video

Year company founded: 1981
Franchise fee or other initial payment: $29,000
Franchise royalty or other ongoing payment: 5 percent of sales
Advertising royalty or fee: None
Estimated initial investment required: $200,000
Total outlets: 100

Panhandler Shops

Year company founded: 1974
Franchise fee or other initial payment: $25,000
Franchise royalty or other ongoing payment: 6 percent of sales
Advertising royalty or fee: 1 percent of sales
Estimated initial investment required: $125,000
Total outlets: 80

Papa Aldo's

Year company founded: 1981
Franchise fee or other initial payment: $17,500
Franchise royalty or other ongoing payment: 5 percent of sales
Advertising royalty or fee: 2 percent of sales
Estimated initial investment required: $63,500
Total outlets: 80

Parson-Bishop

Year company founded: 1973
Franchise fee or other initial payment: $19,000
Franchise royalty or other ongoing payment: None
Advertising royalty or fee: None
Estimated initial investment required: $500
Total outlets: 50

Party Harty

Year company founded: 1987
Franchise fee or other initial payment: $15,000
Franchise royalty or other ongoing payment: 3 percent of sales
Advertising royalty or fee: None
Estimated initial investment required: $30,000
Total outlets: 30

Paul Davis Systems

Year company founded: 1966
Franchise fee or other initial payment: $37,500
Franchise royalty or other ongoing payment: 2.5 percent of sales
Advertising royalty or fee: None
Estimated initial investment required: $25,000
Total outlets: 120

Pay N Play Racquetball

Year company founded: 1978
Franchise fee or other initial payment: May vary
Franchise royalty or other ongoing payment: 10 percent of sales
Advertising royalty or fee: 2.5 percent of sales
Estimated initial investment required: $5,000
Total outlets: 9

Payless Car Rental

Year company founded: 1971
Franchise fee or other initial payment: $10,000
Franchise royalty or other ongoing payment: 5 percent of sales
Advertising royalty or fee: 3 percent of sales
Estimated initial investment required: $25,000
Total outlets: 116

PCR Computer Rentals

Year company founded: 1983
Franchise fee or other initial payment: $25,500
Franchise royalty or other ongoing payment: 7 percent of sales
Advertising royalty or fee: 1 percent of sales
Estimated initial investment required: $60,000
Total outlets: 37

Pearle Vision

Year company founded: 1962
Franchise fee or other initial payment: $16,000
Franchise royalty or other ongoing payment: 8.5 percent of sales
Advertising royalty or fee: 8 percent of sales
Estimated initial investment required: $100,000
Total outlets: 860

Penguin's Place

Year company founded: 1983
Franchise fee or other initial payment: $25,000
Franchise royalty or other ongoing payment: 4 percent of sales
Advertising royalty or fee: 4 percent of sales
Estimated initial investment required: $160,000
Total outlets: 140

Pennysaver

Year company founded: 1973
Franchise fee or other initial payment: $24,500
Franchise royalty or other ongoing payment: $500 per month
Advertising royalty or fee: None
Estimated initial investment required: $8,000
Total outlets: 410

Pepe's

Year company founded: 1967
Franchise fee or other initial payment: $15,000
Franchise royalty or other ongoing payment: 4 percent of sales
Advertising royalty or fee: 3 percent of sales
Estimated initial investment required: $200,000
Total outlets: 65

Perkins Family Rest.

Year company founded: 1950
Franchise fee or other initial payment: $30,000
Franchise royalty or other ongoing payment: 4 percent of sales
Advertising royalty or fee: 4 percent of sales
Estimated initial investment required: $950,000
Total outlets: 330

Perma Ceram

Year company founded: 1975
Franchise fee or other initial payment: $19,500
Franchise royalty or other ongoing payment: None
Advertising royalty or fee: None
Estimated initial investment required: $1,000
Total outlets: 130

Perma-Glaze

Year company founded: 1978
Franchise fee or other initial payment: None
Franchise royalty or other ongoing payment: None
Advertising royalty or fee: None
Estimated initial investment required: $19,500
Total outlets: 65

Perma-Guard

Year company founded: 1974
Franchise fee or other initial payment: $32,000
Franchise royalty or other ongoing payment: 5 percent of sales
Advertising royalty or fee: 5 percent of sales
Estimated initial investment required: $32,000
Total outlets: 45

Personnel Pool

Year company founded: 1946
Franchise fee or other initial payment: $20,000
Franchise royalty or other ongoing payment: 5 percent of sales
Advertising royalty or fee: None
Estimated initial investment required: $50,000
Total outlets: 200

Pet Valu

Year company founded: 1976
Franchise fee or other initial payment: $20,000
Franchise royalty or other ongoing payment: 6 percent of sales
Advertising royalty or fee: None
Estimated initial investment required: $70,000
Total outlets: 85

Petland

Year company founded: 1967
Franchise fee or other initial payment: None
Franchise royalty or other ongoing payment: 4 percent of sales
Advertising royalty or fee: ,5 percent of sales
Estimated initial investment required: $40,000
Total outlets: 162

Physicians Weight Loss

Year company founded: 1979
Franchise fee or other initial payment: $32,500
Franchise royalty or other ongoing payment: 10 percent of sales
Advertising royalty or fee: $1,000
Estimated initial investment required: $47,500
Total outlets: 350

Pinnacle 1

Year company founded: 1981
Franchise fee or other initial payment: $14,000
Franchise royalty or other ongoing payment: None
Advertising royalty or fee: None
Estimated initial investment required: $10,000
Total outlets: 40

Pioneer Take-Out

Year company founded: 1961
Franchise fee or other initial payment: $35,000
Franchise royalty or other ongoing payment: 5.9 percent of sales
Advertising royalty or fee: 3.9 percent of sales
Estimated initial investment required: $25,000
Total outlets: 226

PIP Printing

Year company founded: 1965
Franchise fee or other initial payment: $40,000
Franchise royalty or other ongoing payment: 6 percent of sales
Advertising royalty or fee: 2 percent of sales
Estimated initial investment required: $50,000
Total outlets: 1120

Pizza Delight

Year company founded: 1968
Franchise fee or other initial payment: $25,000
Franchise royalty or other ongoing payment: 6 percent of sales
Advertising royalty or fee: 3 percent of sales
Estimated initial investment required: $225,000
Total outlets: 190

Pizza Factory

Year company founded: 1982
Franchise fee or other initial payment: $20,000
Franchise royalty or other ongoing payment: 3 percent of sales
Advertising royalty or fee: 1 percent of sales
Estimated initial investment required: $55,000
Total outlets: 40

Pizza Hut

Year company founded: 1958
Franchise fee or other initial payment: $15,000
Franchise royalty or other ongoing payment: May vary
Advertising royalty or fee: May vary
Estimated initial investment required: May vary
Total outlets: 6000

Pizza Inn

Year company founded: 1960
Franchise fee or other initial payment: $17,500
Franchise royalty or other ongoing payment: 4 percent of sales
Advertising royalty or fee: 1.5 percent of sales
Estimated initial investment required: $150,000
Total outlets: 690

Pizza Man

Year company founded: 1971
Franchise fee or other initial payment: $25,000
Franchise royalty or other ongoing payment: 4 percent of sales
Advertising royalty or fee: 4 percent of sales
Estimated initial investment required: $75,000
Total outlets: 56

Pizza Movers

Year company founded: 1985
Franchise fee or other initial payment: $16,000
Franchise royalty or other ongoing payment: 8.5 percent of sales
Advertising royalty or fee: 3 percent of sales
Estimated initial investment required: $110,000
Total outlets: 70

Pizza Pizza

Year company founded: 1968
Franchise fee or other initial payment: $20,000
Franchise royalty or other ongoing payment: 6 percent of sales
Advertising royalty or fee: 6 percent of sales
Estimated initial investment required: $60,000
Total outlets: 160

Pizzeria Uno

Year company founded: 1943
Franchise fee or other initial payment: $15,000
Franchise royalty or other ongoing payment: 5 percent of sales
Advertising royalty or fee: 1 percent of sales
Estimated initial investment required: $250,000
Total outlets: 45

PKG's

Year company founded: 1983
Franchise fee or other initial payment: $13,500
Franchise royalty or other ongoing payment: 2 percent of sales
Advertising royalty or fee: 2 percent of sales
Estimated initial investment required: $12,000
Total outlets: 70

Playorena

Year company founded: 1981
Franchise fee or other initial payment: $7,000
Franchise royalty or other ongoing payment: 6 percent of sales
Advertising royalty or fee: None
Estimated initial investment required: $13,000
Total outlets: 63

Pofolks

Year company founded: 1975
Franchise fee or other initial payment: $37,000
Franchise royalty or other ongoing payment: 1.5 percent of sales
Advertising royalty or fee: May vary
Estimated initial investment required: $600,000
Total outlets: 150

Ponderosa Steakhouse

Year company founded: 1965
Franchise fee or other initial payment: $25,000
Franchise royalty or other ongoing payment: 4 percent of sales
Advertising royalty or fee: .4 percent of sales
Estimated initial investment required: $100,000
Total outlets: 700

Popeyes

Year company founded: 1972
Franchise fee or other initial payment: $25,000
Franchise royalty or other ongoing payment: 5 percent of sales
Advertising royalty or fee: 3 percent of sales
Estimated initial investment required: $250,000
Total outlets: 715

Port of Subs

Year company founded: 1975
Franchise fee or other initial payment: $13,500
Franchise royalty or other ongoing payment: 5.5 percent of sales
Advertising royalty or fee: 1 percent of sales
Estimated initial investment required: $75,000
Total outlets: 30

Precision Tune

Year company founded: 1975
Franchise fee or other initial payment: $15,000
Franchise royalty or other ongoing payment: 7.5 percent of sales
Advertising royalty or fee: 9 percent of sales
Estimated initial investment required: $86,000
Total outlets: 417

Print Masters

Year company founded: 1976
Franchise fee or other initial payment: $34,500
Franchise royalty or other ongoing payment: 4 percent of sales
Advertising royalty or fee: 2 percent of sales
Estimated initial investment required: $91,000
Total outlets: 80

Print Shack

Year company founded: 1982
Franchise fee or other initial payment: $17,500
Franchise royalty or other ongoing payment: 6 percent of sales
Advertising royalty or fee: None
Estimated initial investment required: $50,200
Total outlets: 116

Print Three

Year company founded: 1970
Franchise fee or other initial payment: $29,500
Franchise royalty or other ongoing payment: 6 percent of sales
Advertising royalty or fee: 3 percent of sales
Estimated initial investment required: $21.000
Total outlets: 125

Priority Management

Year company founded: 1984
Franchise fee or other initial payment: $27,500
Franchise royalty or other ongoing payment: 9 percent of sales
Advertising royalty or fee: 1 percent of sales
Estimated initial investment required: $10,000
Total outlets: 145

Pro IMage

Year company founded: 1985
Franchise fee or other initial payment: $16,500
Franchise royalty or other ongoing payment: 4 percent of sales
Advertising royalty or fee: 3 percent of sales
Estimated initial investment required: $68,500
Total outlets: 98

Pro-Cuts

Year company founded: 1982
Franchise fee or other initial payment: $25,000
Franchise royalty or other ongoing payment: 6 percent of sales
Advertising royalty or fee: 5 percent of sales
Estimated initial investment required: $60,000
Total outlets: 75

Professional Carpet

Year company founded: 1978
Franchise fee or other initial payment: $15,000
Franchise royalty or other ongoing payment: $100 per month
Advertising royalty or fee: None
Estimated initial investment required: $15,600
Total outlets: 180

ProForma

Year company founded: 1978
Franchise fee or other initial payment: $27,500
Franchise royalty or other ongoing payment: 7 percent of sales
Advertising royalty or fee: 1 percent of sales
Estimated initial investment required: $5,000
Total outlets: 80

Profusion Systems

Year company founded: 1980
Franchise fee or other initial payment: $20,500
Franchise royalty or other ongoing payment: 6 percent of sales
Advertising royalty or fee: None
Estimated initial investment required: $10,500
Total outlets: 120

proVenture

Year company founded: 1981
Franchise fee or other initial payment: $18,000
Franchise royalty or other ongoing payment: 6 percent of sales
Advertising royalty or fee: None
Estimated initial investment required: $30,000
Total outlets: 10

Putt Putt Golf

Year company founded: 1954
Franchise fee or other initial payment: $15,000
Franchise royalty or other ongoing payment: 3 percent of sales
Advertising royalty or fee: 2 percent of sales
Estimated initial investment required: $58,000
Total outlets: 325

Quaker State Minit-Lube

Year company founded: 1977
Franchise fee or other initial payment: $25,000
Franchise royalty or other ongoing payment: 5 percent of sales
Advertising royalty or fee: 10 percent of sales
Estimated initial investment required: $75,000
Total outlets: 300

Quality Inn/Comfort Inn

Year company founded: 1941
Franchise fee or other initial payment: $30,000
Franchise royalty or other ongoing payment: 3 percent of sales
Advertising royalty or fee: May vary
Estimated initial investment required: $76,000
Total outlets: 950

Rainbow International

Year company founded: 1981
Franchise fee or other initial payment: $15,000
Franchise royalty or other ongoing payment: 7 percent of sales
Advertising royalty or fee: None
Estimated initial investment required: $8,000
Total outlets: 1450

RainSoft

Year company founded: 1953
Franchise fee or other initial payment: $4,000
Franchise royalty or other ongoing payment: None
Advertising royalty or fee: None
Estimated initial investment required: $20,000
Total outlets: 305

Rally's

Year company founded: 1984
Franchise fee or other initial payment: $20,000
Franchise royalty or other ongoing payment: 4 percent of sales
Advertising royalty or fee: 4 percent of sales
Estimated initial investment required: $280,000
Total outlets: 80

Ramada Inn

Year company founded: 1954
Franchise fee or other initial payment: $25,000
Franchise royalty or other ongoing payment: 3 percent of sales
Advertising royalty or fee: 3.5 percent of sales
Estimated initial investment required: $3,000,000
Total outlets: 590

Rax Restaurants

Year company founded: 1978
Franchise fee or other initial payment: $25,000
Franchise royalty or other ongoing payment: 4 percent of sales
Advertising royalty or fee: 4 percent of sales
Estimated initial investment required: $500,000
Total outlets: 520

REMAX

Year company founded: 1973
Franchise fee or other initial payment: $10,000
Franchise royalty or other ongoing payment: May vary
Advertising royalty or fee: May vary
Estimated initial investment required: $2,800
Total outlets: 1400

Realty Executives

Year company founded: 1965
Franchise fee or other initial payment: $15,000
Franchise royalty or other ongoing payment: May vary
Advertising royalty or fee: None
Estimated initial investment required: $10,000
Total outlets: 70

Realty World

Year company founded: 1974
Franchise fee or other initial payment: $9,900
Franchise royalty or other ongoing payment: 3 percent of sales
Advertising royalty or fee: 2 percent of sales
Estimated initial investment required: $6,000
Total outlets: 1760

Recognition Express

Year company founded: 1972
Franchise fee or other initial payment: $23,500
Franchise royalty or other ongoing payment: 6 percent of sales
Advertising royalty or fee: 2 percent of sales
Estimated initial investment required: $45,000
Total outlets: 96

Red Carpet/Scottish Inns

Year company founded: 1972
Franchise fee or other initial payment: $25,000
Franchise royalty or other ongoing payment: 2 percent of sales
Advertising royalty or fee: .5 percent of sales
Estimated initial investment required: $275,000
Total outlets: 250

Red Carpet Real Estate

Year company founded: 1966
Franchise fee or other initial payment: $9,500
Franchise royalty or other ongoing payment: 8 percent of sales
Advertising royalty or fee: None
Estimated initial investment required: $8,800
Total outlets: 460

Red Robin Burger

Year company founded: 1976
Franchise fee or other initial payment: $25,000
Franchise royalty or other ongoing payment: 4,5 percent of sales
Advertising royalty or fee: 2.5 percent of sales
Estimated initial investment required: $500,000
Total outlets: 48

Rent a Wreck

Year company founded: 1970
Franchise fee or other initial payment: $3,000
Franchise royalty or other ongoing payment: 5 percent of sales
Advertising royalty or fee: 1.5 percent of sales
Estimated initial investment required: $30,000
Total outlets: 355

Rent-a-Dent

Year company founded: 1976
Franchise fee or other initial payment: $3,500
Franchise royalty or other ongoing payment: 7 percent of sales
Advertising royalty or fee: 2 percent of sales
Estimated initial investment required: $10,000
Total outlets: 100

Residence Inn

Year company founded: 1975
Franchise fee or other initial payment: May vary
Franchise royalty or other ongoing payment: 4 percent of sales
Advertising royalty or fee: 2.5 percent of sales
Estimated initial investment required: $5,000,000
Total outlets: 90

Ritzy's

Year company founded: 1980
Franchise fee or other initial payment: $17,000
Franchise royalty or other ongoing payment: 3.5 percent of sales
Advertising royalty or fee: None
Estimated initial investment required: $200,000
Total outlets: 75

Robin's Donuts

Year company founded: 1975
Franchise fee or other initial payment: $35,000
Franchise royalty or other ongoing payment: 4 percent of sales
Advertising royalty or fee: 3 percent of sales
Estimated initial investment required: $150,000
Total outlets: 124

Rocky Mountain Chocolate Factory

Year company founded: 1981
Franchise fee or other initial payment: $20,000
Franchise royalty or other ongoing payment: 5 percent of sales
Advertising royalty or fee: 1 percent of sales
Estimated initial investment required: $39,000
Total outlets: 60

Rodeway Inns

Year company founded: 1961
Franchise fee or other initial payment: $15,000
Franchise royalty or other ongoing payment: 3 percent of sales
Advertising royalty or fee: 1 percent of sales
Estimated initial investment required: May vary
Total outlets: 160

Romac

Year company founded: 1966
Franchise fee or other initial payment: $40,000
Franchise royalty or other ongoing payment: 8 percent of sales
Advertising royalty or fee: 1 percent of sales
Estimated initial investment required: $40,000
Total outlets: 40

Roth Young Personnel

Year company founded: 1962
Franchise fee or other initial payment: $50,000
Franchise royalty or other ongoing payment: 8 percent of sales
Advertising royalty or fee: 2 percent of sales
Estimated initial investment required: $92,700
Total outlets: 31

Roto Rooter

Year company founded: 1935
Franchise fee or other initial payment: $500
Franchise royalty or other ongoing payment: May vary
Advertising royalty or fee: None
Estimated initial investment required: $10,000
Total outlets: 750

Roto-Static International

Year company founded: 1977
Franchise fee or other initial payment: $5,000
Franchise royalty or other ongoing payment: 5 percent of sales
Advertising royalty or fee: None
Estimated initial investment required: $11,500
Total outlets: 100

Round Table Pizza

Year company founded: 1959
Franchise fee or other initial payment: $25,000
Franchise royalty or other ongoing payment: 4 percent of sales
Advertising royalty or fee: 3 percent of sales
Estimated initial investment required: $235,000
Total outlets: 550

Roy Rogers Restaurants

Year company founded: 1968
Franchise fee or other initial payment: $25,000
Franchise royalty or other ongoing payment: 4 percent of sales
Advertising royalty or fee: 4 percent of sales
Estimated initial investment required: $500,000
Total outlets: 570

Runza Drive-Inns

Year company founded: 1960
Franchise fee or other initial payment: $17,000
Franchise royalty or other ongoing payment: 5 percent of sales
Advertising royalty or fee: 1 percent of sales
Estimated initial investment required: May vary
Total outlets: 50

Sales Consultants

Year company founded: 1957
Franchise fee or other initial payment: $20,000
Franchise royalty or other ongoing payment: 5 percent of sales
Advertising royalty or fee: .5 percent of sales
Estimated initial investment required: $15,000
Total outlets: 133

Sandler Systems

Year company founded: 1983
Franchise fee or other initial payment: $20,000
Franchise royalty or other ongoing payment: $750
Advertising royalty or fee: None
Estimated initial investment required: $3,000
Total outlets: 60

Sandwich Tree, The

Year company founded: 1977
Franchise fee or other initial payment: $25,000
Franchise royalty or other ongoing payment: 4.5 percent of sales
Advertising royalty or fee: 3 percent of sales
Estimated initial investment required: $125,000
Total outlets: 70

Sanford Rose Associates

Year company founded: 1959
Franchise fee or other initial payment: $29,500
Franchise royalty or other ongoing payment: 3 percent of sales
Advertising royalty or fee: None
Estimated initial investment required: $15,000
Total outlets: 85

Saucy's Pizza

Year company founded: 1982
Franchise fee or other initial payment: $16,000
Franchise royalty or other ongoing payment: 5 percent of sales
Advertising royalty or fee: $300 per month
Estimated initial investment required: $30,000
Total outlets: 77

Sbarro

Year company founded: 1977
Franchise fee or other initial payment: $35,000
Franchise royalty or other ongoing payment: 5 percent of sales
Advertising royalty or fee: 1 percent of sales
Estimated initial investment required: $350,000
Total outlets: 275

Scandia Down Shops

Year company founded: 1970
Franchise fee or other initial payment: $25,000
Franchise royalty or other ongoing payment: 5 percent of sales
Advertising royalty or fee: 3 percent of sales
Estimated initial investment required: $120,000
Total outlets: 80

Schlotzsky's

Year company founded: 1971
Franchise fee or other initial payment: $15,000
Franchise royalty or other ongoing payment: 4 percent of sales
Advertising royalty or fee: 1 percent of sales
Estimated initial investment required: $90,000
Total outlets: 222

Seafood America

Year company founded: 1976
Franchise fee or other initial payment: $10,000
Franchise royalty or other ongoing payment: 2 percent of sales
Advertising royalty or fee: $300 per month
Estimated initial investment required: $105,000
Total outlets: 30

Second Cup

Year company founded: 1975
Franchise fee or other initial payment: $15,000
Franchise royalty or other ongoing payment: 9 percent of sales
Advertising royalty or fee: 2 percent of sales
Estimated initial investment required: $160,000
Total outlets: 132

Second Sole

Year company founded: 1976
Franchise fee or other initial payment: $15,000
Franchise royalty or other ongoing payment: 5 percent of sales
Advertising royalty or fee: .5 percent of sales
Estimated initial investment required: $100,000
Total outlets: 60

Service America

Year company founded: 1965
Franchise fee or other initial payment: $15,000
Franchise royalty or other ongoing payment: May vary
Advertising royalty or fee: 3 percent of sales
Estimated initial investment required: May vary
Total outlets: 86

ServiceMaster

Year company founded: 1947
Franchise fee or other initial payment: $6,000
Franchise royalty or other ongoing payment: 10 percent of sales
Advertising royalty or fee: None
Estimated initial investment required: $8,700
Total outlets: 3875

ServPro

Year company founded: 1967
Franchise fee or other initial payment: $17,800
Franchise royalty or other ongoing payment: 3 percent of sales
Advertising royalty or fee: None
Estimated initial investment required: $15,000
Total outlets: 650

7-Eleven Stores

Year company founded: 1927
Franchise fee or other initial payment: May vary
Franchise royalty or other ongoing payment: May vary
Advertising royalty or fee: None
Estimated initial investment required: $42,500
Total outlets: 12000

Shakey's Pizza

Year company founded: 1954
Franchise fee or other initial payment: $20,000
Franchise royalty or other ongoing payment: 4.5 percent of sales
Advertising royalty or fee: 4.5 percent of sales
Estimated initial investment required: $300,000
Total outlets: 360

Shefield & Sons

Year company founded: 1976
Franchise fee or other initial payment: $10,000
Franchise royalty or other ongoing payment: 2 percent of sales
Advertising royalty or fee: None
Estimated initial investment required: $70,000
Total outlets: 60

Sheraton Inns

Year company founded: 1937
Franchise fee or other initial payment: $30,000
Franchise royalty or other ongoing payment: 5 percent of sales
Advertising royalty or fee: None
Estimated initial investment required: May vary
Total outlets: 500

Shine Factory

Year company founded: 1979
Franchise fee or other initial payment: $10,000
Franchise royalty or other ongoing payment: 8 percent of sales
Advertising royalty or fee: 5 percent of sales
Estimated initial investment required: $40,000
Total outlets: 24

Shoney's

Year company founded: 1959
Franchise fee or other initial payment: $25,000
Franchise royalty or other ongoing payment: 3 percent of sales
Advertising royalty or fee: 4 percent of sales
Estimated initial investment required: $60,000
Total outlets: 625

Showbiz Pizza Time

Year company founded: 1980
Franchise fee or other initial payment: $25,000
Franchise royalty or other ongoing payment: 3 percent of sales
Advertising royalty or fee: 3.3 percent of sales
Estimated initial investment required: $750,000
Total outlets: 265

Silk Plants, Etc.

Year company founded: 1985
Franchise fee or other initial payment: $25,000
Franchise royalty or other ongoing payment: 6 percent of sales
Advertising royalty or fee: 1 percent of sales
Estimated initial investment required: $45,000
Total outlets: 160

Sir Goony

Year company founded: 1960
Franchise fee or other initial payment: None
Franchise royalty or other ongoing payment: None
Advertising royalty or fee: None
Estimated initial investment required: $36,800
Total outlets: 45

Sir Speedy Printing

Year company founded: 1968
Franchise fee or other initial payment: $17,500
Franchise royalty or other ongoing payment: 6 percent of sales
Advertising royalty or fee: 2 percent of sales
Estimated initial investment required: $45,000
Total outlets: 830

Sizzler

Year company founded: 1959
Franchise fee or other initial payment: $30,000
Franchise royalty or other ongoing payment: 4.5 percent of sales
Advertising royalty or fee: 4.5 percent of sales
Estimated initial investment required: $256,000
Total outlets: 600

Skipper's

Year company founded: 1969
Franchise fee or other initial payment: 10,000
Franchise royalty or other ongoing payment: 5 percent of sales
Advertising royalty or fee: 4 percent of sales
Estimated initial investment required: $75,000
Total outlets: 215

Skyline Chili

Year company founded: 1949
Franchise fee or other initial payment: $15,000
Franchise royalty or other ongoing payment: 4 percent of sales
Advertising royalty or fee: 2 percent of sales
Estimated initial investment required: $80,000
Total outlets: 78

Slumberland

Year company founded: 1967
Franchise fee or other initial payment: $10,000
Franchise royalty or other ongoing payment: 3 percent of sales
Advertising royalty or fee: None
Estimated initial investment required: $84,000
Total outlets: 21

Snelling & Snelling

Year company founded: 1951
Franchise fee or other initial payment: $14,000
Franchise royalty or other ongoing payment: 7 percent of sales
Advertising royalty or fee: 1 percent of sales
Estimated initial investment required: $30,000
Total outlets: 500

Snelling Temporary

Year company founded: 1951
Franchise fee or other initial payment: $10,000
Franchise royalty or other ongoing payment: 4.5 percent of sales
Advertising royalty or fee: .5 percent of sales
Estimated initial investment required: $65,000
Total outlets: 75

Soap Opera Washateria

Year company founded: 1984
Franchise fee or other initial payment: $20,000
Franchise royalty or other ongoing payment: $580 per month
Advertising royalty or fee: $180 per month
Estimated initial investment required: $26,450
Total outlets: 25

Softwaire Center

Year company founded: 1981
Franchise fee or other initial payment: $25,000
Franchise royalty or other ongoing payment: 2.5 percent of sales
Advertising royalty or fee: 1 percent of sales
Estimated initial investment required: $235,000
Total outlets: 40

Software City

Year company founded: 1980
Franchise fee or other initial payment: $12,500
Franchise royalty or other ongoing payment: 5 percent of sales
Advertising royalty or fee: 1.5 percent of sales
Estimated initial investment required: $82,000
Total outlets: 90

Sonic Drive-Ins

Year company founded: 1954
Franchise fee or other initial payment: $15,000
Franchise royalty or other ongoing payment: 3 percent of sales
Advertising royalty or fee: 3 percent of sales
Estimated initial investment required: $70,000
Total outlets: 1100

Sirloin Stockade

Year company founded: 1964
Franchise fee or other initial payment: $15,000
Franchise royalty or other ongoing payment: 3 percent of sales
Advertising royalty or fee: 1 percent of sales
Estimated initial investment required: $600,000
Total outlets: 70

60 Minute Tune

Year company founded: 1979
Franchise fee or other initial payment: $25,000
Franchise royalty or other ongoing payment: 6 percent of sales
Advertising royalty or fee: 6 percent of sales
Estimated initial investment required: $65,000
Total outlets: 50

Sonitrol

Year company founded: 1964
Franchise fee or other initial payment: $20,000
Franchise royalty or other ongoing payment: 2.5 percent of sales
Advertising royalty or fee: None
Estimated initial investment required: $100,000
Total outlets: 170

Sonny's Real Pit BarBQ

Year company founded: 1968
Franchise fee or other initial payment: $25,000
Franchise royalty or other ongoing payment: 2.5 percent of sales
Advertising royalty or fee: 1 percent of sales
Estimated initial investment required: $125,000
Total outlets: 75

Sparkle Wash

Year company founded: 1965
Franchise fee or other initial payment: $7,500
Franchise royalty or other ongoing payment: 5 percent of sales
Advertising royalty or fee: None
Estimated initial investment required: $12,500
Total outlets: 176

Sparks Tune-Up

Year company founded: 1972
Franchise fee or other initial payment: $25,000
Franchise royalty or other ongoing payment: 6 percent of sales
Advertising royalty or fee: $1,920
Estimated initial investment required: $100,000
Total outlets: 160

Sparky Coin-Op

Year company founded: 1948
Franchise fee or other initial payment: None
Franchise royalty or other ongoing payment: None
Advertising royalty or fee: None
Estimated initial investment required: $42,900
Total outlets: 270

Speedy Muffler King

Year company founded: 1956
Franchise fee or other initial payment: $18,500
Franchise royalty or other ongoing payment: 5 percent of sales
Advertising royalty or fee: 5 percent of sales
Estimated initial investment required: $135,000
Total outlets: 560

Speedy Transmission

Year company founded: 1983
Franchise fee or other initial payment: $15,000
Franchise royalty or other ongoing payment: 7 percent of sales
Advertising royalty or fee: 3 percent of sales
Estimated initial investment required: $45,000
Total outlets: 23

Sport Shack

Year company founded: 1974
Franchise fee or other initial payment: $17,500
Franchise royalty or other ongoing payment: 4 percent of sales
Advertising royalty or fee: 2 percent of sales
Estimated initial investment required: $120,000
Total outlets: 40

Sport-About

Year company founded: 1978
Franchise fee or other initial payment: $22,500
Franchise royalty or other ongoing payment: 4 percent of sales
Advertising royalty or fee: 1.5 percent of sales
Estimated initial investment required: $130,000
Total outlets: 61

Sports Fantasy

Year company founded: 1986
Franchise fee or other initial payment: $15,000
Franchise royalty or other ongoing payment: 5 percent of sales
Advertising royalty or fee: None
Estimated initial investment required: $90,000
Total outlets: 25

Spotless Office Systems

Year company founded: 1970
Franchise fee or other initial payment: $3,000
Franchise royalty or other ongoing payment: 5 percent of sales
Advertising royalty or fee: None
Estimated initial investment required: $3,000
Total outlets: 118

Spring Crest Drapery

Year company founded: 1955
Franchise fee or other initial payment: $12,500
Franchise royalty or other ongoing payment: 3 percent of sales
Advertising royalty or fee: 2 percent of sales
Estimated initial investment required: $35,000
Total outlets: 315

Spring-Green

Year company founded: 1977
Franchise fee or other initial payment: $12,900
Franchise royalty or other ongoing payment: 6 percent of sales
Advertising royalty or fee: 2 percent of sales
Estimated initial investment required: $15,000
Total outlets: 140

St. Clair Paint

Year company founded: 1939
Franchise fee or other initial payment: $20,000
Franchise royalty or other ongoing payment: None
Advertising royalty or fee: None
Estimated initial investment required: $150,000
Total outlets: 175

St. Hubert Bar-B-Q

Year company founded: 1936
Franchise fee or other initial payment: $25,000
Franchise royalty or other ongoing payment: 3 percent of sales
Advertising royalty or fee: 3 percent of sales
Estimated initial investment required: $450,000
Total outlets: 850

Staff Builders

Year company founded: 1961
Franchise fee or other initial payment: $39,500
Franchise royalty or other ongoing payment: May vary
Advertising royalty or fee: None
Estimated initial investment required: $100,000
Total outlets: 132

Stained Glass Overlay

Year company founded: 1974
Franchise fee or other initial payment: $34,000
Franchise royalty or other ongoing payment: 5 percent of sales
Advertising royalty or fee: 2 percent of sales
Estimated initial investment required: $30,000
Total outlets: 325

Stanley Steemer

Year company founded: 1947
Franchise fee or other initial payment: $20,000
Franchise royalty or other ongoing payment: 7 percent of sales
Advertising royalty or fee: None
Estimated initial investment required: $34,000
Total outlets: 225

Steak Escape

Year company founded: 1982
Franchise fee or other initial payment: $27,000
Franchise royalty or other ongoing payment: 8 percent of sales
Advertising royalty or fee: None
Estimated initial investment required: $133,000
Total outlets: 40

Steamatic

Year company founded: 1948
Franchise fee or other initial payment: $13,000
Franchise royalty or other ongoing payment: 3 percent of sales
Advertising royalty or fee: None
Estimated initial investment required: $21,000
Total outlets: 240

Sterling Optical

Year company founded: 1912
Franchise fee or other initial payment: $15,000
Franchise royalty or other ongoing payment: 8 percent of sales
Advertising royalty or fee: 6 percent of sales
Estimated initial investment required: $200,000
Total outlets: 235

Steve's Ice Cream

Year company founded: 1980
Franchise fee or other initial payment: $25,000
Franchise royalty or other ongoing payment: 6 percent of sales
Advertising royalty or fee: 1.5 percent of sales
Estimated initial investment required: $100,000
Total outlets: 52

Sub Station II

Year company founded: 1975
Franchise fee or other initial payment: $10,500
Franchise royalty or other ongoing payment: 3.5 percent of sales
Advertising royalty or fee: 2 percent of sales
Estimated initial investment required: $55,000
Total outlets: 125

SUBWAY

Year company founded: 1965
Franchise fee or other initial payment: $7,500
Franchise royalty or other ongoing payment: 8 percent of sales
Advertising royalty or fee: 2.5 percent of sales
Estimated initial investment required: $27,400
Total outlets: 2400

Suddenly Slender

Year company founded: 1969
Franchise fee or other initial payment: $20,000
Franchise royalty or other ongoing payment: May vary
Advertising royalty or fee: 1 percent of sales
Estimated initial investment required: $38,100
Total outlets: 280

Sunshine Polishing

Year company founded: 1983
Franchise fee or other initial payment: $975
Franchise royalty or other ongoing payment: None
Advertising royalty or fee: None
Estimated initial investment required: $2,800
Total outlets: 335

Super 8 Motels

Year company founded: 1972
Franchise fee or other initial payment: $20,000
Franchise royalty or other ongoing payment: 4 percent of sales
Advertising royalty or fee: 2 percent of sales
Estimated initial investment required: $150,000
Total outlets: 430

SuperCuts

Year company founded: 1975
Franchise fee or other initial payment: $25,000
Franchise royalty or other ongoing payment: 10 percent of sales
Advertising royalty or fee: 5 percent of sales
Estimated initial investment required: $55,000
Total outlets: 510

Swensen's Ice Cream

Year company founded: 1948
Franchise fee or other initial payment: $20,000
Franchise royalty or other ongoing payment: 6 percent of sales
Advertising royalty or fee: 1 percent of sales
Estimated initial investment required: $100,000
Total outlets: 50

Swiss Colony Stores

Year company founded: 1926
Franchise fee or other initial payment: $5,000
Franchise royalty or other ongoing payment: 4 percent of sales
Advertising royalty or fee: None
Estimated initial investment required: $100,000
Total outlets: 100

Sylvan Learning Center

Year company founded: 1979
Franchise fee or other initial payment: $35,000
Franchise royalty or other ongoing payment: 8 percent of sales
Advertising royalty or fee: 1.5 percent of sales
Estimated initial investment required: $52,500
Total outlets: 460

T-Shirts Plus

Year company founded: 1975
Franchise fee or other initial payment: $30,000
Franchise royalty or other ongoing payment: 6 percent of sales
Advertising royalty or fee: 1 percent of sales
Estimated initial investment required: $80,000
Total outlets: 176

T.J. Cinnamons

Year company founded: 1985
Franchise fee or other initial payment: $25,000
Franchise royalty or other ongoing payment: 5 percent of sales
Advertising royalty or fee: 2 percent of sales
Estimated initial investment required: $125,000
Total outlets: 220

Taco Bell

Year company founded: 1962
Franchise fee or other initial payment: $35,000
Franchise royalty or other ongoing payment: 5.5 percent of sales
Advertising royalty or fee: 4.5 percent of sales
Estimated initial investment required: $100,000
Total outlets: 2760

Taco John's

Year company founded: 1969
Franchise fee or other initial payment: $16,500
Franchise royalty or other ongoing payment: 4 percent of sales
Advertising royalty or fee: 2 percent of sales
Estimated initial investment required: $70,000
Total outlets: 440

Taco Villa

Year company founded: 1965
Franchise fee or other initial payment: $20,000
Franchise royalty or other ongoing payment: 5 percent of sales
Advertising royalty or fee: 5 percent of sales
Estimated initial investment required: $100,000
Total outlets: 150

TacoTime

Year company founded: 1959
Franchise fee or other initial payment: $18,000
Franchise royalty or other ongoing payment: 5 percent of sales
Advertising royalty or fee: .5 percent of sales
Estimated initial investment required: $125,000
Total outlets: 275

Tastee Freez

Year company founded: 1950
Franchise fee or other initial payment: $10,000
Franchise royalty or other ongoing payment: 4 percent of sales
Advertising royalty or fee: 1 percent of sales
Estimated initial investment required: $140,000
Total outlets: 500

Taylor Rental

Year company founded: 1945
Franchise fee or other initial payment: $20,000
Franchise royalty or other ongoing payment: 2.75 percent of
    sales
Advertising royalty or fee: None
Estimated initial investment required: $250,000
Total outlets: 360

TCBY

Year company founded: 1981
Franchise fee or other initial payment: $20,000
Franchise royalty or other ongoing payment: 4 percent of sales
Advertising royalty or fee: 3 percent of sales
Estimated initial investment required: $72,000
Total outlets: 1075

Temp Force

Year company founded: 1959
Franchise fee or other initial payment: None
Franchise royalty or other ongoing payment: May vary
Advertising royalty or fee: None
Estimated initial investment required: $75,000
Total outlets: 74

Temps & Co.

Year company founded: 1968
Franchise fee or other initial payment: $12,500
Franchise royalty or other ongoing payment: May vary
Advertising royalty or fee: May vary
Estimated initial investment required: $57,940
Total outlets: 16

Tender Sender

Year company founded: 1982
Franchise fee or other initial payment: $20,000
Franchise royalty or other ongoing payment: 6 percent of sales
Advertising royalty or fee: 2 percent of sales
Estimated initial investment required: $50,000
Total outlets: 90

Texas State Optical

Year company founded: 1935
Franchise fee or other initial payment: $11,000
Franchise royalty or other ongoing payment: 8.5 percent of sales
Advertising royalty or fee: 8 percent of sales
Estimated initial investment required: May vary
Total outlets: 170

TGI Friday's

Year company founded: 1965
Franchise fee or other initial payment: $50,000
Franchise royalty or other ongoing payment: 4 percent of sales
Advertising royalty or fee: 4 percent of sales
Estimated initial investment required: $2,000,000
Total outlets: 130

That Muffler & Brake Place

Year company founded: 1987
Franchise fee or other initial payment: $4,900
Franchise royalty or other ongoing payment: $500
Advertising royalty or fee: $500
Estimated initial investment required: $25,000
Total outlets: 10

Three Star Muffler

Year company founded: 1977
Franchise fee or other initial payment: $15,000
Franchise royalty or other ongoing payment: 7 percent of sales
Advertising royalty or fee: 2 percent of sales
Estimated initial investment required: $53,000
Total outlets: 10

Thrifty Rent-a-Car

Year company founded: 1962
Franchise fee or other initial payment: $10,000
Franchise royalty or other ongoing payment: 3 percent of sales
Advertising royalty or fee: 5 percent of sales
Estimated initial investment required: $20,000
Total outlets: 668

Tidy Car

Year company founded: 1976
Franchise fee or other initial payment: $12,500
Franchise royalty or other ongoing payment: 9 percent of sales
Advertising royalty or fee: 3 percent of sales
Estimated initial investment required: $35,000
Total outlets: 300

Tim Horton Donuts

Year company founded: 1964
Franchise fee or other initial payment: $15,000
Franchise royalty or other ongoing payment: 3 percent of sales
Advertising royalty or fee: 3 percent of sales
Estimated initial investment required: $195,000
Total outlets: 370

Tinder Box, The

Year company founded: 1928
Franchise fee or other initial payment: $24,000
Franchise royalty or other ongoing payment: 4 percent of sales
Advertising royalty or fee: 3 percent of sales
Estimated initial investment required: $90,000
Total outlets: 186

TKD

Year company founded: 1964
Franchise fee or other initial payment: $11,000
Franchise royalty or other ongoing payment: 8 percent of sales
Advertising royalty or fee: 1.4 percent of sales
Estimated initial investment required: $34,000
Total outlets: 130

Togo's Eatery

Year company founded: 1972
Franchise fee or other initial payment: $10,000
Franchise royalty or other ongoing payment: 5 percent of sales
Advertising royalty or fee: 2
Estimated initial investment required: $100,000
Total outlets: 120

Tony Roma's

Year company founded: 1972
Franchise fee or other initial payment: $50,000
Franchise royalty or other ongoing payment: 4 percent of sales
Advertising royalty or fee: 1 percent of sales
Estimated initial investment required: $600,000
Total outlets: 102

Tool Shack

Year company founded: 1978
Franchise fee or other initial payment: $30,000
Franchise royalty or other ongoing payment: 3 percent of sales
Advertising royalty or fee: 3 percent of sales
Estimated initial investment required: $65,000
Total outlets: 40

Travel Agents International

Year company founded: 1980
Franchise fee or other initial payment: $29,500
Franchise royalty or other ongoing payment: $585 per month
Advertising royalty or fee: May vary
Estimated initial investment required: $10,000
Total outlets: 330

Travel Network

Year company founded: 1982
Franchise fee or other initial payment: $27,500
Franchise royalty or other ongoing payment: May vary
Advertising royalty or fee: $200 per month
Estimated initial investment required: $50,000
Total outlets: 75

Travel Travel

Year company founded: 1978
Franchise fee or other initial payment: $10,000
Franchise royalty or other ongoing payment: May vary
Advertising royalty or fee: May vary
Estimated initial investment required: $45,000
Total outlets: 240

Travelodge

Year company founded: 1947
Franchise fee or other initial payment: $15,000
Franchise royalty or other ongoing payment: 3 percent of sales
Advertising royalty or fee: 4 percent of sales
Estimated initial investment required: $500,000
Total outlets: 470

TRC Temporary

Year company founded: 1980
Franchise fee or other initial payment: May vary
Franchise royalty or other ongoing payment: May vary
Advertising royalty or fee: None
Estimated initial investment required: $75,000
Total outlets: 40

Treadway Inns

Year company founded: 1912
Franchise fee or other initial payment: May vary
Franchise royalty or other ongoing payment: None
Advertising royalty or fee: None
Estimated initial investment required: May vary
Total outlets: 100

Treats

Year company founded: 1977
Franchise fee or other initial payment: $25,000
Franchise royalty or other ongoing payment: 8 percent of sales
Advertising royalty or fee: 2 percent of sales
Estimated initial investment required: $55,000
Total outlets: 125

Trendy Tidy's

Year company founded: 1978
Franchise fee or other initial payment: $15,000
Franchise royalty or other ongoing payment: 6 percent of sales
Advertising royalty or fee: 2 percent of sales
Estimated initial investment required: $10,000
Total outlets: 50

TriMark

Year company founded: 1969
Franchise fee or other initial payment: $24,900
Franchise royalty or other ongoing payment: None
Advertising royalty or fee: None
Estimated initial investment required: $5,000
Total outlets: 105

Triple Check

Year company founded: 1968
Franchise fee or other initial payment: None
Franchise royalty or other ongoing payment: May vary
Advertising royalty or fee: None
Estimated initial investment required: $500
Total outlets: 250

Tuff-Kote Dinol

Year company founded: 1964
Franchise fee or other initial payment: $4,000
Franchise royalty or other ongoing payment: 8 percent of sales
Advertising royalty or fee: 1 percent of sales
Estimated initial investment required: $43,000
Total outlets: 131

Tuffy Service Center

Year company founded: 1970
Franchise fee or other initial payment: $18,500
Franchise royalty or other ongoing payment: 5 percent of sales
Advertising royalty or fee: 5 percent of sales
Estimated initial investment required: $70,000
Total outlets: 114

TV Focus

Year company founded: 1979
Franchise fee or other initial payment: $1,800
Franchise royalty or other ongoing payment: May vary
Advertising royalty or fee: None
Estimated initial investment required: $5,000
Total outlets: 215

TV Tempo

Year company founded: 1974
Franchise fee or other initial payment: $30,000
Franchise royalty or other ongoing payment: $110
Advertising royalty or fee: None
Estimated initial investment required: $3,000
Total outlets: 85

Twistee Treat

Year company founded: 1983
Franchise fee or other initial payment: $8,000
Franchise royalty or other ongoing payment: 8 percent of sales
Advertising royalty or fee: 2.5 percent of sales
Estimated initial investment required: $50,000
Total outlets: 38

U&R Tax Service

Year company founded: 1972
Franchise fee or other initial payment: $4,500
Franchise royalty or other ongoing payment: 40 percent of sales
Advertising royalty or fee: None
Estimated initial investment required: $7,500
Total outlets: 100

UBI Business Brokers

Year company founded: 1969
Franchise fee or other initial payment: $27,500
Franchise royalty or other ongoing payment: 6 percent of sales
Advertising royalty or fee: 2 percent of sales
Estimated initial investment required: $50,000
Total outlets: 100

Ugly Duckling

Year company founded: 1977
Franchise fee or other initial payment: $6,000
Franchise royalty or other ongoing payment: 6 percent of sales
Advertising royalty or fee: 2 percent of sales
Estimated initial investment required: $50,000
Total outlets: 475

Ultra Wash

Year company founded: 1981
Franchise fee or other initial payment: $35,000
Franchise royalty or other ongoing payment: 8 percent of sales
Advertising royalty or fee: None
Estimated initial investment required: $10,000
Total outlets: 25

Uniclean

Year company founded: 1976
Franchise fee or other initial payment: $6,000
Franchise royalty or other ongoing payment: 5 percent of sales
Advertising royalty or fee: 2 percent of sales
Estimated initial investment required: $1,000
Total outlets: 90

Uniforce Temporary

Year company founded: 1961
Franchise fee or other initial payment: $15,000
Franchise royalty or other ongoing payment: May vary
Advertising royalty or fee: May vary
Estimated initial investment required: $50,000
Total outlets: 75

Uniglobe

Year company founded: 1979
Franchise fee or other initial payment: $42,500
Franchise royalty or other ongoing payment: .75 percent of sales
Advertising royalty or fee: $591 per month
Estimated initial investment required: $60,000
Total outlets: 580

United Chiropractic

Year company founded: 1983
Franchise fee or other initial payment: $3,500
Franchise royalty or other ongoing payment: $250 per month
Advertising royalty or fee: $300 per month
Estimated initial investment required: $250
Total outlets: 190

United Consumers Club

Year company founded: 1971
Franchise fee or other initial payment: $50,000
Franchise royalty or other ongoing payment: 22 percent of sales
Advertising royalty or fee: 5 percent of sales
Estimated initial investment required: $35,000
Total outlets: 70

USA Baby

Year company founded: 1975
Franchise fee or other initial payment: $7,500
Franchise royalty or other ongoing payment: 3 percent of sales
Advertising royalty or fee: .5 percent of sales
Estimated initial investment required: $185,000
Total outlets: 27

ValCom

Year company founded: 1983
Franchise fee or other initial payment: $30,000
Franchise royalty or other ongoing payment: 8 percent of sales
Advertising royalty or fee: 1 percent of sales
Estimated initial investment required: $250,000
Total outlets: 180

Via de France Bakery

Year company founded: 1978
Franchise fee or other initial payment: $20,000
Franchise royalty or other ongoing payment: 4 percent of sales
Advertising royalty or fee: 1 percent of sales
Estimated initial investment required: $571,500
Total outlets: 88

Video Biz

Year company founded: 1981
Franchise fee or other initial payment: $19,000
Franchise royalty or other ongoing payment: 2.5 percent of sales
Advertising royalty or fee: 2.5 percent of sales
Estimated initial investment required: $65,000
Total outlets: 170

Video Data

Year company founded: 1980
Franchise fee or other initial payment: $14,950.
Franchise royalty or other ongoing payment: $500 per year
Advertising royalty or fee: None
Estimated initial investment required: $2,000
Total outlets: 237

Video Galaxy

Year company founded: 1981
Franchise fee or other initial payment: $20,000
Franchise royalty or other ongoing payment: 5 percent of sales
Advertising royalty or fee: $100 per month
Estimated initial investment required: $161,000
Total outlets: 38

Village Inn

Year company founded: 1958
Franchise fee or other initial payment: $25,000
Franchise royalty or other ongoing payment: 5 percent of sales
Advertising royalty or fee: None
Estimated initial investment required: $55,000
Total outlets: 270

VR Business Brokers

Year company founded: 1979
Franchise fee or other initial payment: $35,000
Franchise royalty or other ongoing payment: 6 percent of sales
Advertising royalty or fee: 2 percent of sales
Estimated initial investment required: $50,000
Total outlets: 205

Wallpapers to Go

Year company founded: 1977
Franchise fee or other initial payment: $40,000
Franchise royalty or other ongoing payment: 8 percent of sales
Advertising royalty or fee: 5 percent of sales
Estimated initial investment required: $160,000
Total outlets: 100

Wash on Wheels

Year company founded: 1964
Franchise fee or other initial payment: $7,500
Franchise royalty or other ongoing payment: 3 percent of sales
Advertising royalty or fee: 1 percent of sales
Estimated initial investment required: $7,500
Total outlets: 120

Weed Man

Year company founded: 1970
Franchise fee or other initial payment: $30,000
Franchise royalty or other ongoing payment: May vary
Advertising royalty or fee: May vary
Estimated initial investment required: $7,500
Total outlets: 100

Wendy's

Year company founded: 1969
Franchise fee or other initial payment: $25,000
Franchise royalty or other ongoing payment: 4 percent of sales
Advertising royalty or fee: 4 percent of sales
Estimated initial investment required: $250,000
Total outlets: 3650

West Coast Video

Year company founded: 1983
Franchise fee or other initial payment: $32,500
Franchise royalty or other ongoing payment: 5 percent of sales
Advertising royalty or fee: 2 percent of sales
Estimated initial investment required: $130,000
Total outlets: 220

Western Auto

Year company founded: 1909
Franchise fee or other initial payment: None
Franchise royalty or other ongoing payment: None
Advertising royalty or fee: None
Estimated initial investment required: $150,000
Total outlets: 1800

Western Medical

Year company founded: 1948
Franchise fee or other initial payment: $4,000
Franchise royalty or other ongoing payment: May vary
Advertising royalty or fee: None
Estimated initial investment required: May vary
Total outlets: 66

Western Sizzlin

Year company founded: 1962
Franchise fee or other initial payment: $25,000
Franchise royalty or other ongoing payment: 3 percent of sales
Advertising royalty or fee: None
Estimated initial investment required: $75,000
Total outlets: 590

Western Temporary

Year company founded: 1948
Franchise fee or other initial payment: $4,000
Franchise royalty or other ongoing payment: May vary
Advertising royalty or fee: None
Estimated initial investment required: May vary
Total outlets: 330

Whataburger

Year company founded: 1950
Franchise fee or other initial payment: $15,000
Franchise royalty or other ongoing payment: 5 percent of sales
Advertising royalty or fee: None
Estimated initial investment required: $500,000
Total outlets: 405

White Hen Pantry

Year company founded: 1965
Franchise fee or other initial payment: $10,000
Franchise royalty or other ongoing payment: 13.5 percent of sales
Advertising royalty or fee: None
Estimated initial investment required: $35,300
Total outlets: 350

Wicks N Sticks

Year company founded: 1968
Franchise fee or other initial payment: $35,000
Franchise royalty or other ongoing payment: 6 percent of sales
Advertising royalty or fee: None
Estimated initial investment required: $145,000
Total outlets: 312

Wienerschnitzel

Year company founded: 1961
Franchise fee or other initial payment: $30,000
Franchise royalty or other ongoing payment: 5 percent of sales
Advertising royalty or fee: 4 percent of sales
Estimated initial investment required: $40,000
Total outlets: 276

Wild Birds Unlimited

Year company founded: 1981
Franchise fee or other initial payment: $5,000
Franchise royalty or other ongoing payment: 3 percent of sales
Advertising royalty or fee: None
Estimated initial investment required: $15,000
Total outlets: 30

Winchell's Donut House

Year company founded: 1948
Franchise fee or other initial payment: $30,000
Franchise royalty or other ongoing payment: 5 percent of sales
Advertising royalty or fee: 3 percent of sales
Estimated initial investment required: $150,000
Total outlets: 680

Window Man

Year company founded: 1983
Franchise fee or other initial payment: $30,000
Franchise royalty or other ongoing payment: 6 percent of sales
Advertising royalty or fee: 1 percent of sales
Estimated initial investment required: $30,000
Total outlets: 30

Window Works

Year company founded: 1978
Franchise fee or other initial payment: $17,500
Franchise royalty or other ongoing payment: 4 percent of sales
Advertising royalty or fee: 1 percent of sales
Estimated initial investment required: $25,000
Total outlets: 90

World Bazaar

Year company founded: 1965
Franchise fee or other initial payment: $15,000
Franchise royalty or other ongoing payment: 8 percent of sales
Advertising royalty or fee: None
Estimated initial investment required: $150,000
Total outlets: 300

Worldwide Refinishing

Year company founded: 1971
Franchise fee or other initial payment: $6,9550
Franchise royalty or other ongoing payment: 5 percent of sales
Advertising royalty or fee: None
Estimated initial investment required: $5,000
Total outlets: 48

WOW Inc.

Year company founded: 1966
Franchise fee or other initial payment: $2,500
Franchise royalty or other ongoing payment: 3 percent of sales
Advertising royalty or fee: 1 percent of sales
Estimated initial investment required: $9,490
Total outlets: 120

Yogi Bear Jellystone

Year company founded: 1969
Franchise fee or other initial payment: $15,000
Franchise royalty or other ongoing payment: 6 percent of sales
Advertising royalty or fee: 1 percent of sales
Estimated initial investment required: $100,000
Total outlets: 105

Zack's

Year company founded: 1977
Franchise fee or other initial payment: $20,000
Franchise royalty or other ongoing payment: 5 percent of sales
Advertising royalty or fee: 3 percent of sales
Estimated initial investment required: $85,400
Total outlets: 210

Ziebart

Year company founded: 1954
Franchise fee or other initial payment: $20,000
Franchise royalty or other ongoing payment: 8 percent of sales
Advertising royalty or fee: 5 percent of sales
Estimated initial investment required: $60,000
Total outlets: 575

Zippy Print

Year company founded: 1979
Franchise fee or other initial payment: $40,000
Franchise royalty or other ongoing payment: 5 percent of sales
Advertising royalty or fee: 5 percent of sales
Estimated initial investment required: $95,000
Total outlets: 80

Appendix B
Statistical Comparison

Abbreviations Used in Appendix B:

Init. Fee = Initial Fee

Rty. = Royalty

Adv. = Advertising

FRANCHISOR	OUTLETS
1. MCDONALD'S	13900
2. 7-ELEVEN STORES	12000
3. H&R BLOCK	8800
4. KENTUCKY FRIED CHICKEN	7700
5. CENTURY 21	7000
6. PIZZA HUT	6000
7. DAIRY QUEEN	5000
8. DOMINO'S PIZZA	4600
9. SERVICEMASTER	3875
10. JAZZERCISE	3800
11. WENDY'S INTERNATIONAL	3650
12. BUDGET RENT A CAR	3600
13. BASKIN-ROBBINS	3450
14. HARDEE'S	3000
15. ELECTRONIC REALTY ASSOCIATES	2840
16. TACO BELL	2760
17. SUBWAY	2400
18. DIET CENTER INC.	2330
19. MIDAS	2200
20. LITTLE CAESAR'S	2000
21. ARBY'S	2000
22. CHEM-DRY	1840
23. WESTERN AUTO	1800
24. REALTY WORLD	1760
25. DUNKIN' DONUTS	1735
26. HOLIDAY INN	1600
27. DOLLAR RENT A CAR	1600
28. GOODYEAR TIRE CENTERS	1570
29. CHURCH'S FRIED CHICKEN	1500
30. LONG JOHN SILVER'S	1500
31. AMERICAN INTERNATIONAL	1500
32. RAINBOW INTERNATIONAL	1450
33. RE/MAX	1400
34. NATIONAL VIDEO	1400
35. DENNY'S	1390
36. JANI-KING	1300
37. FANTASTIC SAM'S	1275
38. PIP PRINTING	1120
39. PACKY THE SHIPPER	1120
40. SONIC DRIVE-INS	1100
41. BEN FRANKLIN STORES	1100
42. TCBY	1075
43. ONE HOUR MARTINIZING	1000
44. NUTRI SYSTEM	1000
45. KWIK KOPY	1000
46. ALMOST HEAVEN HOT TUBS	975
47. COAST TO COAST STORES	965
48. QUALITY INN/COMFORT INN	950
49. JACK IN THE BOX	940
50. AAMCO TRANSMISSION	920

FRANCHISOR	OUTLETS
51. JIFFY LUBE	920
52. COVERALL	900
53. PEARLE VISION	860
54. ST. HUBERT BAR-B-Q	850
55. SIR SPEEDY PRINTING	830
56. MINUTEMAN PRESS	820
57. GODFATHER'S PIZZA	810
58. CULLIGAN WATER CONDITIONING	806
59. ADVENTURELAND	800
60. COMPUTERLAND	800
61. BECKER MILK CO.	784
62. BIG BOY RESTAURANTS	780
63. CARVEL	750
64. ROTO ROOTER	750
65. ORANGE JULIUS	745
66. MEDICINE SHOPPE	740
67. MEINEKE DISCOUNT MUFFLER	720
68. DECORATING DEN	720
69. POPEYES	715
70. PONDEROSA STEAKHOUSE	700
71. DAYS INN	700
72. PIZZA INN	690
73. NOVUS WINDSHIELD REPAIR	685
74. WINCHELL'S DONUT HOUSE	680
75. THRIFTY RENT-A-CAR	668
76. SERVPRO	650
77. KAMPGROUNDS OF AMERICA	640
78. SHONEY'S	625
79. DURACLEAN	615
80. BONANZA	610
81. MISTER DONUT	610
82. MR. BUILD	605
83. MAIL BOXES ETC. USA	600
84. GENERAL BUSINESS SERVICE	600
85. SIZZLER	600
86. RAMADA INN	590
87. WESTERN SIZZLIN	590
88. CAPTAIN D'S	590
89. UNIGLOBE	580
90. ZIEBART	575
91. ROY ROGERS RESTAURANTS	570
92. SPEEDY MUFFLER KING	560
93. ROUND TABLE PIZZA	550
94. AM/PM MINI-MARKETS	550
95. ICE CREAM CHURN	530
96. A&W RESTAURANTS	525
97. RAX RESTAURANTS	520
98. SUPERCUTS	510
99. AMERICAN SPEEDY PRINTING	508
100. SNELLING & SNELLING	500

FRANCHISOR	OUTLETS
101. SHERATON INNS	500
102. ATHLETE'S FOOT	500
103. TASTEE FREEZ	500
104. FASHION CROSSROADS	480
105. UGLY DUCKLING	475
106. TRAVELODGE	470
107. MERRY MAIDS	470
108. HEALTH MART	466
109. ADIA PERSONNEL	460
110. RED CARPET REAL ESTATE	460
111. SYLVAN LEARNING CENTER	460
112. CARL'S JR.	460
113. INTL. HOUSE OF PANCAKES	458
114. HOWARD JOHNSON	450
115. MIRACLE EAR	445
116. MAACO	440
117. TACO JOHN'S	440
118. ECONO LODGE	440
119. SUPER 8 MOTELS	430
120. PRECISION TUNE	417
121. PENNYSAVER	410
122. WHATABURGER	405
123. HAIRCRAFTERS	400
124. BOJANGLES	380
125. TIM HORTON DONUTS	370
126. TAYLOR RENTAL	360
127. INSTY PRINTS	360
128. SHAKEY'S PIZZA	360
129. RENT A WRECK	355
130. HELP U-SELL	353
131. GYMBOREE	350
132. WHITE HEN PANTRY	350
133. PHYSICIANS WEIGHT LOSS	350
134. HICKORY FARMS OF OHIO	340
135. COMPREHENSIVE ACCOUNTING	340
136. DUNHILL PERSONNEL	340
137. MR. GATTI'S	338
138. MOLLY MAID	336
139. SUNSHINE POLISHING	335
140. PERKINS FAMILY RESTAURANTS	330
141. MANAGEMENT RECRUITERS	330
142. TRAVEL AGENTS INTERNATIONAL	330
143. WESTERN TEMPORARY	330
144. STAINED GLASS OVERLAY	325
145. PUTT PUTT GOLF	325
146. INTERNATIONAL BLIMPIE	320
147. SPRING CREST DRAPERY	315
148. WICKS N STICKS	312
149. RAINSOFT	305
150. BRESLER'S	300

FRANCHISOR	OUTLETS
151. QUAKER STATE MINIT-LUBE	300
152. BIG O TIRES	300
153. WORLD BAZAAR	300
154. GREAT EXPECTATIONS	300
155. TIDY CAR	300
156. LAWN DOCTOR	290
157. HAIR PERFORMERS	290
158. COST CUTTERS	290
159. ABC SEAMLESS	280
160. DIP N STRIP	280
161. SUDDENLY SLENDER	280
162. LEE'S	280
163. WIENERSCHNITZEL	276
164. MOTO PHOTO	275
165. ARMSTRONG WORLD INDUSTRIES	275
166. MR. SUBMARINE	275
167. SBARRO	275
168. HILTON INN	275
169. TACOTIME	275
170. SPARKY COIN-OP	270
171. VILLAGE INN	270
172. DOCKTOR PET	270
173. COMMAND PERFORMANCE	267
174. MEDICAL PERSONNEL	265
175. SHOWBIZ PIZZA TIME	265
176. HOMES & LAND MAGAZINE	264
177. GALLERY OF HOMES	260
178. FRONTIER FRUIT & NUT	260
179. DECK THE WALLS	254
180. TRIPLE CHECK	250
181. RED CARPET/SCOTTISH INNS	250
182. FOUR SEASONS GREENHOUSE	250
183. DIPPER DAN	250
184. DRY CLEAN USA	245
185. NORELL TEMPORARY	240
186. TRAVEL TRAVEL	240
187. COUSTIC-GLO	240
188. STEAMATIC	240
189. COLOR-GLO	240
190. VIDEO DATA	237
191. GINGESS FORMALWEAR	235
192. DRAKE PERSONNEL	235
193. STERLING OPTICAL	235
194. ALLISON'S PLACE	230
195. ALPHAGRAPHICS	230
196. PIONEER TAKE-OUT	226
197. ARTHUR MURRAY	225
198. STANLEY STEEMER	225
199. NATIONAL MAINT. CONTR.	224
200. SCHLOTZSKY'S	222

FRANCHISOR	OUTLETS
201. NUVISION OPTICAL	220
202. WEST COAST VIDEO	220
203. T.J. CINNAMONS	220
204. SKIPPER'S	215
205. TV FOCUS	215
206. ZACK'S	210
207. MAZZIO'S PIZZA	210
208. GRANDY'S	205
209. VR BUSINESS BROKERS	205
210. MIGHTY DISTRIBUTING	200
211. MICROAGE	200
212. PERSONNEL POOL	200
213. DAVID'S COOKIES	200
214. CRUSTY'S PIZZA	200
215. BASKIN-ROBBINS/SILICORP	200
216. FOSTER'S FREEZE	200
217. GROUND ROUND, THE	200
218. DESCAMPS	195
219. ENTRE COMPUTER CENTERS	195
220. HANDLE WITH CARE	190
221. PAK MAIL	190
222. UNITED CHIROPRACTIC	190
223. PIZZA DELIGHT	190
224. AJAX RENT A CAR	190
225. MONEY MAILER	190
226. TINDER BOX, THE	186
227. EVERYTHING YOGURT	185
228. CUTLERY WORLD	185
229. PROFESSIONAL CARPET	180
230. HAMPTON INNS	180
231. VALCOM	180
232. NUTRA BOLIC	180
233. SPARKLE WASH	176
234. T-SHIRTS PLUS	176
235. ST. CLAIR PAINT	175
236. ATHLETIC ATTIC	175
237. I CAN'T BELIEVE/YOGURT	175
238. MR. STEAK	175
239. SONITROL	170
240. ACA JOE	170
241. PACER RACER	170
242. VIDEO BIZ	170
243. TEXAS STATE OPTICAL	170
244. MAIDS, THE	165
245. PETLAND	162
246. PIZZA PIZZA	160
247. GREAT CLIPS	160
248. FREEDOM RENT-A-CAR	160
249. SPARKS TUNE-UP	160
250. SILK PLANTS, ETC.	160

FRANCHISOR	OUTLETS
251. RODEWAY INNS	160
252. MARIE CALLENDER	160
253. JAPAN CAMERA	150
254. MR. PHILLY	150
255. TACO VILLA	150
256. MAJOR VIDEO	150
257. POFOLKS	150
258. DRUG EMPORIUM	150
259. COTTMAN TRANSMISSION	150
260. PRIORITY MANAGEMENT	145
261. MAGICUTS	145
262. MINI MAID	140
263. AFFORDABLE USED CAR	140
264. AFFORDABLE	140
265. SPRING-GREEN	140
266. MR. TRANSMISSION	140
267. PENGUIN'S PLACE	140
268. HASTY MARKETS	135
269. FRIENDSHIP INN	135
270. BATHCREST	135
271. SALES CONSULTANTS	133
272. SECOND CUP	132
273. STAFF BUILDERS	132
274. GREASE MONKEY	131
275. TUFF-KOTE DINOL	131
276. CHAMPION AUTO	130
277. PERMA CERAM	130
278. TKD	130
279. TGI FRIDAY'S	130
280. DIAL-A-GIFT	130
281. MARCOIN	130
282. LANGENWALTER DYE CONCEPT	130
283. AAA EMPLOYMENT	130
284. TREATS	125
285. EUROPEAN TANSPA	125
286. SUB STATION II	125
287. PRINT THREE	125
288. ROBIN'S DONUTS	124
289. TOGO'S EATERY	120
290. COMPUFUND NETWORK	120
291. CAR-X MUFFLER	120
292. LITTLE PROFESSOR	120
293. AIR BROOK LIMOUSINE	120
294. PROFUSION SYSTEMS	120
295. WASH ON WHEELS	120
296. WOW INC.	120
297. PAUL DAVIS SYSTEMS	120
298. SPOTLESS OFFICE SYSTEMS	118
299. PRINT SHACK	116
300. PAYLESS CAR RENTAL	116

FRANCHISOR	OUTLETS
301. AMERICAN ADVERTISING DISTRIBUTORS	115
302. FOX'S PIZZA DEN	115
303. ECONO LUBE N TUNE	115
304. TUFFY SERVICE CENTER	114
305. CROSSLAND FURNITURE RESTORATION	110
306. ALOETTE COSMETICS	108
307. MIRACLE METHOD	107
308. FUDDRUCKERS	106
309. EXPRESS SERVICES	105
310. TRIMARK	105
311. YOGI BEAR JELLYSTONE	105
312. MINUTE MUFFLER	105
313. LEE MYLES TRANSMISSION	104
314. TONY ROMA'S	102
315. WEED MAN	100
316. NURSEFINDERS	100
317. UBI BUSINESS BROKERS	100
318. WALLPAPERS TO GO	100
319. FOOD N FUEL	100
320. PALMER VIDEO	100
321. BETTER HOMES REALTY	100
322. MISTER TRANSMISSION	100
323. ANNIE'S BOOK STOP	100
324. TREADWAY INNS	100
325. SWISS COLONY STORES	100
326. KOENIG ART EMPORIUM	100
327. RENT-A-DENT	100
328. ROTO-STATIC INTERNATIONAL	100
329. HOUSEMASTER	100
330. U&R TAX SERVICE	100
331. PRO IMAGE	98
332. EL CHICO	96
333. RECOGNITION EXPRESS	96
334. CAMERA AMERICA	95
335. AMERICAN LEAK DETECTION	95
336. GREAT FRAME UP	95
337. MIKE'S RESTAURANTS	95
338. J. HIGBY'S YOGURT	94
339. FRANKLIN'S	92
340. HEIDI'S	90
341. HUNTINGTON LEARNING CENT	90
342. CARLINE MUFFLER	90
343. EARL KEIM REALTY	90
344. FASTFRAME	90
345. UNICLEAN	90
346. AMERICLEAN	90
347. RESIDENCE INN	90
348. WINDOW WORKS	90
349. CHICKEN DELIGHT	90
350. SOFTWARE CITY	90

FRANCHISOR	OUTLETS
351. TENDER SENDER	90
352. VIA DE FRANCE BAKERY	88
353. FLOWERAMA	88
354. CALIFORNIA CLOSET CO.	87
355. AID AUTO	86
356. SERVICE AMERICA	86
357. SANFORD ROSE ASSOCIATES	85
358. JUST PANTS	85
359. MERLE HARMON'S FAN FAIR	85
360. ENDRUST	85
361. FOUR STAR PIZZA	85
362. BREADEAUX PISA	85
363. TV TEMPO	85
364. PET VALU	85
365. JOHN CASABLANCA	81
366. GIBRALTAR TRANSMISSIONS	80
367. PADGETT BUSINESS SERVICE	80
368. PANHANDLER SHOPS	80
369. PAPA ALDO'S	80
370. DR. VINYL	80
371. JANIMASTER INTERNATIONAL	80
372. PROFORMA	80
373. BATHTIQUE	80
374. SCANDIA DOWN SHOPS	80
375. DUDS N SUDS	80
376. INACOMP	80
377. PRINT MASTERS	80
378. ZIPPY PRINT	80
379. RALLY'S	80
380. FRESHENS	80
381. SKYLINE CHILI	78
382. DEBIT ONE	77
383. SAUCY'S PIZZA	77
384. FOREMOST LIQUORS	76
385. BOSTON PIZZA	76
386. LITTLE KING	76
387. TRAVEL NETWORK	75
388. CONROY'S	75
389. KITS CAMERA	75
390. UNIFORCE TEMPORARY	75
391. SONNY'S REAL PIT BARBQ	75
392. SNELLING TEMPORARY	75
393. RITZY'S	75
394. PRO-CUTS	75
395. TEMP FORCE	74
396. HEADQUARTERS COMPANY	72
397. EMPLOYERS OVERLOAD	72
398. DICTOGRAPH	72
399. CANTERBURY NEW ZEALAND	70
400. SANDWICH TREE, THE	70

FRANCHISOR	OUTLETS
401. FAMOUS AMOS	70
402. LIVING LIGHTING	70
403. PIZZA MOVERS	70
404. BEN & JERRY'S	70
405. PKG'S	70
406. SIRLOIN STOCKADE	70
407. UNITED CONSUMERS CLUB	70
408. MEDICAP PHARMACY	70
409. REALTY EXECUTIVES	70
410. CARPETERIA	70
411. BRIGHAM'S	70
412. HOUSE OF ALMONDS	68
413. WESTERN MEDICAL	66
414. PEPE'S MEXICAN RESTAURANTS	65
415. DAWN DONUT	65
416. BOARDWALK FRIES	65
417. PERMA-GLAZE	65
418. L'IL PEACH	65
419. COMMUNICATIONS WORLD	65
420. KING BEAR	64
421. BUDGETEL	63
422. PLAYORENA	63
423. MUNDUS COLLEGES	63
424. COLT DRAPERY	63
425. CHEM-CLEAN	62
426. NUMERO UNO	62
427. JOHN ROBERT POWERS	62
428. SPORT-ABOUT	61
429. JERRY'S SUBS	60
430. ROCKY MOUNTAIN CHOCOLATE	60
431. MIFAX	60
432. MOUNTAIN MIKE'S	60
433. MR. GROCER	60
434. SECOND SOLE	60
435. SANDLER SYSTEMS	60
436. LE PEEP	60
437. BIGHORN SHEEPSKIN CO.	60
438. BINEX	60
439. CULTURES FRESH FOOD	60
440. EMPRESS TRAVEL	60
441. KIDDIE KOBBLER	60
442. SHEFIELD & SONS	60
443. CHECK-X-CHANGE	58
444. GRAND SLAM USA	57
445. PIZZA MAN	56
446. MIRACLE AUTO PAINTING	56
447. FOSTER'S DONUTS	55
448. CLUB NAUTICO	55
449. ATHLETIC TRAINING EQUIPMENT	55
450. ONE POTATO TWO	54

FRANCHISOR	OUTLETS
451. STEVE'S ICE CREAM	52
452. LARRY'S	52
453. CHEZ CHOCOLAT	52
454. INK WELL, THE	50
455. COPY MAT	50
456. JACKSON HEWITT TAX SVC.	50
457. HEALTH FORCE	50
458. TRENDY TIDY'S	50
459. 60. MINUTE TUNE	50
460. HOMETREND	50
461. PARSON-BISHOP	50
462. F-O-R-T-U-N-E	50
463. LEMON TREE	50
464. MAID BRIGADE	50
465. IN N OUT FOOD STORES	50
466. SWENSEN'S ICE CREAM	50
467. RUNZA DRIVE-INNS	50
468. AUTOSPA	50
469. BENIHANA OF TOKYO	50
470. DAN HANNA AUTO WASH	50
471. NAKED FURNITURE	50
472. ALL AMERICAN HERO	50
473. BEEFSTEAK CHARLIE'S	48
474. RED ROBIN BURGER	48
475. MINUT-TUNE	48
476. APPLAUSE VIDEO	48
477. MR. SIGN	48
478. WORLDWIDE REFINISHING	48
479. EL POLLO ASADO	47
480. MING AUTO BEAUTY	47
481. OLGA'S KITCHEN	47
482. BLUE CHIP COOKIES	47
483. LIEN CHEMICAL	46
484. COOKIE FACTORY	46
485. MRS. VANELLI'S PIZZA	46
486. PERMA-GUARD	45
487. PIZZERIA UNO	45
488. FORTUNATE LIFE	45
489. LONDON FISH & CHIPS	45
490. SIR GOONY	45
491. MERLIN'S MAGIC MUFFLER	44
492. NAMCO	43
493. MAD HATTER MUFFLERS	42
494. MRS. POWELL'S	42
495. JRECK SUBS	41
496. BUILDING INSPECTOR, THE	41
497. CINDY'S CINNAMON ROLLS	41
498. ROMAC	40
499. STEAK ESCAPE	40
500. PIZZA FACTORY	40

FRANCHISOR	OUTLETS
501. PINNACLE 1	40
502. SPORT SHACK	40
503. TOOL SHACK	40
504. INTERNATIONAL MERGERS & ACQUISITIONS	40
505. ERNIE'S WINE & LIQUORS	40
506. BELLINI JUVENILE	40
507. KERNELS	40
508. TRC TEMPORARY	40
509. SOFTWAIRE CENTER	40
510. CALIFORNIA SMOOTHIE	38
511. VIDEO GALAXY	38
512. TWISTEE TREAT	38
513. MARCO'S PIZZA	38
514. FOLIAGE DESIGN	38
515. GLORIA JEAN'S COFFEE BEA	37
516. PCR COMPUTER RENTALS	37
517. ATLANTIC PERSONNEL	36
518. HEALTHCARE RECRUITERS	36
519. CINNAMON SAM'S	36
520. MOTRA TRANSMISSION	35
521. FRUSEN GLADJE	35
522. FAT BOY'S BAR-B-Q	34
523. ASI SIGN SYSTEMS	34
524. ELS INTERNATIONAL	34
525. CARBONE'S PIZZERIA	32
526. BATH GENIE	32
527. ROTH YOUNG PERSONNEL	31
528. M.G.M. LIQUOR WAREHOUSE	30
529. CHAD'S RAINBOW	30
530. MOVIELAND USA	30
531. BRYANT BUREAU	30
532. PARTY HARTY	30
533. DOMESTIC AIDE	30
534. SEAFOOD AMERICA	30
535. K&W TAX SERVICE	30
536. WILD BIRDS UNLIMITED	30
537. PORT OF SUBS	30
538. WINDOW MAN	30
539. CLASSY MAIDS	30
540. DR. NICK'S TRANSMISSIONS	30
541. FRAMING EXPERIENCE	30
542. GELATO CLASSICO	30
543. GIORGIO	30
544. USA BABY	27
545. ELDORADO STONE	26
546. MILEX TUNE-UP	26
547. G. FRIED CARPETLAND	26
548. CARPET TOWN	26
549. CEILING DOCTOR	25
550. HILLARY'S	25

FRANCHISOR	**OUTLETS**
551. ULTRA WASH	25
552. BEST INNS	25
553. MOM'S CINNAMON ROLLS	25
554. ISLAND WATER SPORTS	25
555. AEROWEST	25
556. HEAVENLY HAM	25
557. FLAKEY JAKE'S	25
558. SOAP OPERA WASHATERIA	25
559. SPORTS FANTASY	25
560. FLEET FEET	24
561. KALE'S COLLISION	24
562. SHINE FACTORY	24
563. SPEEDY TRANSMISSION	23
564. SLUMBERLAND	21
565. CELLULAND	21
566. COFFEE BEANERY	20
567. AMERICAN WHOLESALE THERM	20
568. GOURMET CUP	20
569. BAILEY EMPLOYMENT	20
570. ACC-U-TUNE	18
571. BARTER EXCHANGE	18
572. ADVANTAGE PAYROLL	17
573. TEMPS & CO.	16
574. CHILDREN'S ORCHARD	16
575. NEW YORK PIZZA DEPTARTMENT	14
576. CAPS NURSING SERVICE	11
577. PROVENTURE	10
578. THAT MUFFLER & BRAKE PLACE	10
579. THREE STAR MUFFLER	10
580. PAY N PLAY RACQUETBALL	9
581. LAZER MASE	9
582. CAREER BLAZERS	5
583. ALL MY MUFFINS	5

Apparel Franchises

FRANCHISOR	INIT. FEE	RTY.	ADV.	OUTLETS
ACA JOE	$30,000	NONE	3%	170
ALLISON'S PLACE	$99,500	3.5%	2%	230
ATHLETE'S FOOT	$15,000	3%	.5%	500
ATHLETIC ATTIC	$7,500	3%	NONE	175
CANTERBURY NEW ZEALAND	$18,000	2%	2%	70
CHILDREN'S ORCHARD	$13,500	6%	1%	16
FASHION CROSSROADS	$3,000	NONE	NONE	480
FLEET FEET	$12,500	2.4%	NONE	24
GINGESS FORMALWEAR	$15,000	6%	1%	235
JUST PANTS	$15,000	5%	3%	85
KIDDIE KOBBLER	$20,000	4%	1%	60
SECOND SOLE	$15,000	5%	.5%	60
T-SHIRTS PLUS	$30,000	6%	1%	176

Automotive Franchises

FRANCHISOR	INIT. FEE	RTY.	ADV.	OUTLETS
60 MINUTE TUNE	$25,000	6%	6%	50
AAMCO TRANSMISSION	$25,000	9%	VAR.	920
ACC-U-TUNE	$18,000	7%	7%	18
AFFORDABLE	$3,500	VAR.	NONE	140
AFFORDABLE USED CAR	$3,500	VAR.	NONE	140
AID AUTO	$15,000	$400/M	$600/M	86
AJAX RENT A CAR	$15,000	7%	NONE	190
AMERICAN INTERNATIONAL	$25,000	8%	NONE	1500
AUTOSPA	$25,000	7%	4%	50
BIG O TIRES	$10,000	2%	4%	300
BUDGET RENT A CAR	$15,000	5%	2.5%	3600
CAR-X MUFFLER	$18,500	5%	5%	120
CARLINE MUFFLER	NONE	NONE	NONE	90
CHAMPION AUTO	NONE	NONE	NONE	130
COTTMAN TRANSMISSION	$22,500	7.5%	13%	150
DAN HANNA AUTO WASH	$24,000	3%	2%	50
DOLLAR RENT A CAR	$7,500	9%	NONE	1600
DR. NICK'S TRANSMISSIONS	$21,500	7%	$1,200	30
ECONO LUBE N TUNE	$79,500	6%	8%	115
ENDRUST	$30,000	NONE	NONE	85
FREEDOM RENT-A-CAR	$5,000	3.5%	1%	160
GIBRALTAR TRANSMISSIONS	$30,000	7%	NONE	80
GOODYEAR TIRE CENTERS	VAR.	NONE	NONE	1570
GREASE MONKEY	$25,000	5%	6%	131
JIFFY LUBE	$25,000	5%	8%	920
KALE'S COLLISION	$15,000	6%	$1,000	24
KING BEAR	$19,900	$150/M	$300/M	64
LEE MYLES TRANSMISSION	$20,000	6%	4.5%	104
MAACO	$25,000	8%	$2,000	440
MAD HATTER MUFFLERS	$17,500	8%	4%	42
MEINEKE DISCOUNT MUFFLER	$22,500	7%	10%	720
MERLIN'S MAGIC MUFFLER	$22,000	4.9%	5%	44
MIDAS	$10,000	5%	5%	2200
MIGHTY DISTRIBUTING	$15,000	5%	.5%	200
MILEX TUNE-UP	$17,500	5%	5%	26
MING AUTO BEAUTY	$25,000	5%	4%	47
MINUT-TUNE	$20,000	5%	5%	48
MINUTE MUFFLER	$10,000	NONE	NONE	105
MIRACLE AUTO PAINTING	$35,000	5%	5%	56
MISTER TRANSMISSION	$20,000	7%	VAR.	100
MOTRA TRANSMISSION	$17,500	7%	VAR.	35
MR. TRANSMISSION	$19,500	8%	10%	140
NOVUS WINDSHIELD REPAIR	$2,900	6%	2%	685
PAYLESS CAR RENTAL	$10,000	5%	3%	116
PERMA-GUARD	$32,000	5%	5%	45
PRECISION TUNE	$15,000	7.5%	9%	417

FRANCHISOR	INIT. FEE	RTY.	ADV.	OUTLETS
QUAKER STATE MINIT-LUBE	$25,000	5%	10%	300
RENT A WRECK	$3,000	5%	1.5%	355
RENT-A-DENT	$3,500	7%	2%	100
SHINE FACTORY	$10,000	8%	5%	24
SPARKS TUNE-UP	$25,000	6%	$1,920	160
SPARKY COIN-OP	NONE	NONE	NONE	270
SPEEDY MUFFLER KING	$18,500	5%	5%	560
SPEEDY TRANSMISSION	$15,000	7%	3%	23
SUNSHINE POLISHING	$975	NONE	NONE	335
TKD	$11,000	8%	1.4%	130
THAT MUFFLER & BRAKE PLACE	$4,900	$500	$50	10
THREE STAR MUFFLER	$15,000	7%	2%	10
THRIFTY RENT-A-CAR	$10,000	3%	5%	668
TIDY CAR	$12,500	9%	3%	300
TUFF-KOTE DINOL	$4,000	8%	1%	131
TUFFY SERVICE CENTER	$18,500	5%	5%	114
UGLY DUCKLING	$6,000	6%	2%	475
WASH ON WHEELS	$7,500	3%	1%	120
WESTERN AUTO	NONE	NONE	NONE	1800
ZIEBART	$20,000	8%	5%	575

Automotive Rental Franchises

FRANCHISOR	INIT. FEE	RTY.	ADV.	OUTLETS
AFFORDABLE USED CAR	$3,500	VAR.	NONE	140
AJAX RENT A CAR	$15,000	7%	NONE	190
AMERICAN INTERNATIONAL	$25,000	8%	NONE	1500
BUDGET RENT A CAR	$15,000	5%	2.5%	3600
DOLLAR RENT A CAR	$7,500	9%	NONE	1600
FREEDOM RENT-A-CAR	$5,000	3.5%	1%	160
PAYLESS CAR RENTAL	$10,000	5%	3%	116
RENT A WRECK	$3,000	5%	1.5%	355
RENT-A-DENT	$3,500	7%	2%	100
THRIFTY RENT-A-CAR	$10,000	3%	5%	668
UGLY DUCKLING	$6,000	6%	2%	475

Business Service Franchises

FRANCHISOR	INIT. FEE	RTY.	ADV.	OUTLETS
AAA EMPLOYMENT	$10,000	10%	NONE	130
ASI SIGN SYSTEMS	$50,000	5%	1%	34
ADIA PERSONNEL	$17,500	35%	NONE	460
ADVANTAGE PAYROLL	$10,000	NONE	NONE	17
ALPHAGRAPHICS	$47,000	3%	1%	230
AMERICAN ADV. DISTR.	$19,500	VAR.	NONE	115
AMERICAN SPEEDY PRINTING	$39,500	4%	2%	508
AMERICAN WHOLESALE THERM	$38,500	5%	NONE	20
ATLANTIC PERSONNEL	$8,500	7%	NONE	36
BAILEY EMPLOYMENT	$40,000	8%	NONE	20
BINEX	$11,500	NONE	NONE	60
BRYANT BUREAU	$10,000	5%	1%	30
CAPS NURSING SERVICE	$25,000	6%	NONE	11
CAREER BLAZERS	$15,000	VAR.	VAR.	5
CELLULAND	$25,000	3.5%	1%	21
COMMUNICATIONS WORLD	$10,000	4%	1%	65
COMPREHENSIVE ACCOUNTING	$30,000	VAR.	NONE	340
COMPUTERLAND	$15,000	5%	1%	800
COPY MAT	$40,000	7%	1%	50
DEBIT ONE	$20,000	8%	1%	77
DRAKE PERSONNEL	$15,000	7%	NONE	235
DUNHILL PERSONNEL	$15,000	3%	1%.	340
EMPLOYERS OVERLOAD	$15,000	5%	.5%	72
ENTRE COMPUTER CENTERS	$15,000	5.5%	.5%	195
EXPRESS SERVICES	$9,000	6%	2%	105
F-O-R-T-U-N-E	$30,000	7%	1%	50
FRANKLIN'S	$25,000	5%	1.5%	92
GENERAL BUSINESS SERVICE	$25,000	7%	NONE	600
HANDLE WITH CARE	$12,500	5%	1%	190
HEADQUARTERS COMPANY	$30,000	1%	VAR.	72
HEALTH FORCE	$39,500	8.5%	.05%	50
HEALTHCARE RECRUITERS	$25,000	10%	1%	36
INACOMP	$5,000	5%	NONE	80
INK WELL, THE	$20,000	5%	2.5%	50
INSTY PRINTS	$40,000	3%	2%	360
INTL. MERGERS & ACQ.	$10,000	3%	1%	40
KWIK KOPY	$22,000	4%	NONE	1000
MAIL BOXES ETC. USA	$19,500	5%	2%	600
MANAGEMENT RECRUITERS	$20,000	5%	,5%	330
MARCOIN	$30,000	8.5%	.5%	130
MEDICAL PERSONNEL	$15,000	5%	NONE	265
MICROAGE	$15,000	4%	1%	200
MIFAX	$13,800	NONE	NONE	60
MINUTEMAN PRESS	$24,500	6%	NONE	820
MONEY MAILER	VAR.	NONE	NONE	190
MR. SIGN	$17,500	5%	2%	48

FRANCHISOR	INIT. FEE	RTY.	ADV.	OUTLETS
NAMCO	$25,000	15%	NONE	43
NORELL TEMPORARY	$15,000	VAR.	NONE	240
NURSEFINDERS	$15,000	5%	NONE	100
PCR COMPUTER RENTALS	$25,500	7%	1%	37
PIP PRINTING	$40,000	6%	2%	1120
PKG'S	$13,500	2%	2%	70
PACKY THE SHIPPER	$995	VAR.	NONE	1120
PADGETT BUSINESS SERVICE	$14,500	9%	NONE	80
PAK MAIL	$15,500	5%	1%	190
PARSON-BISHOP	$19,000	NONE	NONE	50
PERSONNEL POOL	$20,000	5%	NONE	200
PINNACLE 1	$14,000	NONE	NONE	40
PRINT MASTERS	$34,500	4%	2%	80
PRINT SHACK	$17,500	6%	NONE	116
PRINT THREE	$29,500	6%	3%	125
PRIORITY MANAGEMENT	$27,500	9%	1%	145
PROFORMA	$27,500	7%	1%	80
PROVENTURE	$18,000	6%	NONE	10
RECOGNITION EXPRESS	$23,500	6%	2%	96
ROMAC	$40,000	8%	1%	40
ROTH YOUNG PERSONNEL	$50,000	8%	2%	31
SALES CONSULTANTS	$20,000	5%	.5%	133
SANDLER SYSTEMS	$20,000	$750	NONE	60
SANFORD ROSE ASSOC.	$29,500	3%	NONE	85
SIR SPEEDY PRINTING	$17,500	6%	2%	830
SNELLING & SNELLING	$14,000	7%	1%	500
SNELLING TEMPORARY	$10,000	4.5%	.5%	75
SOFTWAIRE CENTER	$25,000	2.5%	1%	40
SOFTWARE CITY	$12,500	5%	1.5%	90
STAFF BUILDERS	$39,500	VAR.	NONE	132
TRC TEMPORARY	VAR.	VAR.	NONE	40
TV FOCUS	$1,800	VAR.	NONE	215
TV TEMPO	$30,000	$110	NONE	85
TEMP FORCE	NONE	VAR.	NONE	74
TEMPS & CO.	$12,500	VAR.	VAR.	16
TENDER SENDER	$20,000	6%	2%	90
TRIMARK	$24,900	NONE	NONE	105
UBI BUSINESS BROKERS	$27,500	6%	2%	100
UNIFORCE TEMPORARY	$15,000	VAR.	VAR.	75
VR BUSINESS BROKERS	$35,000	6%	2%	205
VALCOM	$30,000	8%	1%	180
WESTERN MEDICAL	$4,000	VAR.	NONE	66
WESTERN TEMPORARY	$4,000	VAR.	NONE	330
ZIPPY PRINT	$40,000	5%	5%	80

Construction and Maintenance Franchises

FRANCHISOR	INIT. FEE	RTY.	ADV.	OUTLETS
ABC SEAMLESS	$12,000	VAR.	.5%	280
AEROWEST	$1,000	50%	NONE	25
AMERICAN LEAK DET.	$40,000	8%	NONE	95
AMERICLEAN	$15,000	4%	2%	90
ARMSTRONG WORLD IND.	$8,000	NONE	NONE	275
BATH GENIE	NONE	NONE	NONE	32
BATHCREST	$3,500	NONE	NONE	135
CALIFORNIA CLOSET CO.	$25,000	5%	NONE	87
CARPET TOWN	VAR.	NONE	VAR.	26
CARPETERIA	$50,000	4%	.25%	70
CEILING DOCTOR	$10,000	6%	2%	25
CHEM-CLEAN	$18,000	NONE	NONE	62
CHEM-DRY	$1,350	$100/M	NONE	1840
CLASSY MAIDS	$5,900	6%	NONE	30
COLOR-GLO	VAR.	5%	$60/MO	240
COLT DRAPERY	$5,000	5%	NONE	63
COUSTIC-GLO	$9,750	5%	1%	240
COVERALL	$3,250	10%	1%	900
CROSSLAND FURNITURE RESTORATION	NONE	5%	3%	110
CULLIGAN WATER CONDITIONING	NONE	VAR.	VAR.	806
DECORATING DEN	$6,900	6%	2%	720
DICTOGRAPH	$15,000	6%	NONE	72
DIP N STRIP	NONE	6%	NONE	280
DOMESTIC AIDE	$7,500	7%	2%	30
DR. VINYL	$20,000	4%	1%	80
DURACLEAN	$9,500	2%	NONE	615
ELDORADO STONE	$3,400	4%	NONE	26
FOUR SEASONS GREENHOUSE	$5,000	NONE	NONE	250
G. FRIED CARPETLAND	NONE	2%	NONE	26
JANI-KING	$6,500	10%	.5%	1300
JANIMASTER INTERNATIONAL	$7,995	6%	NONE	80
LANGENWALTER DYE CONCEPT	$14,500	NONE	$100/M	130
LAWN DOCTOR	NONE	10%	VAR.	290
LIEN CHEMICAL	$9,000	5%	NONE	46
LIVING LIGHTING	$25,000	7%	5%	70
MAID BRIGADE	$15,000	6%	2%	50
MAIDS, THE	$12,900	4.5%	2%	165
MINI MAID	$8,900	$350/M	NONE	140
MIRACLE METHOD	$19,950	7.5%	3%	107
MOLLY MAID	$16,900	4%	2%	336
MR. BUILD	$6,000	VAR.	$300/M	605
NATIONAL MAINT. CONTR.	$2,500	20%	NONE	224
PERMA CERAM	$19,500	NONE	NONE	130
PERMA-GLAZE	NONE	NONE	NONE	65
PROFESSIONAL CARPET	$15,000	$100/M	NONE	180
PROFUSION SYSTEMS	$20,500	6%	NONE	120

FRANCHISOR	INIT. FEE	RTY.	ADV.	OUTLETS
RAINSOFT	$4,000	NONE	NONE	305
RAINBOW INTERNATIONAL	$15,000	7%	NONE	1450
ROTO ROOTER	$500	VAR.	NONE	750
ROTO-STATIC INTL.	$5,000	5%	NONE	100
SERVPRO	$17,800	3%	NONE	650
SERVICE AMERICA	$15,000	VAR.	3%	86
SERVICEMASTER	$6,000	10%	NONE	3875
SONITROL	$20,000	2.5%	NONE	170
SPARKLE WASH	$7,500	5%	NONE	176
SPOTLESS OFF. SYST.	$3,000	5%	NONE	118
SPRING CREST DRAPERY	$12,500	3%	2%	315
SPRING-GREEN	$12,900	6%	2%	140
ST. CLAIR PAINT	$20,000	NONE	NONE	175
STAINED GLASS OVERLAY	$34,000	5%	2%	325
STANLEY STEEMER	$20,000	7%	NONE	225
STEAMATIC	$13,000	3%	NONE	240
TRENDY TIDY'S	$15,000	6%	2%	50
ULTRA WASH	$35,000	8%	NONE	25
UNICLEAN	$6,000	5%	2%	90
WALLPAPERS TO GO	$40,000	8%	5%	100
WEED MAN	$30,000	VAR.	VAR.	100
WINDOW MAN	$30,000	6%	1%	30
WINDOW WORKS	$17,500	4%	1%	90
WORLDWIDE REFINISHING	$6,9550	5%	NONE	48

Educational Service Franchises

FRANCHISOR	INIT. FEE	RTY.	ADV.	OUTLETS
ARTHUR MURRAY	NONE	5%	2%	225
ELS INTERNATIONAL	$20,000	5%	NONE	34
GYMBOREE	$8,000	6%	2%	350
HUNTINGTON LEARNING	$10,000	6%	2%	90
JOHN CASABLANCA	$6,500	7%	3%	81
JOHN ROBERT POWERS	$30,000	10%	$150/M	62
MUNDUS COLLEGES	$15,000	NONE	NONE	63
SYLVAN LEARNING CENTER	$35,000	8%	1.5%	460

Entertainment Franchises

FRANCHISOR	INIT. FEE	RTY.	ADV.	OUTLETS
ATHLETIC TRAINING EQUIP.	$6,000	6%	NONE	55
CLUB NAUTICO	$15,000	10%	2%	55
ISLAND WATER SPORTS	$25,000	NONE	VAR.	25
KAMPGROUNDS OF AMERICA	$20,000	8%	2%	640
LAZER MASE	$15,000	5%	2%	9
PACER RACER	NONE	NONE	NONE	170
PAY N PLAY RACQUETBALL	VAR.	10%	2.5%	9
PUTT PUTT GOLF	$15,000	3%	2%	325
SIR GOONY	NONE	NONE	NONE	45
YOGI BEAR JELLYSTONE	$15,000	6%	1%	105

Food Service Franchises

FRANCHISOR	INIT. FEE	RTY.	ADV.	OUTLETS
A&W RESTAURANTS	$15,000	4%	4%	525
ALL AMERICAN HERO	$20,000	6%	3%	50
ALL MY MUFFINS	$20,000	6%	2%	5
ARBY'S	$25,000	3.5%	.07%	2000
BASKIN-ROBBINS	NONE	.5%	1.5%	3450
BASKIN-ROBBINS/SILICORP	$25,000	.055%	4%	200
BEEFSTEAK CHARLIE'S	$25,000	5%	3%	48
BEN & JERRY'S	$21,000	NONE	4%	70
BENIHANA OF TOKYO	$50,000	5%	.5%	50
BLUE CHIP COOKIES	$33,000	6%	3%	47
BOARDWALK FRIES	$25,000	7%	2%	65
BOB'S BIG BOY	$25,000	3%	4%	780
BOJANGLES	$25,000	4%	1%	380
BONANZA	$30,000	4.8%	3%	610
BOSTON PIZZA	$30,000	7%	2.5%	76
BREADEAUX PISA	$15,000	5%	2%	85
BRESLER'S	$10,000	6%	3%	300
BRIGHAM'S	$31,500	5%	1%	70
CALIFORNIA SMOOTHIE	$25,000	5%	2%	38
CAPTAIN D'S	$10,000	3%	6%	590
CARBONE'S PIZZERIA	$10,000	3%	1%	32
CARL'S JR.	$35,000	4%	4%	460
CARVEL	$25,000	VAR.	VAR.	750
CHICKEN DELIGHT	$15,000	5%	2%	90
CHURCH'S FRIED CHICKEN	$15,000	4%	5%	1500
CINDY'S CINNAMON ROLLS	$25,000	5%	NONE	41
CINNAMON SAM'S	$25,000	5%	2%	36
COOKIE FACTORY	$20,000	5%	1%	46
CRUSTY'S PIZZA	$15,000	5%	5%	200
CULTURES FRESH FOOD	$30,000	5%	2%	60
DAIRY QUEEN	$30,000	4%	3.5%	5000
DAVID'S COOKIES	$25,000	NONE	NONE	200
DAWN DONUT	$15,000	4.5%	4.5%	65
DENNY'S	$35,000	4%	2%	1390
DIPPER DAN	NONE	NONE	NONE	250
DOMINO'S PIZZA	$1,300	5.5%	3%	4600
DUNKIN' DONUTS	$30,000	4.9%	5%	1735
EL CHICO	$35,000	4%	1%	96
EL POLLO ASADO	$25,000	4%	3%	47
EVERYTHING YOGURT	$30,000	5%	1%	185
FAMOUS AMOS CHOC. CHIP	$25,000	4%	3%	70
FAT BOY'S BAR-B-Q	$15,000	3%	1%	34
FLAKEY JAKE'S	$20,000	3%	.5%	25
FOSTER'S DONUTS	$35,000	5%	.5%	55
FOSTER'S FREEZE	$25,000	4%	3%	200
FOUR STAR PIZZA	$9,000	5%	1%	85

FRANCHISOR	INIT. FEE	RTY.	ADV.	OUTLETS
FOX'S PIZZA DEN	$8,000	$200/M	NONE	115
FRESHENS	$19,500	4%	4%	80
FRUSEN GLADJE	$25,000	NONE	1.5%	35
FUDDRUCKERS	$50,000	5%	NONE	106
GELATO CLASSICO	$25,000	NONE	NONE	30
GIORGIO	$30,000	5%	4%	30
GLORIA JEAN'S COFFEE BEAN	$19,500	6%	1%	37
GODFATHER'S PIZZA	$15,000	5%	5%	810
GRANDY'S	$15,000	4%	.8%	205
GROUND ROUND, THE	$30,000	3%	2%	200
HARDEE'S	$15,000	3.5%	5%	3000
HEIDI'S	$22,000	4%	4%	90
HILLARY'S	$28,000	5%	$500/Y	25
I CAN'T BELIEVE/YOGURT	$20,000	5%	2%	175
ICE CREAM CHURN	$7,500	VAR.	VAR.	530
INTERNATIONAL BLIMPIE	$15,000	6%	3%	320
INTL. HOUSE OF PANCAKES	$50,000	4.5%	3%	458
J. HIGBY'S YOGURT	$20,000	4%	2.5%	94
JACK IN THE BOX	$25,000	4%	5%	940
JERRY'S SUBS	$30,000	5%	3%	60
JRECK SUBS	$10,000	5%	2%	41
KENTUCKY FRIED CHICKEN	$20,000	4%	5%	7700
LARRY'S	$15,000	1%	3%	52
LE PEEP	$30,000	5%	1%	60
LEE'S	$10,000	3%	1%	280
LITTLE CAESAR'S	$15,000	5%	VAR.	2000
LITTLE KING	$19,500	5%	NONE	76
LONDON FISH & CHIPS	$7,500	6%	NONE	45
LONG JOHN SILVER'S	$20,000	4%	5%	1500
MARCO'S PIZZA	$12,000	4.5%	2.5%	38
MARIE CALLENDER	$25,000	3%	2%	160
MAZZIO'S PIZZA	$20,000	3%	1%	210
MCDONALD'S	$22,500	12%	4%	9500
MIKE'S	$40,000	5%	3%	95
MISTER DONUT	$25,000	4.9%	3.5%	610
MOM'S CINNAMON ROLLS	$20,000	5%	3%	25
MOUNTAIN MIKE'S	$12,500	4%	2%	60
MR. GATTI'S	$10,000	4%	1%	338
MR. PHILLY	$21,500	4%	6%	150
MR. STEAK	$16,000	3%	1%	175
MR. SUBMARINE	$15,000	5%	3%	275
MRS. POWELL'S	$25,000	5%	2%	42
MRS. VANELLI'S PIZZA	$25,000	6%	2%	46
NEW YORK PIZZA DEPTARTMENT	$10,000	5%	3%	14
NUMERO UNO	$25,000	5.5%	4.5%	62
OLGA'S KITCHEN	$25,000	5%	3%	47

FRANCHISOR	INIT. FEE	RTY.	ADV.	OUTLETS
ONE POTATO TWO	$20,000	6%	2%	54
ORANGE JULIUS	$30,000	6%	3.5%	745
PAPA ALDO'S	$17,500	5%	2%	80
PENGUIN'S PLACE	$25,000	4%	4%	140
PEPE'S MEXICAN REST.	$15,000	4%	3%	65
PERKINS FAMILY REST.	$30,000	4%	4%	330
PIONEER TAKE-OUT	$35,000	5.9%	3.9%	226
PIZZA DELIGHT	$25,000	6%	3%	190
PIZZA FACTORY	$20,000	3%	1%	40
PIZZA HUT	$15,000	VAR.	VAR.	6000
PIZZA INN	$17,500	4%	1.5%	690
PIZZA MAN	$25,000	4%	4%	56
PIZZA MOVERS	$16,000	8.5%	3%	70
PIZZA PIZZA	$20,000	6%	6%	160
PIZZERIA UNO	$15,000	5%	1%	45
PLAYORENA	$7,000	6%	NONE	63
POFOLKS	$37,000	1.5%	VAR.	150
PONDEROSA STEAKHOSUE	$25,000	4%	.4%	700
POPEYES	$25,000	5%	3%	715
PORT OF SUBS	$13,500	5.5%	1%	30
RALLY'S	$20,000	4%	4%	80
RAX RESTAURANTS	$25,000	4%	4%	520
RED ROBIN BURGER	$25,000	4,5%	2.5%	48
RITZY'S	$17,000	3.5%	NONE	75
ROBIN'S DONUTS	$35,000	4%	3%	124
ROUND TABLE PIZZA	$25,000	4%	3%	550
ROY ROGERS RESTAURANTS	$25,000	4%	4%	570
RUNZA DRIVE-INNS	$17,000	5%	1%	50
SUBWAY	$7,500	8%	2.5%	2400
SANDWICH TREE, THE	$25,000	4.5%	3%	70
SAUCY'S PIZZA	$16,000	5%	$300/M	77
SBARRO	$35,000	5%	1%	275
SCHLOTZSKY'S	$15,000	4%	1%	222
SEAFOOD AMERICA	$10,000	2%	$300/M	30
SHAKEY'S PIZZA	$20,000	4.5%	4.5%	360
SHONEY'S	$25,000	3%	4%	625
SHOWBIZ PIZZA TIME	$25,000	3%	3.3%	265
SIRLOIN STOCKADE	$15,000	3%	1%	70
SIZZLER	$30,000	4.5%	4.5%	600
SKIPPER'S	$10,000	5%	4%	215
SKYLINE CHILI	$15,000	4%	2%	78
SONIC DRIVE-INS	$15,000	3%	3%	1100
SONNY'S REAL PIT BARBQ	$25,000	2.5%	1%	75
ST. HUBERT BAR-B-Q	$25,000	3%	3%	850
STEAK ESCAPE	$27,000	8%	NONE	40
STEVE'S ICE CREAM	$25,000	6%	1.5%	52

FRANCHISOR	INIT. FEE	RTY.	ADV.	OUTLETS
SUB STATION II	$10,500	3.5%	2%	125
SWENSEN'S ICE CREAM	$20,000	6%	1%	50
T.J. CINNAMONS	$25,000	5%	2%	220
TCBY	$20,000	4%	3%	1075
TGI FRIDAY'S	$50,000	4%	4%	130
TACO BELL	$35,000	5.5%	4.5%	2760
TACO JOHN'S	$16,500	4%	2%	440
TACO VILLA	$20,000	5%	5%	150
TACOTIME	$18,000	5%	.5%	275
TASTEE FREEZ	$10,000	4%	1%	500
TIM HORTON DONUTS	$15,000	3%	3%	370
TOGO'S EATERY	$10,000	5%	2	120
TONY ROMA'S	$50,000	4%	1%	102
TREATS	$25,000	8%	2%	125
TWISTEE TREAT	$8,000	8%	2.5%	38
VIA DE FRANCE BAKERY	$20,000	4%	1%	88
VILLAGE INN	$25,000	5%	NONE	270
WENDY'S	$25,000	4%	4%	3650
WESTERN SIZZLIN	$25,000	3%	NONE	590
WHATABURGER	$15,000	5%	NONE	405
WIENERSCHNITZEL	$30,000	5%	4%	276
WINCHELL'S DONUT HOUSE	$30,000	5%	3%	680
ZACK'S	$20,000	5%	3%	210

Lodging Franchises

FRANCHISOR	INIT. FEE	RTY.	ADV.	OUTLETS
BEST INNS	$10,000	2%	1%	25
BUDGETEL	$20,000	5%	1%	63
DAYS INN	VAR.	6.5%	NONE	700
ECONO LODGE	$20,000	4%	2.5%	440
FRIENDSHIP INN	$12,500	VAR.	NONE	135
HAMPTON INNS	$35,000	4%	2.5%	180
HILTON INN	$25,000	5%	NONE	275
HOLIDAY INN	VAR.	4%	1.5%	1600
HOWARD JOHNSON	$30,000	5%	VAR.	450
QUALITY INN/COMFORT INN	$30,000	3%	VAR.	950
RAMADA INN	$25,000	3%	3.5%	590
RED CARPET/SCOTTISH INNS	$25,000	2%	.5%	250
RESIDENCE INN	VAR.	4%	2.5%	90
RODEWAY INNS	$15,000	3%	1%	160
SHERATON INNS	$30,000	5%	NONE	500
SUPER 8	$20,000	4%	2%	430
TRAVELODGE	$15,000	3%	4%	470
TREADWAY INNS	VAR.	NONE	NONE	100

Personal Service

FRANCHISOR	INIT. FEE	RTY.	ADV.	OUTLETS
AIR BROOK LIMOUSINE	$7,000	40%	NONE	120
ALOETTE COSMETICS	$60,000	5%	NONE	108
BARTER EXCHANGE	$30,000	NONE	NONE	18
COMMAND PERFORMANCE	$21,500	6%	NONE	267
COST CUTTERS	$12,500	4%	4%	290
DIET CENTER INC.	$12,000	VAR.	NONE	2330
DRY CLEAN USA	$25,000	5%	2%	245
DUDS N SUDS	$25,000	4%	1%	80
EUROPEAN TANSPA	$5,000	VAR.	NONE	125
FANTASTIC SAM'S	$25,000	$145/M	$67/M	1275
FORTUNATE LIFE	$9,000	10%	VAR.	45
GREAT CLIPS	$12,500	6%	5%	160
GREAT EXPECTATIONS	$18,000	6%	2%	300
H&R BLOCK	$600	VAR.	NONE	8800
HAIR PERFORMERS	$15,000	6%	2%	290
HAIRCRAFTERS	$20,000	6%	NONE	400
JACKSON HEWITT	$3,000	VAR.	VAR.	50
JAZZERCISE	$500	VAR.	NONE	3800
K&W TAX SERVICE	$8,500	50%	8%	30
LEMON TREE	$7,500	6%	$400/M	50
MAGICUTS	$18,000	7%	2%	145
MIRACLE EAR	$12,500	VAR.	NONE	445
NUVISION OPTICAL	$10,000	8.5%	7%	220
NUTRA BOLIC	$17,900	5%	NONE	180
NUTRI SYSTEM	$13,000	7%	NONE	1000
ONE HOUR MARTINIZING	$20,000	2.4%	4%	1000
PAUL DAVIS SYSTEMS	$37,500	2.5%	NONE	120
PEARLE VISION	$16,000	8.5%	8%	860
PENNYSAVER	$24,500	$500/M	NONE	410
PHYSICIANS WEIGHT LOSS	$32,500	10%	$1,000	350
PRO-CUTS	$25,000	6%	5%	75
SOAP OPERA WASHATERIA	$20,000	$580/M	$180/M	25
STERLING OPTICAL	$15,000	8%	6%	235
SUDDENLY SLENDER	$20,000	VAR.	1%	280
SUPERCUTS	$25,000	10%	5%	510
TEXAS STATE OPTICAL	$11,000	8.5%	8%	170
TRIPLE CHECK	NONE	VAR.	NONE	250
U&R TAX SERVICE	$4,500	40%	NONE	100
UNITED CHIROPRACTIC	$3,500	$250/M	$300/M	190
UNITED CONSUMERS CLUB	$50,000	22%	5%	70

Retail Franchises

FRANCHISOR	INIT. FEE	RTY.	ADV.	OUTLETS
7-ELEVEN STORES	VAR.	VAR.	NONE	12000
ALMOST HEAVEN HOT TUBS	NONE	NONE	NONE	975
AM/PM MINI-MARKETS	$30,000	4%	2%	550
ANNIE'S BOOK STOP	$17,500	3.5%	1%	100
BATHTIQUE	$25,000	5%	NONE	80
BECKER MILK CO.	$25,000	5%	NONE	784
BELLINI JUVENILE	$25,000	50%	NONE	40
BEN FRANKLIN STORES	$245,000	NONE	NONE	1100
BIGHORN SHEEPSKIN CO.	NONE	NONE	NONE	60
CAMERA AMERICA	$18,000	3.5%	2%	95
CHAD'S RAINBOW	$35,000	5%	2%	30
CHEZ CHOCOLAT	VAR.	5%	NONE	52
COAST TO COAST STORES	$5,000	$100/M	VAR.	965
COFFEE BEANERY	$17,500	4%	2%	20
CONROY'S	$75,000	7.75%	3%	75
CUTLERY WORLD	$20,000	6.5%	1%	185
DESCAMPS	NONE	NONE	NONE	195
DOCKTOR PET	$15,000	4.5%	NONE	270
DRUG EMPORIUM	$25,000	1%	.1%	150
ERNIE'S WINE & LIQUORS	$10,000	1%	NONE	40
FASTFRAME	$25,000	7.5%	5%	90
FLOWERAMA	$17,500	5%	NONE	88
FOLIAGE DESIGN	$8,000	4%	NONE	38
FOOD N FUEL	$10,000	4%	NONE	100
FOREMOST LIQUORS	VAR.	1.5%	1%	76
FRAMING EXPERIENCE	$16,000	5%	NONE	30
FRONTIER FRUIT & NUT	$15,000	6%	NONE	260
GOURMET CUP	$25,000	6%	2%	20
GREAT FRAME UP	$19,500	6%	2%	95
HASTY MARKETS	$32,500	6%	.05%	135
HEALTH MART	NONE	NONE	NONE	466
HEAVENLY HAM	$25,000	4%	1%	25
HICKORY FARMS OF OHIO	$20,000	6%	2%	340
HOUSE OF ALMONDS	$15,000	5%	2%	68
IN N OUT FOOD STORES	$15,000	3.75%	1.75%	50
JAPAN CAMERA	$40,000	8%	3.5%	150
KERNELS	$25,000	8%	NONE	40
KITS CAMERA	$19,500	6%	1.5%	75
KOENIG ART EMPORIUM	$25,000	6%	NONE	100
L'IL PEACH	$10,000	15%	NONE	65
LITTLE PROFESSOR	$21,000	2.75%	.5%	120
M.G.M. LIQUOR WAREHOUSE	$25,000	VAR.	1%	30
MEDICAP PHARMACY	$15,000	4%	1%	70
MEDICINE SHOPPE	$18,000	5.5%	2%	740
MERLE HARMON'S FAN FAIR	$15,000	5%	1%	85
MOTO PHOTO	$35,000	6%	.5%	275

FRANCHISOR	INIT. FEE	RTY.	ADV.	OUTLETS
MR. GROCER	NONE	3.85%	.75%	60
NAKED FURNITURE	$16,500	4%	NONE	50
PANHANDLER SHOPS	$25,000	6%	1%	80
PARTY HARTY	$15,000	3%	NONE	30
PET VALU	$20,000	6%	NONE	85
PETLAND	NONE	4%	5%	162
PRO IMAGE	$16,500	4%	3%	98
ROCKY MOUNTAIN CHOCOLATE	$20,000	5%	1%	60
SCANDIA DOWN SHOPS	$25,000	5%	3%	80
SECOND CUP	$15,000	9%	2%	132
SHEFIELD & SONS	$10,000	2%	NONE	60
SILK PLANTS, ETC.	$25,000	6%	1%	160
SLUMBERLAND	$10,000	3%	NONE	21
SPORT SHACK	$17,500	4%	2%	40
SPORT-ABOUT	$22,500	4%	1.5%	61
SPORTS FANTASY	$15,000	5%	NONE	25
SWISS COLONY STORES	$5,000	4%	NONE	100
TAYLOR RENTAL	$20,000	2.75%	NONE	360
TINDER BOX, THE	$24,000	4%	3%	186
TOOL SHACK	$30,000	3%	3%	40
USA BABY	$7,500	3%	.5%	27
WICKS N STICKS	$35,000	6%	NONE	312
WILD BIRDS UNLIMITED	$5,000	3%	NONE	30
WORLD BAZAAR	$15,000	8%	NONE	300

Travel Franchises

FRANCHISOR	INIT. FEE	RTY.	ADV.	OUTLETS
EMPRESS TRAVEL	$35,000	VAR.	VAR.	60
TRAVEL AGENTS INTL.	$29,500	$585/M	VAR.	330
TRAVEL NETWORK	$27,500	VAR.	$200/M	75
TRAVEL TRAVEL	$10,000	VAR.	VAR.	240
UNIGLOBE	$42,500	.75%	$591/M	580

Video Rental Franchises

FRANCHISOR	INIT. FEE	RTY.	ADV.	OUTLETS
ADVENTURELAND	$15,500	4.5%	3%	800
APPLAUSE VIDEO	$15,000	5%	1%	48
MAJOR VIDEO	$25,000	4%	1%	150
MOVIELAND USA	$10,000	4%	1%	30
NATIONAL VIDEO	$29,900	4.9%	3%	1400
PALMER VIDEO	$29,000	5%	NONE	100
VIDEO BIZ	$19,000	2.5%	2.5%	170
VIDEO DATA	$14,950	$500/Y	NONE	237
VIDEO GALAXY	$20,000	5%	$100/M	38
WEST COAST VIDEO	$32,500	5%	2%	220

Index

Dennis L. Foster is a foremost authority on franchising and the author of 24 books, including *The Rating Guide to Franchises, The Complete Franchise Book, Franchising For Free,* and *Franchise Marketing Techniques.* He is chairman of the board of Franchise Associates International, a diversified corporation involved in consulting, franchising, software development, and technical education, and is also president of The Development Group, a franchise development firm.